NATIONAL
GEOGRAPHIC

FOODS *for* HEALTH

NATIONAL
GEOGRAPHIC

FOODS
for
HEALTH

◆

Choose and Use the Very Best Foods
for Your Family and Our Planet

Barton Seaver
P. K. Newby, Sc.D., M.P.H.

NATIONAL GEOGRAPHIC
WASHINGTON, D.C.

CONTENTS

TOWARD A COMMUNION OF THE COMMONS: EATING JOYFULLY AND RESPONSIBLY

✦ ✦ ✦

BARTON SEAVER

I grew up in a multicultural neighborhood in Washington, D.C. While the majority of the neighborhood hailed from El Salvador, there were large populations of Ethiopians, Guatemalans, Hondurans, Koreans, Chinese, Thai, and African Americans.

It was a Noah's Ark of people. Each of these groups had little bodegas that served their needs, importing to their new world a taste of home. I vividly remember exploring the aisles of these shops and being blown away by the heady, seductive spices, the exotic fruits and vegetables, and the variety of meats available, not to mention the cuts of meat not easily found in our regular stores. I warmly remember answering the dinner bell's clang and saying goodbye to my friends after an intense afternoon of street soccer. Arriving home I would find my father, tie off, apron donned, at work at the stove. My father was an excellent cook and was not shy to use new ingredients. Some nights the aroma of an East Indian curry filled the house. Other nights I would be put to work pressing out the moistened masa harina dough to form the tortillas, dry-fried, and then stuffed with fresh ingredients for taco night.

Muliticultural Food

Food was always an exploration for me. A window onto a world of new flavors, textures, aromas, experiences. But as much as dinner brought some new corner of the world into our house, these ingredients, dishes, and flavors also represented the cultures of the boys and girls with whom I spent my days. Just as these new ingredients and dishes helped me to better know the physical world, they also allowed me to better know the people who populated my life. I realized early on that food is an exploration of geography, of physical senses, of history, of culture, and is an expression of the needs that we all share as neighbors on this planet.

I was fortunate to spend a few weeks every summer on the shores of the Patuxent River in Maryland, a tributary of the Chesapeake Bay. There, every morning at the crack of dawn I would wake and begin my search for food. Walking down the dock I would deftly scoop up the blue crabs that had anchored on the pilings. I would cast my line into the deep water and with every third toss reel in a striped bass, bluefish, perch, croaker, spot, or mackerel. There was bounty in these waters, and our dinners were a reflection of whatever we were blessed to have received from the bay that day.

Respecting Earth's Resources

Years later I was offered my first executive chef position. As I created my menu, I asked myself what I wanted to communicate to my guests? I went back to those summer memories and hoped to share that same joy with my clientele. I phoned my fish purveyor and said, "Send me striped bass, crab, oysters. I want bluefish. I want mackerel." He gave a brief chuckle and dryly stated, "Sorry kid, we ate all of those. What else do you want?"

I was speechless. How could something that was part of my identity be gone? It turned out my fish supplier was right. Our demand for those species had been so great that they were effectively gone. Efforts were in place to restore the health of the bay, but for the time being I had to look elsewhere for my menu.

I realized at that moment that the guiding hand of natural selection in this world is quite firmly holding a fork. What we choose to eat describes how we choose to use the world. And in this case, we had used it all up.

I began to talk to friends in the conservation community and learned a great deal about how marine ecosystems work, how fishing pressure can diminish the health of our oceans, and how most people were unaware of the crisis. I looked back into the cannon of environmental literature and found out about the "tragedy of the commons." This idea, put forth beautifully in an essay by Dr. Garret Hardin, has become a cornerstone of modern environmentalism, and states that men and women acting in rational self-interest will ultimately bring ruin to our shared common. And this has given rise to a style of environmentalism that focuses on how humans negatively impact ecosystems.

People Create Solutions

Now I was a chef selling hospitality in a restaurant. I needed to come up with another perspective on the common story—describe how humans have a positive role to play in our relationship with nature. If humans can bring destruction to ecosystems through their quest for food, if humans can then use that food to give rise to unprecedented rates of diabetes, heart disease, obesity; if humans can make the earth and themselves sick by the choices that they make for dinner, then the opposite was also true—they could make the very same choices in order to heal. Heal their bodies and their planet.

In other words, we are the problem, and that means that we are also the solution. I began to call this perspective the communion of the commons. It's a narrative of how humans are impacted by ecosystems, a consideration of our role in nature that is more hopeful, useful, and human.

Sustainability

One of my favorite authors, E. B. White wrote, "I wake each morning torn, not knowing whether to save the earth or to savor it." Fortunately we don't have to make that choice, we cannot create more food, bulldoze more rainforests, find more fish in the sea. But we can learn how to balance our relationship with what nature provides. Sustainability and human health are about nourishing ourselves and our communities with the foods that we already produce.

Sustainable food production is a continuously advancing effort. But it alone is not enough. We must also achieve a simultaneous behavioral shift that encourages and teaches us to use food sustainably. It's all about balance, finding the best products and then using them wisely. The same principles apply to sustaining environments and sustaining humans.

We eat to sustain ourselves, and food is the basis of all health. We eat for calories, nutrients, vitamins, and a host of biological interactions to serve our physiological needs, some known, others not. Nutrition allows for us to understand how foods impact the body, and why some are good and others less so. This biological approach to food is the science of nutrition, which is a science of discovery, revealing the inner workings of the human body's biochemistry. Understanding nutrition gives us an opportunity to gain wisdom on how best to use food to sustain our bodies.

SPRING

AN EARLY SPRING CELEBRATION
THE RETURN OF THE VEGETABLES

Spring heralds the return of tender young vegetables.
Farmer's markets sprout up as eagerly as do the first shoots
of asparagus after a long winter's hiatus. This menu celebrates
the new flavors and crisp textures of the season

BEVERAGE
These heady-scented lemons, a holdover from the winter, make for a beguiling treat. Sweeten the lemon juice with maple syrup and add soda or flat water to your taste.

MEYER LEMONADE

VEGETABLE
Asparagus is easily combined with many flavors. Here the crisp stalks are paired with the creamy egg, the salty bite of shaved Parmesan, and the sweet crunch of toasted barley.

ROASTED ASPARAGUS WITH POACHED EGG, TOASTED BARLEY, AND PARMESAN

ENTRÉE
Fisheries begin anew in the warming spring weather. Halibut is one of the markers of the season and its snowy, white flesh is a perfect match to the sweet and delicate flavors of roasted carrots and crisp snap peas tossed in vinaigrette with pea shoots.

ROASTED ALASKAN HALIBUT, PEAS AND CARROTS SALAD WITH TENDER PEA SHOOTS

DESSERT
Pannacotta is the wonderfully simple thickened cream dessert of Italy. Similar to a crème brulée in texture, this creamy dessert is a perfect foil to the aromatic burst of the first of season strawberries.

PANNACOTTA WITH MACERATED STRAWBERRIES

CRISP CALIFORNIA SAUVIGNON BLANC

WINE
A crisp California sauvignon blanc pairs easily with many of the foods of spring dessert.

Fads versus Prudent Choices

Too often in the past, nutrition has been perceived incorrectly as a science of invention. People have looked to nutrition to alleviate their ills that have resulted from mismanagement of everyday health habits. Instead of changing our habits, we prefer to believe that doctors will invent a miracle cure or a magic pill that allows us to continue in our poor dietary habits that have hurt our health.

Invention is a part of human behavior and culture and responds to the cycles of popular preferences and trends. We see this often in the ever-recurring "new diet" that will radically change our appearance and life. Such promises offer more than an instant cure; they support the notion that our health can be guaranteed by science and not by our own prudent choices throughout our lives.

We do not need to reinvent the human diet. We have been getting along acceptably for the past 10,000 years, and the human relationship to food has been one of immense reward, allowing our diverse societies to succeed in magnificent ways. However, a part of the modern food industry has largely convinced us of the need to reinvent food, not for reasons of better health, but for their profit. What we need and fortunately are moving towards is a return to a more rational relationship with the foods that have sustained us throughout history.

SUMMER

A MIDSUMMER'S FEAST
THE PLAYFUL DELIGHTS OF SUMMER

Summer is when cooking gets really easy.
The straightforward flavors of ripe fruit and produce
are best when left to speak for themselves.
The cook's role here is to buy great ingredients
and then let them shine.

BEVERAGE
Blackberries are a sweet-sour treat. Muddle a few berries with mint and sugar then stir into soda water or sparkling wine.

BLACKBERRY SODA

SHAVED ZUCCHINI AND FENNEL SALAD WITH MUSTARD VINAIGRETTE

SALAD
Raw zucchini makes for a delicious dish when shaved thin with a peeler into long, thin ribbons. The aromatic crunch of fennel and the cool tang of mustard rounds this dish out.

ENTRÉE
Fresh sockeye salmon takes to smoke like a fish to water. Spike your grill with woodchips and cook slowly. Romesco is a classic Catalan sauce of roasted then puréed vegetables.

GRILL-SMOKED SALMON WITH ROMESCO

SPELT AND ALMOND PILAF

SIDE DISH
Spelt is delightful when paired with nutty sweetness of almonds. Start by toasting the spelt in olive oil with garlic then add almonds and water. Simmer till the spelt is soft.

GRILLED PEACHES WITH BALSAMIC VINEGAR AND ICE CREAM

DESSERT
Grilling peaches couldn't be simpler. Pair the smoky, sweet fruit with the tang of balsamic for a balanced dessert.

Craft Your Own Diet

This is not a plea that we all return to a farm to charm from the soil our daily bread. We do not need to cast aside our culinary preferences and cultural identities to adhere to a strict dietary prescription. The offerings in this book aim to encourage people to make food—its preparation, culture, and enjoyment—a pleasurable priority in our everyday life.

Good nutrition is not the result of denying ourselves the foods we love. It is not an all or nothing proposition. A hamburger now and then is not going to kill you. *Foods for Health* shares that it's not so much the unhealthy food we choose, but how much of it we consume.

So much of healthy eating is about behavior—setting expectations of what we hope food to accomplish in our lives and realigning our consumption behaviors to match our goals. Good nutrition is the result of eating a diverse range of foods within the framework of dietary guidelines, and delicious taste must always be of primary importance. You have to enjoy food in order to want to eat it again. And food is an incredibly personal topic. It represents the most intimate relationship we have with anything in our natural world, second only to our families and partners.

There is no right answer, no one answer, for how we eat. *Foods for Health* presents information and our own passions for fresh, natural ingredients to help you to understand the amazing opportunity available in every meal you craft.

Enjoying Delicious Food

To help you discover and experiment more, we offer many of our favorite ingredients

AUTUMN

AUTUMN'S SPLENDOR
A HARVEST CELEBRATION

There is much to celebrate in the Fall,
and this meal invites you to do just that.
Gather your friends and family and give a culinary
tip-of-the-hat to the seasons as they change.

APERITIF
A glass of warmed apple cider begs for a dash of brandy!

SPICE-MULLED APPLE CIDER

ROASTED SQUASH PANZANELLA WITH PEAR AND WALNUT

SALAD
Panzanella is a salad of croutons and vegetables that combine for a well-textured dish.

QUINOA CAKES, ROASTED SWEET POTATOES WITH CILANTRO-ALMOND PESTO, AND BRAISED BROCCOLI WITH RAISINS AND ALMONDS

ENTRÉE
A bevy of vegetables to celebrate the harvest is a perfect send-off to the bounty of the year.

DESSERT
Peel, core, and bake your favorite heirloom apple with a dash of cider in a covered pan. When soft, fill with cool plain yogurt sweetened with maple syrup and top with crunchy granola.

BAKED APPLES STUFFED WITH YOGURT AND GRANOLA

A VIBRANT OREGON PINOT NOIR

WINE
A refreshing yet luscious pinot noir is an excellent pairing for the earthy flavors of autumn.

and suggestions on how to approach these foods. Here you can find the groundwork to create or expand your relationship with food in a way that enables you to feel satisfaction and well-being.

When we eat we nourish more than just our bodies—we nourish our spirits. Through food we extend hospitality to ourselves and to others. We create bonds that transcend nationality, age, race, and beliefs. We nourish a complicated hunger in that we use food to connect to each other, to our past. Through food we also participate in tradition and acknowledge our place in the natural systems of this world. Ultimately, what and how we eat defines our health, and the myriad ways food comes into our lives defines the health of our planet.

Nutrition helps us to understand our biological needs, and sustainability helps us to understand what we can rationally expect our world to provide for us. When we combine these two efforts we find that we have a rare opportunity to acknowledge our dependence upon nature for our wellbeing and as a result embrace our relationship with nature and honor its ecosystems. Health and sustainability are social constructs with a singular purpose: to both savor and save the blessing of our time here on earth, one delicious bite at a time.

Our goal is for *Foods for Health* to inspire you to think about what you eat and how it can optimize your health and improve the environment. We hope that you use this book to increase the joy of eating and of eating together, so that we might all be reminded of what unites us on this beautiful, remarkable planet.

WINTER

Winter's Comfort
A MEAL TO BRING PEOPLE TOGETHER

In the winter months we want to snuggle
into the comfort of our homes
and gather around the warming fires of the kitchen.
The foods we crave are rich and filing.
The ingredients at market yield nothing new
as we settle into the dormant months on a farm.

SALAD
Spinach gives us a burst of fresh flavor, especially when this slightly bitter green is paired with the sweet, creamy taste of caramelized onion.

VEGETABLE
Cauliflower has a beautiful flavor and is well suited to a long-simmered dish like this. Cut into florets and simmer with canned, diced tomatoes, onions, and slivered almonds. Finish with fresh mint and olive oil.

Spinach and Caremelized Onion Salad

⁜

Braised Cauliflower with Mint and Almond

⁜

ENTRÉE
Lots and lots of vegetables are what make this stew. Turnips, parsnips, carrots, potatoes, kohlrabi all add a unique twist to this balanced stew of flavors. You'll find yourself picking around the beef just to get to the vegetables!.

Vegetable and Beef Stew

⁜

Rich California Cabernet

⁜

WINE
The rich foods of winter are well matched with fuller bodied red wines.

Hot Chocolate

BEVERAGE
Rich cocoa stirred into warmed milk is a perfect foil for the evening's chill. Carry a mug with you to the fire and snuggle in for the night.

FROM FARM TO FORK: WHY WHAT WE EAT MATTERS

✦ ✦ ✦

P. K. NEWBY, Sc.D., M.P.H.

When you get right down to it, food is practically the whole story every time, wrote Kurt Vonnegut in his 1985 novel, *Galápagos*. Wise words indeed, for food is as fundamental to human life as it is to for the development of civilization itself.

A source of pleasure, a celebration of culture, and a foundation of health, food practically is the whole story every time.

Vonnegut's words certainly ring true in my own life. My love affair with food began as a child, baking and gardening at my mother's side. I began working in restaurants as a teenager and worked as a part-time cook in a local vegetarian restaurant in college. Despite my love of the culinary arts, I became increasingly fascinated with the larger role food plays in our lives, farm to fork, spoon to society. From examining the effects of food on health and disease to studying why we eat what we do and the impacts of our choices on the environment, I have dedicated my scientific career to understanding why what we eat matters. These days, I spend more time in the kitchen than the laboratory, where I work to communicate what we know about food—and we know a lot—to people like you. My goal is simple: to help individuals translate principles of sound science and sustainable eating to their plates in delectable ways. After all, if food doesn't taste good, no one's going to eat it, no matter how good it is for you.

As one of life's purest joys, there are plenty of occasions for indulgence when it comes to food and drink: moderation is a key facet of a healthful diet. Even so, some foods are better for our bodies and the environment than others. The foods we eat regularly that form our everyday diet have the power and potential to help us reduce our risk of disease, maintain a healthy body weight, and maybe, just maybe, save the planet in so doing. It is to this life- and planet-saving topic—foods for health—that this book is dedicated.

Eating "Whole"

I envision this book sitting on a kitchen shelf or coffee table, providing you with at-a-glance information to help guide your individual body and our planetary home toward better health. Our goal is to provide you with a compendium that brings together key elements of what we grow and eat in easy-to-use fashion. Each section includes

historical and agricultural food facts as well as science-based nutritional information, health benefits, and environmental considerations. We've also included a few of our favorite methods, techniques, and tips for selecting and preparing foods in ways you and your family will enjoy. Through its pages, I hope you will gain an increased appreciation for why what you eat matters, farm to fork.

The book is arranged alphabetically within each food category: vegetables, fruits, proteins, whole grains, fats, and oils, and beverages. Organizing the book one food at a time makes logical sense when it comes to reading, but less so when it comes to eating. For while we might snack on a handful of juicy blueberries or crunchy almonds, our diet includes a mixture of foods and drinks that, together, create an indelible impact on our health and the planet. In other words, when it comes to diet, the whole is greater than the sum of its parts.

Combining Foods

This is certainly obvious from a taste perspective: combining foods in delectable ways creates memorable meals, and we all have our favorite examples of things that just "go together." Eating foods in mixtures also provides a major health benefit, as nutrients often interact with each other in the body. Fat-soluble vitamins, for example, are better absorbed if consumed alongside fat, as their name implies. Thus, not only is our salad more flavorful with a zesty vinaigrette, it also helps us gain the maximum nutritional value from all of those nutrient-rich vegetables—more so than if we had eaten the salad without any dressing at all.

The whole is also greater than the sum of its parts when it comes to individual foods, as foods are complex packages that include vitamins, minerals, and phytonutrients (powerful chemicals found in plants), many of which work in concert to impact our health. Scientific studies have shown that whole foods evoke a greater benefit to our bodies than consuming any one particular nutrient. Moreover, foods undoubtedly include a host of beneficial elements that scientists have not yet discovered: what we don't know about an individual food may turn out to be just as important to our health as what we know now.

For these reasons, it's best to fill your diet with whole foods that have been minimally processed so as to preserve and maximize their health benefits. Stripping away the germ and bran from grains, for instance, results in a far less nutritious food than consuming its "whole" counterpart. (Think: bread or pasta made from the whole wheat kernel rather than the "white" version.) And eating the whole fruit rather than just extracting the sweet juice will deliver more nutrients and less sugar than simply drinking the liquid. While it's necessary to wash produce to remove unwanted dirt and chemical residues, consuming the fiber- and (phyto)nutrient-rich peels alongside the flesh delivers more nutrients than removing the skins. By consuming all the different parts of foods, root to leaf, we also reduce our methane-producing, climate-warming food waste that gets dumped into landfills—much of it perfectly edible.

Your Personal Plate

While most people eat pretty much everything, it is the degree to which we do so that defines our overall dietary pattern, our whole diet. There are obvious examples of how we might classify the way we eat, like omnivore or vegetarian. Yet even within those groups exists considerable variation in what we cook, colored by geography

and culture as much as taste, cost, convenience, and healthfulness. Are you a meat-and-potatoes person who enjoys traditional comfort foods, or do you enjoy global cuisine? Do you have a penchant for sweet or salty foods, or do you consume alcohol? Is your diet filled with fast-food favorites like burgers, fries, and pizza or does it burst with whole grains, fruits, and vegetables? More so than the consumption of any one particular food, it is the combination of all the foods you eat regularly (alongside other genetic and lifestyle factors) that ultimately influences your health, your weight, your risk of disease, and your carbon footprint. And, whatever your plate looks like, employing the three fundamental tenets of variety, balance, and moderation will go a long way towards building a healthy diet.

Variety, Balance, Moderation

Certainly you've heard that variety is the spice of life. So, too, is variety the spice of a salubrious diet: the greater the diversity in color and

• SPRING •

The Start of Seasonal Produce
CELEBRATING SPRING DELIGHTS

Spring in Boston marks the opening of the seasonal markets that last until November. A time of transition, my meals feature ephemeral delicacies like asparagus, fava beans, and strawberries. Whether part of a garden party luncheon or a light supper, these dishes celebrate spring and welcome warmer days to come.

BEVERAGE
Infusions bursting with berries, flowers, and herbs are my go-to beverage, perfect for a sunny afternoon. Serve with a lemon wedge or sprig of mint for a delightful drink that's calorie- and sugar-free.

BEAN SALAD
A labor of love, I prepare fresh favas every spring. Dress with olive oil, lemon juice, salt, pepper, and whatever herbs strike your fancy. Watermelon radishes with their pink and green center are a gorgeous complement. (Parmesan shards optional.)

ICED HIBISCUS AND WILD BERRY HERBAL INFUSION

✛

FAVA BEAN SALAD WITH WATERMELON RADISHES AND HERBS

✛

SPINACH SALAD WITH STRAWBERRIES, SCALLIONS, AND TOASTED PECANS

✛

LEMON-SCENTED ASPARAGUS WITH SPRING GARLIC

✛

STRAWBERRY GELATO

GREEN SALAD
Juicy berries, scallions, and toasted pecans lie atop a bed of spinach, glorious with an orange-balsamic vinaigrette. (Add farro or blue cheese for variety, or try other spring lettuces like mesclun or arugula.)

VEGETABLE
Simple as can be, just toss asparagus with olive oil, lemon zest, and crushed garlic; season with a bit of salt and ground black pepper; and toast in a hot oven until crisp-tender. Be on the lookout for purple asparagus!

DESSERT
Not for everyday eating, gelato is a special treat I make only when sumptuous local berries are at their best: red, sweet, and delicious. Simply amazing. Serve with a mint sprig garnish for a pop of color.

kind of foods we eat, the healthier our diet tends to be. No doubt this is why humans evolved as omnivores. Because each food contains different components, we increase the probability of avoiding nutritional deficiencies by consuming a wide array of foods. As some nutrients are toxic at high amounts, loading up on just a few foods can even be fatal. Therefore, treating a single food or nutrient as a magic pellet is not the road to health if other foods are neglected: forget the "superfood" du jour and focus on eating broadly.

Balance in diet, as in life, can be a tricky concept to put into practice, in part because there are different paths to a healthy diet. Sardinians consume a Mediterranean diet high in fat, primarily due to olive oil, with moderate wine intake; Okinawans enjoy a high carbohydrate diet filled with soy foods and green tea; and Seventh Day Adventists in Loma Linda, California, are vegetarians who eat a

high fiber diet and don't drink alcohol. While all three groups eat primarily plant-based diets, the range of foods and beverages consumed vary greatly and are nestled firmly in their distinct geography, culture, traditions, and beliefs. As a result, the balance of the key energy-containing macronutrients fat, carbohydrate, and protein also differs. Nonetheless, these three diverse groups from three different parts of the globe share one important feature: the greatest longevity among the world's populations. Happily, there are numerous ways to achieve balance; one size does not fit all when it comes to diets that will get you to your hundredth birthday.

Moderation is the third pillar of the dietary triad, and it's arguably the most fun to implement when we're reveling in some of our favorite foods. Unlike vegetables and fruits, which should be eaten in abandon given most of us don't consume nearly enough, there are

SUMMER

SUMMER'S BOUNTY
A SALAD BUFFET FOR A HOT DAY

From colorful squashes and lettuces to luscious berries and stone fruit,
I can make almost my entire supper from local produce
during the height of summer. Below is selection of favorites
I might serve as part of an evening buffet on a balmy day.
(Can you tell I eat a lot of salad?)

APERITIF
Mix puréed cucumber—keep the skin for fiber and color—with fresh lime juice, basil simple syrup, and sparkling water for a flavorful, pretty drink. For an alcoholic version, substitute gin.

CUCUMBER BASIL SPARKLER

STARTER
Grilled peaches are sublime in summer (and make a terrific dessert). Plate with seared sea scallops and baby chard and dress with a peach vinaigrette for a salad that is as lovely as it is nutritious.

WARM SCALLOP SALAD WITH GRILLED PEACHES AND BABY CHARD

CORN SALAD
Top thinly sliced squash with a mixture of sun gold cherry tomatoes, corn, white onion, and parsley dressed with olive oil, white balsamic vinegar, and garlic. Summer on a plate, made even more divine with a scattering of chèvre.

CORN SALAD WITH SUN GOLD CHERRY TOMATOES

HERBED QUINOA SALAD WITH BLUEBERRIES AND PIGNOLIS

GRAIN SALAD
Toss a selection of lettuces and herbs together with quinoa, blueberries, and toasted pine nuts for a dinner salad that won't leave you wanting. Dress with a lemon-herb vinaigrette, or keep it simple with oil and vinegar.

POACHED RHUBARB AND BLACKBERRIES WITH MASCARPONE

DESSERT
I put these together when I found both at the market one spring day. Poached in port, orange peel, and spices and topped with a dollop of mascarpone, this is a wonderful dessert that can be served at room temperature.

other foods and dishes in which a moderate approach is best. Chocolate and alcohol come to mind, and you can easily envision dishes you adore that fall under the heading of "moderation." Your beloved, high-calorie dishes should not be totally eschewed, and complete denial can lead to an unhealthy relationship with food for some. Moderation is indeed part of a healthy diet and allows you to savor the divine pleasures of food and drink.

Plant-Based Diets

Building a diet that suits your palate and preferences upon a foundation of variety, balance, and moderation will go a long way toward creating healthy habits. Yet the one principle of nutrition and sustainable eating that will ultimately transform your health—and if billions of human beings do it, will in time restore the Earth—is following a plant-based diet. In Albert Einstein's words, "Nothing will benefit human health and increase chances for survival of life on Earth as much as the evolution to a vegetarian diet."

But with all this talk of variety, balance, and moderation combined with the recognition that the diet of early humans was omnivorous, must plants really take the lead in today's twenty-first century diets?

In fact, decades of research have shown the beneficial effect of diets high in plant foods such as vegetables, fruits, whole grains, beans, and legumes when it comes to human health, longevity, and disease prevention. While there are numerous forms a plant-based diet may take, paramount is the high intake of a variety of plant foods consumed in balance with each other and with physical activity to maintain a healthy body weight. Although science has shown it is not necessary to shun meat completely to obtain positive health benefits, filling our plates with plant foods of all kinds is vital.

A Healthy Planet

Science is also clear that plant-based diets are best for the health of our planet, primarily due to the high cost in fuel, feed, land, and water in producing animal foods. It's

AUTUMN

Shifting Seasons
harvesting boston's best

As the days grow shorter and temperatures begin to drop,
late summer produce is still around at the markets,
but my attention turns to fall fare. These selections are early
autumn favorites that bridge the seasons, comprising here a
buffet for a board of directors' meeting for my theater company.

Wine

Kale Salad with Caramelized
Brussels Sprouts and Toasted Almonds

Smoked Mussel and Corn Chowder

Warm Heirloom Tomato Salad with
Mustard Greens and Gorgonzola

Butternut Squash Salad with
Dried Cranberries, Toasted Walnuts,
and Chive Blossoms

GREEN SALAD
I fell in love with kale a few years back, greatly expanding my salad horizons. Chop the crucifer into thin strips and toss in a cider vinaigrette with caramelized Brussels sprouts. Top with sliced scallions and a sprinkle of dry roasted, unsalted almonds.

WINE
Alongside water at dinnertime, heart-healthy wine is a common libation for me. I keep bottles of red, white, and rosé on hand so people can select what they like.

CHOWDER
Traditional corn chowder is made with bacon and loaded in cream. My version substitutes smoked mussels for richness and includes diced zucchini and red peppers. Freshly shucked corn and stock made from the cobs makes all the difference.

TOMATO SALAD
A selection of brightly colored heirlooms needs little else but a drizzle of olive oil and vinegar, salt and pepper. Take things up a notch by roasting, plating over mustard greens tossed in a balsamic vinaigrette, and scattering with gorgonzola.

SQUASH SALAD
No autumn menu would be complete without winter squash. Cubes of roasted butternut pair beautifully with ruby red cranberries and toasted walnuts; pretty chive blossoms add elegance and flavor. Dress with maple-Dijon vinaigrette.

sorely inefficient to transform precious natural resources into meat and wreaks a greater burden on the environment. Further, there are numerous externalities associated with meat production that do not occur when growing plants, including the production of methane from ruminant animals, a greenhouse gas twenty-one times more powerful than carbon dioxide. For this reason, the impact of "food miles"—the environmental cost of how far a food travels to get to your plate—must be considered in the context of other more potent drivers of environmental damage. In general, food transportation affects climate change far less than food production: the "what" is usually more important than the "how far" when it comes to greening up your diet. While there are plenty of fantastic reasons to support your local farmers market and select fresh foods in season, reducing your consumption of animal products will go much further in limiting the deleterious effects of your diet on the earth's soil, waterways, and atmosphere.

The time has arrived for you to embark on your journey into *National Geographic Foods for Health: Choose and Use the Very Best Foods for Your Family and Our Planet*. Drink in each chapter. Ponder how you might incorporate these teachings into your own diet to achieve variety, balance, and moderation. Recall that the whole food—and the whole diet—are greater than the sum of their individual parts. Give plants the starring role in your diet, remembering that moving toward a plant-based diet is better for your own health as well as the planet.

Be inspired. Get into the kitchen. Begin here. Start now.

From farm to fork, what you eat indeed matters.

WINTER

MIDWINTER GATHERING
TANTALIZE THE TASTE BUDS, WARM THE SOUL

Winter markets arrived in Boston a few years back, so I get fabulous food that supports Massachusetts farmers all year long. And did I mention there's a fishmonger who provides local oysters? I'm a lucky woman indeed. These are some of my favorite dishes I might serve as part of a multi-course dinner party to celebrate the holidays.

OYSTERS ON THE HALF SHELL WITH SPICY-SWEET MIGNONETTE

ARUGULA SALAD WITH BEETS, ORANGES, AND TOASTED HAZELNUTS

CAULIFLOWER-ARTICHOKE SOUP WITH LEEKS

SLOW-ROASTED SALMON WITH OLIVE OIL, HERBS, AND WARM LENTIL SALAD

HOT TEA

STARTER
Oysters are one of the most sustainable foods you can consume. I serve these tasty mollusks with a mignonette including sriracha (Asian chili sauce) and a touch of agave. Simple yet sublime.

BEET SALAD
My dad adores beets, which is how I learned to love them when I was a little girl. Roasted beets and orange segments on bed of arugula are terrific when dressed with an orange-balsamic vinaigrette; add toasted hazelnuts or pistachios for crunch.

SOUP
Roasting cauliflower maximizes flavor, and the addition of artichokes, leeks, garlic, and a touch of Romano cheese and cream make this soup dinner-party worthy. Add whole grain croutons for a satisfying dinner all on its own.

ENTRÉE
Select whichever fish is in season and sustainably caught: most will work just fine when slow-roasted in olive oil and fresh herbs. (Include a splash of white wine and lemon juice, too, if you like.) Serve atop a warm salad of brown lentils, red peppers, parsley, and onions.

BEVERAGE
A habit I learned from my mother, I often enjoy a cup of hot tea in the evening. Whether green or an herbal infusion like chamomile or peppermint, it's especially welcomed on a cold winter's night.

VEGETABLES

In 2007, during a campaign stop in Adel, Iowa, then–U.S. presidential candidate Barack Obama made a remark about the price of arugula. Some media pundits seized upon that comment as proof that the Illinois senator was elitist and out of touch with middle America, because who buys arugula in Iowa? Who even knows what it is? But you can indeed purchase arugula in Iowa, where it is commonly known as rocket. Many Iowans enjoy eating this leafy green, technically an herb, and they grow it in that state as well.

While not everyone may be aware of it, the United States is in the midst of a fresh-food revolution. If you need convincing, take a stroll through the vegetable aisle at your local supermarket. You will find a greater assortment of produce on display there than was available at any previous time in the nation's history. Supermarkets in every state in the country now stock an extensive variety of vegetables, both conventionally raised and organically grown.

Abundant and Available

You might see heirloom tomatoes, enoki mushrooms, bok choy, radicchio, purple potatoes, and yes, even arugula, at your grocery store. Seasonal produce, such as asparagus and tomatoes, that once made a cameo appearance in supermarkets only at certain times of the year are now imported from warmer climates, or grown hydroponically, and have become available year-round. In response to consumer demand for fresh local produce, the number of farmers markets in the United States has surged, growing almost 10 percent from 2011 to 2012. There's plenty of room to grow from there: Food from farmers markets accounts for less than half a percent of national consumption, though the figure is significantly higher when accounting for locally sourced produce sold through groceries.

Another sign of the shift in consumers' attitudes toward what they eat: Sales of vegetarian foods have doubled in the United States. Ten percent of Americans now say that they follow a "vegetarian-inclined" diet, and though strict veganism is still relatively uncommon, the practice of "Meatless Mondays" is a growing phenomenon. Supermarkets serve burgeoning immigrant communities by regularly stocking so-called ethnic foods, such as daikon radishes, yucca, lemongrass, plantains, and seaweed, and the average American palate has become more adventurous by virtue of being exposed to so many intriguing new ingredients.

Heirloom Legacy

Yet, in the midst of this bounty, Americans have never been so unhealthy. Today, U.S. citizens have shorter life spans and experience

more illness than people in other comparably affluent countries. Two-thirds of American adults are obese or overweight, and childhood obesity has grown into a national epidemic. The reasons for this national health crisis are complex, but a sedentary lifestyle with large portions and eating habits that exceed caloric needs combined with the low cost and convenience of energy-dense foods that are high in sugar and fat are likely at the core of the problem.

Many people are convinced that part of the solution may be found in the vegetable aisle—not in one particular plant, but in the bountiful and healthful array of produce now available to most Americans. It seems as if every day a new study comes out that has media outlets touting one plant or another as a miracle food that can cure cancer, restore memory and sexual prowess, trim thighs, and sculpt and strengthen muscles. Pop-up ads singing the praises of the latest vegetable du jour, from kale to kohlrabi, skitter across our computer desktops.

The truth is that food fads come and go just as quickly as those annoying Internet ads, and a single food has yet to be discovered that will help you live forever—and probably never will be. In fact, it can be dangerous to rely solely on any one food, no matter how healthy and nutrient-dense it may be.

Planetary Consciousness

As is true in most areas of life, variety, balance, and moderation are essential. Many vegetables have unique health properties, but eating an array of healthy foods in appropriate portions every day is the best way to ensure that your body gets all the nutrients it requires. Based on many decades of research, the consensus among nutritionists

*For the sake of our national health,
it's time we moved veggies to the center of the plate.*

is that a plant-based diet that incorporates a variety of nutrient-dense, minimally processed foods can promote health and physical well-being and substantially reduce the risk of obesity, heart disease, type 2 diabetes, stroke, and many cancers, as well as other chronic maladies ranging from arthritis to depression.

Adopting a plant-based diet may also be the single most important thing a person can do to combat global warming. The practices of commercial livestock production in the United States undermine the health of the planet every day by producing greenhouse gases, using vast amounts of water, and generating animal and chemical waste. Choosing "forks over knives" represents a commitment to a more sustainable way of life, and over time relatively simple choices such as what we eat can have a huge cumulative impact.

Earth's Abundance

Nonetheless, while vegetarianism isn't for everyone, the good news is that even the most devoted carnivores will benefit from adding more plant foods to their diet, particularly vegetables. Despite growing up with the repeated commandment to "Eat your vegetables" resounding in their ears, most Americans eat far fewer than the recommended amount of two and a half cups of vegetables per day. This is a low bar to reach. Current guidelines of the U.S. Department of Agriculture and Harvard School of Public Health are for filling half your plate with veggies. And don't overlook dark-orange, red, yellow, and green plants.

In the following pages, you will find information about many vegetables from artichoke to zucchini, including a profile on seaweed and other sea vegetables, relatively new arrivals on the American culinary scene. Each entry features a current nutritional profile, detailed information about well-established health benefits and significant nutritional studies, and suggestions for food storage and preparation. You'll find information on the origins and history of each plant and learn about the vegetable family to which it belongs.

One of the most satisfying ironies of food history is that the parts of plants typically discarded or used only as food for slaves, peasants, and animals were eventually found to possess the most nutritional value. The following entries stress the benefits of consuming the whole vegetable, root to leaves, and offer tips on how to use all portions of the plant.

Finally, you will learn that not all convenience foods are unhealthy: Many vegetables come prepackaged or precut, frozen or canned, without significant loss of health benefits, enabling you to put a nutritious meal together quickly when life awaits. And vegetables, on the whole, are quite a bit more nutrient-dense than fruit.

So make room on your plate for vegetables. They will do wonders for your health.

ARTICHOKE

The giant bud of a plant that produces blue or pink thistle-like flowers, the artichoke was regarded as a delicacy in some cultures and as an aphrodisiac in others. In 1533, when Catherine de Medici left Italy to wed Henri II of France, she brought along a supply, since she couldn't bear to be without them. Today, nearly all artichokes grown commercially in the United States come from California, primarily from the foggy coastal climate of Monterey County. The Green Globe variety is the most prevalent; baby artichokes and purple varieties can sometimes be found at U.S. farmers markets.

Choose and Use

Look for tightly closed heads that squeak when you squeeze them. To prepare, wash well and trim an inch off the stem and the top and remove the tough leaves (bracts) around the base. Steam over boiling water, bud end down, until tender. To test, insert a sharp knife into the base of the artichoke—it should be soft and yield to the knife easily. Delicious both hot and cold, whole artichokes are eaten by removing one leaf at a time and scraping off the base with one's teeth before discarding the remainder. The hairy, inedible *choke* at the center must be removed before enjoying the fleshy base or *heart*—the prized part of the plant. Artichokes are often served with melted butter or mayonnaise for dipping; a healthier preparation is to dress lightly with olive oil and lemon juice. Halved, with the chokes removed, artichokes may be grilled or roasted after being steamed. Two naturally occurring chemicals present in artichokes, cynarin and chlorogenic acid, can make foods consumed after these delicacies taste sweet. But this reaction does not occur in all people and is temporary and harmless.

GIVES YOU

Dietary fiber
Folate
Vitamin C
Magnesium
Manganese
Potassium
Phosphorus
Copper
Phytonutrients
    flavonoids, phenolic
    acids, flavonolignans)

For Your Health

A large artichoke contains just 75 calories, and more antioxidants than any other cooked vegetable. This low-calorie food is high in dietary fiber and potassium and contains the phytonutrients cynarin and silymarin, both good for the liver.

For Our Planet

Almost all of the commercial U.S. artichokes are from California and require frequent irrigation, but you may find them at your local market in spring. The spiny exteriors allow for shipment without packaging, which reduces waste.

✦ TAKE AWAY

Artichokes make a tasty, low-calorie snack or side dish.

ARUGULA

Also known as rocket, rucola, and Italian cress, this edible herb grows wild in the Mediterranean. In ancient times arugula was grown for its leaves and seeds, used for flavoring oil, and was reputed to be an aphrodisiac. Arugula's distinctive peppery flavor is similar to watercress and dandelion greens. A member of the broccoli and cabbage family, arugula shares some of the cancer-fighting properties of other cruciferous vegetables.

GIVES YOU

Vitamin K
Vitamin C
Folate
Calcium
Iron
Potassium
Magnesium
Phytonutrients
   (glucosinolates,
   flavonoids,
   carotenoids)

CONSIDER ✦ SALAD IN A BAG

Health-conscious grocery shoppers love bagged, prewashed salad mixes for their convenience. However, as with most convenience foods, all this packaging creates waste. Arugula and other salad greens often come in plastic containers that end up in the garbage or recycling bin. Due to the popularity of packaged greens, bunched arugula is sometimes not available. When you can find it, perhaps at a local farmers market or food coop, it's worth the trouble to wash your own. Just be sure to wash it well. You can then store it in the refrigerator in a reusable vegetable bag so that it's ready when you need it.

Mesclun, a Provençal word meaning "mixture," is an assortment of young salad greens that began cropping up in U.S. supermarkets (loose and bagged) in the 1990s. Mesclun traditionally contains equal portions of arugula, chervil, endive, and lettuces, but now may include radicchio, mâche (or lamb's lettuce), frisée, baby spinach, and other tender greens. It's a great choice for adding diverse tastes, textures, and nutrients to your salads.

Choose and Use

When not prebagged arugula is typically sold with roots attached. Choose bunches with fresh green leaves with no signs of wilting or yellowing. Once refrigerated, the leaves should be consumed within a day or two and must be rinsed well just before using to remove grit. Pesticides penetrate these delicate greens and cannot be washed away. The amount of residue is negligible for most healthy adults, but if slight amounts pose a particular concern for you, or out of concern for the environment, you might choose organic. Try combining with sliced red pears, blue cheese, toasted nuts, and a walnut vinaigrette for an elegant salad. (Dress with a light hand and don't toss until right before serving, since the tender leaves break down quickly.) Arugula can also be sautéed, like spinach. It also makes an excellent pesto and pairs wonderfully with eggs when added to frittatas and omelets.

For Your Health

Though tender, arugula's greens pack a nutritional punch. Unlike romaine and iceberg lettuce, which are less nutritious than darker-hued lettuces, raw arugula is an excellent source of the vitamin K, critical for bone health, as well as vitamins C and A. The leaves also contain glucosinolates, flavonoids, and carotenoids, which help boost the human immune system. Full of flavor, this fast-growing salad green has become widely available in U.S. markets.

For Our Planet

Because arugula does not attract many insects, much of the plant grown in the western U.S. is cultivated without pesticides, great news for maintaining soil quality and protecting farmworkers.

ASPARAGUS

Cultivated and enjoyed the world over for thousands of years, the elegant green spears of the asparagus have always signaled spring's arrival. A flowering perennial plant that produces edible shoots, asparagus is actually a member of the lily family. Commercially grown in the United States since the mid-1800s, asparagus is a labor-intensive crop, since each spear must be cut by hand. China is currently the world's largest producer of this vegetable.

GIVES YOU

Vitamin K
Vitamin E
Folate
Vitamin C
Tryptophan
Riboflavin (vitamin B2)
Dietary fiber
Phytonutrients
   (carotenoids,
   flavonoids, saponins)

Choose and Use

This springtime favorite is now available year-round, though it costs less in season. Choose bunches of long, bright green spears with closed, compact tips. Spears are available in varying thicknesses, but thicker spears are generally more succulent. Green asparagus is most common in U.S. markets, though sometimes one finds purple too. White or light green asparagus, grown without sunlight, is more popular in Europe than the green variety. Immerse the base of a bunch in an inch or two of water and store upright in the refrigerator until use. Best consumed within two days of purchase, asparagus may be parboiled, steamed, stir-fried, roasted, pickled, or eaten raw. Thin spears require less cooking time; choose thicker spears for grilling and roasting. Try roasting asparagus with a little olive oil and then wrapping the spears in savory smoked salmon for a treat. A traditional French preparation, roasted asparagus also makes a wonderful bed for fried eggs.

For Your Health

Asparagus contains vitamin K, a fat-soluble vitamin that aids in blood clotting and bone health. Just four spears contain almost 40 percent of vitamin K needed for the day. Serving asparagus with a heart-healthy salad dressing made from polyunsaturated fats like vegetable and nut oils helps in vitamin absorption, as with any vegetable with fat-soluble nutrients. Low in calorie and high in fiber and protein, asparagus is also an excellent source of glutathione, one of the body's best cancer fighters. It is rich in beta-carotene. An excellent source of the antioxidants lutein and zeazanthin, asparagus is also high (for a plant) in choline. Some people notice their urine has a pungent odor after they eat asparagus—a harmless reaction to the body's metabolizing of sulfur.

For Our Planet

In North America, the growing season for asparagus extends from January to June, and it's a vegetable that for many marks the arrival of spring. According to the Environmental Working Group, asparagus is one of the "Clean 15" crops with the fewest pesticide residues if you can't access organic.

PREP TIP ✦ IT'S A SNAP

The bottom of asparagus stalks can be tough and fibrous. Trim them by hand rather than with a knife by bending each stalk until it snaps; it will naturally break at the point where it becomes tender. But don't throw out the ends! The asparagus stubs make a fine soup: simmer in water with some chopped onion, then puree with a few tablespoons of yogurt.

AVOCADO

Sometimes called the alligator pear because of its shape and pebbled skin, the avocado is botanically a fruit that masquerades as a vegetable due to its common culinary use. Avocado pits have been found in pre-Incan tombs, and evidence suggests avocado trees were cultivated in the Americas as early as 5000 BC. Available year-round, the creamy green flesh may be processed into avocado oil and used in cooking and cosmetics.

Choose and Use

Avocados sold in markets are usually hard, but they are climacteric fruits that will ripen in a day or two when left on a kitchen counter. Store at room temperature. A ripe avocado yields slightly to the touch; avoid those with soft or brown spots. Bisect the avocado lengthwise with a knife; when the blade hits the pit, rotate the knife around the avocado, then twist the two halves in opposite directions to separate. Sinking a blade carefully into the pit and twisting will dislodge it. Use a soupspoon to easily remove all the fruit cleanly from the skin. Lime or lemon juice rubbed on the cut surface prevents browning. Avocados are usually eaten raw.

GIVES YOU

Dietary fiber
Vitamin K
Vitamin E
Riboflavin
Niacin (vitamin B3)
Folate
Vitamin C
Pantothenic acid
Potassium
Pyridoxine (vitamin B6)
Copper
Monounsaturated fats
Phytonutrients
  (carotenoids,
  phytosterols,
  polyhydroxylated
  fatty alcohols)

Serve sliced into salads, or spread on bread. The buttery texture also pairs beautifully with citrus. Guacamole is a cinch to make too, including only mashed avocado, chopped onion, garlic, and lemon juice; it stays green longer when you leave the pit in the bowl. Cover the mixture with plastic wrap directly covering the puree to prevent oxidation.

For Your Health

Though high in calories (about 200 in a single avocado), avocados are rich in a protein that contains all the essential amino acids. Studies have shown that avocados contain an abundance of oleic acid, another heart-healthy fat, this time monounsaturated, which also contributes to the vegetable's satiating power. Avocados also have a small amount of heart- and brain-healthy polyunsaturated omega-3 fatty acids. Of the two types available in the U.S., the California avocado is richer in oil than the Florida variety.

For Our Planet

A place to consider the complexities of carbon emissions, while avocados grown in California may be closer (for some), they require extensive irrigation compared to those from Mexico.

BEET

A folk belief says that two people who eat from the same beet will fall in love. Typically a deep garnet-red—though ranging from golden to purple and even striped like a candy cane—beets have been long associated with physical passion: pictures of the root adorned the walls of a brothel in ancient Pompeii. Originally, the beet's root resembled a carrot, but preference through the centuries for a plumper juicier shape eventually resulted in the modern, swollen root one finds on market shelves today. Both roots and greens are good to eat.

Choose and Use

Beets are at their most tender from late June through early October, when they are picked fresh. The most flavorful are small to medium size, with the greens still attached. If selecting beets with the greens removed, check that some portion of the stem is still attached, the root is firm, and the skin smooth with no cracks. Separate the greens from the root and refrigerate both until ready to use. Rinse well under running water before preparing.

Highly versatile, beets add vivid color and sweetness to various recipes. Eastern Europeans make borscht, a traditional cold beet soup. The root may be grated and served raw or pickled in salads, or cooked by boiling or steaming. Roasting in particular concentrates the flavors. Cook beets whole, rub off the skins with your hands, and slice afterward on a cutting board

PAIRINGS ✦ GREAT WITH NUTS

Beets make a fine side salad, especially when teamed with chopped walnuts. Cut up roasted beets and toss with olive oil and a little balsamic vinegar, add crumbled cheese such as feta or goat cheese (chevre), then sprinkle with toasted nuts. Beets also pair well with arugula, anchovies, and sour cream.

The raw beet's skin can be removed with a vegetable peeler or a paring knife, but an easier trick is to roast or boil the beet until tender, cool slightly, then rub off the skin with your hands or a clean kitchen towel you don't mind getting stained. The cooked skin should slip off easily.

GIVES YOU
ROOTS:
Folate
Manganese
Dietary fiber
Potassium
Tryptophan
Phytonutrients
  (betalains)

GIVES YOU
GREEN:
Vitamin K
Ascorbic acid
Potassium
Manganese
Riboflavin
Magnesium
Dietary fiber
Calcium
Iron
Copper
Phytonutrients
  (carotenoids,
  phenolic acids)

you don't mind staining; latex gloves will protect your hands. Root vegetables grown in contaminated soil will appropriate those contaminants (such as lead), a good reason to choose organic. Try sliced or grated beets with your favorite greens, toasted pecans or walnuts, and blue cheese for a colorful salad.

Too often discarded, beet greens are actually the most nutritious part of the vegetable. They may be cooked like any other dark leafy green such as Swiss chard or spinach; they are wonderful simply sautéed with olive oil and garlic.

For Your Health
Beets have the highest sugar content of any vegetable but are low in calories. Raw beets contain folate, a vitamin beneficial in cancer and heart disease prevention, but cooking diminishes this nutrient. Nutritional studies indicate that table beets are rich in antioxidants that promote cardiovascular health. They are also a good source of fiber. Consuming these roots may turn urine and stools red, a harmless (though alarming) condition. Beet greens contain almost nine times the recommended daily value of vitamin K, a bone nutrient and heart protector.

For Our Planet
Beets with attached greens are often sold bundled in markets with no additional packaging, reducing the carbon cost of processing. Consuming both the greens and roots also reduces unnecessary methane-producing food waste.

BOK CHOY

Also called Chinese white cabbage, *pak choi*, and white mustard cabbage, bok choy has been grown in China for more than 6,000 years and is still associated primarily with Asian cuisine. Bok choy means "white vegetable" in Cantonese, a reference to the snowy white stalks of the plant.

Choose and Use

Now available in the United States, Canada, and the Philippines, bok choy has been slower to catch on elsewhere in the world. Two varieties commonly found in U.S. markets are Shanghai bok choy with its white stalks and tender dark green leaves, and light green baby bok choy. In Hong Kong, one may find 20 different varieties of this vegetable.

Choose bunches with firm white stalks and crisp green leaves. Refrigerated, bok choy will keep for three to four days in the refrigerator. This mild-tasting leafy green may be steamed, braised, stir-fried, or added to soups. The stems take longer to cook than the leaves. The Korean pickled cabbage known as kimchi is sometimes made with bok choy. Used raw, it adds a pleasant crunch to salads.

GIVES YOU

Vitamin C
Vitamin K
Folate
Calcium
Iron
Phytonutrients
(carotenoids,
glucosinolates)

PREP TIP ✦ USE IT LIKE CABBAGE

Bok choy may be used as you would cabbage: think steamed or shredded finely for a coleslaw-like presentation. This vegetable also benefits from grilling. First, trim the base of each bunch and remove and clean the stalks. Lightly oil and season both sides with salt and cracked black pepper and grill until leaves are crisp at the edges.

PAIRINGS
✦
SIMPLE OR SPICY STIR-FRY

Like other Asian greens, bok choy is wonderful when prepared simply, with garlic and olive oil. For bigger flavors, try peanut oil and a pinch of crushed red pepper. Combining bok choy with other vegetables, like carrots and red peppers, makes a colorful and delicious side dish or bed for a piece of fish. Or toss with pasta for a quick, nutritious dinner.

✦ TAKE AWAY

For centuries this Chinese cabbage has added flavor, nutrients, and a satisfying crunch to meals.

For Your Health

Bok choy is an excellent source of carotenoids and vitamins C and K, as well as folate and calcium. It is low in oxalate, which binds calcium and impedes absorption, so the calcium in bok choy can be more readily absorbed than that in other leafy greens. This relative of the cabbage also contains carotenoids like beta-carotene, which may help prevent heart disease and stroke as well as some cancers. As with other cruciferous vegetables, chopping bok choy before cooking increases the bioavailability of cancer-preventive compounds.

For Our Planet

Imported bok choy seems to have fewer pesticides than domestic, but today many small farmers have begun growing and selling this Asian treat at local markets.

BROCCOLI

Beloved by ancient Romans who consumed it several times in the course of a single banquet, broccoli was sometimes referred to as "the five green fingers of Jupiter." Native to Italy, this leafy green vegetable was first commercially cultivated in the United States by Italian immigrants in the 1920s. When overcooked, broccoli can be sulfurous and mushy, traits that have led to the plant's periodic bouts with unpopularity. Today, many celebrate broccoli, and its star rides high again in the vegetable firmament.

Choose and Use

Fresh broccoli can be found in markets year-round, though peak season is October through April. Choose bunches with sturdy stems and compact, bluish green heads; pass on those with cracked bases and yellowing florets. Sometimes purple and white varieties become available, as well as the astonishing lime-green Romanesco broccoli, a living fractal, with its cluster of spiraling heads. Frozen broccoli is just as nutritious as fresh. The stems are edible and nutritious and are particularly tender in "baby" broccoli varieties. This vegetable can be steamed, sautéed, stir-fried, or roasted. Slice the stem into pieces and prepare along with the separated florets. Cooked broccoli may also be pureed into a soup; roasting with olive oil and garlic first brings in the most flavors. A member of the mustard family, broccoli is most healthful when cooked as little as possible, until crisp-tender and retaining its bright green color, and served simply—without calorie-laden sauces.

For Your Health

It is difficult to overstate the benefits of broccoli. This cruciferous vegetable is rich in beta-carotene as well as lutein and

GIVES YOU

Vitamin C
Vitamin K
Folate
Manganese
Dietary fiber
Tryptophan
Potassium
Pyridoxine
Riboflavin
Thiamine
Phosphorus
Calcium
Phytonutrients
(carotenoids,
flavonoids [higher in
raw], glucosinolates,
phenolic acids, lignans)

zeaxanthin, meaning it helps prevent age-related macular degeneration, and it promotes heart health. People who eat an abundance of broccoli appear to have a reduced incidence of bladder and prostate cancer. Although most people prefer it cooked, raw broccoli also makes a great salad addition.

For Our Planet
A sturdy vegetable, broccoli is often found with relatively little packaging—which reduces the resources used to process broccoli and cuts down packaging waste.

PREP TIP ✦ DON'T FORGET THE GREENS!

The neatly trimmed heads of broccoli displayed in most produce aisles bear only a partial resemblance to the living plant itself: the large mass of flower heads grows surrounded by leaves that can be prepared just like broccoli rabe or collard greens, with delicious and healthy results. If you find the discarded greens at your local farmers market, ask if you can take some home for your supper table.

BROCCOLI RABE

Related to both the cabbage and the turnip family, broccoli rabe (pronounced *rahb*), also called rape, or rapini, is used in the cuisines of southern Europe, Portugal, the Netherlands, and China. Many Americans are unfamiliar with this leafy green, though it is a favorite vegetable in Italian immigrant communities throughout the United States. The plant has six- to nine-inch stalks, ruffled green leaves, scattered clusters of broccoli-like buds, and a distinctively bitter taste that complements starchy foods such as pasta and rice.

Choose and Use

Broccoli rabe makes its appearance in the market from late summer through the fall and winter, though it may be elusive in some regions. Look for bunches of slender stems, crisp green leaves, and compact florets; avoid wilted or yellowed broccoli rabe, though a few yellow flowers should not trouble you. Store in the refrigerator in a reusable plastic container for no more than five days, and wash well before cooking. The stems of this vegetable tend to be tough, so trim off a couple inches before use. One method for reducing the bitter flavor of this green is to quickly blanch it in boiling water, followed by an ice-water dip; then it can be sautéed, stir-fried, or braised. Serve broccoli rabe on its own as a side dish, combine with potatoes or pasta, or add to broth. The chopped leaves may be added to salads.

✦ TAKE AWAY

Broccoli rabe adds a flavorful variation to rice or pasta.

PREP TIP ✦ **BRAISE LONG AND SLOW**

For many, broccoli rabe can be a tough vegetable to love, but braising slowly tames its bitterness. Heat some sliced onions in a small amount of olive oil, then add the chopped broccoli rabe and a couple tablespoons of raisins. Add some water, cover, and let simmer for an hour or more. Finish with a handful of chopped almonds right before serving. For those less sensitive to bitter flavors—taste buds differ among humans—a simple sauté in olive oil and garlic is a quicker, easier preparation.

FOOD SCIENCE ✦ THE BRASSICA GENUS

Brassica is a genus of plants in the mustard family and one of the most popular food crops worldwide. Collectively known as cruciferous vegetables (Latin for cross-bearing, because of the shape of their flowers), this family includes cabbage, cauliflower, broccoli, kale, Brussels sprouts, bok choy, turnips, and other nutritional green leaf vegetables—generally considered to be healthy foods with cancer-fighting properties. Cruciferous vegetables are rich in sulfuraphanes, which help protect arteries from disease by boosting the body's own natural defense mechanisms. Plants in this beneficial family contain isothiocyanates and phytochemicals known as organosulfur compounds, which are powerful anticarcinogens.

GIVES YOU

Vitamin K
Vitamin C
Folate
Vitamin E
Thiamine (vitamin B1)
Niacin
Riboflavin
Pyridoxine
Manganese
Iron
Calcium
Phosphorus
Potassium
Tryptophan
Phytonutrients
  (carotenoids,
  glucosinolates)

For Your Health

Broccoli rabe is a rich source of glucosinolates, which the body converts to cancer-fighting compounds. Studies credit nutrient-dense broccoli rabe with many other benefits as well, such as strengthening bones, lowering the risk of heart disease, and detoxifying the liver.

For Our Planet

The entire plant of broccoli rabe can be enjoyed, which means less ends up in landfills.

BRUSSELS SPROUTS

Another member of the cancer-fighting family of cruciferous (*Brassica*) vegetables, which include cauliflower and broccoli, Brussels sprouts grow along a towering stalk, crowned with a cabbage rose. Ancient Romans called them *bullata gemmifera* (diamond-making bubbles) because they were reputed to increase mental clarity. The modern Brussels sprout was first extensively cultivated in Belgium and named after that country's capital city. Alas, many English and American cooks boiled this highly nutritious vegetable into a sulfurous lump, earning it a reputation as culinary Kryptonite. Today, the practice of oven roasting them is gaining in popularity and the much-maligned Brussels sprout seems to be enjoying a renaissance.

Choose and Use

Brussels sprouts are usually trimmed and sold in net bags or baskets, though they can increasingly be found on their impressive stalks at farmers markets. Look for small, bright green sprouts with tightly packed leaves. Use soon after purchasing since they begin losing their sweetness as soon as they are picked. Frozen sprouts are a good option as they retain most of their flavor and nutrients. This fall/winter crop often appears on Thanksgiving menus paired with chestnuts.

To prepare, rinse, pull off any loose outer leaves, and trim a bit off each base. An X cut into the base of each will hasten cooking. Leave sprouts whole, or halve them, or just use the individual leaves. They may be roasted, boiled, steamed, pan fried, or chopped finely and used raw in a slaw. Overcooking greatly reduces their nutritional value and creates bitter flavors. Roasting Brussels sprouts coaxes out a nutty sweetness from

GIVES YOU

Vitamin K
Vitamin C
Manganese
Folate
Dietary fiber
Potassium
Pyridoxine
Tryptophan
Thiamine
Iron
Phosphorus
Phytonutrients
 (flavonoids,
 glucosinolates,
 carotenoids, lignans)

the caramelized sugars in the plant. Finish under the broiler to lightly char the outer leaves. Brussels sprouts pair beautifully with nuts, mustard, garlic, caraway seeds, and lemon.

For Your Health
Brussels sprouts offer the same benefits as other members of the *Brassica* genus and contain more antioxidants than broccoli ounce for ounce. The carotenoids lutein and zeaxanthin, present in Brussels sprouts, promote eye health.

For Our Planet
Most U.S. production is in California, but many small farms also grow Brussels sprouts, a great opportunity to support your local farmer come autumn.

✦ TAKE AWAY

You can roast, boil, steam, or fry Brussels sprouts, but be careful not to overcook them.

PREP TIP ✦ ROAST UNTIL NUTTY AND SWEET

Roasting coaxes out a wonderful nutty sweetness that even a lifelong sprout hater may find impossible to resist. Finish under the broiler if desired to lightly char the outer leaves.

CABBAGE

Nutritionally rich, cabbage has been used throughout history as both a medicine and a food. In preparation for a night of overindulgence, ancient Romans ingested it to ward off hangovers, and 17th-century explorers brought it along on ocean voyages to prevent scurvy, since the vegetable is a good source of ascorbic acid, or vitamin C. Cabbage has also served as a subsistence food in many cultures. As a result, the privileged classes have tended to look down their noses at it, and the unpleasant smell of overcooked cabbage has contributed to its disfavor. Still, the humble cabbage with its pleasant crunch deserves a place at every health-conscious table.

GIVES YOU

Vitamin K
Vitamin C
Folate
Dietary fiber
Manganese
Pyridoxine
Potassium
Phytonutrients
    (carotenoids,
    glucosinolates,
    phytosterols,
    flavonoids/phenolic
    acids [in red
    cabbage], lignans)

Choose and Use

When selecting a head of cabbage, choose one that is firm, glossy, and feels heavy for its size. Cabbage keeps in the refrigerator for about a week but tastes best when eaten right away. To prepare, first discard any wilted outer leaves and rinse. Cabbage may be boiled, steamed, braised, or stir-fried, as well as stuffed and baked; the quickest cooking methods will preserve the most nutrients. Do not cook cabbage in an aluminum pot—a chemical reaction will discolor the vegetable. Finely chopped or grated, raw cabbage adds a spicy crunch to salads and slaws. The nutritious core, which people often discard, may be grated into a slaw.

For Your Health

Along with broccoli and Brussels sprouts, cabbage is a cruciferous vegetable with proven cancer-fighting properties. The three main types are green, red/purple, and Savoy, all of which are low in calories and high in fiber (red has more fiber than green, and Savoy has the most). Since the different colors contain different cancer-fighting glucosinolates, it's wise to eat a mix. Chopping cabbage and then allowing it to aerate for five minutes on the cutting board enables an enzyme in the vegetable to convert these glucosinolates into isothiocyanates, which enhance the body's natural detoxification systems. Steam cabbage to increase its cholesterol-lowering powers.

For Our Planet

Conventionally grown cabbages retain fewer pesticide residues than many other fruits and vegetables. Cabbages also transport well from farm to purchase, so they are usually sold unwrapped, which reduces unnecessary packaging waste.

✦ TAKE AWAY

Use many types of cabbage to make your meals more colorful and nutritious.

PREP TIP ✦ HOLD THE MAYO

Classic coleslaw recipes tend to drown shredded cabbage in a sea of mayonnaise, which adds a lot of extra calories and dilutes the crunch and flavor cabbage provides. Try substituting a smaller amount of nonfat Greek yogurt for the mayo for a change. Sliced cabbage can also be served simply with vinegar and, if left to sit, will quickly pickle for an interesting side dish.

CARROT

A carrot's greens might tip you off that this root is a member of the parsley family, related to Queen Anne's lace. The earliest carrots were actually skinny and purple or yellow, and probably originated in Afghanistan. We have Dutch horticulturalists to thank for the large bright orange carrots so common in markets today, which they fed to cows to ensure that butter made from their milk had a rich yellow hue, imparted from the orange-hued carotenoids found in carrots.

Choose and Use

Harvested beginning midsummer through fall, carrots are available year-round. They are often sold trimmed and packed in plastic bags, or in bunches with the greens attached. Choose bunches with firm carrots and fresh-looking greens, and avoid those with cracks or hairlike rootlets. Green tops rob the root of nutrients, so remove before refrigerating. (They can be stored in the freezer for use in a homemade vegetable stock.) Carrots keep for weeks but do lose some flavor as they sit. Also avoid storing them near apples, pears, and potatoes, which emit ethylene gas that can give carrots a bitter taste. As long as carrots are washed thoroughly their skins can be eaten.

GIVES YOU

Vitamin A
Dietary fiber
Vitamin C
Potassium
Phytonutrients
  (carotenoids,
  polyacetylenes,
  phenolic acids,
  lignans)

FOOD SCIENCE ✦ PURPLE CARROTS

A purple carrot might look like a science fair project gone awry, but it harks back to the original carrot, which was not orange but purple. Today, carrots are bred in a rainbow of colors, including purple, maroon, red, orange, yellow, and white. Different colors signal the presence of different phytonutrients. The anthocyanins in purple carrots act as powerful antioxidants. This pigment may also reduce the risk of heart disease by slowing blood clotting. Alas, they lose much of their color during cooking but make a gorgeous addition to salads when served raw.

The bagged carrots that now dominate the market are not "baby" carrots at all, but mature carrots milled down to a uniform small size, then soaked in water containing chlorine. The waste products from this process are used to make shredded carrots and the peel for cattle feed. Simply prepared carrot sticks you cut yourself are more flavorful and avoid unnecessary packaging and energy use.

This versatile tuber may be prepared any number of ways: boiled, steamed, sautéed, stir-fried, or grated raw over salads. As with other vegetables, roasting deepens their flavor and converts some of their starches into sugars. Spices such as caraway, dill, cumin, cinnamon, and coriander all enhance this vegetable. The carrot's natural sweetness makes it a favorite in cakes and muffins too.

For Your Health

A ten-year-long study conducted in the Netherlands on the impact of different-colored fruits and vegetables on cardiovascular disease determined that those with darker shades of orange and yellow offered the most protection, with carrots ranking highest in this category. Eating these roots as part of a plant-based diet also guards against cancer and diabetes. Beta-carotene, which the body converts into vitamin A, improves night vision and protects skin from sun damage. Alpha-carotene, also present in carrots, has been shown to significantly reduce one's risk of death from cardiovascular disease, cancer, and other diseases. Carotenoid value may increase when carrots are boiled rather than steamed. Dressing carrots with olive oil or butter aids in absorption of the fat-soluble nutrients in these vegetables.

For Our Planet

Carrots can be enjoyed root to leaf, so reduce your personal food waste by keeping the skins on—make sure to wash well—and use the bright-tasting greens in a pesto or stock.

CAULIFLOWER

This member of the *Brassica* genus is well named, since it truly is a flower, or rather thousands of tiny flower buds packed into larger buds that make up the head's snowy bouquet. The outer leaves of the cabbage-like plant are tied closed over the young heads of white cauliflower to block sunlight and "blanch" them as they grow, making cauliflower one of the most labor-intensive crops. This delicately flavored winter vegetable, which pairs wonderfully with spices, is a staple of Indian cooking as well as classic French cuisine, but it leaves many American cooks cold. Eye-catching new varieties in orange and vivid purple pigments may help raise the profile of this nutritious, delicious, low-calorie vegetable.

Choose and Use

Choose cauliflower with compact florets, no discoloration, and fresh green leaves (which are edible). Wrapped in plastic, it will keep for up to two weeks in the crisper. Rinse and pat dry, then cut out the large core on the underside of the head, or curd. Avoid cooking cauliflower in aluminum or iron pots, which will discolor it. Cauliflower may be divided into florets and steamed, boiled, sautéed, or eaten raw. The whole head may also be steamed (stem end up), or baked. Different colors vary slightly in taste, but all cauliflowers taste delicious with sharply flavored ingredients such as mustard and spices. Roasting at a high heat makes it crispy and sweet, and mashing it with a little garlic and olive oil is a lower-calorie and more healthful alternative to potatoes.

For Your Health

Low in calories and high in fiber, this cruciferous vegetable may reduce the risk of bladder, breast, colon, prostate, and ovarian cancer, thanks to sulforaphanes, the compounds responsible for many of its health benefits. Cauliflower also contains a compound called glucoraphanin, which protects the stomach and intestines. Different colors of cauliflower provide different nutrients in varying amounts—for instance, orange cauliflower contains 25 times more beta-carotene than the white variety.

For Our Planet

Cauliflower is a great choice to conserve your food dollars and reduce your food waste by eating the whole vegetable: core, flowers, and leaves. If possible, choose organic to invest in sustainable farming.

GIVES YOU

Vitamin C
Vitamin K
Folate
Choline
Pyridoxine
Potassium
Dietary fiber
Manganese
Phytonutrients
 (glucosinolates,
 phytosterols,
 carotenoids, phenolic
 acids, lignans)

PREP TIP ✦ ROAST IT, MASH IT

If you've never tried it before, roasted cauliflower is a revelation. Preparing it this way also seems to reduce the bloating and flatulence that some people experience after eating this vegetable. Cauliflower cooked until soft and mashed with yogurt and some extra-virgin olive oil also makes an excellent, low-calorie substitute for mashed potatoes.

CORN

Maize, known in the United States and Canada as corn, has been so essential to human survival in North American cultures that native peoples regarded the plant as a deity. Originally a wild grain, corn was domesticated thousands of years ago in Mexico. Today, it's the number one field crop in the United States and the source of more than 800 processed foods, including breakfast cereals, flour, grits, syrup, and oil. Ethanol fuel, ink, medicine, and plastic containers are also made from corn. Sweet corn, the type categorized and consumed as a vegetable, is a sugar-rich variety of grain harvested when immature. Dried corn, including popcorn and corn flour, is considered a grain.

GIVES YOU

Dietary fiber
Folate
Vitamin C
Niacin
Pantothenic acid
Phytonutrients
(flavonoids [in purple corn], carotenoids, phenolic acids)

Choose and Use

Eat fresh corn as soon off the stalk as possible, when it's the sweetest: Corn that sits in the refrigerator will still be good to eat but will become less tasty as some of its simple sugars are converted to starch. Choose ears with bright green, snugly fitting husks, and gold-brown silk. Peel back the very top of the husk and look for plump, evenly spaced kernels. This vegetable comes in a variety of colors, with yellow and white the most common; "butter and sugar" corn, with its combination of yellow and white kernels, is a summer favorite. Corn tastes best when cooked until just tender, either by immersing the husked cobs in unsalted water and bringing just to a boil for a few minutes, steaming, or by cutting off the cob and sautéing. You can also soak the ears and then grill corn in its husk, a tasty summertime treat. Place corn in its husk directly on the middle rack of the oven and bake at 350 degrees for approximately half an hour for an infallible side dish. Eventually, the kernels will caramelize, resulting in a delicacy for corn aficionados.

For Your Health

A good source of dietary fiber, corn can help boost weight loss by making one feel full. It also contains lutein and zeaxanthin, antioxidant phytonutrients that keep the eyes healthy as they age.

For Our Planet

The United States produces more corn, by far, than anywhere else in the world. Forty percent of this crop is used to produce ethanol, a corn-based biofuel. Overall, U.S. corn production has become more sustainable. According to the Field to Market alliance for sustainable agriculture, corn production saw a 30 percent decrease per bushel in greenhouse gas emissions between 1987 and 2007.

✦ TAKE AWAY

Choose the freshest ears available, and boil, steam, or grill them.

CONSIDER ✦ CORN IN THE FOOD CHAIN: ANIMAL FEED

Only a small percentage of the U.S. corn crop is destined for human consumption. Most of the corn grown in North America is dent, or field corn destined for livestock feed because it's cheap and plentiful. Ruminants such as cattle have trouble digesting corn; this leads to a host of physical problems that then need to be controlled with antibiotics, another problem with conventionally raised cattle.

EGGPLANT

Eggplants belong to the nightshade family, as do potatoes and tomatoes, and initially people in many world cultures believed them to be poisonous. The Italian word *melanzana* derives from an older name: *mela insana,* or "insane apple," but the eggplant is actually a large berry—botanically a fruit that is categorized and consumed as a vegetable. The original American eggplant was small and white, hence the name; in the U.K. and in France they are called aubergines. Eggplant today lends its silky texture and bulk to Mediterranean, Chinese, Indian, and Middle Eastern cuisines.

GIVES YOU

Dietary fiber
Thiamine
Pyridoxine
Phytonutrients
 (phenolic acids,
 flavonoids, nasunin)

Choose and Use

The best-tasting eggplants tend to be smaller, since larger ones may be seedy and bitter. The large, deep purple variety is most commonly seen in U.S. markets, but one also finds smaller white eggplants, striped varieties, and the slender, purple kind known as Japanese eggplants. A green cap and firm, unblemished skin signal freshness. This summer vegetable should be stored in the refrigerator crisper drawer. Slice or cube the vegetable (leave the edible skin on for an extra nutritional boost). Large eggplants may also be baked whole and then mashed, or sliced and grilled. Smaller types have more tender skins and may be stir-fried, sautéed, or roasted.

For Your Health

Eggplants get their rich purple color from anthocyanins, antioxidants that may lower the risks of cancer and heart disease. A powerful antioxidant, nasunin is found only in the skin of eggplants and is responsible for its purple color. Eggplant's high fiber and meaty texture create a feeling of fullness with very few calories.

For Our Planet

Keep the skin for maximum nutrition and to avoid food waste.

✦ TAKE AWAY

Try roasted or baked eggplant instead of meat—its thick texture will leave you satisfied.

PAIRINGS ✦ A SIMPLE RATATOUILLE

Eggplant tastes delicious teamed with other summer vegetables, such as tomatoes and zucchini. A simple version of ratatouille can be made by cutting eggplant into chunks and braising it with tomatoes and garlic. Finish with some chopped fresh basil. More adventurous cooks might enjoy using eggplant in a traditional Indian dish such as curried eggplant.

FENNEL

Over millennia, a host of medicinal and magical benefits have been attributed to this hardy perennial herb. Revered by the ancient Greeks and Romans as an appetite suppressant, fennel was also reputed to increase strength, improve vision, stimulate lactation in nursing mothers, and ward off evil spirits. According to Greek mythology, when Prometheus stole fire from the gods, he hid it in a fennel stalk. The type of bulbous fennel found in most markets is called Florence fennel, which lends its licorice flavor to absinthe. Fennel seeds, a popular herb, are actually the dried fruits of another variety of the fennel plant.

GIVES YOU

Vitamin C
(especially the fronds)
Dietary fiber
Potassium
Manganese
Folate
Calcium
Phytonutrients
   (anethole, flavonoids)

Choose and Use

Look for fennel with stalks intact and clean, crisp bulbs. Refrigerate, tightly wrapped, until ready to use. All parts of the plant are edible and can be eaten raw or cooked in a variety of ways, including braising, baking, and sautéing. The feathery fronds may be snipped like dill and used as a garnish or as part of a delightful herb salad. Closely related to carrots, parsley, dill, and coriander, fennel marries well with all of these ingredients. Its anise-like character diminishes when cooked; sometimes chefs add a little anisette to boost the licorice flavor. Fish, especially salmon, taste wonderful with this vegetable.

For Your Health

Far more nutritious than celery, fennel provides the same low-calorie crunch. The folate in fennel aids in brain function and limits the risk of heart disease and stroke. When consumed by pregnant women, fennel can also reduce brain and spine defects in newborns. The high amount of ascorbic acid supports the immune system, and its flavonoids contribute antioxidants. Anethole, the primary component of fennel's volatile oil, has been shown to have anti-inflammatory and anticancer properties. In India, fennel seeds are traditionally offered after meals to freshen breath and aid in digestion.

For Our Planet

Reduce your food waste by enjoying the entire fennel plant: bulbs, roots, stems, seeds, and fronds. Fennel's distinct aroma seems to discourage insect pests, which means fewer pesticides are used to grow it. Most fennel sold in markets is in bulk, which reduces packaging waste.

✦ TAKE AWAY

Use all parts of the fennel plant to boost flavor and add essential nutrients.

PAIRINGS ✦ COLESLAW WITH AN ADULT FLAIR

Shaved very thin with a mandoline or a sharp kitchen knife, fennel makes a wonderful substitute for cabbage in a twist on traditional coleslaw, especially when dressed with lemon juice and a sprinkling of fennel seeds. The addition of the fronds to an herb salad is also a refreshing change.

GARLIC

One of the oldest cultivated plants on earth, garlic belongs to the lily family, along with chives, leeks, and onions. Heads of garlic have been discovered tucked into the tombs of Egyptian pharaohs, and the slaves who built these tombs ate garlic to increase their physical strength and endurance. In the Middle Ages, people believed that ingesting garlic could render one immune to the bubonic plague. Proponents of herbal medicine prescribe garlic to prevent colds, the flu, and other infectious diseases, and around the world people enjoy the aromatic range of flavor that it brings to food.

Choose and Use
Purchase bulbs, or heads, of garlic with firm, plump cloves and dry skins. Avoid garlic with small green sprouts or mold, both signs of age. Stored in an open container in a cool, dark place, a head of garlic will keep about eight weeks. The individual cloves are usually peeled before use, and they may be eaten raw or cooked, depending on the flavor desired. Pressing garlic produces a sharper flavor than chopping or slicing it. When cooking

GIVES YOU

Manganese
Vitamin B6
Vitamin C
Selenium
Calcium
Tryptophan
Phytonutrients
   (organosulfur
   compounds, lignans)

PREP TIP ✦ ROAST THE WHOLE HEAD

Roasting garlic radically changes its character, transforming it into a sweet and caramelized paste that can be used in a broad range of dishes, from flavoring mashed potatoes or smashed cauliflower to spreading on a sandwich. Fill an ovenproof casserole with a half-inch of water, then place several heads of garlic upright inside and cover. Roast for 30 minutes, or until soft, in a 375-degree oven. Or drizzle with extra-virgin olive oil and put in a dish or wrap in foil before roasting. Water will leach off some nutrients, and the oil preparation will add more calories; it's a matter of taste and trade-offs.

Crushed or sliced garlic is a super way to add robust flavor to a wide variety of foods and dishes. But have you ever seen it take on a bluish-green hue in a hot oven, or when it's pickled? This is because of an enzymatic reaction due to the sulfur components in garlic (and other aromatics), which breaks down in high heat or acidic environments. Don't worry, though: the colorful garlic may take you by surprise, but it's perfectly safe to eat.

garlic at high heat, take care not to let it burn or it will turn bitter. Garlic can enhance all sorts of savory dishes. Raw garlic may cause indigestion in some people.

For Your Health

One hears many grandiose claims about the health benefits of garlic. While some have been bolstered by science, other studies have proved inconclusive. The widely held folk belief that garlic helps ward off the common cold has yet to be fully substantiated. Sulfur-containing compounds in garlic, specifically hydrogen sulfide, are the source of many of its health-promoting effects. Colorectal and ovarian cancer rates drop in populations that regularly ingest a lot of garlic. There also appears to be a correlation between allium foods and reduced gastric cancer risk. And not the least of garlic's benefits is its ability to elevate the taste of bland food. Chopping or crushing garlic helps release a chemical called allicin; wait at least 15 minutes before using to increase its healthful properties.

For Our Planet

Heads of garlic are typically transported and sold without additional packaging waste. But chemicals are heavily applied to fumigate the soil in which garlic is grown, so buying organic if possible is a more sustainable option to protect the Earth.

GREEN BEAN

Though consumed throughout the Americas, green beans were not raised commercially in the United States until 1836. These legumes became so popular that growers once marketed them as "The Ninth Wonder of the World," and they still rank high on Americans' list of favorite vegetables. Also called string beans or snap beans, green beans are related to other so-called common beans, including kidney, navy, pinto, and black beans. Harvesting earlier results in the fresh green character of this vegetable, which pairs well with lemon, vinegar, dill, parsley, garlic, and almonds. Other varieties include pale yellow wax beans and purple beans.

Choose and Use

Green beans are available year-round, with peak season between May and October. Look for bright green beans that snap, not bend. The freshest beans have slightly fuzzy skins; avoid bumpy looking ones where the beans are visible under the pod. Unwashed green beans stored in a plastic bag will keep for about five days in the crisper. As with any vegetable, rinse well before using. The entire bean pod is edible and may be consumed raw or cooked by steaming, boiling, braising, and stir-frying. Pickled green beans taste great too. In many Middle Eastern recipes, green beans are slow-cooked until meltingly soft, but they retain more of their phytonutrients, vitamins, and minerals when steamed quickly just until tender-crisp. An ice bath after cooking preserves their bright green color and prevents overcooking. Green beans are also sold frozen and canned; make sure to choose brands with no added sodium or sugar.

For Your Health

Green beans contain a wide variety of carotenoids (such as lutein and beta-carotene) and flavonoids (such as quercetin),

GIVES YOU

Vitamin C
Vitamin K
Manganese
Dietary fiber
Folate
Molybdenum
Magnesium
Iron
Phytonutrients
  (carotenoids,
  flavonoids, lignans)

which have antioxidant properties that have been shown to support cardiovascular health. They also afford a good source of the mineral silicon, which can help build strong bones and support the growth of connective tissue in the body.

For Our Planet

Sixty percent of all conventionally produced green beans are grown in the United states, in Illinois, Michigan, New York, Oregon, and Wisconsin. Food miles is just one part of the carbon emissions equation, though: efficiently transported green beans from afar can sometimes have a smaller footprint.

PREP TIP ✦ THINK CELERY SUB

If you're craving a green, crunchy snack, skip the celery and try some raw green beans. They taste great and offer far more nutritional benefits than celery, and you don't have to cut them into sticks. For a real treat, see if you can find purple pole beans at your local market, which are similar in flavor to green beans. Toss with a little olive oil, vinegar, and garlic and lightly season with salt and pepper for a colorful, snappy salad.

HEARTY GREENS: COLLARD, MUSTARD, CHARD

Easily cultivated, fast growing, and highly nutritious, cooking greens provided sustenance for the many enslaved persons, sharecroppers, and migrants who labored on U.S. plantations. Inexpensive and available year-round, mixed greens are most popular in the American South, where they are typically cooked with butter, lard, or oil and flavored with fatback, also called salt pork, or a ham hock. Often lumped together as a "mess" of greens, each has a distinct flavor, with chard being the mildest and mustard the most peppery. While they can be consumed raw, making for a robust if somewhat bitter salad green, slow cooking (braising) or sautéing is more common. The practice of cooking down the leafy greens and drinking the juices, or "pot likker," stems from African heritage. All cruciferous vegetables, these greens are nutritional powerhouses.

Choose and Use

Greens wilt easily, so select the freshest-looking bunches with the greenest leaves. Unwashed greens may keep longer than a week if wrapped in dampish paper towels and stored in the crisper. Rinse thoroughly before cooking to flush out the dirt trapped between the ribs of the collard and chard, in particular. Both stems and leaves are edible, and the quickest preparation is to chop and cook the entire plant together; the slower-cooking stems will yield a satisfying crunch. Swiss chard has white stalks and glossy green leaves; ruby chard has red ribs and stalks and a stronger flavor. Sometimes varieties are bunched together and labeled "rainbow chard." The oxalic acid in chard will discolor an aluminum pot. Collards may be prepared in the same manner as spinach or cabbage. Raw mustard greens add a peppery bite to salads, but may also be steamed, braised, or sautéed.

GIVES YOU

Vitamin K
Vitamin C
Folate
Manganese
Calcium
Potassium
Copper
Iron
Phytonutrients
   (glucosinolates, phenolic
   acids, flavonoids,
   carotenoids)

For Your Health

Greens are rich in vital minerals, such as iron, copper, and manganese, and bone-building vitamin K and calcium, which help ward off osteoporosis. Mustard greens, which stave off breast cancer and heart disease and keep bones healthy when consumed as part of a plant-based diet, may be especially beneficial for menopausal women. Chard also helps prevent cancers, especially those of the digestive tract. Collard greens outrank all other common cruciferous vegetables in their ability to lower cholesterol.

For Our Planet

Especially prone to damage, conventionally grown leafy greens often require lots of chemicals—especially troublesome for farmers growing them for your dinner table. Selecting organic is an investment in sustainable growing practices and also protects farmworkers.

PAIRINGS ✦ A HEALTHIER MIX

Southern greens are traditionally cooked with fatty meats, which reduces their healthfulness. A more nutritious preparation for both you and the planet is to sauté them—either mixed together or singly—in a little olive oil with freshly chopped garlic and a bit of salt and pepper. A splash of lemon juice or vinegar adds a bright finish.

KALE

Modern kale, which resembles collard greens with frilly leaves, comes in many varieties and colors, including red and purple. It still bears a striking resemblance to fossils of wild grasses that grew on Earth billions of years ago. A member of the mighty *Brassica* genus, kale thrives in a cold climate. This hardy winter vegetable is usually harvested after the first frost, which intensifies its flavor, making it sweeter and more tender. Kale was the most widely eaten green vegetable in Europe until the end of the Middle Ages, when it was eclipsed by its cousin the cabbage.

Choose and Use

Choose relatively small bunches with sprightly leaves and no wilting or discolorations. The unwashed greens will keep for several days in a cold refrigerator. Wash well and cut out the tough midrib of each leaf before use—these can be simmered in water to make a broth, or sliced thinly and served with the greens. To preserve its rich stores of vitamins K, A, and ascorbic acid, it's best to cook kale quickly in minimal water or, better yet, sauté it with olive oil and a bit of garlic. Steaming kale concentrates its cholesterol-lowering powers. Brighten the flavor of kale with a splash of lemon juice or vinegar.

✦ TAKE AWAY

Add kale to salads and dishes for its cancer-fighting antioxidants.

PREP TIP ✦ GREAT ON THE GRILL

For a more tender salad, dress the kale and let it sit overnight (less time will suffice), which helps tenderize the leaves. First remove the large rib, which can be tough unless sliced thinly, and cut the leaves very thin, then toss with a vinaigrette. Sprinkling with lemon juice before letting it sit enhances kale's phytonutrient concentration.

PAIRINGS ✦ A HEALTHIER SALAD GREEN

A hearty green, kale's colors include red, green, and purple. Texture also varies, including a flatter leaf or one with crinkles. Whichever you choose, kale makes a beautiful salad when paired with toasted nuts and cheese. Topped with a piece of grilled fish or tofu, it makes a fine dinner on its own.

GIVES YOU

Vitamin K
Vitamin C
Manganese
Dietary fiber
Copper
Tryptophan
Calcium
Pyridoxine
Potassium
Iron
Folate
Phytonutrients
(carotenoids,
flavonoids,
glucosinolates,
lignans)

For Your Health

Of late, kale has been hailed as a superfood, and the label seems largely justified. A 2010 study published in the *American Journal of Clinical Nutrition* showed that eating a diet rich in the antioxidant vitamin K reduces one's risk of developing or dying from cancer. Studies have also shown that ingesting kale can slow cognitive decline, prevent rheumatoid arthritis and heart disease, and slow age-related macular degeneration. The carotenoids, flavonoids, and vitamin K in kale are fat-soluble nutrients and must be eaten as part of a meal including fat to increase absorption. Try consuming as part of a winter salad with a heart-healthy vegetable oil such as olive or canola.

For Our Planet

Like other greens, conventionally grown kale often requires a lot of pesticides to obtain a thriving crop. If you are able to find and afford organic, buy it to protect the earth as well as those who grew it for you: the farmers.

LEEK, ONION, GREEN ONION

For centuries, members of the pungent tribe known as the allium family have lent their versatile character to all manner of savory dishes, and countless recipes begin with the simple act of chopping an onion. Our ancestors worshipped onions long before they ventured to eat them, however. Egyptian tomb paintings depict onions more than any other plant. The word *onion* derives from the Latin *unus*, meaning "one," and ancient Romans regarded the plant's multilayered sphere as a symbol of the universe.

Today these noble bulbs are inexpensive and readily available, and they work all manner of magic in the cuisines of the world. "Dry" onions range in size and sharpness, from large yellow, white, and red onions to sweet varieties such as the Vidalia, to diminutive pearl onions. Green onions are slender onions without bulbs, a favorite ingredient in Asian dishes. The mildest-tasting member of this fraternity and the soul of vichyssoise, the leek has been cherished by gourmets for thousands of years, though it has yet to make much headway in American kitchens.

GIVES YOU

LEEK:
Vitamin K
Manganese
Vitamin C
Folate
Pyridoxine
Iron
Dietary fiber
Phytonutrients
(carotenoids,
flavonoids,
organosulfur
compounds)

ONION:
Vitamin C
Dietary fiber
Pyridoxine
Folate
Tryptophan
Phytonutrients
(phytosterols,
flavonoids,
organosulfur
compounds)

GREEN ONION:
Vitamin K
Vitamin C
Dietary Fiber
Folate
Calcium
Iron
Phytonutrients
(flavonoids,
carotenoids,
organosulfur
compounds)

Choose and Use

When choosing dry onions, look for firm bulbs with glossy papery skins. Avoid any that have sprouted or have soft or moldy spots or an odor. Onions should not be refrigerated. Kept in a cool, dry place with good air circulation, they should last approximately two months. Cutting onions causes tearing (a result of certain sulfuric compounds). If this bothers you, try wearing glasses or goggles made for this purpose. The sharper the knife, the fewer the tears. The onion adds flavor to almost anything you cook, and its culinary uses are practically infinite. This versatile vegetable may be fried, braised, boiled, sautéed, roasted, baked, or eaten raw. When cooked slowly, the high sugar content in onions

PREP TIP ✦ LEEKS: CUT, RINSE, REPEAT

Grown in sandy soil, the leek tends to trap dirt in its bulb and must be cleaned carefully before use. To ensure that no residual grit finds its way into the cooking pot, chop the white stalk (and the green leaves, if you plan to use them) and immerse the pieces in several changes of water to rinse away the grit, then toss in a colander to drain. A salad spinner is a useful tool for this task.

caramelizes, resulting in a wonderfully mellow flavor. The very sweetest varieties, such as Vidalia and Walla Walla onions, may even be eaten out of hand, like an apple.

Green onions are usually sold in bunches; the stalks should look fresh and crisp. Wrapped in plastic, they last up to two weeks in the refrigerator. Rinse before using, and trim off the rootlets. Sliced raw green onion may be sprinkled over foods or soups or added to salads, or stir-fried with other vegetables.

Leeks no larger than two inches in diameter with a slightly limber stem are the most tender. Choose those with brightly colored leaves and an unblemished white bulb. Bagged in plastic, leeks will last in the crisper for about five days. If using whole leek, trim off the root end, slit lengthwise, and rinse well under running water, to flush out the grit between the plant's many layers. People often discard the green leaves and use only the bulb, but the leaves are edible too—though they take longer to tenderize. Leeks have a more delicate flavor than dry onions. They may be braised, steamed, and grilled, or chopped and added to soups or salads.

For Your Health

Ingesting onions can boost immunity, lower blood pressure, help prevent stroke, and decrease one's risk of developing colorectal, ovarian, pancreatic, and prostate cancer. An onion's

FOOD SCIENCE ✦ ALLIUM

A genus of the lily family, alliums include garlic, chives, shallots, and scallions, which look almost identical to green onions but are a distinct variety. Many plants in this group were cultivated as herbal medicines long before they were used to flavor food. Research shows that eating alliums adds anticancer, anti-inflammatory, and antioxidant compounds to one's diet. With all of their shapes, sizes, colors, and flavors, mix them up in your diet to gain the maximum health benefits.

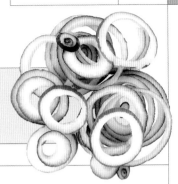

PREP TIP ✦ USE RED ONIONS WHEN USING ONIONS RAW

Raw onions can have a sharp taste that some people find unpleasant. In recipes calling for raw onion, opt for the red ones, which are sweeter and have a more balanced flavor than yellow or white onions. They are especially wonderful on salad, where they add flavor as well as color.

cancer-fighting power is directly related to its pungency: The strongest-tasting onions, such as the New York Bold, prove most effective at reducing one's cancer risk. Onions are rich in cancer-fighting antioxidants called flavonoids. Because many of these flavonoids are concentrated in the onion's outer layers, overpeeling can result in a significant loss of these phytonutrients. Take care to remove only the onion's papery outer skin. Onions can also help improve bone density. One study showed that eating an onion a day helped postmenopausal women reduce their risk of hip fracture.

For Our Planet
Some commercial onion producers, notably Gills Onions in California, have pioneered sustainability practices to reduce plant waste in onion production. This grower converts 100 percent of its daily onion waste (unusable tops, tails, and skins) into emissions-free electricity and uses drip irrigation systems to conserve water.

✦ TAKE AWAY

Onions add a range of flavors and essential nutrients to many dishes.

MUSHROOM

Neither animal nor plant but something in between, the mysterious mushroom is classified as a fungus. Mushrooms come in a fantastic array of sizes, shapes, and colors. People in every age and culture have eaten them as food, but they have also served as medicines or as hallucinogens in religious ceremonies. Most of the mushrooms eaten in the United States are cultivated inside darkened buildings where temperature and humidity are controlled. Wild mushrooms, which may be cultivated or foraged, offer a more exotic range of flavors than the typical white supermarket mushroom, with a higher price tag.

Choose and Use

Medium-sized white button mushrooms and brown criminis (baby portobellos) are the most common varieties stocked in supermarkets. Select firm mushrooms with tightly closed caps and no gills showing, and store in the refrigerator for as much as a week. To clean, brush off caps with a damp paper towel. Mushrooms can be eaten raw in salads, or sautéed and added to pasta, omelets, soups, and other dishes to impart a wonderful earthiness to a recipe. The larger portobello mushroom grills beautifully and provides an excellent substitute for meat in a vegetarian diet. Try one as part of a vegetarian "burger." More exotic varieties, such as the shiitake, oyster, and chanterelle, can be found in many markets, along with canned mushrooms and dried wild mushrooms.

GIVES YOU

Selenium
Riboflavin
Copper
Niacin
Pantothenic acid
Potassium
Phosphorus
Vitamin D
Ergothioneine
Phytonutrients
   (beta glucans)

FOOD SCIENCE ✦ WASHING MUSHROOMS

Despite kitchen folklore, it is a myth that mushrooms absorb excess liquid and become soggy when cleaned in water. While they should not be submerged, rinsing mushrooms gently but thoroughly under water, like other vegetables and fruit, will ensure your fungi are free of dirt and ready to be used in your favorite recipe.

PREP TIP
+
MUSHROOM DIVERSITY

Fresh and dried mushrooms are found in a wide array of shapes and sizes, textures and flavors. Some mushrooms, like shiitake, have tough stems that should be trimmed and composted. Dried mushrooms are a shelf-stable food that will last for months in your pantry. Once the mushrooms are rehydrated in a hot water bath, the soaking liquid can be used in your favorite soup or stew.

+ **TAKE AWAY**

Raw or cooked, mushrooms can enhance the flavor and texture of your dishes.

For Your Health

Studies show that mushrooms may play a role in both cancer prevention and treatment. The B vitamins and antioxidants in mushrooms support cardiovascular health, and they also represent one of the few food sources of bone-building vitamin D. Mushrooms also contain glutamic acid, a nonessential amino acid that the body makes on its own but that helps brain function and muscle recovery. This low-calorie but filling food can aid in weight loss by satisfyingly replacing meat in regular meals. Cultivated mushrooms provide the same benefits as more expensive wild varieties.

For Our Planet

Mushrooms are a crop that grows rapidly and yields high returns. Many organizations regard mushroom cultivation as playing an important role in moving the planet toward sustainability.

PEPPERS: RED, ORANGE, YELLOW, GREEN

Native to the Americas, and related to the eggplant, potato, and other edible members of the nightshade family, these colorful vegetables are also called sweet peppers to distinguish them from their fiery cousins, the chilis. Each color signals a different stage of maturity: green bell peppers turn yellow, orange, and then red as they ripen and grow sweeter. Peppers can also be found in white and purple varieties.

GIVES YOU

Vitamin C
Pyridoxine
Folate
Dietary fiber
Vitamin E
Potassium
Phytonutrients
  (flavonoids,
  carotenoids, phenolic
  acids, phytosterols,
  lignans)

Choose and Use

Look for firm peppers that feel heavy for their size and have shiny skin and bright green stems. Leave the stem intact and store in a crisper for a week or longer, then rinse well before use. Sliced raw peppers add a pleasant crunch to salads. With the top sliced off and seeds and ribs removed, peppers may be stuffed and baked. Add them to stir-frys or grill them. To roast peppers, spear one with a fork and rotate slowly over a gas flame until the skin blackens and blisters. Let the roasted pepper sweat in a sealed paper bag until cool, then peel off the skin (don't wash off the juices), and remove the stem and seeds. Olive oil, onions, and tomatoes all pair well with peppers.

For Your Health

Although red peppers are lower in the carotenoids beta-carotene and alpha-carotene than green peppers, they have more vitamins and nutrients, including the antioxidant lutein, a potential agent for cancer prevention. Red peppers contain more than three times the vitamin C of oranges. Pairing them with iron-rich foods helps increase absorption of this mineral. Peppers of all colors are very high in antioxidants.

For Our Planet

All colors of commercially grown bell peppers have been classified by the Environmental Working Group as one of the "Dirty Dozen" vegetables that retain high levels of pesticide residues. If you're able, selecting organic is a good choice.

✦ TAKE AWAY

Prepare peppers in a variety of ways to benefit from their antioxidants and sweet, tangy taste.

RADICCHIO

Radicchio (pronounced *ra-DEE-kyoh)* is a type of red-leafed chicory related to both endive and escarole. It was listed in an ancient Roman encyclopedia as a blood purifier and a cure for insomnia. Once virtually unknown in the United States, this distinctive Italian immigrant has made its way into practically every supermarket, where it often contributes a striking dash of color and a bracing bitter flavor to the mixed salad greens called mesclun. Most varieties of radicchio are named for different regions in Italy. Heads of radicchio di Chioggia, the most common type sold in the United States, resemble small cabbages with pretty variegated white and wine-red leaves.

Choose and Use

Choose heads with crisp-looking outer leaves with no discolorations. This cool-season plant may be purchased year-round and will keep for many weeks in the vegetable crisper. Green salads can benefit from the color and pleasantly bitter taste of radicchio leaves. It tastes good baked with rice or mixed into risotto, or braised on its own as a side dish. Radicchio pairs well with balsamic vinegar or dressings with a touch of sweetness. The leaves may be brushed lightly with olive oil and grilled or roasted, which mellows their flavor.

GIVES YOU

Vitamin K
Copper
Folate
Vitamin C
Vitamin E
Potassium
Phytonutrients
(flavonoids,
carotenoids)

PAIRINGS ✦ RADICCHIO SALAD

The pretty purple and white leaves of radicchio are lovely to look at but the bitter flavor can be too much for some. Combining it with sweeter salad greens like spinach alongside avocado, pears, or toasted nuts keeps the pleasing color and provides balance.

PREP TIP
✦
GRILLED RADICCHIO

Everyone loves to barbecue during summertime but few are familiar with grilling lettuce. Grilled radicchio is beautiful and the high heat cuts down its bitter flavors. Cut the heads in half length-wise, drizzle with olive oil, and season with salt and pepper then toss onto the grill at high heat. Enjoy as a side dish on its own, or toss with whole wheat pasta, garlic, and parmesan for a quick supper.

✦ TAKE AWAY

Radicchio adds a tasty bitterness to salads and is a traditional ingredient in risotto.

For Your Health

Radicchio is an excellent source of vitamin K, important for bone health and which may play a role in the treatment of Alzheimer's disease. This leafy vegetable contains the antioxidants zeaxanthin and lutein, which help protect the eyes against age-related macular degeneration. Radicchio gets its bitter flavor from lactucopicrin, which has a sedative and pain-killing effect in the body.

For Our Planet

If you enjoy gardening, radicchio is easy to raise and requires less water than many other crops. And, if you're really adventurous, enjoy the whole plant: its roots can be used to brew chicory coffee.

RADISH

First cultivated in China, the radish is the edible root of a mustard-like plant, which accounts for its peppery flavor. A close relative of the cabbage, turnip, and cauliflower, this crucifer is often relegated to the status of a decorative garnish on American plates—a regretful waste of a beneficial and flavorful vegetable. Varieties include the red globe, and the black radish, widely used in eastern Europe. The large white daikon radish has multiple uses in Asian cuisine.

Choose and Use

Red globe radishes, the pretty red ones sold in bunches at the market, have a mild peppery flavor. Bright color and crisp green leaves indicate freshness. Avoid the largest ones, which may be pithy, and any with cracks. Remove the green tops, which leach off nutrients, and store in the refrigerator. Most radishes grow more pungent as they mature, so use them within a few days of purchase, although they last in the fridge for weeks if stored in a plastic bag. Many people discard radish tops, but they are nutritious and tasty, either eaten raw in salads, sautéed along with the radishes, or used as you would other greens. Wash roots and tops well before using, to rinse away any residue and grit. Raw

GIVES YOU
Vitamin C
Potassium
Pyridoxine
Phytonutrients
    (glucosinolates,
    phenolic acids,
    flavonoids)

PREP TIP ✦ WATERMELON RADISH

An heirloom variety of the daikon radish that originated in China, the watermelon radish masks its wonders inside an unassuming white exterior. Slicing one open reveals a striking magenta core, which tastes mild and sweet and resembles the beloved summer fruit. Watermelon radishes lose their brilliant color when cooked, so you may prefer to showcase them raw in salads or pickle them.

✦ TAKE AWAY

Add radish greens or the red bulbs to your salads, or eat the spicy roots as snacks.

radishes make a low-calorie snack or an unexpected addition to salsa. Cooked (by braising, stir-frying, or steaming), they lose their bite and taste more like turnips. Chopped daikon added to soups and sauces softens during cooking and adds texture.

For Your Health

Radishes offer many of the same cancer-fighting benefits as other vegetables in the *Brassica* genus. They are also a good source of vitamin C, an antioxidant that boosts the immune system. Don't peel radishes, since many of the antioxidants are thickly concentrated in the peel.

For Our Planet

Radishes are grown in most U.S. states, with California and Florida being the largest producers. Enjoy green tops in addition to the root to reduce your food waste. These plants are easy to cultivate and grow quickly, so anyone with a vegetable plot can raise their own.

SEAWEED

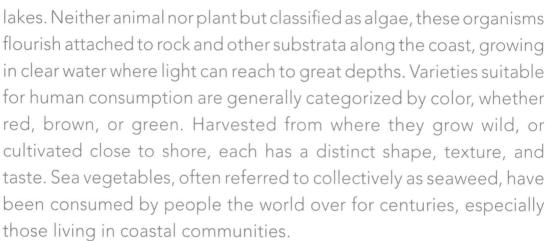

Thousands of varieties of seaweed grow in the Earth's oceans as well as in freshwater lakes. Neither animal nor plant but classified as algae, these organisms flourish attached to rock and other substrata along the coast, growing in clear water where light can reach to great depths. Varieties suitable for human consumption are generally categorized by color, whether red, brown, or green. Harvested from where they grow wild, or cultivated close to shore, each has a distinct shape, texture, and taste. Sea vegetables, often referred to collectively as seaweed, have been consumed by people the world over for centuries, especially those living in coastal communities.

Today, seaweed makes up 25 percent of the Japanese diet. It can also be found in the cuisines of Scotland, Ireland, and Wales, as well as in China, Korea, Vietnam, and Malaysia, where people welcome the range of flavors and abundant nutrients sea vegetables bring to the table. Nonetheless, most Americans are still largely unfamiliar with seaweed, though they have been unknowingly ingesting it all their lives. Additives made from seaweed are used as stabilizers, emulsifiers, and thickening agents in processed foods such as ice

FOOD SCIENCE ✦ CARRAGEENAN

While most people don't know exactly what carrageenan is, they might recognize the term from an ingredient list. Carrageenan is extracted from some red seaweeds and its various forms are used as thickeners, gels, and stabilizers in a wide variety of foods. Incredibly versatile, its properties vary according to type, important to know if you're using it in home cooking. Agar-agar is one form of carrageenan known for its exceptional gelling properties.

PREP TIP
REHYDRATING SEAWEED

Rehydrating dried seaweed is a cinch: separate the dried pieces, being careful not to prick your hands; place in a large pan; and cover with water. Seaweed will swell as it absorbs water, rehydrating completely in about 30–40 minutes; add more water as needed. Plain water works perfectly, but you could use a no-sodium seafood or vegetable stock for more flavor.

GIVES YOU

Vitamin K
Folate
Magnesium
Calcium
Iron
Iodine
Phytonutrients
   (fucoidans, flavonoids)

cream, pudding, and pie fillings, like the familiar carrageenan found on so many ingredient labels.

The most popular sea vegetables include nori, used to make edible wrappers for sushi rolls; kombu and wakame, simmered to flavor broth, such as for miso soup; and hijiki, which resembles black, wiry pasta. Kelp, the North American equivalent of kombu, is often roasted and processed into flakes. Dulse, harvested from the frigid waters off the north Atlantic and the northern Pacific coast, is soft and chewy and is sometimes sold as a snack food. The Western palate has become more cosmopolitan, and adventurous cooks will doubtless find ways to add this versatile, healthy, and highly sustainable food to their diets.

Choose and Use

Sold in many health food and specialty stores, sea vegetables also may be ordered online. As with any food sourced from the sea, water quality is a concern—it's wise to purchase from suppliers who guarantee the purity of their seaweed. In the future, different varieties will likely become more widely available in supermarkets. Look for this food in various forms, such as in sheets (nori), whole pieces (dulse), or in flakes (kelp). Stored at room temperature in tightly sealed packages, it should keep for at least six months. A versatile and convenient food, seaweed needs no cooking, but many varieties require soaking for five to ten minutes, depending on the desired consistency. To prepare, follow the directions on the package.

For anyone unfamiliar with this food, incorporating it into the diet can pose a challenge. Using seaweed as a seasoning is a great place to start. Sea vegetables come in flaked and powdered forms that can be added to other foods, to impart a fifth taste, umami, a savory flavor that is neither sweet, salty, sour, nor bitter. Flaked kelp may be used as a seasoning at the dinner

---

PAIRINGS
✦
SEAWEED SALAD

The familiar seaweed salad served in sushi restaurants is easy to prepare at home. The healthiest option is to rehydrate dried seaweed. (You can buy seaweed that's ready to go, but watch out for added sodium.) Chop the seaweed into strips and toss with a simple dressing of rice vinegar, sesame oil, soy sauce, grated ginger, and garlic. Thinly sliced cucumber and a sprinkle of toasted white sesame seeds add color and crunch.

PREP TIP ✦ SIMMER INTO SOUPS

Given how healthy and sustainable seaweed is, it's time to start simmering it into some of your favorite stews and soups. The most traditional dish is miso soup, but it can be added to any Asian-style recipe for flavor and body.

table. (Certain seaweeds have a high sodium content.) Try sampling a few varieties to learn which ones you like best. Experiment with adding chopped sea vegetables to salads, rice, pasta, stir-frys, and soups. Dulse makes a tasty bacon substitute, since it turns crispy when fried.

For Your Health

One of the healthiest foods on earth, sea vegetables contain the same range of minerals that the human body requires, in quantities far exceeding those in land vegetables. Seaweed can also protect against radiation. Kelp has a beneficial isotope that prevents the thyroid from absorbing radioactive iodine-131, a byproduct of nuclear energy production. The sodium alginate in this sea vegetable also helps the body excrete radiation and heavy metals. Unique phytonutrients found in seaweed have anti-inflammatory, antiviral, and anti-cancer properties, and reduce the risk of blood clots in addition to lowering blood LDL ("bad") cholesterol. Seaweed is also a natural source of iodine, necessary for the proper functioning of the thyroid gland, which regulates the body's metabolism.

✦ TAKE AWAY

Experiment with seaweed, which has higher amounts of essential nutrients than any land vegetable.

For Our Planet

Sea vegetables represent the ultimate sustainable food. A World Bank study showed that the production process of seaweed farms could actually have a *negative* carbon footprint, since they could potentially absorb 20 percent more carbon dioxide than they emit. In the future, seaweed may be one of the key foods sustaining the world's growing population.

SPINACH

Spinach grew wild in ancient Persia (modern Iran) before the Moors introduced it to Spain. Related to Swiss chard and beets, this dark leafy green became known across Europe as the "Spanish vegetable." Today, people everywhere associate spinach with super strength, thanks to its well-known evangelist, the cartoon character Popeye.

Choose and Use

Spinach is often sold in bunches. Look for crisp, fresh-smelling leaves, with no wilting or yellowing. Wrapped in plastic, this leafy green may keep well for a week in the vegetable crisper. Stems are edible but can be trimmed if tough. Immerse in several changes of water to remove sand. Rinse well even when the package says, "triple washed." These greens may be cooked by steaming or sautéing, and eaten on their own or combined with many other ingredients. Spinach cooks quickly and reduces considerably in volume, so allow one-fourth to one-half pound of raw spinach per person. Raw spinach also makes a fine salad, especially wonderful when served with sliced avocado, citrus, and toasted nuts. Frozen spinach is handy to have around for addition to stews and sauces; make sure to select a no-sodium variety if using canned spinach.

✦ TAKE AWAY

Spinach, high in protein and other nutrients, is delicious raw or cooked.

CONSIDER ✦ A SWEETER SPINACH

Like other salad and cooking greens, spinach can be purchased as large, often curly leaves or as its smaller, sweeter, and more tender counterpart known as "baby spinach." Adding spinach to a salad, whether for lunch or dinner, will give you a boost of vitamins and nutrients that paler salad greens won't provide. If you're not used to the stronger flavor, combine it with other lettuces while your palate adjusts.

PREP TIP ✦ NUTRITION BOOST

Spinach from the frozen food aisle is just as nutritious as fresh, as it's picked and processed at the height of ripeness. It's great to keep on hand to help your children eat more vegetables. Adding spinach to soups, stews, and tomato sauce will add nutrition and flavor—and your kids probably won't even notice.

GIVES YOU

Vitamin K
Manganese
Folate
Magnesium
Iron
Vitamin C
Riboflavin
Calcium
Potassium
Pyridoxine
Tryptophan
Vitamin E
Dietary fiber
Protein
Phytonutrients
  (carotenoids,
  flavonoids, phenolic
  acids, phytosterols)

For Your Health

Popeye was right: Spinach is good for you. Rich in vitamin K, for bone health, spinach also protects against various forms of cancer and promotes cardiovascular and eye health. It is also a good source of vegetable protein. Spinach loses some nutrients when cooked, but heating makes the protein in spinach easier to break down, and one can eat considerably more cooked spinach than raw at a sitting due to its high water content.

For Our Planet

Particular prone to pests, pesticide residues in conventionally grown spinach have earned it a spot on the Environmental Working Group's 2013 "Dirty Dozen" list. Buying organic is a good idea, but if you can't it's still better to be like Popeye and eat your spinach—however grown.

SUMMER SQUASH: ZUCCHINI, PATTYPAN, YELLOW

We know that early farmers in Mexico and Central America cultivated summer squash more than 10,000 years ago, because the preserved seeds of these vegetables have been found in ancient caves. Native Americans referred to them as one of the "three sisters," along with corn (maize) and beans. Related to the hard-shelled winter squash, as well as to melons, cucumbers, and other cucurbits, summer squashes are actually a type of gourd with a thin, edible skin and high water content. The most common varieties are the zucchini (known as courgette in the United Kingdom and France), the bright yellow crookneck, and the pattypan or scallop squash, which comes in a variety of colors. Formerly called Italian squash, the versatile zucchini is a relative latecomer to American kitchens, but it is a featured ingredient in many of the world's cuisines.

GIVES YOU

Vitamin C
Molybdenum
Pyridoxine
Riboflavin
Potassium
Folate
Dietary fiber
Phytonutrients
    (carotenoids, lignans)

Choose and Use

Available all year, these vegetables are especially plentiful during the summer months. Choose brightly colored small- to medium-sized squashes, which have more flavor. Their cut ends should look fresh, and their skin should be smooth and unbruised. Wash them well, but don't peel them before cooking. Unlike their tough winter sisters, summer squashes are highly perishable and won't usually last longer than a week in the refrigerator. Mildly flavored, and slightly sweet, they pair well with many other foods and may be eaten raw or cooked.

✦ TAKE AWAY

Delicate in flavor, summer squash pairs well with herbs and other summer vegetables.

PREP TIP ✦ ZUCCHINI'S VERSATILITY

The most popular of summer squashes, zucchini also bears brilliant orange flowers. They make a delightful side dish when stuffed simply with goat cheese and herbs or with a combination of grains, nuts, cheese, and diced zucchini. Or use them as a garnish for a special dish. No matter what, zucchini makes a great summer dish.

Squash can be sliced and steamed, sautéed, fried, roasted, broiled, or grilled. The most common variety of zucchini has dark green skin, but a bright yellow variety is sometimes available. All summer squash cooks quickly, and the line between crisp-tender and mushy is a fine one, so stay vigilant. All parts, including the flowers, are edible, and stuffed squash blossoms are considered a special seasonal treat. Summer squash retain much of their antioxidant values after steaming, which is not the case when they are boiled or microwaved. Squash tastes lovely garnished with herbs such as parsley, dill, and basil, and paired with other summer vegetables such as tomatoes.

For Your Health

The bright green and yellow skins of different varieties of summer squash are an advertisement for the many nutritional benefits found in their colorful phytonutrients. Recent studies have highlighted the antioxidant benefits from lutein of summer squash, which protects the eyes against age-related macular degeneration and the development of cataracts. To obtain full antioxidant benefits, one needs to ingest the skins and seeds of

PAIRINGS
✦
SUMMER STIR-FRY

The height of summer is the perfect time to feature the local bounty—and nothing's more plentiful than squash. Select a combination that pleases you to create a colorful array, and grab a red pepper, onion, and garlic to add texture and flavor. For a quick stir-fry, just sauté with garlic and olive oil. More adventurous cooks might try a combination of soy, ginger, and sesame oil and garnish with toasted almonds for Chinese flair.

PREP TIP ✦ **ENJOY IT RAW**

While usually cooked, summer squash also makes a great addition to a crudité platter when raw. Creating long, thin strips using a vegetable peeler or mandoline creates healthful salad when tossed simply with olive oil, lemon juice and a bit of salt and pepper.

the squash. Of the many varieties of summer squash, zucchini are especially low in calories and contain no saturated fats; adding them to your diet can help support weight loss as part of a high fiber, plant-based diet.

For Our Planet
Summer squashes are usually sold in bulk, which limits packaging waste. Many are commercially grown in the United States, but quantities are also imported from Mexico. If you opt to grow your own, remember that zucchini is a notorious overproducer—better find a good recipe for zucchini bread and some neighbors for sharing the harvest.

✦ **TAKE AWAY**

Add summer squash to your dishes to incorporate valuable antioxidants.

SWEET POTATO

The sweet potato travels under various aliases. Not a potato at all but a large edible root belonging to the morning glory family, it is sometimes called a yam, though it bears no botanical relation to the true yam, a tuber native to Africa. Two varieties of this New World plant are common in U.S. supermarkets: one with reddish brown skin and orange flesh (the so-called yam) and one with tan skin and pale yellow flesh. Red and purple varieties are often harder to find but worth the effort. Growers subject both kinds to a curing process: once unearthed, the tubers are held in a heated, high-humidity environment for four to six days to increase their sweetness and retard spoilage.

✦ TAKE AWAY

More nutritious than white potatoes, sweet potatoes cook quickly and are delicious chopped or mashed.

PREP TIP ✦ **THE OTHER BAKED POTATO**

Sweet potatoes aren't just for Thanksgiving all dressed up fancy. They can be prepared the same way as a baked potato—piercing and cooking in a hot oven—for a more nutritious alternative to white. Eat the skins, too: they're loaded in fiber and nutrients.

PAIRINGS ✦ A BED OF SMASHED POTATOES

Like white potatoes, sweet potatoes are terrific mashed or, if you leave some in larger chunks, smashed. You can keep the skins on, too. Add a bit of olive oil, cumin, and garlic, and you've got a satisfying, tasty side dish. Smashed potatoes also make a colorful bed for a piece of fish or chicken. For an elegant (and indulgent) alternative, add a bit of truffle oil and goat cheese.

GIVES YOU

Vitamin C
Manganese
Pyridoxine
Tryptophan
Potassium
Dietary fiber
Pantothenic acid
Copper
Thiamine
Riboflavin
Niacin
Phytonutrients
  (carotenoids,
  flavonoids [in purple])

Choose and Use

Available year-round, these tubers taste best in fall and early winter. Sweet potatoes are more perishable than they appear and should be used within a week of purchase, if possible. Until then, store them in a cool, dry place. Older potatoes can be used in soup or mashed for a more nutritious alternative to white potatoes. Choose medium-sized ones with smooth skins that taper at the ends. The flesh of the red variety is sweeter and more moist than that of the starchier yellow type. Both can be roasted whole and eaten hot from the oven or enjoyed cold the next day. Cut in pieces and boiled or steamed, they cook quickly. Puréed sweet potatoes make a rich-tasting side dish. The skins are perfectly edible and fiber-rich. People often blanket their "yams" with marshmallows in typical Thanksgiving attire, but these naturally sweet roots don't really require additional sugar.

For Your Health

Like other yellow-orange vegetables, sweet potatoes are an excellent source of beta-carotene, which the body converts to vitamin A. Consuming them as part of a preparation or meal that includes fat aids in absorption of this nutrient, which is fat soluble. Though sweet, these tubers are not high in calories—just higher than most vegetables. Look for purple-fleshed varieties, which are rich in anthocyanins with anti-inflammatory and antioxidant properties.

For Our Planet

North Carolina produces about 40 percent of the U.S. sweet potato crop, followed by California. A planet-friendly vegetable, sweet potatoes can be conventionally grown without a lot of pesticides and require little nitrogen (a common fertilizer) or irrigation.

TOMATO

Like its cousin the eggplant, the tomato is an anomaly—botanically speaking it is a fruit, but it is consumed as a vegetable. Europeans were slow to welcome this edible member of the nightshade family into their diet, fearing it was toxic. Eventually, it became a cornerstone of Italian cuisine. Today the average American ingests 22 pounds of tomatoes a year, mostly processed into ketchup and tomato sauce. For decades, commercially grown tomatoes have been selectively bred for firmness and uniformity, resulting in a practically tasteless product. Efforts to restore the tomato's flavor have led to the increasing availability of heirloom varieties.

Choose and Use

Available all year in many different shapes, sizes, and colors, the tomato is a summer fruit that tastes best in season. Ripe tomatoes should be used soon after purchase. Store at room temperature, since refrigeration causes enzymatic reactions that compromise its sweetness and kill flavor. The versatile tomato may be eaten raw or cooked in countless ways, including broiling, stewing, or sautéing. Roasting intensifies its flavor. Tomatoes can be stuffed and baked, or made into hot and cold soups or condiments such as ketchup and salsa. Sun-dried tomatoes taste great in salads or egg dishes.

GIVES YOU

Vitamin C
Vitamin K
Potassium
Molybdenum
Dietary fiber
Glutamic acid
Phytonutrients
   (flavonoids, phenolic
   acids, carotenoids,
   phytosterols)

PREP TIP ✦ KEEP CANS ON HAND

Nothing beats a sweet, summer-fresh tomato when in season. But there are a whole host of canned tomato products that contain even more lycopene (the tomato's main antioxidant) than fresh. Always keeping an array of canned tomatoes in your pantry, including crushed, diced, sauce, whole, and paste, is a good way to help you get a meal together in a flash.

Fresh tomatoes taste delicious and bring acidity and texture to a dish. However, research has shown that cooking tomatoes, including canned products, boosts their nutritional value, specifically the carotenoid lycopene; the bioavailability of this fat-soluble phytonutrient further improves in the presence of oil. But you can feel great about substituting healthful canned tomatoes for fresh in a recipe, so keep these products handy in your pantry shelves. Canned tomatoes are also a low-cost way to enjoy these summer plants out of season.

For Your Health
In addition to many other phytonutrients, the low-calorie tomato is rich in lycopene, a carotenoid associated with prostate cancer risk reduction and cardiovascular health. A recent study indicated that the lycopene in orange tomatoes may be more readily absorbed than that in red tomatoes. Eating tomatoes may also help prevent pancreatic and colorectal cancer.

For Our Planet
Buying sweet tomatoes at the height of summer treats your taste buds and supports local farmers. Or try your hand at growing your own tomatoes, easily raised in your garden or on your windowsill.

TURNIP

A hardworking yeoman of the vegetable kingdom and part of the cruciferous family, the humble turnip has many virtues. Easily grown, even in nutrient-poor soil, turnips provide a nourishing food during the cold winter months. They filled our ancestors' bellies when other food was scarce, and served as fodder for their farm animals. Sometimes this pale root with the purple shoulders even provided a source of illumination, since (according to an Irish myth) the very first jack-o-lantern was a turnip.

Choose and Use

Choose turnips that are smooth and firm. Smaller equals sweeter—all the better if fresh green leaves are still attached. Turnip roots keep for a few weeks in the refrigerator, but the greens lose their nutrients rapidly and should be eaten right away. The root is hard, and should be peeled unless the turnip is very small, and you'll need a heavy knife to chop it into pieces. Then it may be braised, roasted, boiled, or steamed. The earthy flavor of the turnip blends well with other root vegetables in stews, or puréed into a creamy soup. Roasting brings out its sweetness, but if cooked using other methods it may benefit from a little added sugar, such as honey. Eaten raw, a baby turnip tastes peppery, like a radish.

PAIRINGS ✦ ROASTED TURNIP "FRIES"

Mild in flavor, turnips are particularly good when roasted. Cut into wedges or strips, toss with oil, season lightly with salt and pepper, and roast at high heat until tender. For more flavor, add cumin or chili powder or a selection of fresh herbs.

PREP TIP ✦ TURNIP GREENS

Those accustomed to discarding their turnip tops on the compost heap should be advised that the majority of a turnip's nutrients are concentrated in its nutritious greens. Cooked, the greens provide more than six times the recommended daily value of bone-building vitamin K, as well as high levels of vitamins A and C, folate, manganese, and fiber. The presence of calcium gives the greens their bitter flavor. Turnip greens contain even more cancer-preventing glucosinolates than cabbage, kale, and broccoli. A quick sauté with a little vegetable oil and garlic is all that's needed to enjoy turnip greens, or add them to your next soup or stew.

✦ TAKE AWAY

Turnips are full of antioxidants; include green tops for added nutritional benefits.

GIVES YOU

Vitamin C
Dietary fiber
Potassium
Manganese
Copper
Potassium in greens
Calcium
Pyridoxine
Folate
Phytonutrients
  (glucosinolates/
  organosulfides,
  flavonoids,
  carotenoids in
  greens)

For Your Health

Adding these crucifers to your diet can lower your risk of developing cancer of the breast, bladder, lung, and prostate. Turnip tops contain flavonoids, antioxidants that neutralize free radicals in the body and help protect against these cancers. They also provide a rich source of Vitamin C (diminished somewhat by cooking), which boosts cardiovascular health. Even more benefits may be gained by eating the turnip greens.

For Our Planet

Eating turnips roots to leaves is another fantastic way to save your food dollars and reduce your personal food waste. This way, edible food doesn't end up in landfills—where it creates methane, a potent greenhouse gas.

WINTER SQUASH: BUTTERNUT, ACORN, SPAGHETTI, PUMPKIN

This uniquely American plant is actually a type of gourd, a fleshy fruit protected by a tough rind. Thousands of years of cultivation culminated in the sweet, dense squash we enjoy today. However, the first squash grew wild in Central America, where it was loved only for its seeds, since its flesh was thin and bitter. Traveling north with migrating peoples, squash became a staple of Native American agriculture, and European colonists soon recognized the value of a crop that could last through the winter in a cellar without spoiling.

Harvested when fully mature, winter squashes have harder shells, larger seeds, and more nutrients than summer squash. They vary widely in appearance and flavor: the large, pear-shaped butternut, the compact green acorn, the familiar Halloween pumpkin, and more

FOOD SCIENCE ✦ ROASTED SEEDS (IT'S NOT JUST FOR PUMPKINS)

When it comes to squash seeds, most people think only of pumpkins. Yet a variety of squash seeds can be roasted and enjoyed any time of year. Butternut squash has a smaller, rounder seed that creates a wonderful topping to soups and salads. Whether dry roasted or prepared with a kick of flavor from cumin and a drizzle of maple syrup, enjoy the seeds for extra crunch and nutrition while also reducing your food waste.

GIVES YOU

Vitamin C
Dietary fiber
Manganese
Pyridoxine
Potassium
Vitamin K
Vitamin E
Phytonutrients
(carotenoids)

decorative varieties such as the striped delicata, the turban, and the homely Hubbard, all herald the arrival of autumn, massed in decorative heaps at the market. The spaghetti squash, a relative newcomer whose interior separates into pasta-like strands when cooked, was first grown in Manchuria, China, in the 1890s.

Choose and Use

Choose squashes with dull rinds that are firm, heavy for their size, with no soft spots. Store them in a cool, dark place. Winter squash are far more durable than summer squash and will keep from a week to six months, depending on the variety and storage conditions. Wash under cold water before cutting.

The thick rinds of winter squash demand a heavy knife, and the various shapes of squash can make cutting and peeling a challenge. First slice off the stem and then cut the squash in half (you may have to lean your weight on the back of the knife to accomplish this). Scrape out the seeds, boil them till soft, and

✦ TAKE AWAY

Winter squash can help lower cholesterol, stabilize blood pressure, and support heart and brain health.

then roast with a little oil and salt for a crunchy and nutritious snack or topping for soups. The rest of the squash may then be cut into manageable pieces, or left in halves for roasting. Since winter squash arrive in their own easy-to-cook containers, this is a classic preparation. Simply coat with vegetable oil, season with salt and pepper, and roast approximately one hour, depending on size. For a lower-calorie option, place each cut side in a shallow pan of water and bake in a 400-degree oven. Spaghetti squash (known as vegetable spaghetti in the U.K.) is the exception: roast this whole, then separate the strands with a fork. Its mild flavor combines well with pasta sauces for a healthful noodle alternative. You may leave the skin on some squash before steaming; other types must be peeled. The sunny flesh of the butternut makes a lovely soup on a gray winter day, or try a mix of squashes for variety. Unlike their warm weather counterparts, winter squashes have distinct flavors, so if one variety doesn't appeal, try another.

Don't despair if this prep work seems daunting: squash is also available precut and frozen, perfect for roasting, steaming, or simmering. Add canned pumpkin to sweet breads, muffins, and pies; a high fiber, lower calorie option is to mix some puréed pumpkin with plain Greek-style yogurt and a sprinkle of cinnamon for a protein-rich autumn snack. Winter squash can stand

✦ TAKE AWAY

Each winter squash has a distinct flavor— experiment to find the ones you like best.

PREP TIP ✦ **GOTTA ROAST**

When it comes to bringing out the best in winter squash, nothing beats roasting. Wash and dry the squash then carefully cut it in half and remove the seeds. Season with oil and a bit of salt and pepper and bake for 20–40 minutes. (Time varies by size.) When the squash can be pierced easily with a knife, it's done. Scooping out the flesh and mashing makes a quick side or throw into a pot with sautéed onions, garlic, and vegetable stock, simmer, and purée for soup. Spaghetti squash strings when dragged with a fork, creating a pasta-like shape.

up to an assertive array of seasonings, including nutmeg, cardamom, ginger, rosemary, and thyme.

For Your Health

Winter squash, like many orange-fleshed vegetables, is a great source of health-supportive carotenoids, including alpha-carotene and beta-carotene. The soluble fiber in the flesh can help lower cholesterol. The seeds from any of the squashes can be toasted and consumed; pumpkin seeds are particularly rich in magnesium and heart- and brain-healthy omega-3 fatty acids; together, the two work together to stabilize blood sugar and blood pressure.

For Our Planet

Nothing says the arrival of autumn more than a colorful selection of winter squash. Particularly tasty when in season, a trip to the farmers market may be worthwhile, and eating the seeds reduces your food waste. And, armed with its own protective shell, winter squash can be shipped and stored without the need for excess packaging, great news from a petrochemical perspective.

The peach and plum with their pits as hard as a nutshell, the kiwi with its ring of black specks in green flesh, the apple with shiny dark teardrops enclosed in a fibrous core—all fruits represent the ingenious strategy of a plant to disperse its seeds and perpetuate its kind. Birds and mammals eat the fruit and later sow the undigested seeds (complete with natural fertilizer) at some distant location by defecating on the ground.

Plants gain nothing when animals feed upon their roots, leaves, or stems—the parts we call vegetables. But the life cycle of many plants absolutely depends on this pas de deux between fruit and beast. Thus fruit has evolved over many millions of years to attract and please would-be seed dispersers. At just the right season for sowing, the fruit ripens, flashing brilliant color to contrast with surrounding foliage, and sending out a plume of fragrance.

For tens of millions of years, human ancestors have responded to this promise of a sweet, nutritious, and highly seasonal meal. Our closest living relatives, the great apes, prefer fruit. And the diets of many Paleolithic hunter-gatherers certainly included fruits.

Humans' preference for sweetness and accessible calories may be responsible for latter-day misadventures in the baked-goods aisle of the local supermarket. One researcher even suggests that alcoholism may have evolved from an ability to recognize and locate ripening fruit by the odorous ethanol it emits. But seeking out the fruit itself gave people of the Stone Age a survival advantage—and the same holds true today.

Relatively mobile hunter-gatherers suffered less malnutrition than the farming peoples who succeeded them, largely, scientists believe, because hunter-gatherers ate a variety of plant foods, while early agriculturalists relied on just a few foods.

Enjoy More Fruits

Today, the nutritional variety offered by whole, seasonal fruits remains every bit as important to good health. Scientists have observed, time and again, that people who routinely eat plenty of fruits and vegetables as part of a plant-based diet are less likely to develop heart disease, type 2 diabetes, and certain cancers—diseases that are largely preventable through diet.

In many contemporary societies, grocery stores offer nutritional variety. Gone are the days when residents of New York or London might lose their teeth from scurvy for lack of a vitamin C–rich fruit in wintertime. Indeed, modern consumers have access, year-round, to an unprecedented array of fruit, from tropical bananas to North Woods blueberries, including off-season produce grown locally in hothouses or warehouses. However, only a third of American adults consume the minimum two servings of fruit per day recommended by the U.S. Department of Agriculture.

The antidote, according to many nutritionists, is for each of us to adopt dietary changes that mesh with our lives, choosing fruits that are appealing, reasonably convenient, and affordable. You like canned peaches? Add some to warm breakfast cereal or toss them in a salad. Dried apricots? Munch them on your evening commute. If the high calories of dried fruit are an issue, pack an apple. Fresh strawberries are a pleasure, but frozen are lovely too, especially when fresh berries are out of season and shipped unripe from distant ports. Organic fruit give you sticker shock?

Buy it occasionally or when shopping for products that are particularly burdensome on the environment. Don't let anything limit your enjoyment of fruits and vegetables, which, even when conventionally grown and/or processed, are among the healthiest and most environmentally sound foods you can eat.

Eat a Variety of Fruits

Ironically, while Americans on average consume too little fruit, fads regularly surface that encourage people to binge on "super fruits" or identify the one element in, say, cranberries or pomegranates that imparts optimal health, which they then swallow in high-dose supplements. Again, variety is the key, and that includes all of the vitamins, minerals, fiber, and phytonutrients that, working together in the body, make a whole fruit good to eat. Consuming more of one particular component is not necessarily better, as science has shown.

It's fascinating to learn that colorful-pigments in some fruits may help prevent vision loss, heart disease, and cancer, or that vitamin C helps arrest cell damage that results naturally when the body reacts with oxygen, a contributor to aging. But much of this evidence is produced in the laboratory, and individual plant components, when tested in human trials using supplements, have often proved disappointing. In short, although diets rich in fruits, vegetables, and beta-carotene can reduce the risk of heart disease and cancer, studies have shown that long-term use of beta-carotene supplements increases lung cancer risk for smokers.

Fruit isn't medicine, but something far more valuable. If we live by Hippocrates's words "Let food be thy medicine," food is

> *"Let food be thy medicine."*
> —Hippocrates

also something elemental. The way we produce, market, and consume fruit today affects human health in the broadest sense, by impacting our bodies, our natural environment, and our cultures, both globally and locally.

Local and Seasonal

Today's high crop yields and worldwide distribution bring to our tables a luxuriant supply of fruits that Americans a century ago might never have glimpsed, let alone eaten regularly. But this comes with a cost. Turning over vast tracts of land to a single crop—monoculture—often damages local ecosystems and increases susceptibility to pests, which increases the use of pesticides. Certain crops and intensive land use in general require more fertilizer. Manufacturing these chemicals produces the emissions that are warming our planet. Shipping all that fruit around the world by sea, air, and land—even trucking it from orchard to roadside stand—churns out even more greenhouse gases. Given economies of scale and different growing and transportation methods, it's not always the case that a local food has a smaller carbon footprint than does a food shipped from afar. And to keep prices down in a competitive international market, growers must hold down labor costs; farm workers are among the most impoverished in the

world. Finally, uneaten fruit ends up in landfills, contributing to the release of methane, a greenhouse gas twenty-one times more potent than carbon dioxide.

All this tends to recommend an updated version of an old-fashioned way of life. Yet, it's not practical to eat only locally grown fruits. (Some 19th-century Bostonians did without fruit through the winter and got through on salt cod and beans—hardly desirable.) But it makes sense to be aware of which fruits grow locally and when they're in season. Pass up the flavorless midwinter cantaloupe from Central America for a New York apple or a California navel orange when in season; they'll taste far better. Supplement liberally with frozen and canned fruits (with no added sodium or sugar), often harvested and processed at peak nutritional value. Sure, processing increases the carbon footprint, but plant foods generally are far more eco-friendly than animal products. It's a balancing act. What's most appetizing, nutritious, affordable, and responsibly produced doesn't always come together in one satisfying bite. Then again, sometimes it does—when you find a basket of berries at the farmers market or roadside stand, fragrant and ripened on a stem not far away. Enjoy their sublime taste in good health.

APPLE

Today's cultivated apple—crisp, fleshy, and sweet—comes to us as a gift from the ancient human past. The apple tree with its gnarled limbs and blush-colored blossoms may be one of the first trees ever cultivated. The progenitor of today's commercial apples still grows in the forests of Kazakhstan in Central Asia. Centuries ago, traders carried its seeds along the Silk Road to Western Europe, the tree hybridizing with local wild varieties along the way. European colonists, in turn, brought their beloved apple varieties to the New World. Nurseryman Johnny Appleseed distributed seeds across the American Midwest.

Choose and Use

Though local apples bought soon after the autumn harvest may be especially tasty, apples store and ship well, holding their texture and nutritional value over months. Varieties with a hint of tartness, such as Jonathans, are often favored for baking, while a crunchy, sweet apple such as the newer Honeycrisp or Gala makes good eating. There are so many varieties available today outside of the supermarket, ask the farmers at your local green market for suggestions of new ones to try.

GIVES YOU

Vitamin C
Dietary fiber
Phytonutrients
   (flavonoids,
   phenolic acids)

CONSIDER ✦ APPLE SNACKS: CUT UP, PEEL ON

Cut and peeled apple wedges can be purchased at the store, but you'll reduce your packaging waste and get more flavor and nutrition by doing it yourself. Select a variety of colors and leave the peel on for a simple snack that kids love, best in autumn when apples are in season. For a protein and energy boost, serve with a nut butter like peanut, almond, or cashew.

There's a downside to peeling: Antioxidants and fiber are concentrated in an apple's skin. Applesauce (homemade is best) retains much of the apple's nutritional value, and there's no reason to remove the skins, which add texture, nutrients, and color. Apple juice, on the other hand, is largely stripped of healthy phytochemicals and fiber found in the whole fruit.

✦ TAKE AWAY

Bite into a refreshing apple rich in flavor and antioxidants.

For Your Health

Apples are a major source of flavonoids and phenolic acids in the American diet. Together with vitamin C (an apple provides ten percent of the recommended daily allowance), these plant compounds make the apple a potent anti-oxidant package, helping the body resist cell damage that can result from natural metabolic processes involving oxygen and lead to cancer.

Will an apple a day really keep the doctor away? Population studies have indeed linked regular apple consumption to reduced risk of lung cancer, heart disease, asthma, and type 2 diabetes.

Apples are also especially high in pectin, a water-soluble fiber that turns to gel in the small intestine and takes up cholesterol and sugars, slowing their absorption into the bloodstream.

For Our Planet

Intensive pesticide use is the norm among conventional growers of the fruit, which is particularly vulnerable to bugs and disease. Washing and peeling helps but does not eliminate pesticide residues. In 2012, the nonprofit Environmental Working Group listed apples as the single most-contaminated produce item. That's one reason organic apples are among the top-selling organic products, accounting for about 6 percent of U.S. apple-growing acreage.

APRICOT

The apricot tree with its trim, tender-fleshed fruit is a close relative of the plum. It got its name, *Prunus armeniaca*, from the assumption among Europeans that it originated in Armenia. It has been cultivated there for at least two thousand years, but scientists believe it originated further east, perhaps in western China. The tradition of drying apricots goes back thousands of years in the area of the Fertile Crescent. Turkey and Iran are the world's biggest apricot growers today. Turkey is the largest exporter of dried apricots; the U.S. is its biggest customer. A tarter, less fleshy variety has entered the marketplace in recent years.

GIVES YOU

Phytonutrients
    (carotenoids)
Vitamin C
Vitamin E
Iron
Dietary fiber
Potassium

Choose and Use

Look to sweet scent, tender flesh, and sharp orange color in finding a good, ripe apricot during its May to July or August season. It will be excellent eaten raw as a dessert, or with nuts, cheeses, and whole-grain crackers. Dried apricots are often found in Middle Eastern stews featuring lamb or chicken or a whole grain pilaf such as rice or oats. Drying removes much of an apricot's vitamin C, but ounce for ounce, the dried fruit contains more iron, carotenoids, protein, and fiber than its fresh equivalent.

For Your Health

Ounce for ounce, a fresh apricot packs more ascorbic acid than a peach and provides roughly five times the carotenoids (including beta-carotene and lycopene), those orange, yellow, pink, and red pigments that, like ascorbic acid (vitamin C), act against cell damage from oxidation. This compact fruit also delivers twice the peach's fiber and potassium, one important in reducing cholesterol levels, the other a vital part of a diet to maintain healthy blood pressure.

For Our Planet

California is the source of most U.S. apricots, with roughly 40 percent of the crop going to processors for drying, freezing, canning, and juicing. The bulk of imports are Turkish dried apricots, with some fresh winter fruit coming from South America. California production on mostly small farms is in decline due to labor costs, less consumer demand for canned product, urban growth, and competition from cheaper imports.

✦ TAKE AWAY

Serve apricots as a stand-alone desert or as a tasty component in a wide range of dishes to experience this fruit's health benefits.

PAIRINGS ✦ DRIED OR FRESH, PERFECT WITH CHEESE

Sweet apricots are wonderful with cheese for a simple, French-inspired dessert. Choose dried in winter, which are loaded with even more vitamin A, and save the juicy, fresh version for when apricots are in season, at their best.

BANANA

The banana is native to Southeast Asia. The earliest evidence of banana cultivation dates to at least 6,500 years ago in the Western Highlands of Papua New Guinea. Portuguese sailors carried the first bananas to the Americas in the 16th century. After the U.S. Civil War came the rise of multinational banana companies growing the fruit in so-called banana republics of Central America. Cheap, conveniently packaged, and exotically sweet, the banana became America's most popular fruit by the 1920s.

Choose and Use

American groceries offer a single variety of banana—the robust, yellow-skinned Cavendish. Though less flavorful than some heirloom varieties, the Cavendish has come to dominate because of transport and storage concerns. Because bananas ripen naturally after picking, that's the factor to consider when choosing a bunch. Why does sealing them in a bag accelerate ripening? It traps in ethylene gas, a natural plant hormone produced by bananas that promotes ripening. Add hard peaches or pears to the bag, and the ethylene will ripen them too.

For Your Health

Scientists have found that a diet rich in potassium and low in sodium helps control blood pressure, a key risk factor for cardio-vascular disease. It's the ratio of these two minerals that matters, and, given that most Americans get way too much salt, a medium-sized banana offers an ideal balance: very little sodium, with 12 percent of an average adult's daily potassium needs. Bananas are generally higher in sugar than many fruits, but those that are not fully ripe are a source of resistant starch and release their energy into the bloodstream slowly, preventing blood-sugar spikes and crashes. Unlike most fruits, bananas are also a good source of

GIVES YOU

Potassium
Pyridoxine (vitamin B6)
Vitamin C
Dietary fiber
Magnesium

pyridoxine, a vital player in the breakdown of stored glucose and the synthesis of important chemical messengers in the brain.

For Our Planet

For decades the banana business was notorious for exploiting workers and replacing great swaths of Central American rainforest with chemical-intensive plantations—leading to erosion, flooding, and soil and water pollution. There have been improvements since the 1990s, with more than 15 percent of all bananas in international trade now certified by the nonprofit Rainforest Alliance as meeting environmental and social standards. Look for the green frog seal.

Banana monoculture is another problem. Growers' planting of a single variety of banana leaves plantations vulnerable to disease. Indeed a fungal wilt called Panama disease struck plantations in Southeast Asia during the 1990s, and there's great concern that it will sweep through Latin America and Africa as well, devastating international supply.

✦ TAKE AWAY

Add bananas to your diet for a sweet source of potassium and other vital minerals.

CONSIDER ✦ BABY BANANAS: PERFECT FOR KIDS

Baby bananas were once available only in places like Thailand. Often red but sometimes yellow, baby bananas are slowly making their way to America. About half the size of a regular banana, they're the perfect portion for kids.

BLACKBERRY

Blackberries—a kind of bramble—grow wild in much of the Northern Hemisphere. Human foragers have likely plucked these purple berries from their thorny canes for millennia. Indeed it seems that no serious efforts at cultivating the berries were made until the 19th century.

Choose and Use

Blackberries should be plump and very nearly black; lighter red or blue berries are unripe. Though they are sturdier and less perishable than some other berries, to avoid spoilage they should not be washed until just before eating. Like dark foliage in a summer garden, blackberries add visual interest and intense flavor to a mixed-berry salad. Toss the berries with a light sprinkling of sugar and let them marinate, then add a small dollop of whipped cream and a sprig of mint for an elegant, healthful dessert.

For Your Health

These ink-dark, tart and seedy berries are an embarrassment of riches nutritionally. Endowed with multiple compounds thought to lower risk of cardiovascular disease, they boast the essential vitamins C, E, and folate as well as the purple pigments (anthocyanins) that are a type of flavonoid. One promising clinical trial testing the effects of berries themselves (as opposed to

GIVES YOU

Vitamin C
Vitamin K
Manganese
Dietary fiber
Vitamin E
Folate
Phytonutrients
    (flavonoids,
    phenolic acids)

PREP TIP ✦ THINK BEYOND SWEET

Like other berries, blackberries are often found in sweets but bring flair and elegance to a host of savory presentations. A handful of blackberries are terrific paired with citrus and fennel in an elegant dinner salad, or they can be combined with grains and herbs for a spa-like lunch. At the height of the season, try pickling blackberries in a simple brine to enjoy in colder months.

✦ TAKE AWAY

Enjoy this pleasantly tart berry full of essential vitamins.

supplements) found that, in 72 middle-aged subjects, eating a mixture of berries twice daily for two months lowered blood pressure, increased "good" HDL cholesterol, and slowed blood-platelet function (which can mean fewer blood clots).

For Our Planet

Oregon is the biggest blackberry-growing state in the U.S., with California second. Since blackberries grow well in many areas, local specimens may be available in the summer season. Off-season, the berries typically come from Mexico. Picking berries is hard, careful work performed mainly by migrant and seasonal workers, who may endure poor working conditions (including high pesticide exposure) and earn subpoverty wages.

BLUEBERRY

This tender round berry of dusky hue is a native of North America. Indigenous peoples of the continent gathered it for food and medicinal uses.

It wasn't domesticated until the twentieth century, when a U.S. Department of Agriculture researcher, Frederick Colville, began the research that would lead to the "highbush" blueberry and its successful commercial cropping in 1908. The U.S. remains the fruit's biggest producer, with Maine the dominant grower of lowbush or "wild" blueberries and Michigan leading in the plump highbush type.

GIVES YOU

Vitamin C
Vitamin K
Manganese
Dietary fiber
Phytonutrients
   (flavonoids,
   resveratrol)

FOOD SCIENCE ✦ SUPERFOOD DU JOUR

The indigo-colored juice from blueberries was once used as a textile dye. It's that same color that's responsible for many of the health properties of blueberries, perhaps why it's known as one of today's "superfoods." Loading up on a single food doesn't generally work when it comes to good nutrition, though: enjoy your blueberries along with other vegetables and fruits for the best health.

CONSIDER ✦ THE SAVORY SIDE OF BLUEBERRIES

The sweet, mild flavor of this beloved round berry make it a popular ingredient in baked goods like pies, muffins, and scones, but it's also a terrific addition to savory dishes, hot and cold. A salad including greens, nuts, herbs, and grains topped with fresh blueberries makes a nutrient-filled and satisfying supper on hot summer nights. Blueberries sautéed in oil with minced shallot and finished with balsamic vinegar will break down to create a zesty sauce for fish, chicken, or even tofu.

Choose and Use

Berries are ripe when wholly blue, not reddish; wrinkled skins suggest they're past their peak. Fresh, in-season berries taste best, but frozen are nearly as healthy, and even baked blueberries retain most of their nutritional value. Fresh berries keep in the fridge for up to two weeks; wash just before serving.

For Your Health

A cup of mild-flavored blueberries provides a quarter of the vitamin C you need in a day, and about the same proportion of the recommended intake of vitamin K and manganese, both of which are important for bone integrity. In addition, these berries boast a diverse mix of antioxidant phytonutrients linked with reduced risk factors for cardiovascular disease. They get their indigo color from a high concentration of anthocyanins, a type of flavonoid that, in laboratory experiments, has slowed the proliferation of cancer cells. Population research has also hinted that people who eat the most strawberries and blueberries experience slower cognitive decline as they age compared with those who consume few berries.

For Our Planet

The blueberry is native to North America. Many small farms grow and sell the berries locally or even invite customers to pick their own. Blueberries found in the supermarket will have been grown in the U.S. or in Canada during the summer months and in Chile or other South American countries from November through March. Interestingly, testing in 2013 by the nonprofit Environmental Working Group found that domestic blueberries had more pesticide residues than imports.

CANTALOUPE

This melon is so high in water that its pale orange flesh goes down like a refreshing drink on a summer's day. To produce the sumptuous fruit, vines need hot, sunny days, warm nights, and a long frost-free growing season. Such was the climate of ancient Persia, the cantaloupe's place of first cultivation some 5,000 years ago, and of Cantalupo, the Italian town where the fruit, planted in papal gardens in the 16th century, is said to have gotten its name.

Choose and Use

The sign of a good, ripe cantaloupe is its sweet fragrance. Look for a fruit that feels heavy for its size and is free of mushy spots. Go for U.S.-grown cantaloupes, available from late spring to early fall when in season, as these are generally tastier than the ones shipped from Mexico and Central America in winter. Because they grow in contact with the soil and have porous, netted rinds, cantaloupes are susceptible to hosting colonies of bacteria that can make you sick. Wash the outside thoroughly in hot water, and wipe it dry before cutting to avoid introducing bacteria inside the cantaloupe. Refrigerate cut melon to discourage bacterial growth.

GIVES YOU

Vitamin C
Vitamin A (carotenoids)
Potassium

PREP TIP ✦ KEEP WHOLE UNTIL USING

Tender cantaloupe is a summertime favorite and it's especially sweet when purchased in season. Once ripened on the countertop, however, it's best to store the melon in the refrigerator whole until ready to be used. Like other fruits and vegetables, pre-cutting fruit days before use will decrease its shelf life. And try snacking on frozen cubes, too, on a hot summer's day.

For Your Health

Due to its extremely high water content, cantaloupe is filling yet has vanishingly few calories. Plus, it's highly nutritious. It's full of vitamin C; a medium-sized wedge provides more than 40 percent of the recommended daily intake. And it's loaded with natural plant pigments called carotenoids, in particular, beta-carotene and alpha-carotene. These carotenoids have pro–vitamin A activity, meaning that the body can convert them to vitamin A; a wedge of melon helps provide nearly half the recommended daily supply of this essential vitamin. Though studies on the benefits of taking supplements have failed to show any benefit (indeed beta-carotene supplements boosted lung-cancer risk for smokers), population research shows that people who consume diets high in beta-carotene and other carotenoids are less likely to develop cardiovascular disease and certain cancers. It is also worth noting that, although honeydew melon shares many of the cantaloupe's nutritional benefits, its orange counterpart is much higher in beta-carotene.

For Our Planet

California is the biggest U.S. producer of cantaloupes, followed by Arizona and Texas. According to the Environmental Working Group's survey, cantaloupe flesh is low in pesticide residues, perhaps due to its thick rind. Varieties with lengthwise ridges and relatively little netting don't ship well but are delicious when available from local sources. Melon harvest is labor-intensive handwork often performed by low-paid seasonal and migrant workers.

✦ TAKE AWAY

Indulge multiple senses with this aromatic melon that is abundant in taste and nutrients yet low in calories.

CHERRY

The cherry as a cultivated food probably originated some 2,500 years ago in the area of present-day Greece or Turkey. With the rise of the Roman Empire and flourishing trade routes, the vivid, firm-fleshed fruit spread into the Mediterranean Basin and east through Asia. Early English and French settlers brought cherries to North America. Today, the U.S. is the world's second-largest producer of cherries, after Turkey.

Choose and Use

Sweet cherries like the plump red Bing are usually enjoyed fresh, while tart cherries such as the Montmorency are widely frozen and give intense flavor to traditional pies and jams. Both sweet and tart are available in dried forms. These are highly nutritious and a delight to the eyes and palate when sprinkled onto salads, savory rice dishes, and desserts. A small handful is also a healthy snack.

For Your Health

Sour cherries not only have a little more ascorbic acid than sweet cherries (a serving provides a quarter of the day's recommended consumption), they also are richer in carotenoids contained in red-yellow-orange pigments that can be converted to vitamin A in the body.

Both cherry types are rich in flavonoids like quercetin and the purple-tinting anthocyanins, thought to have anti-inflammatory

GIVES YOU

Vitamin C
Dietary fiber
Potassium
Phytonutrients
  (flavonoids, phenolic
  acids, carotenoids)

PAIRINGS ✦ TRAIL MIX AND BEYOND

Dried fruit is a common addition to a trail mix. With its dark red hue, dried cherries add sweetness and color alongside a selection of mixed nuts and other fruits like raisins. Dried cherries are also wonderful in baked goods, and fresh or dried cherries pair especially well with dark chocolate when you want a little something sweet.

Dried cherries can be sweet or tart, depending on the variety. While often enjoyed out of hand as a snack, dried cherries also quickly rehydrate into a tender fruit if given a hot water bath. Or add them to porridge or pilaf and they'll rehydrate in the dish itself, adding sweetness and depth to the meal.

✦ TAKE AWAY

Satisfy an array of taste buds with cherries that range in flavor from sweet to tart.

properties. Small randomized, placebo-controlled human trials have found that regular consumption of tart cherry juice decreased blood markers for inflammation and lessened muscle pain after long-distance running. Another study suggests that consuming the fruit may reduce attacks of gout, a painful condition involving joint inflammation.

For Our Planet

These densely flavored summer fruits are a chance to go local, since few are imported off-season, and, when they are, they are quite expensive. Some orchards host pick-your-own events. The West Coast grows the great bulk of the sweet cherries available in the U.S., and Michigan produces the preponderance of tart cherries.

CRANBERRY

The Pilgrims likely did not savor cranberry sauce with their fowl during the first Thanksgiving dinner; for one thing, they had no sugar. But 19th-century founders of the holiday may be forgiven for not including cranberry, an authentic American fruit whose native range extends from North Carolina to Newfoundland. The tricky process of learning to cultivate the cranberry—it grows only in bogs layered with sand and organic matter—had been accomplished not long before Thanksgiving became a national holiday in 1863. It happened in 1816, when Revolutionary War veteran Captain Henry Hall first grew cranberries on Cape Cod.

Choose and Use

Fresh cranberries appear on shelves during their short autumn season, but the robust fruit holds up well to freezing. A versatile food suited to sweet and savory dishes alike, cranberries add a burst of color and flavor to relishes, chutneys, and compotes. They're great in pies and quick breads, and added fresh (or dried, although these are usually sugar-sweetened) to porridge.

For Your Health

Between traditional antioxidant nutrients, vitamin C, and manganese and a rich array of phytonutrients (some associated with

GIVES YOU

Vitamin C
Dietary fiber
Manganese
Vitamin E
Phytonutrients
  (flavonoids, phenolic
  acids, resveratrol)

PREP TIP ✦ MAKE YOUR OWN SAUCE

Thanksgiving wouldn't be complete without tangy cranberry sauce. Store-bought brands of this sweet-tart sauce can be loaded in sugar or salt, though, and it's simple to make at home by boiling fresh cranberries with water, simmering, and sweetening with sugar, honey, or agave nectar. Adding orange zest or toasted walnuts is a nice variation.

More than bucolic, cranberries grown in bogs may also be healthier: there are more anthocyanins in cranberries at the water's surface due to their increased exposure to sunlight. A cranberry is more than the sum of its individual nutrients, though, and recent studies have found that consuming either juice or extract does not provide the same benefits as consuming the whole fruit.

the berry's brilliant color), cranberries have one of the highest antioxidant values of any fruit. Theoretically, at least, this could translate into protection against the "diseases of aging" associated with damage from free radicals, the volatile molecules produced as cells react with oxygen, and from the inflammation that results. Small human trials have hinted that consuming cranberry juice daily may affect risk factors for cardiovascular disease—reducing "bad" LDL cholesterol (oxidized) or increasing "good" HDL cholesterol, for example.

Cranberry juice has long been promoted as a remedy for urinary tract infections (UTIs). In the laboratory, the juice appears to prevent bacteria from sticking to the walls of the urinary tract. One 2012 systematic review of the evidence found that cranberry's effect on UTIs may not be as efficacious as originally thought, but more research is needed.

For Our Planet

Wisconsin produces more than half of the nation's cranberries, followed by Massachusetts. According to a survey by the University of Wisconsin, 98 percent of the state's cranberry producers are family owned. Most participate in recycling programs and test their soil and plants for nutrient needs to avoid overfertilizing, which would have a negative impact on the marine life found in the bogs.

GRAPE

The fruit of the vine, first domesticated in the South Caucasus some 8,000 years ago, spread westward through the Middle East. From their earliest beginnings as a cultivated food, grapes have been fermented to make wine, a mainstay of the religious and daily lives of Ancient Israelites, Egyptians, Greeks, and Romans. "White" grapes evolved from red grapes by means of genetic mutations that switched off the grapes' ability to make anthocyanins, natural purplish pigments. Most but not all white wines are made with these light-colored grapes; the key difference lies in the fact that the white wines do not include the grape skin.

Choose and Use

Fresh grapes make a delightful finger food, especially if you partake of the many varieties available these days, from the popular Flame Seedless to the delicately flavored golden Muscat. Pair them with a hard cheese and whole grain crackers. Or take advantage of their high sugar content: Freeze them for a summertime dessert as tempting as an ice pop.

For Your Health

Americans dramatically upped their consumption of red wine in the early 1990s after researchers suggested the libation might explain why French people suffer relatively little cardiovascular disease despite their (relatively) high-fat diet. While red wine

GIVES YOU

Vitamin C
Vitamin K
Phytonutrients
   (flavonoids,
   resveratrol)
Dietary fiber

PREP TIP ✦ CHOKING HAZARD

Kids love the sweet taste of grapes, whether red or green, and they come in the perfect bite size package, easy for eating. But avoid giving them to toddlers whole: they are a choking hazard.

Fresh grapes are more than 80 percent water. Take away the water, and you've got a raisin. Although drying removes a significant amount of vitamin C, otherwise the raisin simply concentrates the grape's constituents—its antioxidants, sugars, calories, etc.—in a smaller, chewier package. Like other dried fruits, raisins are very slow to spoil and convenient to carry. Raisins and protein-rich nuts make the classic "trail mix," a lightweight, sweet and salty, high-energy snack. A little goes a long way.

✦ TAKE AWAY
Incorporate these nutritional fruits into another dish or eat them alone as a wholesome, juicy snack.

may be beneficial, animal studies have shown that the levels needed to evoke a protective effect are incredibly high, much greater than would normally be consumed as part of a diet including moderate alcohol consumption; the French Paradox probably has as much to do with such unglamorous factors as portion size and increased physical activity.

Still, in the laboratory, the flavonoids and resveratrol present in the skins of red grapes (and in red wine) have been found to combat inflammation, blood clotting, and oxidation of "bad" low-density lipoprotein (LDL) cholesterol—all factors in the buildup of fatty deposits in blood vessels. Research suggests purple grape juice confers similar benefits, helpful knowledge for those who don't consume alcohol. Grapes are also a great source of ascorbic acid, with a single cup providing a quarter of the recommended daily intake.

For Our Planet
Most fresh grapes you find in U.S. supermarkets hail from California, except in the off-season (January through April), when they're often shipped from Chile. Farmers markets are the best source for seasonal local grapes. Subject to rot, grapes are often liberally treated with fungicides and come in at number three on the Environmental Working Group's 2013 list of contaminated fruits and vegetables. Organic is a good way to go, if you can afford it. Always wash grapes before serving.

GRAPEFRUIT

Somewhere in the Caribbean islands, before the mid-18th century, the large, acid-green pomelo crossed with the Jamaican sweet orange. The result was grapefruit. In his 1750 *Natural History of Barbados*, the Rev. Griffith Hughes described it as "the forbidden fruit," and quite delicious.

In keeping with its status as a relative newcomer, the grapefruit is essentially an American fruit. In the 19th century, settlers planted grapefruit in Florida and, later, Texas, where it thrived as a commercial crop. The U.S. remains the largest producer and consumer of grapefruit worldwide.

Choose and Use

Look for a fruit that's heavy—bursting with juice—but not squishy, which may indicate it's overripe. Most grapefruits come from Florida or Texas, and their peak season is winter, roughly January through April. Peel and eat the bittersweet fruit like an orange for maximum fiber, slice it onto salads, or cut it in half along its equator and broil it with a little brown sugar and spices for a low-calorie dessert.

For Your Health

Sit down to a half a grapefruit in the morning, and you'll be spooning up 65 percent of the vitamin C you need for the day, but a mere 2 percent of the calories. (It makes a terrific dessert too.) Though vitamin C is much overrated as a cure for the common cold (high doses may slightly reduce symptoms), it is an antioxidant that's vital to tissue repair. The body neither makes nor stores it—excess amounts are flushed out in the urine—so it's important to get enough in your diet. Pink and red grapefruits provide much more of the pigments called carotenoids than do white grapefruit. Carotenoids are antioxidants and produce vitamin A in the body, required for normal vision, skin,

GIVES YOU
Vitamin C
Phytonutrients
  (carotenoids)
Dietary fiber
Potassium

Forbidden fruit seems an odd handle for such an apparently wholesome food, but grapefruit must indeed be considered off-limits by people taking any of more than 40 common medications. Natural compounds in the fruit, called furanocoumarins, interfere with liver and intestinal enzymes that break down drugs. This can lead to excessive blood levels of the medicine—drug toxicity—or block the drug from working. Drugs susceptible to this interaction include cholesterol-lowering, antianxiety, and some heart medications. Check with your doctor if you're not certain.

bones, and immune function. The flavonoid paringin found in white grapefruit has been linked to lower lung-cancer risk.

For Our Planet

Some of Florida's citrus groves are along the ecologically delicate Indian River Lagoon, which flanks 156 miles of Atlantic Coastline. Chemical-laden runoff can lead to smothering algae blooms, but government agencies, environmentalists, and growers are working to protect and restore the lagoon. The Environmental Working Group ranks grapefruit as one of the least pesticide-tainted fruits or veggies available, possibly due to its thick rind.

✦ **TAKE AWAY**

Quench your thirst and appetite with this nourishing fruit high in dietary fiber and restorative antioxidants.

KIWI

The kiwifruit is native to China's Yangtze valley. Chinese traditional medicine categorizes the "yang-tao" or "strawberry peach" as a "cooling" food that can balance digestion. But it remained exclusively wild-growing until about 300 years ago. New Zealand, which handily dominates production today, began cultivating the fruit in the twentieth century, naming it kiwi, or kiwifruit as a marketing effort in the 1960s. Before, it had been known as the Chinese gooseberry.

Choose and Use

Fresh fruit from California arrives October through May, with imports from New Zealand and Chile available April to November. Purchase kiwis that are firm but not hard; they will ripen (and sweeten) if left at room temperature for a few days. The Hayward variety that dominates U.S. groceries has a thin skin that can be eaten along with the succulent flesh for added nutrients and fiber.

GIVES YOU

Vitamin C
Vitamin K
Vitamin E
Potassium
Dietary fiber
Folate
Phytonutrients
  (flavonoids,
  carotenoids)

For Your Health

This strange little fruit of translucent green flesh dotted with tiny black seeds boasts a significantly higher density of vitamin C than an orange—along with significant amounts of potassium and vitamin E. All are considered important to healthy blood vessels. Kiwi also contains two carotenoids, lutein and zeaxanthin, linked to improvement of age-related macular degeneration, an eye disease affecting many older people.

In the lab, a kiwi extract proved better than an (vitamin C) solution at protecting DNA from oxidative damage, suggesting there are components beyond its ascorbic acid that make the kiwi a power fruit important in the prevention of cancer. (Of course, extracts tend to concentrate nutrients and provide much larger amounts than would ordinarily be consumed in a serving of the actual fruit.) Another study found that eating two or three kiwis per day for a month lowered plasma triglycerides (an undesirable fat found in the blood) and inhibited the clumping of blood platelets, both factors in cardiovascular diseases like atherosclerosis.

For Our Planet

Zespri, the world's largest marketer of kiwis from New Zealand and other countries, reports that shipping accounts for 35 percent of its total emissions. The company is taking steps to reduce greenhouse-gas emissions by maximizing use of space on vessels, using very large vessels, and shipping at slow, fuel-efficient speeds.

✦ TAKE AWAY

Throw an exotic twist into your daily diet with the kiwi's distinct texture and flavor.

PREP TIP ✦ EAT THE FUZZ

With their fuzzy exterior and speckled green interior, kiwis are a fun fruit for children. No need to peel the edible skin, either: teaching kids to eat the fuzz early on will help them learn to enjoy it and avoids unnecessary food waste.

LEMON AND LIME

Lemons and limes are so closely linked in food culture that they seem almost like varieties of a single fruit. Both are small citrus fruits not often eaten alone but used to flavor and garnish a huge variety of dishes and drinks. Both grow in warm climates on glossy-leaved evergreen shrubs, though the lemon's birthplace is thought to be eastern India, while the lime originated in Indonesia. Both spread ultimately to the Middle East, the lemon appearing in Italy by around A.D. 200. By A.D. 1000 both fruits were taking root throughout the Mediterranean region; a half-century later, they arrived in the Americas with the explorer Christopher Columbus.

Choose and Use

Choose fruit that are heavy for their size, barely soft to pressure, and thin skinned with great aroma when gently scratched. Use lemons and limes in place of vinegars on salads and instead of salt for savory dishes such as chicken. Flavor water with a twist of lemon or lime for flair. The zest of these fruits is particularly aromatic and flavorful, an excellent addition to baked goods, salads, and seafood dishes. Vitamin C helps the body absorb iron, so squeeze some lemon or lime onto an iron-rich protein (such as beans) or dark greens (spinach, collards, kale).

GIVES YOU

Vitamin C
Phytonutrients
(limonoids)

CONSIDER ✦ JUICING CITRUS

When a recipe calls for citrus juice, using fresh is worth the effort (and avoids packaging). Sometimes the fruit is particularly hard and doesn't feel juicy. Giving it a roll on your counter or popping it into the microwave for ten seconds will get the juices flowing.

PAIRINGS ✦ A ZESTY VINAIGRETTE

Vinaigrette is often made with oil and vinegar, as its name implies. But lemon or lime juice also makes a tasty salad dressing: a Greek dressing commonly uses lemon juice, for example, while a Mexican salad is perfect with lime.

For Your Health

Laboratory studies have shown that limonoids, natural plant compounds found in citrus fruits, are toxic to certain types of cancer cells. But a more certain asset is this: A single ounce of lemon juice packs 20 percent of the day's recommended intake of vitamin C, and a scant 7 calories. That makes lemon (or lime) a great way to give food a satisfying dash without laying on the salt, sugars, and calories.

For Our Planet

Most of the lemons in U.S. grocery stores are grown in California or Arizona. By the end of the twentieth century, a bacterial disease called citrus canker helped dramatically shrink lime groves in Florida, once a major source. An outbreak that began in the 1990s has resulted in the burning of millions of citrus trees. Fortunately, this flavorful tangy green fruit is still readily available from Mexico.

✦ TAKE AWAY

Squeeze either of these citrus fruits into food or drink for a zesty flavor.

MANGO

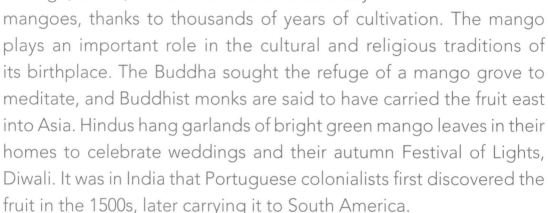

Mangos have grown around the Sea of Bengal—in the area of present-day India, Bangladesh, and Myanmar (Burma)—for millions of years, though the first fruits were not nearly so large, sweet, and smooth-fleshed as today's mangoes, thanks to thousands of years of cultivation. The mango plays an important role in the cultural and religious traditions of its birthplace. The Buddha sought the refuge of a mango grove to meditate, and Buddhist monks are said to have carried the fruit east into Asia. Hindus hang garlands of bright green mango leaves in their homes to celebrate weddings and their autumn Festival of Lights, Diwali. It was in India that Portuguese colonialists first discovered the fruit in the 1500s, later carrying it to South America.

Choose and Use

Depending on the variety, a ripe mango may be yellow, green, or red. Choose a plump, slightly tender fruit that emits a sweet aroma at the stem. Mangoes add a velvety texture to fruit salads and a cool, mild flavor to the piquancy of many chutneys and salsas. Try this tropical fruit in a mango lassi, a traditional drink made of mango, yogurt, and milk popular in India and Pakistan, or combine it with chopped peppers and lime juice for a bright, summery fruit salsa.

GIVES YOU

Vitamin C
Pyridoxine
Vitamin E
Dietary fiber
Phytonutrients
  (carotenoids)

PREP TIP ✦ SNACKING ON MANGO, FRESH OR FROZEN

Mango's juicy, sweet flesh with its bright orange color is something most kids love. Carefully remove the peel with a sharp knife (it's bitter and inedible) and then cut into chunks for a healthy snack. Throwing long wedges into the freezer on a hot summer day is almost like stick-free ice pops.

For Your Health

The rich, almost creamy orange flesh of a mango provides many of the same nutritional advantages as the similarly colored cantaloupe. Mango has a bit more calories but also more dietary fiber. Like cantaloupe it packs a hearty supply of vitamin C, required for tissue growth and repair, and carotenoids, which the body can convert to vitamin A, essential for healthy vision, especially in low light. Like cantaloupe, mango is also distinguished by the sheer variety of vitamins and minerals it contains in modest amounts—including folate and pyridoxine (vitamin B6), which help control blood levels of a key marker for heart disease (homocysteine); vitamin E, an antioxidant; and vitamin K, which helps the body use calcium to build bones.

For Our Planet

The U.S. is the world's leading importer of this tropical fruit. Most mangoes on U.S. shelves come from Mexico, Peru, Ecuador, and Brazil. A limited number are certified by the Rainforest Alliance or Fair Trade USA, which check that growers meet standards for treatment of workers and environmental stewardship. Testing in 2013 by the Environmental Working Group found mangoes to be low in pesticide residues.

ORANGE

Beginning in the Renaissance, wealthy European families considered it most desirable to outfit their estates with an elegant, glass-enclosed greenhouse filled with orange trees—glossy-leaved evergreens that produce waxy, five-pointed white flowers and of course the coveted exotic fruit. The tree was a relative newcomer to the continent, having arrived with Portuguese sailors or perhaps Spanish traders before 1500. Christopher Columbus brought its seeds to the Caribbean in 1493. The orange's place of origin is Asia, probably China in particular, where it's been cultivated for millennia.

Choose and Use

Look for navel oranges in the winter months, choosing fruit that is neither hard nor spongy-soft. Simply peel and eat. So-called juice oranges, available late winter through fall, have a thinner skin and a few seeds, but their flesh is every bit as tasty. They are refreshing in seafood and poultry marinades, or joined in a sun-splashed salad with beets and spinach, good sources of iron. Mandarin oranges packed in their own juice make an easy, nutritious, and affordable alternative to keep handy on pantry shelves. The clementine, a variety of Mandarin orange

GIVES YOU

Vitamin K
Vitamin C
Folate
Dietary fiber
Manganese
Vitamin B6
Potassium
Phytonutrients
   (carotenoids,
   glucosinolates,
   phytosterols,
   flavonoids/phenolic
   acids, lignans)

PREP TIP ✦ KEEP IT WHOLE

It takes about a pound of oranges to make eight ounces of juice. You do get plenty of vitamins in that little drink, but you also get a lot more sugar and calories than you would in a whole orange—with almost none of the fiber. Juice is less satiating, and, like other sweet drinks (even those from naturally occurring, not added, sugars), OJ can raise your blood glucose and insulin sharply, a risk factor for type 2 diabetes and heart disease.

usually eaten fresh during its winter season, provides the same sweet, nutritious refreshment as its larger cousin in a natural snack-sized package.

For Your Health

Oranges and orange juice are a critical source of vitamin C in American diets, and it's not surprising—an extra-large orange provides more than the recommended daily intake, along with about 20 percent of an adult's daily fiber needs. A leading antioxidant, (vitamin C) may help the body ward off the cell damage that contributes to aging and disease.

Data from one large population study, published in 2010, showed that smokers who consumed more citrus fruits were less likely to develop the type of lung cancer most closely linked to smoking. In another population study, researchers found that women who consumed the most flavonones (a type of flavonoid) had almost 20 percent lower rates of clot-induced stroke compared with those who consumed the least amount of these phytonutrients. In the large American study, fully 82 percent of the flavonones consumed came from oranges and orange juice.

For Our Planet

Most of the fresh oranges available in supermarkets come not from the Sunshine State, but from California. Though Florida dominates orange production in the U.S., its fruit is mostly processed into juice—and that's how Americans consume the bulk of their oranges. Often "not from concentrate" juice mixes domestic juice with product imported from Brazil. Processing, long-term storage, and packaging also add to the carbon footprint.

✦ TAKE AWAY

Peel back an orange's dimpled skin to taste its sweet, fibrous flesh, highly nutritious in its raw form.

PAPAYA

The papaya "tree"—actually a large, shrub-like herb—is a tropical plant to the Americas. From somewhere in the region of southern Mexico it spread throughout Central America, into the Caribbean, and, in the 16th century, to India, landing in Europe in the 17th century. Today the major papaya-growing countries are India, Brazil, Indonesia, Nigeria, and Mexico.

Choose and Use
Papayas are yellow and sweet smelling when ripe but can be purchased green and allowed to ripen at room temperature. Slice the fruit lengthwise, scoop out its black seeds, and use it as a bowl for fruit salads or in a spicy fruit salsa. Roast it like butternut squash or grill it like a pepper for an interesting side dish. Add shredded green papaya to marinades to tenderize meat or poultry.

For Your Health
Rich and dense as this opulent fruit may seem, half a large papaya—an ample serving—has fewer calories than an apple or pear. It packs a one-two punch of vitamin C and carotenoids, which are supplied in part by the orange and yellow pigments and which the body converts to vitamin A. A diet high in these pigments has been associated with reduced risk of cardiovascular disease and some cancers.

GIVES YOU

Vitamin C
Folate
Vitamin E
Potassium
Dietary fiber
Phytonutrients
  (carotenoids,
  flavonoids)

PREP TIP ✦ CUT OR SCOOP

It's simple to cut a ripe papaya in half lengthwise with a sharp knife. (When working with harder green papaya be sure to hold the fruit firmly.) A large spoon will easily remove the seeds. Using a melon baller to remove circular chunks means you don't have to peel it!

PAIRINGS ✦ ASIAN SALAD

Indigenous to many Asian countries, papaya is often used in flavorful Pan-Asian cooking. The less-familiar green papaya, an unripened version of the familiar orange-fleshed fruit, is often used in Thai salads when combined with red or yellow peppers, onions, sprouts, and chopped peanuts; a traditional dressing including fish sauce, lime juice, garlic, and a bit of sugar completes this colorful dish.

Ounce for ounce, the fruit has more than half the potassium of a banana, a key component of the low-sodium, high-fiber diet recommended to control blood pressure. Papaya also is the source of papain, a digestive enzyme used commercially as a meat tenderizer that may have pain-killing and anti-inflammatory effects, although studies looking at its use as a supplement have not uncovered definite benefits.

For Our Planet

Though Hawaii once was an important papaya producer, American grocers now get most of their papaya as fresh fruit from Mexico and Belize. Since a major outbreak of papaya ringspot virus in the 1990s devastated the Hawaiian papaya industry, growers there have bounced back by planting a variety genetically modified to resist the virus, thought to have saved the Hawaiian papaya industry. Hawaii's major buyer, Japan, approved the GM papaya after extensive safety testing. Few of these "Rainbow" and "SunUp" papayas are sold in the continental U.S.

PEACH

The ancient Chinese began cultivating their native peach tree some 4,000 years ago, nurturing a tradition that prizes both the wood and the fruit as symbols of long life and good fortune. Testament to the peach's continued popularity in China, the country still produces about a third of the world's peaches, mostly on small farms, and consumes nearly all of them domestically.

The Silk Road carried the peach west to Persia (present-day Iran) and into the Mediterranean region. In the 16th century, European explorers brought the peach to America—perhaps Florida—where it naturalized extensively and was cultivated and eaten by Native Americans.

Choose and Use

A ripe peach may sport more or less blushing pink color depending on the variety. (There are also white peaches, as well as aptly named donut peaches.) But it won't be green, and it will give off a nectar-sweet aroma. A classic ingredient in desserts from cobbler to sorbet, peaches also make a fine poultry glaze or base for herbaceous salads using mint, cilantro, or ginger. Grilling or roasting peaches makes a terrific dessert, especially on an outdoor grill in the heart of summer. Canned (in juice), frozen, and dried peaches retain much of their nutritional value and are convenient, affordable alternatives to fresh.

CONSIDER ✦ FRESH, FROZEN, OR CANNED?

While nothing beats a juicy, fresh peach when in season, frozen and canned are fine alternatives to keep on hand. They are just as nutritious as fresh—as long as you choose brands with no added sugar or sodium—and make a great dessert or snack.

GIVES YOU

Vitamin C
Niacin (vitamin B3)
Dietary fiber
Potassium
Phytonutrients
  (carotenoids)

✦ TAKE AWAY

Velvety, succulent peaches add color and flavor to many recipes, both savory and sweet.

For Your Health

Though not as packed with vitamins A and C as, say, papayas or cantaloupe, yellow peaches are a good source of both these essential vitamins. A large peach also contains about 10 percent of a day's recommended intake of potassium, which balances the sodium in your body, helping to maintain healthy fluid balance and blood pressure. Peaches are also one of the few fruits to contain a significant amount of niacin, a water-soluble vitamin that the body neither makes nor stores but which it needs to convert carbohydrates into glucose it can use as fuel.

For Our Planet

California supplies roughly half the country's fresh peaches, but this summer fruit grows in 28 states. This offers a great opportunity to go easy on the environment—and enjoy full-flavored, peak-season, tree-ripened peaches—by buying locally. In-season peaches sold not far from the orchard will taste delicious, and your dollars will be supporting local businesses and farmers. If it's a practical option, buying organic peaches is also an excellent way to support organic farming. In the Environmental Working Group's 2013 testing, peaches ranked fifth among fruits in pesticide residues.

PEAR

Pears appear to have grown wild in much of Europe and Asia for millennia, giving rise to two basic types: the European pear (Bosc, D'Anjou, Bartlett) common in American grocery stores, and the Asian pear, which is round and crisp like an apple. Both have ancient roots in the human diet. Burned remains of European pear have been discovered in Neolithic sites in Switzerland and elsewhere. The ancient Greeks and Romans cultivated pears; the fruit is mentioned with apples, figs, grapes, and other fruits in Homer's *Odyssey*.

Choose and Use

Pears are in season in fall and winter. A slightly yielding neck indicates ripeness. Pair them with apples and a tangy cheese, slice them onto a peanut butter sandwich, toss them into salads, or poach them with white wine, balsamic vinegar, and water, or red wine with a cinnamon stick and cloves. No need to remove the peel, which is full of fiber and phytonutrients and highly palatable. Eating the skins will reduce your food waste too.

For Your Health

A pear, though smooth as silk, provides more fiber than an apple, orange, or banana. Plenty of fiber helps prevent constipation, reduce "bad" LDL cholesterol, and regulate blood sugar (glucose). Pears are especially rich in phytonutrients. In 2012 data on more than 12,000 cases of diabetes among pooled populations from three separate studies showed that consuming large quantities of certain flavonoids called anthocyanins—and specifically a combination of apples and pears—reduced risk for type 2 diabetes.

A subclass of phenolic acids called cinnamic acids, abundant in pears, may have some activity against gastric cancer. A Mexico City study examined 257 cases of the cancer compared

GIVES YOU

Dietary fiber
Vitamin C
Phytonutrients
  (flavonoids,
  phenolic acids)

✦ TAKE AWAY

Complete your dish with slices of juicy pear, known for its flowery aroma and phytonutrients.

with age- and gender-matched healthy controls, and found that high intake of cinnamic acids reduced risk. The biggest dietary sources of these phytonutrients in the study were pears, mangoes, and beans.

For Our Planet

Most U.S. pears come from the West Coast states, with imports from Argentina and Chile available off season, from late winter to early summer. New York was once the leading pear-growing state, but a disease called fire blight that thrives in moist conditions, along with cold winters, led to the decline of East Coast commercial pear cultivation by around 1900.

PAIRINGS ✦ **PEARS WITH BLUE CHEESE AND WALNUTS**

A fall favorite, a gorgeous red pear is reminiscent of autumn leaves. Pears are classically paired with blue cheese and walnuts. Whether part of a cheese tray or tossed with your favorite lettuce for an elegant salad, keep the peel for color and fiber.

PINEAPPLE

In 1493, Christopher Columbus encountered pineapple on the island of Guadeloupe, becoming the first European to sample the strange, sweet-and-sour, prickly-skinned thing natives of the Caribbean called the "excellent fruit." Later, American colonists thought it excellent, too. Rare, expensive, and exotically sweet before the widespread availability of sugar, the pineapple became the ultimate dinner-party offering and a symbol of hospitality. In recent decades, fresh pineapple consumption has again shot up in America, partly on the strength of a new, super-sweet variety known as the MD2.

Choose and Use

Pineapples do not ripen after picking, so choose one that's ready to enjoy: a sweet-smelling fruit that weighs heavy in the hand. For much of the twentieth century, Americans ate a lot more canned pineapple than fresh, but fresh pineapples have become increasingly popular since the 1990s; they're more work to prepare, but typically deliver superior flavor and more vitamin C.

For Your Health

The pineapple is a bromeliad, but like a citrus fruit it's very acidic and has plenty of vitamin C—nearly as much as an orange. Unlike citrus fruits, though, a serving of pineapple contains three quarters of the recommended daily consumption of manganese, a mineral studied for its possible role in slowing bone loss in post-menopausal women and easing symptoms of premenstrual syndrome. Pineapple is the only food to contain a group of protein-digesting enzymes called bromelain, used in supplement form by Europeans to reduce inflammation after sinus and other surgeries. Natives of South and Central America used the fruit itself as a poultice to treat wounds.

GIVES YOU

Vitamin C
Manganese
Thiamin (vitamin B1)
Vitamin B6
Dietary fiber
Bromelain

For Our Planet

Costa Rica is the largest exporter of pineapples to the U.S. and Europe, having taken over the role from Hawaii toward the end of the twentieth century. The product, perhaps thanks to its tough skin, is relatively free of pesticide residues, according to the Environmental Working Group. But environmental and labor groups have complained that Costa Ricans face harsh working conditions and contamination of local soil and water from pineapple-field runoff.

PLUM

There are many varieties of the plum tree, which are sprinkled with white blossoms in spring, followed by purplish, pitted fruit. More than two thousand years ago the ancient Chinese domesticated *Prunus salicina*, which came to be called Japanese plum after widespread cultivation there. The smaller and more oval-shaped European plum has its origins in the Caucasus. North America has its own wild plums, but Americans today generally eat Japanese plums.

Choose and Use

Look for a fruity aroma, deep color with a whitish blush, an unwrinkled skin, and slight give in the flesh. Though plums ripen after picking, if harvested too early they will remain sour. Eat them raw or stew them a few minutes with a little sugar and water for an intensely colored topping to pancakes, oatmeal, ice cream, or yogurt.

For Your Health

A juicy plum is a decent source of essential vitamins C and A as well as dietary fiber. But it's the diminutive fruit's ample supply of phytonutrients—plant compounds called phenolic acids and pigments known as flavonoids—that shoot plums up the charts when it comes to antioxidant power, at least as measured in the lab. Plums are particularly rich in a reddish-purple pigment

GIVES YOU

Vitamin C
Dietary fiber
Vitamin A
Vitamin K
Phytonutrients
  (flavonoids,
  phenolic acids)

PREP TIP ✦ ENJOY THE VARIETY

You might not know it from the supermarket, but plums come in many colors and sizes. In addition to the common purple and red, there are almost-black, small Italian plums (used to make prunes) and you might also find green plums at your local farm stand.

Marketers are trying to rehabilitate the prune by calling it a "dried plum," and that's just what it is. The drying process concentrates the plum's components, including its vitamins, fiber, and phytonutrients. But this leads to a salutary effect on constipation that's almost medicinal in strength. Prunes contain a high concentration of sorbitol, a sugar that is absorbed very slowly and gathers water as it moves through the bowel. Too much sorbitol may cause gastrointestinal distress. Prunes also concentrate fiber, which adds mass to the stool.

class called anthocyanins. Though cause and effect remain unclear, research suggests that people who eat lots of produce vividly colored with these pigments have a lower risk of cardiovascular disease and cancer.

For Our Planet

Because plums are inexpensive and grow in many regions, they're a good fruit to purchase locally, in season, cutting down on the environmental costs of transportation. Domestic plums, mostly from California, are available June through December. Or you may be able to find them in season at a neighborhood farmers' market. In the off-season, most supermarket plums come from Chile.

POMEGRANATE

Probably domesticated some 5,000 years ago in the area of present-day Iran, the pomegranate with its seeds like polished rubies spread west to Greece and along the Silk Road to China. It had an important place in ancient civilizations. In Greek mythology, Persephone, daughter of Zeus and the harvest goddess Demeter, ate four seeds of a pomegranate in the underworld. As a result she was forced to spend four months of each year there—the winter months when plants go dormant. Many of the world's religions hold it is an important symbol, and it's thought that the original tree fruit in the Garden of Eden was pomegranate, not apple, since the timing is otherwise anachronistic. In twenty-first-century America, U.S. consumers are now embracing the pomegranate as a potent antioxidant.

GIVES YOU

Vitamin C
Vitamin K
Folate
Potassium
Dietary fiber
Phytonutrients
   (ellagitannins,
   flavonoids)

Choose and Use

Look for a fruit that's heavy for its size and has a rich red or reddish-brown color. Try it in Middle Eastern and Greek-style salads and savory dishes featuring couscous, quinoa, lamb, chicken, feta cheese, or mint. It also makes a tasty, nutritious snack all on its own.

For Your Health

Drinking pomegranate juice may reduce risk factors for cardiovascular disease and, in men with prostate cancer, slow increases in prostate-specific antigen levels, a marker for the disease. Scientists believe this may be attributable to the fruit's unusually high level of ellagitannins, phytonutrients with strong antioxidative effects. Pomegranates are also rich in flavonoids, including anthocyanins, which may reduce risk for cardiovascular disease. But so far research has been limited to the laboratory (looking at cultured cells and mice, for example) and small-scale human trials. The fruit itself has some advantages over juice. One pomegranate provides around half the vitamin C and dietary fiber you'll need in a day. Pomegranate juice, on the other hand, has no (vitamin C), very little fiber—and 50 percent more calories than orange juice.

For Our Planet

Most fresh pomegranates on U.S. shelves are grown in California and are in season from September through February. In warm-weather months the fruit is likely to have traveled far, including from India, which processes and packages the seeds (or arils) for sale in U.S. grocery stores.

✦ TAKE AWAY

Slice into a nutrient-packed pomegranate to discover a cache of ruby red seeds, ideal for salads or snacks.

PREP TIP ✦ CLEANING THE JEWELED FRUIT

Pomegranates are a little like crabs; it's not easy to get at the good bits. Cut the pomegranate in half around its equator. Hold one half of the fruit, cut side down in your hand over a bowl. Use the back of a spoon to lightly beat the skin and watch as the seeds fall out, perfectly clean of pith. Continue until all the seeds have been knocked loose. It's probably best to wear an apron for this task.

RASPBERRY

The Latin name for this delicate fruit, *Rubus idaeus*, comes from the Latin *ruber*, for red, and Mount Ida, near the ancient city of Troy in present-day Turkey, where the fruit may have originated. In fact the hardy plants are native to temperate zones throughout Europe, Asia, and North America, springing up in the semishade of forest floors and thriving especially in clearings. The ancient Romans spread the berry across their empire. Native Americans ate their own native raspberries and used the leaves as an astringent and to soothe diarrhea.

Choose and Use

In season during the summer months, raspberries have a sweet-tart flavor and layered texture that make them a wonderful base for salad dressings, jams, cobblers, and all kinds of baked goods. Try them with dark chocolate for an antioxidant-rich dessert. Toss them with summer greens, a mild, creamy goat cheese, and toasted walnuts or pecans for a tasty salad, or add them to a savory herbed whole grain pilaf or wild rice salad. Buy raspberries shortly before eating as they spoil quickly, and wash just before serving to preserve shelf life.

For Your Health

Raspberries are among the amplest sources of anthocyanins, the flavonoids that give them a crimson hue. Population studies have linked high consumption of these phytonutrients with lower risk of cardiovascular disease and cancer. In the lab, scientists have shown that ellagic acid (a product of ellagitannins) thwarts inflammation and the growth of cancer cells. The berries are also very high in manganese, a mineral important to maintaining strong bones, and fiber, which helps lower cholesterol and regulate bowel function. In fact, raspberries have more than twice the fiber of strawberries.

GIVES YOU

Vitamin C
Vitamin E
Vitamin K
Dietary fiber
Manganese
Magnesium
Phytonutrients
  (flavonoids,
  ellagitannins)

For Our Planet

Though Washington, Oregon, and California are the major raspberry-growing states (supplemented by imports from Canada in summer and Mexico off season), the berries lend themselves to cultivation on small farms across the country. Fresh, local berries are generally the tastiest and most eco-friendly; look for them in season at farmers markets, roadside stands, or pick-your-own operations on nearby farms. Plucking these fragile berries from thorny canes is a highly labor-intensive process—one reason why raspberries tend to be expensive. Frozen raspberries are a practical, affordable, and nutritious option.

PREP TIP ✦ STORING

Many people wash fruit and vegetables right after food shopping so they're ready to go. Unfortunately, this step decreases shelf life. Berries in particular are highly perishable, so it's best to store them unwashed in a covered container then rinse gently in cold water right before consuming.

STRAWBERRY

Like so many fruits, today's familiar garden strawberry is a product of the Age of Exploration. It is a cross between two American wild strawberries—a small, flavorful one from eastern North America, and a larger though less tasty berry native to Chile—that took place in 18th century France, after Europeans carried the two American varieties home. In the last century, horticulturalists have bred garden-strawberry hybrids for size and durability in transit. Local berries commonly seen at farmers markets are often smaller, sweeter, darker, and more easily bruised than the larger, pink variety you commonly see in the supermarket.

GIVES YOU

Vitamin C
Folate
Manganese
Dietary fiber
Phytonutrients
    (flavonoids,
    ellagitannins)

PAIRINGS ✦ HEALTHY ELEGANCE

Chocolate-covered strawberries are commonly served at weddings or garden parties, a sumptuous treat everyone loves. Easy to make at home—just dip the washed berries in a bowl of melted dark chocolate and set in the fridge—this is actually one the healthiest desserts out there.

TAKE CARE ✦ ORGANIC

Strawberries are vulnerable to a variety of pests—and conventional growers combat them with an armamentarium of chemicals that are toxic to the environment and farmworkers. Fumigants that sterilize soil before planting have been particularly controversial. Long the fumigant of choice, methyl bromide is being phased out because it depletes the Earth's ozone layer. A proposed alternative, methyl iodide, was withdrawn from the U.S. market in 2012 after widespread alarm over its health risks to farm workers and consumers. For all of these reasons, selecting organic strawberries is better for the planet and for people.

Choose and Use

Look for deep and even coloration and a texture that is yielding to slight pressure. Berries should be red, not green- or white-tipped; they are nonclimacteric and will not ripen after picking. Smell is a false indicator of quality in strawberries. New varieties from California and Florida have been hybridized to be alluringly pungent, but they are barren of flavor. A dash of pepper or sprinkling of fresh basil can bring out the berries' sweetness in savory salads. Squeeze a little lemon or orange juice over berries that need a flavor lift. They're wonderful chopped in a homemade muesli with uncooked oats, other dried and fresh fruits, nuts, yogurt, and milk (cow's, soy, coconut, rice, or almond all work well).

For Your Health

Like raspberries, strawberries contain a plethora of natural plant compounds—including deep red colorants called anthocyanins (a type of flavonoid) and ellagitannins—that may have protective effects against heart disease and cancer. What's more, ounce for ounce, strawberries just about match up with oranges in vitamin C, a powerful antioxidant that's vital for tissue repair.

Several observational studies have linked high strawberry intake with lower risk for cardiovascular disease or death from cardiovascular disease, with one study showing that women who ate the most berries lowered their chance of heart attack by almost a third.

For Our Planet

Available year-round, strawberries are shipped mainly from California, Oregon, or, in winter, Florida. A few imports hail from Mexico. This is a good fruit to purchase in season, locally. Stem-ripened berries from your local market are far more flavorful than varieties bred to withstand long-distance shipment. You'll taste the difference.

CHAPTER THREE

PROTEINS

After water, protein is the most prevalent constituent of the human body. It is an important structural element of every cell, and the major component of muscles, eyes, skin, hair, and bone. Proteins also perform myriad jobs in the body. They act as antibodies, fighting off infection; enzymes, which speed chemical reactions; hormones, the body's chemical messengers; and transport devices that, for example, carry oxygen through the bloodstream.

Proteins are made up of 20 amino acids in different combinations. The body constantly breaks down its proteins into their constituent amino acids and "recycles" them into new proteins. We also replenish our supply of amino acids from the protein we eat in food. In fact, the body cannot make nine of the amino acids that form proteins, so these amino acids are only available through diet.

Like the other two macronutrients, carbohydrates (sugars) and fats, protein in the diet provides energy (or calories) that fuels the body. Fat is the most concentrated source of energy at approximately nine calories per gram; protein and carbohydrates each contain four calories per gram.

Fuel for Life

But the body uses these energy forms in very different ways. It draws immediately on carbohydrates, which break down in the digestive tract and enter the bloodstream as glucose. After this supply of carbohydrates is exhausted, the body can switch metabolic pathways, breaking down and burning stored fat instead. Only after both these energy stores are depleted does the body begin to break down stored protein, much of it found in muscles, and convert it to the body's major fuel source—glucose. While an adaptive response to provide the body energy, this may result in wasting and, ultimately, death if energy intake continues to be inadequate. On the other hand, when the body gets more dietary protein than it needs, along with ample calories, it will convert the excess protein to body fat.

The old-fashioned advice to build a strong body by eating plenty of protein-rich food is not altogether wrong. Everyone needs to consume protein, not so much for its calories but for the raw amino acids needed for growth, maintenance, and repair throughout the body. However, most Americans consume more protein than necessary: Americans get roughly 70 percent of their protein from animal products, the most protein-dense foods. Deficiency is rare even among vegans; they tend to eat more legumes, soy products, whole grains, and nuts, all of which provide protein. Though these plant-based proteins may lack a particular essential amino acid (grains are low in lysine, for example, and legumes are low in methionine), a diet rich in diverse foods generally allows those consuming plant-based diets to easily meet their protein needs.

Protein for a Hungry World

Inadequate dietary protein is a problem for many people in the developing world. They not only lack access to expensive, resource-intensive, nutrient-dense animal products but may also depend heavily on a single staple—such as sorghum, corn, or cassava—which compromises their ability to obtain all nine essential amino acids needed for optimum health.

According to UNICEF, about a third of child deaths under the age of five are attributable to undernourishment. In these cases, protein deficiency often takes place in the context of *energy* deficiency—too few calories—along with deficits in vitamins and minerals. One study examining the diets of

children in an Indian slum found their protein came mostly from plant foods, with animal products (including milk) consumed only once or twice a week. A scant 3 percent of the children had inadequate protein intake with sufficient calories overall, whereas the largest segment—41 percent—got enough protein but too few calories. As a result, their bodies may draw down fat and protein reserves for energy, perhaps stunting their growth.

Healthy Proteins

Meanwhile, wealthier folks' heavy reliance on animal proteins has its own consequences, in terms of health and the global environment. For one thing, full-fat dairy products and many meats are loaded with saturated fat and cholesterol and other stuff too (one ounce of cheddar cheese can have six grams of saturated fat for a third of the recommended daily intake, plus a tenth of your daily cholesterol). Replacing these fats with monounsaturated and polyunsaturated fats—fats found in alternative protein sources like nuts, seeds, and oily fish—significantly reduces blood cholesterol and risk for heart disease, America's number-one killer. Most Americans also don't get enough fiber, which pulls cholesterol from the blood, stabilizes blood sugar, and contributes to healthy bowel functioning. Unlike animal products, which contain no fiber, legumes, whole grains, and nuts are fiber powerhouses that also provide ample servings of protein (although some of these are not complete sources of the essential amino acids). Indeed, the U.S. Department of Agriculture (USDA) dietary guidelines recommend a shift to heart-healthier plant-based protein sources.

As poor nations achieve greater prosperity, their citizens often move away from heart-healthy, plant-based diets and eat more high-protein meat and dairy. This trend is

Heavy reliance on animal proteins has consequences, in terms of health and the global environment.

fueling a global boom in production of animal products—the United Nations Food and Agriculture Organization (UNFAO) projects a doubling of demand for meat in the first half of the 21st century—that the Earth can ill afford.

As it is, livestock production places a heavy burden on the natural world, taking up fully 30 percent of the world's land surface and generating some 18 percent of annual greenhouse gas emissions worldwide. Instead of eating plants ourselves, we grow them (often using fossil-fuel-intensive technologies) to feed animals, an inefficient system that drains the planet of precious natural resources, including land and water.

The rise of "factory" farming, which focuses on intensive production at low economic cost, means food animals are now raised in ways unknown to earlier generations. Use of growth-promoting hormones and antibiotics has increased dramatically in recent decades; 80 percent of all antibiotic use in the U.S. is in farm animals. These spread to water and soil through the animals' waste and agricultural run-off. And the drugs permit animals to grow in very confined, unhealthy conditions that many condemn as inhumane and unethical.

A Way Forward

Change, though, is afoot. People are eating more organic and free-range meat and dairy products, which slightly mitigates environmental impacts and may be more humane to animals. Americans are also eating significantly less meat, at least over the last several years. Schools, other institutions,

and individuals from around the world have joined the U.S. Meatless Monday campaign launched in 2003 by the Johns Hopkins Bloomberg School of Public Health. The aim is not necessarily to cut out these nutrient-dense foods altogether but to enjoy them in moderation and thereby reduce negative impacts on human health and world ecology. According to the Environmental Working Group, if everyone in America ate no meat or cheese one day a week this year, it would be equivalent to taking 7.6 million cars off the road—hardly a solution to the factors driving climate change, but a step in the right direction.

Turning less reflexively to ham and cheese may even open our eyes to wonderfully tasty plant-based proteins that have been with us for millennia—from the little black bean of South America, gleaming with antioxidant pigments, to rich, spreadable nut butters and sea-fresh, iron-dense oysters and clams.

ALMOND

The almond tree grows wild in parts of the Middle East, where it was probably domesticated a few thousand years ago. One of the first nut trees cultivated by people, the almond is mentioned in Genesis, the first book of the Bible. It is not a true nut but a seed—the pit of a plumlike fruit whose outer flesh is tough and green. Learning to grow the tree for food required people to select trees producing a sweet seed. In wild varieties, the "nut" is not only bitter but toxic, producing cyanide when crushed.

Choose and Use

Almonds can be purchased whole, sliced, or slivered, the latter two very nice for adding crunchy protein to Swiss chard, salads, green beans, or casseroles. Try them as a nutritious and more affordable alternative to pine nuts in pesto, or drink low-fat almond milk as a substitute for cow's milk. Blanching removes the almond's brown skin, along with antioxidant flavonoids and, to some tastes, pleasing texture and flavor. Roasting in itself does not appreciably change nutritional content, but look out for added salt, oils, and sugar—which mean extra calories to an already energy-dense food.

GIVES YOU

Protein
Dietary fiber
Riboflavin
Vitamin E
Manganese
Magnesium
Phosphorus
Copper
Calcium
Iron
Monounsaturated and
    polyunsaturated fats
Phytonutrients
    (flavonoids,
    phytosterols,
    phenolic acids)

For Your Health

For the calories (about 160 in a small handful), almonds offer more protein and fiber than most other nuts. They're also high in healthy monounsaturated fats, which lower cholesterol, and have the highest concentration of any nut of alpha-tocopherol, a form of vitamin E. Vitamin E is a potent antioxidant; it prevents the damage that results from the natural process in which cells react with oxygen, producing volatile "free radical" molecules that injure other cells. Oxidation of cholesterol helps it stick to blood-vessel walls, one mechanism in the development of heart disease.

Because of these nutrients some studies show adding almonds to the diet helps lower "bad" low-density lipoprotein (LDL) or total cholesterol, although a 2009 review of studies concludes that they have a "neutral effect" on blood lipids.

For Our Planet

Around 80 percent of the world's almonds are grown in California orchards, and demand is growing. These orchards rely mainly on honeybees to pollinate trees so they can produce fruit (and seeds). In recent years sensitive bee populations have plunged due to a phenomenon known as colony collapse disorder. Scientists now believe pesticides play an important role in the problem. Water demand is also a major concern in California's Central Valley, where the bulk of the world's almond growing takes place. A major state plan to divert water to this valley from Northern California's Sacramento–San Joaquin Delta has been controversial, although the plan also includes restoration of the delta.

✦ **TAKE AWAY**

Try highly nutritious almond products in place of everyday items such as cow's milk and peanut butter.

PREP TIP ✦ **ALMOND BUTTER**

Almonds are lower in saturated fat and higher in calcium, iron, and fiber than peanuts. Their rich, ever so slightly bitter flavor makes a spread that stands up well to fruity jams and holds the interest of sophisticated palates. To be sure, almond butter is a little harder to find and more expensive than peanut butter, but, on occasion at least, well worth it. Added to soba noodles or whole-wheat spaghetti, it makes an easy sesame noodles-style dish.

BEEF

Dating as far back as 20,000 years, cave paintings at Lascaux, France, depict enormous grass-eating beasts along with other wild animals. Aurochs, the prehistoric ancestors of domestic cattle, roamed across much of Asia, Europe, and North Africa for many thousands of years, playing an important part in the development of human societies. People managed to tame and keep aurochs beginning about 8,000 years ago in the Near East, with independent domestication also occurring on the Indian subcontinent. Long before domestication, the cattle best known in North America, *Bos taurus,* split from the humped cattle (or zebu) domesticated in Pakistan.

Choose and Use
Beef is a food best eaten in moderation or used as a flavoring (in broth, for example) for other foods. Lean cuts of beef—flank steak, New York strip steak, lean ground beef, eye round roast—are healthier but require careful cooking. Sear the meat, then cook it slowly on low heat; leaner meat cooks up to a third more quickly than fatty beef. A little cooking oil may be required for

GIVES YOU
Protein
Zinc
Iron
Selenium
Phosphorus
Vitamin B12
Vitamin B6
Riboflavin
Niacin
Vitamin B5

steaks and burgers. Try adding smoked paprika, oregano, fresh herbs, or Worcestershire sauce to lean burgers.

Look for grass-fed beef that is free of hormones and antibiotics. Cattle fed exclusively on pasture grasses (rather than corn and other grains) tend to be leaner in general, with a higher concentration of heart-healthy fatty acids (including polyunsaturated omega-3 fatty acids) than conventionally raised beef.

For Your Health

Beef, it's true, is chock full of saturated fat (and cholesterol). A six-ounce serving of prime rib can dish up more than half the government-recommended daily limit. Research shows that eating fewer saturated fats protects against cardiovascular disease—particularly if those fats are replaced not by refined carbohydrates like high-carbohydrate but nutrient-poor white bread and white pasta but by the healthy fats contained in nuts, seeds, oils, and fish, which have a positive effect on cholesterol levels.

But, to put things in perspective, whole-milk cheese, pizza, baked and dairy desserts, and even chicken contribute more than does beef to Americans' saturated fat intake. And beef is an excellent source of complete, readily absorbable protein, which the body requires to build many of its components and to serve as energy backup when carbohydrates and fats are low.

Beef also has more iron—which carries oxygen in the blood and helps muscles use it—than chicken, fish, or pork.

For Our Planet

High meat consumption, together with the industrialized production systems developed to meet demand, have extremely serious consequences for the environment. All beef is resource intensive; more than two-thirds of the world's agricultural land is devoted not to human food but to growing feed for livestock. It takes about 6.6 pounds of grain and roughly two thousand gallons of water to produce a single pound of beef. Cows are a major contributor to climate change as their distinctive digestive process produces the potent greenhouse gas methane; indeed livestock are responsible for 28 percent of methane generated by human activities, with beef being the principal source. Concentrated feedlot operations where cattle are fattened for slaughter pollute soil and water.

FOOD SCIENCE

✦

CONSIDER THE TRUE COST OF BEEF

Putting cattle out to grow on natural pasture grasses is a slower, more expensive way to raise them. It's also more humane to the animals, less burdensome on the environment, and ultimately less costly to human health. Sure, the price tag on a pound of grass-fed beef is higher than on conventional beef, where the true costs are hidden from the consumer. Consider eating less, and paying more. Beef really shouldn't be a food of default, served up quick and cheap on every corner, but an occasional high-protein treat.

BLACK BEAN

Like the pinto bean and kidney bean, the black bean is a variety of the common bean, *Phaseolus vulgaris*, which comes in many shapes and colors. In prehistoric times wild beans grew in a large area from Mexico to Argentina and were domesticated in two locations—in Peru some 8,000 years ago, and in Mexico about 7,000 years ago. Both the Aztecs of Mexico and the Incas of Peru grew beans along with maize and squash in a combination known as "the three sisters." These plantings complemented one another horticulturally—beans provide nitrogen to the soil and squash plants retain moisture—and nutritionally, since beans and maize together provide all nine essential amino acids.

GIVES YOU

Dietary fiber
Protein
Manganese
Copper
Phosphorus
Magnesium
Iron
Potassium
Zinc
Folate
Thiamine
Phytonutrients
    (flavonoids,
    phenolic acids)

Choose and Use

Dried beans can be soaked overnight, but the quick-soak method is just as good: Rinse the beans and place in a pot with water added to about two inches above the beans. Boil for two minutes, then remove from heat, cover, and let stand for an hour. Cook the beans according to the direction or recipe. Salt beans only after cooking because it slows the process. Canned beans (with no added salt) are a cheap and convenient pantry staple for southwestern scrambles, black-bean hummus, Mexican salads, veggie burgers, soups, and chilis.

For Your Health

For your heart, you can't go wrong with a cup of black beans. It provides protein along with well over half the fiber you'll need in a day. That soluble fiber lowers cholesterol and keeps blood sugar in check, while ample quantities of magnesium (nearly a third of the daily recommended intake) and potassium help control blood pressure. A cup of black beans also provides more than half the daily recommended intake of folate, which helps curb blood levels of homocysteine, a marker for cardiovascular disease.

Like many berries, black beans get their deep color from anthocyanins, which have antioxidant and anti-inflammatory properties important for heart health and cancer prevention.

For Our Planet

Beans can essentially fertilize their own soil; their root systems harbor bacteria that convert atmospheric nitrogen to a form the plant can use. Small grains and corn, which have different nutrient demands, are often grown in rotation with beans, a form of polyculture that protects the soil and avoids the vulnerability to pests that results when a single crop is grown over the long term.

✦ TAKE AWAY

Black beans contain protein, fiber, and other nutrients essential for heart health.

PREP TIP ✦ THE FOUNDATION OF TEX MEX

Black beans are a common ingredient in a wide variety of Tex-Mex dishes, burritos, and beyond. Giving dried beans a quick soak overnight and simmering on the stovetop decreases packaging. They're cheaper than canned and cook very quickly, too.

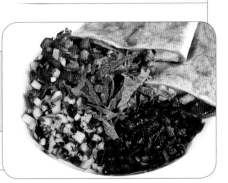

BLACK-EYED PEA

The black-eyed pea, an ivory-colored bean with a distinct black marking, was first cultivated about 5,000 years ago in West Africa. The beans were brought to the American colonies by way of the West Indies, along with enslaved Africans. Thus, in the New World, enslaved people, especially those of the Southern colonies where black-eyed peas took hold, were able to find ingredients for traditional African rice-and-bean dishes that, not incidentally, had provided a complete protein like the maize-squash-beans grouping cultivated by Native Americans. Black-eyed peas became a mainstay of soul food and Southern cuisine, often eaten for good luck on New Year's Day in a dish called "Hoppin' John."

Choose and Use

Though soaking is not strictly required for dried black-eyed peas due to their small size, a quick soak—boil them in water for a few minutes, then let stand, covered, for an hour or so—will reduce cooking time. Frozen are even easier to prepare. While traditionally seasoned with pork, the beans' fresh, earthy flavor can also be enhanced with onions, garlic, sweet and hot peppers, and salt; combine them with collard greens and corn bread for a classic Southern meal.

✦ TAKE AWAY

Black-eyed peas boast high protein, fiber, and vitamins.

FOOD SCIENCE ✦ PEA OR BEAN?

Unlike true peas like snow or sugar snap, black-eyed peas are botanically a legume that preserves soil quality by adding nitrogen; they require relatively little water and are extremely drought tolerant. Thought to bring good luck, black-eyed peas are popular at New Year's, but they're a great choice any time for sustaining our planet's precious natural resources.

For Your Health

Black-eyed peas share the overwhelmingly positive nutritional profile of other beans—plenty of protein and fiber, and lots of B vitamins and minerals. Eating these and other beans regularly along with fruits, vegetables, and grains is a recipe for avoiding heart disease, diabetes, and excess weight. Their phenolic acid is a potent antioxidant.

Black-eyed peas are especially low in calories and high in folate; a cup has well over half the recommended daily intake. Folate is a water-soluble vitamin that may help prevent colorectal cancers from beginning.

For Our Planet

Nigeria and Niger are the biggest producers of black-eyed peas today, though they're also grown in the American South and California. The drought- and heat-tolerant plants are sometimes "double-cropped"—grown after wheat or another cash crop in the same season, which makes the land more productive. Their stalks are often saved for animal fodder, reducing food waste.

GIVES YOU

Dietary fiber
Protein
Manganese
Phosphorus
Copper
Iron
Magnesium
Potassium
Zinc
Folate
Thiamine
B6
Vitamin B5
Phytonutrients
 (phenolic acid)

CASHEW

The humidity-loving cashew tree bears a tasty but highly perishable fruit called the cashew apple. From the bottom of this fruit protrudes the kidney-shaped morsel we know as a cashew—not a nut, in fact, but a seed. The 40-foot evergreen cashew tree is native to coastal areas of Brazil and was an important food for indigenous peoples there. The tree traveled with 16-century Portuguese missionaries to India and East Africa, where it also thrived along the seacoasts. The nutritious nuts are often used in Chinese, Thai, and Indian cooking.

Choose and Use

Unsalted cashews add crunch to savory dishes and can be tossed onto salads or soups to boost the nutrition and texture. They can also be simmered into rice pilafs, soups, or vegetables to flavor the dish and release the nuts' nutrients. Their high oil content makes them subject to spoilage; store in the freezer or in an airtight container for up to six months. They should be crisp and sweet-tasting.

For Your Health

An ounce of cashews (a small handful) has nearly as much protein as an egg. Cashews are particularly high in oleic acid, a monounsaturated fatty acid also found in olive oil, which is heavily consumed in the vaunted Mediterranean diet.

It may well be due to the special fat composition of nuts that eating them very regularly, as opposed to rarely or not at all, seems to reduce rates of cardiovascular disease, and lower risk factors for diabetes and "metabolic syndrome," a very common collection of factors (excess abdominal fat and high blood sugar, cholesterol, and blood pressure) that together dramatically boost heart-disease risk. While quite

GIVES YOU
Protein
Monounsaturated and
    polyunsaturated fats
Thiamin
Vitamin K
Manganese
Copper
Phosphorus
Magnesium
Iron
Zinc
Selenium
Phytonutrients
    (flavonoids,
    phytosterols)

PAIRINGS ✦ STIR-FRY CRUNCH

Starchier than many other nuts and also a good source of fiber and minerals, cashews are a favorite for snacking out of hand. (Go for unsalted.) They are also a common ingredient in Chinese stir-frys, adding crunch and protein as well as heart-healthy fats and minerals. Select 3 to 4 vegetables that are in season and sauté in peanut oil. Add an Asian-inspired sauce along with sliced water chestnuts and cashews for a flavorful dinner served over brown rice or quinoa.

calorically dense, cashews and other nuts can even be part of a successful weight-loss diet as long as they are consumed in moderation.

For Our Planet

Cashew trees stabilize soil and generally do not require pesticides or herbicides. Major producers of cashews include Vietnam, Brazil, India, and parts of East and West Africa. Vietnam has sharply increased cashew production in recent years and is now the top exporter to the U.S.

✦ TAKE AWAY

For a healthy heart, eat a handful of cashews.

CHEESE: HARD, SOFT, COTTAGE

The most basic step in making cheese is fermenting milk with bacteria that convert its sugars to lactic acid. In fact, the craft of cheese making deploys a veritable menagerie of fermenting microorganisms—including a variety of bacteria, molds, and yeasts. The choice of organism is one of the most important elements in determining taste and consistency.

The so-called starter culture begins to curdle the milk, its liquid whey separating from the solid curds. Next comes rennet, a substance found in the stomach linings of young calves that helps them digest their mother's milk (although today most cheeses are produced with genetically engineered rennet). The enzymes in rennet further separate the solid curds from the watery whey. The product is salted, and other organisms such as mold may be introduced. The cheese is allowed to age over a period of days or even years.

Apart from the lightly acidified "fresh" cheeses, such as cottage cheese or ricotta, cheese is easier to store and carry than milk, and—thanks to acid, salt, and low moisture—keeps much longer.

This is one reason people have been making it for millennia. Though the origins of cheese making are obscure, the art apparently arose soon after the domestication of milk-giving beasts in the Near East and, subsequently, Europe. The earliest evidence, dating back 7,200 years, comes from milk-fat deposits in pottery found at sites in Poland.

Choose and Use

The old adage holds true: All things in moderation. A little blue cheese crumbled over vegetables, slabs of creamy feta enjoyed in a Greek salad, or a slice of cheddar with fruit and a hearty bread all please the senses, feed the appetite, and nourish the body. Parmesan and Romano are relatively low in saturated fat compared to other cheeses, keep well, and are excellent grated fresh over pasta or mixed greens. Ricotta is low in salt and high in calcium and protein, a common ingredient in both savory and sweet Italian dishes that can also be spread on bread or fruit.

For Your Health

Cheeses vary a lot in their nutritional content. Most—including such diverse types as cottage cheese, Swiss cheese, mozzarella, and cheddar—are good sources of protein. Cheese also provides plenty of calcium and phosphorus, both important to building strong bones and teeth.

On the other hand, cheese is high in saturated fat, accounting for about 16 percent of Americans' overall consumption. Research shows replacing saturated fats with whole grains and unsaturated fats lowers cardiovascular risk. Cheese is also a salty food, which, especially when potassium intake is low, can contribute to high blood pressure.

GIVES YOU

Protein
Calcium
Phosphorus
Zinc
Vitamin A
Riboflavin
Vitamin B12

FOOD SCIENCE ✦ KEEP IT REAL

Whether you're moved by an interest in personal health, the environment, animal welfare, rich and subtle flavor, or all of the above, hold out for a real cheese that's carefully chosen and responsibly made. Why not eat a little less cheese rather than buy "low-fat" versions souped up with salt, sugar, and flavor additives in an unavailing effort to make up for the absence of fat? And why not pay more for an artisanal or farmstead cheese made with milk from pastured animals? Certified organic products mean no hormones or antibiotics, pesticide-free feed, and, in the case of some companies such as Organic Valley, a policy of humane animal treatment on small farms.

But studies examining whether eating cheese increases a person's risk of heart disease, stroke, and diabetes have produced equivocal results. This may be partly because cheese, like other foods, contains more than just saturated fats and salt and is consumed as part of an overall dietary pattern that will include a host of other foods.

Published in 2012, a review of studies concluded that most population studies fail to link dairy intake with heart disease or stroke, regardless of fat levels. The same review found that fat intake from cheese raises "bad" low-density lipoprotein (LDL)

PREP TIP ✦ LESS IS MORE

The big flavors of cheese mean a little goes a long way. Whether thinly shaving a hard Italian cheese or crumbling a soft chèvre or blue, cheese adds richness and depth to salads and other dishes.

The word "terroir" is most often used when referring to wine, but it is true of many drinks and foods. Animals like cows, goats, and sheep who have dined on grasses where they live creates distinct flavors to their milk and artisans use unique enzymes when making cheese, further imparting terroir to the world's cheeses.

cholesterol less than the same amount of fat from butter. Meanwhile, there's some suggestion that people who eat more low-fat dairy products may have reduced blood pressure and lower risk for stroke and type 2 diabetes.

For Our Planet

The main reason to eat cheese sparingly isn't to save the body from disease but to spare the global environment from the impacts of livestock production. A 2011 report by the Environmental Working Group found that cheese is third only to lamb and beef in greenhouse gas emissions per edible pound. Indeed, the conventional dairy industry is all but indistinguishable from the beef industry. After a few years, dairy cattle are sold for slaughter, making up some 18 percent of U.S. ground-beef supply. Their calves are also sold for meat. All cattle produce methane and consume enormous quantities of feed and water (more than 800 gallons of water are required to make a pound of cheese). Concentrated operations pollute air, water, and soil. U.S. dairy cattle are often given antibiotics to stave off udder and other infections, and nearly one in five is given growth hormones to stimulate milk production, though studies show this tends to increase rates of mastitis and lameness.

✦ TAKE AWAY

Cheese is a good source of protein and calcium, though many are high in saturated fat and salt.

CHICKEN

Now the most common bird in the world, the ubiquitous domestic chicken is most likely a descendant of the Red Junglefowl, which in the wild feeds on insects, seeds, and small animals, and flies only to reach its nest in a tree or other elevated site. Domestication probably took place in Southeast Asia more than 7,500 years ago. Chickens' inability to migrate far means their spread throughout the world was accomplished by people.

In the 1990s, for the first time, Americans began eating more chicken than beef.

Choose and Use

No need to avoid dark meat; though a little higher in saturated fat than white, it's also got a tad more vitamins and, according to many, much more flavor. But going for skinless chicken is well worth it, since fat is heavily concentrated in the skin. Chicken can be grilled, oven roasted, lightly pan fried, or poached in low-sodium broth or wine. Marinate the meat in lemon with a dash of salt and pepper, or bake it with rosemary and other aromatic herbs. Breading and deep-frying, of course, add a great deal of saturated fat, and "nuggets" are often made of reconstituted meat along with corn-based fillers and other additives.

For Your Health

Chicken is an excellent source of animal protein. Compared with 85 percent lean ground beef, a portion of chicken breast has about the same amount of protein but fewer calories and, if you eat it without the fatty skin, about a third the total fat. And the fat is composed differently. Stacked up against beef, pork, and lamb, chicken fat has a significantly higher ratio of cholesterol-lowering monounsaturated and polyunsaturated fats to

GIVES YOU

Protein
Selenium
Phosphorus
Niacin
Vitamin B6

✦ TAKE AWAY

Chicken is low in saturated fat, as long as you remove the skin before cooking.

saturated fats, although fat composition changes based on animals' diets.

Half a roasted chicken breast confers more than half the suggested daily intake of niacin, one of the B vitamins that helps the body convert food to energy and play a basic role in nervous-system functioning. Published in 2004, a study examining the effects of diet in thousands of elderly Chicagoans found that those who consumed lots of niacin in their food had slower age-related mental decline and fewer cases of Alzheimer's disease.

For Our Planet

In its 2011 Meat Eater's Guide to Climate Change and Health, the Environmental Working Group ranked chicken as having the lowest overall greenhouse-gas emissions of any meat, with a higher percentage—about 25 percent—produced during processing rather than in raising the animals. To produce a pound of chicken takes about 468 gallons of water and 2 pounds of grain, a lot less than is required for a pound of beef, pork, or lamb. That said, EWG advises consumers to opt for chickens labeled organic, pasture-raised, or antibiotic-free.

CONSIDER ✦ THE REAL COST OF CHICKEN

Most broilers are raised amid their own droppings on the floors of dark barns that hold thousands of birds—and fed antibiotics to promote fast growth despite this unwholesome confinement. "Free-range" birds have continuous access to an outside space, but government regulations don't characterize the required space; in any event, since the birds are bred for heavy breasts and thighs, many do not avail themselves of the opportunity. The less common term "pasture-raised" has no legal definition but has been adopted by farmers to suggest the chickens are raised on actual pasture. "Organic" is probably the most meaningful term on chicken labels. The chickens must be free-range and raised on organic feed without antibiotics (which means they have to be kept healthy by other means). The higher price tag on organic or antibiotic-free chicken reflects lower costs for the environment, the animals, and human health.

CRUSTACEANS: CRAB, SHRIMP, LOBSTER

Crustaceans, with their tough, jointed exoskeletons, proliferated during the Cretaceous period, 145 to 66 million years ago—long predating the rise of mammals, and certainly the emergence of anatomically modern humans some 200,000 years ago.

From available evidence, it seems that hunter-gatherers added shellfish and other marine resources to their diet of fruits, nuts, and meat as long as 164,000 years ago. This is the date attached to a site on the southern coast of Africa, where a group of *Homo sapiens* had migrated, perhaps driven by climate change that brought cold, dry conditions. They survived by exploiting the ocean's bounty, including whelks and the spiral-shaped giant periwinkle. Not much later, their relatives, the Neanderthals, were collecting shellfish at sites in Spain and Italy.

In ancient times, the Greeks and Romans drew shrimp, lobster, and crab from coastal waters, and ate all three, although their recourse to crab meat was apparently not enthusiastic. Native Americans who lived by coasts and bays also took advantage of protein-rich crustacean populations, catching shrimp and crab in weirs, and harvesting lobster by hand for use as both food and fertilizer.

American shrimp and crab fisheries are among the country's largest and most valuable; lobster is also a high-value U.S. fishery. These rich shellfish are favorites among American consumers, too—especially shrimp, now the most popular seafood in the U.S.

Choose and Use

Crustaceans should have bright, firm shells and give off a sea-fresh aroma, not a rank fishy smell. It's important to keep them cool and prepare or freeze them as soon as possible after purchase.

If buying lobster or crab live, here's how you kill it with compassion: freeze it for twenty minutes to render it insensible. Then, for the crab, stab through its head with a sharp, heavy knife. For the lobster, lay it on its back and swiftly split it along its midline, from the head to the tail. This will destroy its decentralized nervous system. Then steam, boil, or sauté.

Though traditionally eaten with plenty of butter, mayonnaise, and even steak and potatoes, the lightly chilled meat of these animals is so rich that it is happily paired with lighter fare—lemon, fresh herbs such as cilantro or dill, tomatoes, red peppers, avocado, corn, spring greens, or asparagus.

For Your Health

Shrimp, lobster, and crab pack a very generous portion of protein—nearly as much as tuna—with comparatively few calories.

Though known to past generations as high in cholesterol, the buttery flesh of our favorite crustaceans contains negligible amounts of saturated fat, a much bigger dietary contributor to high cholesterol in the blood than dietary cholesterol. In fact research conducted in the late 1990s suggests eating lots of shrimp has no ill effect on overall blood cholesterol. The nine-week study added ten ounces of shrimp a

GIVES YOU

Protein
Vitamin B12
Niacin
Selenium
Phosphorus
Zinc
Copper
Iron
Omega-3 fatty acids
Phytonutrients
   (carotenoids)

CONSIDER ✦ SEA BUGS, LAND BUGS

Crustaceans are arthropods, animals without spines that also include spiders, scorpions, and insects. As ubiquitous in aquatic environments as insects on the earth, crustaceans that crawl along the ocean's floor are often called "sea bugs." While unfamiliar to Americans, "land bugs"—in other words, insects—are consumed around the world and in many places are considered a delicacy. A 2013 report by the Food and Agricultural Organization of the United Nations touted the bright future of insect farming and consumption to address food insecurity and malnutrition.

day to a low-fat diet and tested it against the baseline low-fat diet and the same diet plus two hard-boiled eggs daily. Both the high-cholesterol shrimp and egg diets raised "bad" low-density lipoprotein (LDL) cholesterol, but they also boosted high-density lipoprotein (HDL) cholesterol, an effect most pronounced in the shrimp eaters. HDL cholesterol collects excess cholesterol from the blood and returns it to the liver. It's when HDL levels are low and LDL levels are high that cholesterol builds up in blood vessels and compromises their functioning. The researchers suggested this effect of shrimp might be due to its high levels of healthy polyunsaturated (omega-3) fats.

Finally, these aquatic creatures are loaded with a highly absorbable form of the mineral selenium, as well as a carotenoid coloring called astaxanthin, both of which have demonstrated antioxidant and anti-inflammatory effects in laboratory studies.

For Our Planet

With so many kinds of seafood available from so many sources—not to mention produced and harvested by such diverse methods—finding the most environmentally responsible products is no mean feat. It's simplest to rely on seafood decision guides produced by groups like the Monterey Bay Aquarium, the New England Aquarium, and National Geographic.

PAIRINGS
✦
DITCH THE BUTTER

One of the best-loved seafood dishes in America is steamed lobster, classically served as part of a clambake with melted butter for dipping. Other shellfish (and finfish, too) are also commonly served in rich, buttery sauces. While a little butter can be fine once in a while, olive oil is a healthier choice and pairs beautifully with fishes of all kinds—including lobster—along with a squeeze of fresh lemon juice.

PREP TIP ✦ SAVE THE SHELLS

The shells from your crustaceans put you on your way to creating a broad array of soups from homemade stock, whether clam chowder using clam shells, lobster bisque using lobster shells, or bouillabaisse using the shells from a range of different fishes. It's also a super way to use all parts of the animal and save money: no need to buy store-bought stock.

In 2013, for example, the Monterey Bay Aquarium guide lists 12 types of shrimp, three of which it labels as best avoided. It lists eight kinds of lobster, with only one, the Caribbean spiny lobster from Brazil, getting the thumbs-down. The nonprofit names 14 types of crab, discouraging consumption of one, king crabs trapped in Russia. Fishing and aquaculture practices can change over time, however, so it's important to keep updated when selecting any seafood.

Lobster and crab are generally sustainable choices; most of those that find their way onto a plate in the U.S. were wild-caught in U.S. waters. Shrimp, the most popular seafood in America, poses serious problems. The institute suggests avoiding imported shrimp that's farmed in open systems, which can smother adjacent water and soil with pesticides, waste, and other contaminants; often shrimp farms themselves have replaced mangrove swamps, valuable centers of biodiversity. The trouble is, this kind of shrimp constitutes the bulk of what Americans eat, with 90 percent of it imported, most often from Southeast Asia or Latin America. Systems are improving abroad; meantime, seek out U.S.-farmed or wild-caught shrimp. The information changesoften; so it's best to visit the National Geographic Web site at www.nationalgeographic.com/seafood-decision-guide.

✦ TAKE AWAY

Pair crustaceans with lemon, herbs, or vegetables.

EGG

Since before recorded history, people have gathered eggs from birds' nests for a few mouthfuls of protein. The domestication of the chicken beginning some 7,500 years ago in Southeast Asia made that process much easier, although in ancient Egypt, Greece, Rome, and China its eggs were not necessarily more popular than those of the duck, goose, quail, and pigeon. By the Middle Ages, chickens were fully domesticated in western Europe; both the nobility and peasants ate eggs, which, along with fish, replaced meat on Christian fast days.

For much of U.S. history, egg production has been a domestic undertaking, with backyard chicken coops becoming especially popular in the 19th century. Providing eggs and, on occasion, meat, a brood of chickens often served as a complement to a home vegetable garden.

GIVES YOU

Protein
Vitamin A
Riboflavin
Vitamin B12
Choline
Selenium
Phosphorus
Iron
Phytonutrients
  (carotenoids)

Hard-cooked eggs are used in many dishes, from egg salad to beloved stuffed eggs But have you ever noticed how sometimes they're especially difficult to peel? Nothing at all to do with color, fresher eggs are harder to peel than older eggs. Planning ahead and using older eggs will save you a bit of extra work.

✦ TAKE AWAY

Choose eggs that have been produced ethically and sustainably.

Choose and Use

An egg with a piece of whole-grain toast and a bit of fruit is truly a great way to start the day—filling, relatively low-calorie, and nutritionally balanced.

Are some eggs healthier than others? Whether an egg is white or brown simply reflects the color of the hen. "Vegetarian" eggs come from hens not fed meat and bone meal, a common practice in conventional poultry farming. Eggs advertised as enriched with omega-3 fatty acids come from hens reared on flaxseed and other omega-3-rich foods. That's fine as far as it goes, but consuming the fatty acids directly in salmon and other oily fish (for example) will provide the most valuable fats in greater quantities.

For Your Health

In the 1980s, public health authorities raised the alarm over the sky-high cholesterol content of eggs: A single large egg serves up 70 percent of the recommended daily consumption. But since then scientists have realized that dietary cholesterol is not as important a factor in blood cholesterol as once believed. In fact, a 2013 analysis of eight published population studies concluded that eating up to an egg a day is not associated with a hike in risk for stroke, or, except perhaps in the case of diabetic patients, heart disease. Eggs are also rich in choline, which benefits cell structure and neurotransmitter synthesis.

For Our Planet

The most meaningful distinctions among egg products have to do not with personal dietary preferences or human health but with animal welfare and the environment. The vast majority of laying hens in the U.S. are confined their whole lives in cages (banned in Europe) that prevent natural behaviors or indeed much movement at all; the hens, according to the Humane Society of the United States, "endure constant suffering."

"Free-range" eggs come from hens that at least are permitted to roam in a barn and have continuous access to the outdoors. Certified organic eggs are even better; the birds must be free-range and raised on vegetarian feed (meaning no fish meal or ground-up animal protein) produced organically. They cannot be given antibiotics (another routine practice in conventional egg production). By law, no chickens are given hormones.

FAVA BEAN

Thousands of years ago, while native peoples of Central and South America were cultivating the common bean (varieties include the black bean and kidney bean), across the Atlantic, groups in Eurasia were growing fava beans. This tender legume was domesticated more than 6,000 years ago, probably somewhere in the eastern Mediterranean. Still a favorite dish in parts of the Middle East and Europe, fava beans were the bean Europeans knew until the Age of Discovery, when explorers introduced the common bean, the highly variable *Phaseolus vulgaris*, from the Americas.

Choose and Use

Shelling and peeling the skin from fresh fava beans is a time-consuming chore unless you're ready to make a fun project of it; kids can help. A bag of frozen beans makes the enterprise simple as can be. Boil them for a few minutes, then eat them with Greek yogurt, olive oil, and fresh mint. Or whip up a chunky, rustic hummus in the blender, an enticing nutrient-rich alternative to mayonnaise on a sandwich.

For Your Health

Fava beans have a bit less fiber and protein but also fewer calories and carbohydrates than kidney or black beans. Like other beans they provide an ample quantity of folate, important for cell division, especially in pregnancy, and a smattering of other

GIVES YOU

Protein
Dietary fiber
Folate
Thiamine
Riboflavin
Niacin
Vitamin K
Manganese
Copper
Phosphorus
Magnesium
Iron
Potassium
Phytonutrients
  (flavonoids,
  phytosterols,
  phenolic acids)

PREP TIP ✦ SPRINGTIME FAVORITE

Fava beans are a springtime favorite with a very short season. Preparing fresh favas is a labor of love, however, involving removing them from their pods, steaming, and peeling. Frozen are just as nutritious and can be enjoyed any time of year, without all the work.

B-complex vitamins that are key to converting food into energy the body can use. And fava beans also provide minerals that are required for heart function and healthy bones.

For Our Planet

Canada grows a good deal of fava beans for export to the U.S., but major producers worldwide are China, Ethiopia, the U.K., Egypt, France, and Australia. Grown for animal feed as well as human consumption, like other beans the fava bean is sometimes used as a cover crop to protect soil and retain moisture, or rotated with grain crops to take advantage of the bean's ability to replenish soil with nitrogen. Beans are an environmentally friendly source of calories.

✦ TAKE AWAY

Fava beans have fewer calories and carbohydrates than other types of beans.

GARBANZO BEAN

The garbanzo bean or chickpea is one of the first legumes people learned to cultivate along with grains during the advent of farming in the Neolithic period. The green-leafed annual plant with its trumpet-shaped blossoms and nutritious fleshy seeds was probably domesticated in the area of southeastern Turkey roughly 7,000 years ago, then spread southwest into the Middle East and northwest into southern Europe. Chickpeas are among the most beloved legumes in the world today, the principal ingredient of foods such as falafel and hummus enjoyed throughout the Middle East and beyond.

CONSIDER
✦
DRIED VERSUS CANNED

Buying dried garbanzos reduces packaging and costs less than canned. Preparation requires overnight soaking— or an hour-long soak in a hot water bath— before simmering on the stovetop. Takes time, but it's easy and the beans are firm and fresh tasting. If you keep cans on hand for convenience, make sure to select a no salt added brand.

Once enjoyed only by health food fanatics, hummus is now mainstream. A simple purée of garbanzos, tahini (sesame paste), olive oil, garlic, lemon juice, and water whizzed up in a food processor, homemade hummus is a cinch to make and fresher tasting than store-bought.

✦ TAKE AWAY

Take advantage of garbanzo beans' versatility—whole in salads, mixed into curries or soups, or blended into hummus.

GIVES YOU

Protein
Dietary fiber
Folate
Thiamine
Vitamin B6
Vitamin K
Manganese
Copper
Phosphorus
Iron
Magnesium
Potassium
Calcium
Zinc
Phytonutrients
   (phytosterols,
   phenolic acids)

Choose and Use

For a simple, cheap, and healthy dish, try chickpeas dressed with lemon, olive oil, and garlic. Including additional colorful vegetables makes a pretty and healthful chopped salad. Chickpeas are also great in Indian curries and vegetable dishes. Hummus, a chickpea spread made with tahini (sesame paste), olive oil, lemon, and garlic, is wonderful spread on whole grain bread or dark rye crisps along with tomatoes and sprouts. It's easy to make at home, and store-bought flavors like roasted red pepper or artichoke keep things interesting; be sure to check the ingredient label for sodium content. Frozen green garbanzos are excellent in sautés, minestrone soups, and salads.

For Your Health

Chickpeas share their most impressive assets with other beans: they are fiber-dense and a good source of protein. And that makes them a satisfying food that's healthy for the heart.

Squeeze a little lemon on your bean salad; the vitamin C in lemons aids the absorption of the iron in chickpeas. Magnesium supports nerves and muscles.

A cup of chickpeas provides half the dietary fiber recommended for the day. Most people don't get enough fiber, some of which helps pull cholesterol from the blood and regulate its uptake of sugars.

For Our Planet

U.S. per capita consumption of garbanzo beans has been slowly increasing in recent years, and that's all to the good. The plant is adaptable to weather and requires relatively little water. U.S. supplies come largely from the American West and Canada.

GREEN PEA

The pea plant grows wild in the Near East and Mediterranean basin, where it was likely domesticated some 9,000 years ago as foragers learned to cultivate its nutritious seed. For many centuries the seeds in their peapods were allowed to dry like other legumes and formed the basis of gruels somewhat like the modern split pea soup that helped stave off starvation. By the 19th century, "fresh" immature green peas consumed as a vegetable had become a popular side dish. In the U.S., peas were among the first vegetables to be commercially canned and frozen in the 1920s. Green or garden peas, snap peas, snow peas, and dried "split" peas are all varieties of the legume *Pisum sativum*.

GIVES YOU

Protein
Dietary fiber
Vitamin C
Vitamin A
Vitamin K
Folate
Thiamine
Vitamin B6
Riboflavin
Niacin
Manganese
Magnesium
Phosphorus
Copper
Iron
Potassium
Zinc
Phytonutrients
    (phenolic acids,
    flavonoids,
    carotenoids)

Choose and Use

Green peas, snow peas, snap peas, and split peas have similar nutritional profiles, although only two have edible pods, which are delicious and loaded with fiber. Fresh green peas are crisp and sweet, one of the first vegetables to come in season in the springtime, though often hard to find. Peas also freeze very well. Canned peas (and sometimes frozen) can come heavily salted; choose no-sodium products. For a delicious meal, toss fresh green peas with whole grain pasta and a bit of olive oil and Parmesan in spring and enjoy a split pea soup come winter.

For Your Health

Green peas combine some of the best qualities of beans with certain standout traits of fruits and vegetables. Like beans, they're a good source of fiber and protein (though their protein content is a bit lower) and are replete with B-complex vitamins and minerals. Like many fruits and vegetables, they're also loaded with vitamins C, A, and K, and plenty of phytonutrients, which together may act against cell damage from oxidation and inflammation, processes that accelerate many chronic diseases. Studies have also suggested that when diabetics eat more legumes, they achieve better blood-sugar control and are less likely to die from heart disease.

For Our Planet

Peas capture atmospheric nitrogen in the soil; eco-friendly, they are often used as cover crops to nourish and retain soil. Sustainably grown peas are raised in many states, particularly on the West Coast and in the upper Midwest, although imports from China and Latin America have increased in the last 20 years.

✦ TAKE AWAY

Choose peas for plant-friendly protein.

FOOD SCIENCE ✦ FROZEN PEAS

Green peas are at their sweetest in the heart of summer, and shelling them is a fun way to get kids involved in cooking. Quickly blanched peas can be frozen to enjoy in colder months.

HAZELNUT

The hazel tree was probably domesticated in three separate locations: the Mediterranean (Italy and Spain), Turkey, and Iran, a region where the tree is widely cultivated today for its sweet and crunchy nut. Though it's not clear exactly when people first started growing rather than simply gathering hazelnuts, this transition certainly was accomplished by Roman times. Traditionally called filberts in the United States, hazelnuts are a more commonplace feature of European diets, especially in pastries and chocolate treats. The average Swiss person, for example, eats more than four times the amount of hazelnuts each year as the typical American.

Choose and Use

Familiar as an ingredient in praline candies and the chocolate spread Nutella, hazelnuts can also be toasted and sprinkled onto colorful salads, cooked into rice and vegetable dishes, or eaten out of hand as a filling, protein-rich snack. Check labels for added salt.

GIVES YOU

Protein
Dietary fiber
Monounsaturated and
    polyunsaturated fats
Vitamins E
Thiamine
Vitamin B6
Folate
Manganese
Copper
Magnesium
Iron
Phosphorus
Phytonutrients
    (flavonoids, phenolic
    acids, phytosterols)

For Your Health

Based on a raft of studies, in 2003 the U.S. Food and Drug Administration approved a health claim for nuts saying that eating 1.5 ounces a day as part of a diet low in saturated fat and cholesterol can reduce the risk of heart disease. Like other nuts, hazelnuts are a high-fiber protein source; they also offer robust quantities of antioxidants such as vitamin E and flavonoids called flavanols (as well as anthocyanidins), which studies suggest may be beneficial to the heart. Perhaps the most important heart-protective feature of nuts is their high concentration of healthy unsaturated fats that lower low-density lipoprotein (LDL) cholesterol—and this feature is especially pronounced in hazelnuts. Hazelnuts provide mostly monounsaturated fats (like that found in olive oil)—12.8 grams in an ounce, versus 8.6 grams in almonds and 6.9 grams in peanuts.

For Our Planet

Hazel tree groves are long-lived, help prevent erosion, and require relatively little treatment with pesticides and fertilizers. Turkey is the world's biggest producer, followed by Italy and the U.S.; Oregon produces nearly all American-grown hazelnuts. A fungus called eastern filbert blight made cultivation of the nut impossible in the Northeast and devastated groves in the Northwest in the 1970s, requiring extensive use of fungicides. Today, varieties resistant to the fungus are helping to solve the problem.

✦ TAKE AWAY

High in essential fatty acids, hazelnuts promote heart health.

PAIRINGS ✦ NUTELLA

A chocolate shortage during World War II had confectioners turning to hazelnuts for inspiration, which were cheaper and more plentiful. Thus was born Nutella, the chocolate-filbert spread that's still popular today. Hazelnuts also became a filler for fine chocolates.

KIDNEY BEAN

Like the pinto and black beans so common in Latin American cooking, the red kidney bean is a variety of the common bean, *Phaseolus vulgaris*. The common bean was domesticated in two locations, Peru and Mexico, beginning some 8,000 years ago. Though native peoples of these regions did eat meat (the Aztecs, for example, dined on turkey and dog, while the Incas ate llamas), beans were an important source of protein among pre-Columbian peoples, whose agriculture did not include extensive domestication of food animals.

Choose and Use

Due to high quantities of a protein called phytohemagglutinin, raw kidney beans are toxic. As few as four or five beans may bring on symptoms including nausea and vomiting, and under-cooked beans may be as toxic as raw ones, so be sure to boil kidney beans briskly after soaking. Canned beans (with no salt added) are just about equal in nutritional quality to dried. They are delicious in a traditional chili or rinsed and tossed into a chopped salad or included in a mixed bean salad.

GIVES YOU

Dietary fiber
Protein
Manganese
Copper
Phosphorus
Magnesium
Iron
Potassium
Zinc
Folate
Thiamin
Vitamin B6
Vitamin K
Phytonutrients
   (flavonoids,
   phytosterols,
   phenolic acids)

For Your Health

Kidney beans boast a nutritional profile very similar to their close relative, the black bean. A cup packs 15 grams of protein—more than you'd get in two large eggs. Whereas many protein sources common in Western diets are loaded with saturated fat and cholesterol but mostly devoid of fiber, kidney beans have neither saturated fat nor cholesterol, and they provide nearly half the fiber recommended for a day. Because fiber helps regulate the pace at which sugars are released into the bloodstream, eating plenty of kidney beans is likely to have a positive impact on cholesterol levels. Kidney beans are also a great source of the B-complex vitamin folate and provide a range of minerals in moderate supply. Unlike black beans, a cup of kidney beans contains nearly a fifth of the suggested daily intake of vitamin K, a nutrient that may help direct calcium to the bones where it's needed to build bone matrix, and out of the arteries, where deposits of calcium are a factor in vascular disease.

For Our Planet

Beans do not compete well with weeds and are not tolerant of waterlogged soils, so they may develop fungal diseases requiring application of fungicides. On the other hand, they fix nitrogen from the atmosphere, enriching the soil they grow in, and are often grown in rotation with other crops to replenish fields for replanting. As a low-cost source of plant protein, beans are gentle on the environment.

PREP TIP ✦ BEANS AND RICE

Rice and beans is a dish traditional to many Central and South American cuisines and can be prepared using many different beans seasoned with spices like cumin, garlic, and coriander. With their dark red hue, kidney beans are especially colorful. Don't forget to use brown rice!

LAMB

All sheep are descended from an animal called the mouflon, which may be the first food animal ever domesticated, a process made easier by its relative docility and herding behavior. Humans first brought the animals under domestication for their meat and milk in the area of today's southwestern Iran some 9,000 years ago. A 6,000-year-old small statue of a woolly sheep recovered from a site in Iran suggests that, by then, people were breeding the creature for its fleece as well. New Zealand and Australia are the major producers of sheep meat, accounting for some 90 percent of exports.

Choose and Use

Lamb shank is the leanest cut of this meat, delicious slow-cooked in Mediterranean dishes including tomatoes, onions, garlic, wine, and plenty of spices. Grass-fed lambs will have higher amounts of healthy omega-3 and omega-6 fatty acids than those raised on corn. Organic lamb must meet the U.S. Department of Agriculture's requirement for grass feeding during the pasture season (at least 120 days a year) and will not have been treated with antibiotics.

For Your Health

A lamb chop and sirloin beefsteak provide a similar complex of B vitamins, minerals (including iron), and protein. But there's a big difference in their fat profiles. Lamb generally has even more saturated fat than beef. Unlike beef, it is also quite high in monounsaturated and polyunsaturated fats—"better fats"—as the American Heart Association puts it. A three-ounce serving of sirloin steak has 11.9 mg of polyunsaturated omega-3 fatty acids, whereas a similar portion of lamb chop contains 93.5 mg—not comparable to the prodigious amount of these heart-healthy fatty acids you get in salmon, but worth noting.

CONSIDER
✦
CARBON FOOTPRINT

Among all foods, lamb has the highest carbon footprint. But don't be fooled: it's not because it's usually imported from the other side of the world. One U.K. study found that grass-fed lamb from New Zealand had fewer carbon emissions than factor-farmed lamb from England, highlighting the higher impact of meat production on climate change compared to food miles, or how far it's traveled.

PAIRINGS ✦ MINTED LAMB

One of the most energy-intense foods you can eat, lamb is best enjoyed in moderation, if at all. Although more frequently consumed in Mediterranean countries, lamb is often a favorite for Easter celebrations in the United States. With its big flavors, lamb pairs well with bright herbs like mint. While often in the form of thick jelly, a simpler preparation of olive oil, spices, and fresh mint is a lighter choice.

GIVES YOU

Protein
Vitamin B12
Niacin
Riboflavin
Selenium
Zinc
Phosphorus
Iron
Monounsaturated and
    polyunsaturated fats

Lamb is also higher than beef in polyunsaturated omega-6 fatty acids; though omega-6 fatty acids are controversial because they promote inflammation, research suggests that when they replace saturated and trans fats they help reduce risk for heart disease. The American Heart Association recommends getting at least 5 to 10 percent of calories from omega-6 fats.

For Our Planet

The Environmental Working Group's Meat Eater's Guide to Climate Change and Health lists lamb last on its roster of foods— "worst choice." Overall, beef has a much larger impact on the environment simply because it's produced in vastly larger quantities. However, sheep, like cows, are ruminants that produce methane, a potent greenhouse gas, in their digestive process, while yielding significantly less edible meat per pound of live weight. To produce a pound of lamb requires more than 700 gallons of water and about three pounds of grain. The Environmental Working Group recommends grass-fed lamb over lamb "finished" on grain or grain by-products.

LENTIL

Among the crops that founded agriculture in the Fertile Crescent were wheat, barley, flax, and four legumes—chickpeas, green peas, bitter vetch, and lentils, domesticated at least 9,000 years ago. These crops spread east into Persia (ancient Iran) and India, and west into North Africa and eventually Europe. Protein-dense lentils form the basis of traditional dishes in these parts of the world today, from Indian dal to Middle Eastern mujaddara to hearty European soups that harken back to slow-cooked pottages eaten in medieval times.

Choose and Use
Lentils come in a variety of flavors, colors, and textures, from the yellow split lentil of Indian dal to the peppery French green lentil to the common red and brown lentils of soups and stews. They usually come dried but require no soaking and cook in about 30 minutes. Salt strengthens the structure of beans and will prevent softening, so don't salt until fully cooked. Rather mild-tasting themselves, lentils soak up the flavor of spices and broths. Red lentils break down quickly when cooking, creating an almost-creamy texture to a healthful, beautiful soup, delicious when spiced with cumin, cinnamon, and paprika.

For Your Health
If legumes generally are a very healthy food, it may be fair to say that lentils are the super-legume. A cup of kidney beans or chickpeas provides as much as half the dietary fiber recommended for a day; a cup of lentils provides even more at 63 percent. Most beans provide about 15 grams of protein per cup; lentils provide 18 grams. Lentils have more iron than many legumes, and a cup offers a whopping 90 percent of the day's recommended intake of folate.

GIVES YOU

Protein
Dietary fiber
Folate
Thiamine
B6
Vitamin B5
Niacin
Riboflavin
Manganese
Phosphorus
Iron
Copper
Potassium
Magnesium
Zinc
Phytonutrients
  (phenolic acids,
  flavonoids,
  phytosterols)

Lentils come in assorted colors and textures, commonly enjoyed hot as a side dish or in a soup. Red lentils will break down during cooking, creating an almost creamy texture, whereas others retain their shape. Cooked lentils like green or brown make a delightful salad, warm or cold, when tossed with olive oil, lemon juice, and fresh herbs.

✦ **TAKE AWAY**

Lentils offer more protein, fiber, and folate than other legumes.

A review of ten human trials, published in 2011, found that diets enriched with plenty of legumes lowered "bad" low-density lipoprotein (LDL) cholesterol by an average of 8 mg/dL. In another study, published in 2012, diabetics who added a daily cup of legumes to their diets enjoyed better blood-sugar control and lower blood pressure than those who added whole-wheat products. All of the nutrients in lentils combined together probably play an important role in these benefits.

For Our Planet
Washington, Idaho, and Western Canada are major producers of lentils, though most are exported. The drought-tolerant crop is little bothered by pests or diseases, and contributes nitrogen to the soil; it is often rotated with wheat. Lentils are a very important food in India, which produces and consumes about a quarter of the world's crop.

MOLLUSKS: CLAM, MUSSEL, OYSTER

All over the world, along coastlines and beside streams and rivers, thousands and tens of thousands of years ago, human groups left evidence of their feasting on mollusks. Called shell middens, these heaps of discarded shells are sometimes the leavings of a single meal. In other cases, they show evidence of long occupation, as in the 30-foot pile of oyster shells discovered in Damariscotta, Maine; Native Americans added to this heap for a thousand years, between about 2,200 and 1,000 years ago. The southern coast of South Africa is dotted with 3,500 shell middens, including the earliest known find, dating to 140,000 years ago.

Whether sought out as a marginal food in times of want or incorporated on a large scale into human economies, mollusks, those mouthfuls of protein, clearly played an important part in the diets of many hunter-gatherers as well as early farming peoples.

Clams, mussels, and oysters belong to a class of mollusks called bivalves. Two symmetrical shells joined by a hinge enclose a soft body that includes gills for breathing and sieving food, and a simple digestive tract.

PREP TIP ✦ MAKE SURE THEY'RE ALIVE

Don't wash mollusks until you are ready to use them; soaking them in a water bath with a little flour helps remove excess sand. Mollusks that are opened prior to cooking and do not close when tapped are dead and must be discarded.

Choose and Use

Highly perishable bivalves should be purchased live and kept refrigerated. Expect a fresh sea smell and firmly closed shell; if slightly open, the shell should close when you tap it.

Rinse the shells thoroughly to eliminate sand and grit. Clams, oysters, and mussels can be steamed, baked, or grilled; or you can steam them open, remove the meat, and finish cooking in a soup, stir-fry, or sauté. When steaming, place the bivalves in a wide pot for maximum surface exposure and add liquid—wine and fresh herbs, beer and garlic, water, whatever your recipe calls for. Clams and mussels will open when done (about 6–10 minutes for clams, 3 to 5 for mussels), but oysters may not; tapping on the shell produces a hollow sound when they're cooked, usually after 5–10 minutes.

Of course, some people love nothing better than the delicate, briny taste of raw oysters "on the half shell." Buy them in the half shell, or shuck them yourself. Favorite accompaniments? Just a dash of lemon, or Tabasco, Worcestershire sauce, cocktail sauce, or mignonette made of vinegar, shallots, and lemon juice.

✦ TAKE AWAY

Clams provide high amounts of iron, mussels essential fatty acids, and oysters zinc.

For Your Health

It comes as a surprise to many that mollusks, which seem such delicate morsels, are chock full of protein and iron. Clams in particular pack nearly as much protein as ground beef or chicken, with scarcely any saturated fat. And a serving of clams—about ten small ones—provides all the iron you'll need in a day, and then some.

A tad less impressive than clams on the protein front, at 665 mg per ounce, oysters are among the best sources of the omega-3 fatty acids that promote a healthy heart and eyes and may lower the risk of dementia. Oysters also contain plenty of zinc, which the immune system needs to combat infection. Six steamed oysters have a paltry 60 calories.

Mussels are also a good source of omega-3s, and, like clams and oysters, are loaded with protein, iron, and B-complex vitamins, especially B12. The body can store this essential vitamin in small quantities, but because of reduced absorption many older people are at risk of deficiency, which can cause problems with balance, mood, and memory. A serving of clams provides 14 times the recommended daily intake, oysters about 5 times, and mussels more than 3 times the daily suggested intake. Although most sodium in the diet comes from processed foods, mollusks are naturally high in salt due to their seawater habitat.

GIVES YOU

Protein
Vitamin B12
Riboflavin
Niacin
Vitamin C
Vitamin D
Iron
Zinc
Copper
Manganese
Selenium
Phosphorus
Unsaturated fats

For Our Planet

More good news about mollusks: You can enjoy them knowing you're supporting hard-hit marine-based economies without breaking your own bank or harming the natural world in any way.

Most mussels are farmed, and oysters and clams are widely available both wild and farmed. But the distinction isn't quite as sharp for these shellfish as for other types of seafood. Farmed mollusks live in the ocean. They feed by filtering particles from water, which can actually help keep water it clean. Bivalves are often farmed in cages or on long ropes that hang from floating platforms. These methods have little to no environmental impact.

Wild oyster populations in particular have declined steeply since the 19th century, mostly due to overharvesting, although efforts are under way to restore populations in places such as the Chesapeake Bay and even the harbor of New York City, where fresh local oysters were once a favorite street and bar food. A potential long-term threat to all bivalves is the acidification of the world's oceans. The same human-generated carbon dioxide that is helping to warm the planet also settles into the ocean and makes seawater more corrosive. This seems to make it harder for marine creatures to build shells.

The Monterey Bay Aquarium lists all oysters and mussels as a "best choice"; clams are categorized as either a "best choice" or a "good alternative."

PEANUT

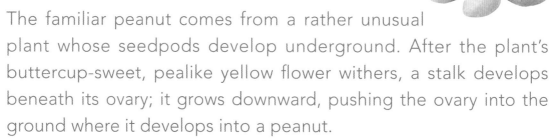

The familiar peanut comes from a rather unusual plant whose seedpods develop underground. After the plant's buttercup-sweet, pealike yellow flower withers, a stalk develops beneath its ovary; it grows downward, pushing the ovary into the ground where it develops into a peanut.

The oldest evidence of peanut consumption comes from Peru, where nut remains and peanut starch on human teeth date back as far as 8,000 years. But scientists believe the plant was domesticated even earlier in Paraguay or Bolivia, where it is native.

George Washington Carver, a botanist and educator born into slavery, promoted peanuts, a nitrogen-fixing crop to rotate with cotton, which had depleted the once-rich loam of the American South. Carver's popular 1916 bulletin on peanuts contained instructions for cultivation and 104 recipes. Peanut consumption took off in the U.S. in the early 1900s, when peanut butter first appeared in supermarkets.

Choose and Use

That little handful of peanuts, while nutritious, packs more than 160 calories. Sugary peanuts pack on nutrients you don't need. The same goes for peanut butter; look for no-salt, no-sugar-added brands that aren't made with trans fats. And skip low-fat peanut butter, which only replaces healthy fats with carbohydrates and sugar.

For Your Health

An ounce of these crunchy, mildly sweet nuts—a small handful—contains seven grams of protein, a little more than an egg. Cook them into a rice dish or spread peanut butter onto wholewheat bread, and you'll have a meal with ample quantities of all the essential amino acids.

GIVES YOU

Protein
Dietary fiber
Niacin
Folate,
Vitamin E (alpha- and
    gamma-tocopherol)
Thiamine
Manganese
Magnesium
Phosphorus
Copper
Iron
Monounsaturated and
    polyunsaturated fats
Phytosterols (stilbenes)

PREP TIP ✦ **PEANUT BUTTER**

Peanuts are among the most popular nuts in America, from ballparks to lunch boxes. And just about everyone loves peanut butter, the creamy spread at its peanuttiest when made only with unsalted nuts and no added oils. Far more healthful than processed meats like bologna, a peanut butter sandwich on whole grain bread is a terrific lunch, whether for kids or adults.

✦ TAKE AWAY

Choose peanuts and peanut butters without added sugar and salt.

Peanuts also offer a modest amount of fiber and vitamin E, an antioxidant that, in the laboratory, has demonstrated activity against the oxidation of cholesterol (a factor in fatty buildup in the arteries) and formation of blood clots, which may cause heart attack or stroke.

In the late twentieth century, peanuts and peanut butter suffered from a reputation as food whose nutrient quality wasn't worth the calories and fat. It's true peanuts are about 50 percent oil, but the type of fat matters when it comes to health: peanuts are primarily unsaturated, heart-healthy fats. Of the 13.9 grams of fat in a small handful of peanuts, only 1.9 grams are saturated fat. Fully 6.9 grams are monounsaturated fat, which helps reduce low-density lipoprotein (LDL) cholesterol. Some research has also shown that peanuts consumed in moderation can also be included as part of a weight-loss diet.

For Our Planet

The U.S. is a major peanut grower, with production concentrated mainly in the Southeast and Southwest. Farmers often rotate the crop with corn and cotton because peanuts supply the soil with nitrogen. Peanut oil has shown potential as a biofuel, although demand for the crop as a food makes it more expensive than corn or soybean to produce.

PECAN

The majestic pecan tree with its bright green pinnate leaves and long, twisting limbs is a native of the south-central United States, where it grows in the moist soil along streams and rivers. Native Americans gathered the hard-shelled nuts in autumn; indeed "pecan" is an Algonquin word that referred to all nuts requiring a stone to crack. Widespread cultivation of pecans did not take place until the 19th century. Even today, in its native range, about half of pecan production comes from wild-growing trees. U.S. production accounts for 80 percent of pecans grown worldwide.

Choose and Use

Smooth-textured and devoid of the slightly bitter nip of walnuts and almonds, pecans make great snacking when not coated with extra salt or sugar. They're also a nutritious addition to fruity quick breads and contribute earthy flavor to salads or cooked vegetables. As with all nuts, lightly toasting in the oven brings out their flavor and crunch. Native Americans use pecan meal to thicken stews.

GIVES YOU

Protein
Dietary fiber
Thiamine
Vitamin E
Manganese
Copper
Iron
Magnesium
Phosphorus
Monounsaturated and
   polyunsaturated fats

For Your Health

A little higher in calories and lower in protein than many nuts, pecans nevertheless are a good source of dietary fiber and especially of the heart-healthy fats that make nut oils more nutritious than animal fat.

A single ounce of pecans contain some 30 percent of recommended daily intake of fat. But well over half that fat is monounsaturated and another 30 percent is polyunsaturated—fats that bring a panoply of benefits, from cutting risk for breast cancer and dementia to improving blood cholesterol levels and perhaps assisting in controlling blood sugar.

One study adding pecans to a diet low in saturated fat and cholesterol found that the pecan-enriched diet delivered more calories as fat than the base diet, but lowered "bad" low-density lipoprotein (LDL) and total cholesterol more than the baseline low-fat diet. Pecans, like peanuts and walnuts, are also high in a form of vitamin E called gamma-tocopherol. Though its health effects are not well understood, some research suggests it may prevent cell damage from oxidation and inflammation.

For Our Planet

Gathering nuts from trees that can live a 100years or more is a sustainable practice, whether the trees are in cultivated orchards or natural stands thinned and nurtured by farmers. Farmers often plant legumes in the orchards to enrich the soil and attract insects that eat pecan aphids and other pests, contributing to a healthy ecosystem. Grazing livestock in pecan groves, where they nibble grasses and fertilize with their manure, is also common.

✦ TAKE AWAY

Pecans make an excellent snack and enliven salads and breads.

PAIRINGS ✦ HEALTHY CRUNCH

Pecans are sweeter than many other nuts and can even be a little chewy when raw. Toasting pecans, like other nuts, really brings out their flavor. Whether you prefer them raw or roasted, make sure to select unsalted. Pecans are a terrific addition to a green salad for crunch and nutrition. A handful of pecans alongside fresh fruits like strawberries, peaches, or plums makes a healthy snack. Or serve with a few pieces of good cheese for a French-inspired dessert.

PINTO BEAN

Pinto beans are one of many varieties of the common bean, *Phaseolus vulgaris,* a major food of pre-Columbian native peoples in South and Central America domesticated in two locations—Peru, some 8,000 years ago, and Mexico, about 7,000 years ago.

These mottled legume seeds are the most popular bean in America and second only to black beans in Mexico. They are a frequent accompaniment to rice and the basis for refried beans, in which the beans are cooked, then mashed into a paste and fried or baked with seasonings like cumin, garlic, and chili power.

Choose and Use

Pinto beans take more time to cook than most—at least two and a half hours, after soaking overnight or using the quick-soak method. Salt and acids such as vinegar or lemon juice delay cooking, so add them late. But cooking with onion or garlic will impart a rich flavor to these mild, creamy beans. For more spur-of-the-moment meals, canned beans retain most of their nutritional value; canning adds sodium, so look for beans labeled no-salt and rinse the beans in cold water for good measure. Serve with seasoned brown rice for a wholesome meal. Spike with lemon juice, extra virgin olive oil, and hot sauce for a satisfying lunch. Peppery greens, beans, and a can of tuna make a great and easy salad or a pasta sauce when gently warmed.

✦ TAKE AWAY

Pair pinto beans with spices or garlic for a creamy, protein-rich dish.

PREP TIP ✦ REFRIED BEANS

Pinto beans are the traditional choice for refried beans. Fry smashed beans in vegetable oil and season with cumin, chili powder, garlic, and onion—add cayenne for kick—for a tasty side. Or stuff into burritos or tacos with salsa for a meatless Mexican meal.

For Your Health

A cup of pinto beans provides a good serving of protein—15 grams—along with well over half the dietary fiber intake recommended for a day, 74 percent of the folate, and 21 percent of minerals potassium and magnesium. All these, in different ways, are good for the cardiovascular system.

Population studies have shown that people who eat lots of legumes (including beans) are less likely to develop heart disease, diabetes, and colon cancer.

For Our Planet

Pintos account for nearly half of all U.S. dry-bean production, concentrated in the northern Great Plains. Though intolerant of moist soils and subject to fungal diseases, beans are relatively untroubled by insects. They are usually planted in rotation with cereal crops that have different nutrient requirements and disease susceptibility. Eating beans, an efficient plant-based source of nutrients, energy, and protein, is a good move for the environment as well as your own health.

GIVES YOU

Protein
Dietary fiber
Folate
Thiamine
Vitamin B6
Vitamin E
Vitamin K
Manganese
Phosphorus
Magnesium
Potassium
Iron
Calcium
Zinc
Copper
Selenium
Phytonutrients
  (phenolic acids)

PISTACHIO

The pistachio is a comely little tree with a dense, bowl-shaped crown and reddish-brown bark. Ten thousand years ago, when hunter-gatherers of the Near East first began the transition to agriculture, pistachio trees mingled with oaks in forests reaching from the eastern Mediterranean to the Zagros Mountains of Iraq and Iran. People had gathered the nuts for thousands of years already, and would combine these foraged nuts with cultivated foods for millennia to come.

Movements associated with Alexander the Great, the Roman Empire, the Muslim expansion, and the Crusades all helped spread pistachios throughout the Mediterranean world. U.S. commercial production of pistachios came much later, in the 1970s. Today's California pistachios are a bit larger and easier to shell than the Turkish (Antep) variety, but some connoisseurs swear by the Turkish nut's sweet crunchiness. Sicilian pistachios are very green and often found slivered onto pastries and other desserts.

✦ TAKE AWAY

Add pistachios to salads and stuffings.

Choose and Use

The most common presentation of this green-tinted nut is as a snack food so heavily salted as to mask its delicate flavor. Try them instead sprinkled in a fruit salad, or with orange slices over peppery greens. Pistachios make terrific pestos, pilafs, stuffings, and crunchy crusts for fish or poultry. Because pistachio growing and processing require a lot of time and labor, the nuts are pricey; try buying them in bulk.

For Your Health

Along with protein, pistachios bring a great deal of fat to the table, but more than half that fat is unsaturated, predominantly monounsaturated fats that, when they replace less healthy fats, might help reduce a person's chances of getting breast cancer, developing age-related macular degeneration or cognitive decline, and suffering flair-ups of arthritis pain. These fats are considered to have salutary effects on cardiovascular health as well.

Indeed, one 2007 study that instructed subjects to take fully 15 percent of their calories from pistachios found they ended up consuming less of their energy in the form of saturated fat and saw small improvements in blood cholesterol. In another study, eating three ounces per day of pistachios over four weeks reduced blood levels of oxidized low-density lipoprotein (LDL) cholesterol—cholesterol that has reacted with oxygen and become, essentially, rancid, a process that promotes buildup on artery walls. This effect might have been in part due to the nuts' lutein, an antioxidant carotenoid that increased in the blood of subjects on the pistachio diet.

For Our Planet

In just 30 years the U.S. has become the world's second-biggest producer of pistachios, after Iran. Growing is centered in California. Each tree requires considerable investment and won't bear until after about 7 years but may continue producing for another 75. Water use is fairly high in pistachio orchards.

GIVES YOU

Protein
Dietary fiber
Vitamin E
   (gamma-tocopherol)
Vitamin B6
Thiamine
Iron
Magnesium
Potassium
Copper
Manganese
Phosphorus
Monounsaturated and
   polyunsaturated fats
Phytonutrients
   (carotenoids
   phytosterols,
   stilbenes, flavonoids)

PORK

Wild boar were among the earliest animals to be domesticated, a process that in their case occurred on multiple occasions and in several locations in Asia and Europe roughly ten thousand years ago. Omnivorous, adaptable, and equipped with a sensitive snout that doubles as a digging instrument, for centuries pigs have been an inexpensive animal to raise, being turned out to forage in the forest, clear crop residues, or indeed gobble the waste from city streets. Pig varieties have diminished sharply as breeders select hogs that perform well in today's intensive production system.

Choose and Use

Add flavor to lean pork by marinating it in lemon juice, vinegar, wine—any acidic liquid—seasoned with plenty of spices and herbs. Then broil, grill, bake, or sear it in a pan using a little olive oil. Lean cuts are best for grilling, whereas fattier cuts lend themselves to barbecuing, slow cooking, and braising.

With the rise of factory farming, old "heritage" hog breeds such as the Berkshire, Hereford, Tamworth, and Red Wattle are harder to find, but repay the effort and expense with juicy, layered flavor.

For Your Health

When it comes to health, all cuts of pork are not created equal. Lean cuts—tenderloin, chops, sirloin or top loin roasts—are comparable to chicken in levels of saturated fat and cholesterol, with both serving up a hefty portion of protein. They also provide iron, B-complex vitamins that help the body break down carbohydrates for energy, and minerals like selenium, which has antioxidant and anti-inflammatory properties.

But processed meats—for example, ham, bacon, and

GIVES YOU

Protein
Thiamine
Niacin
Vitamin B6
Vitamin B12
Selenium
Phosphorus
Zinc
Iron

✦ TAKE AWAY

Choose lean, unprocessed cuts, and avoid processed products high in fat, sodium, and nitrates.

sausage—tend to have a lot more saturated fat and bucketsful of sodium (they're often cured). A single slice of bacon has 43 calories, 30 of which come from fat, a third of which is saturated fat.

In addition, whether because of their saturated fat and salt, nitrate preservatives, chemicals produced during cooking, or a combination of these factors, processed meat consumption has been linked to higher rates of heart disease, diabetes, stroke, and cancer in population studies.

For Our Planet

Once upon a time, pigs were a common and key element in traditional mixed farming, foraging and consuming all manner of farm waste while providing fertilizer as well as meat. Today, most hogs in the U.S. are raised in intensive "factory" farms with thousands of animals. Concentrated in the Midwest and Southeast, these farms may emit hydrogen sulfide, a gas that can cause flulike symptoms in humans, and their enormous waste lagoons pollute soil, air, and water. Crowding and extreme indoor confinement raise serious animal-welfare concerns.

Look for organic, pasture-raised, or free-range pork. Only the organic label is regulated; it means hogs will have organic feed and no antibiotics. Pork labeled "Animal Welfare Approved" will come from pastured animals.

PUMPKIN SEED

In the 1960s, archaeologists discovered seeds and rind from the squash species *Cucurbita pepo*, which includes the pumpkin, in a cave in Oaxaca, Mexico. In the 1990s advanced radiocarbon dating confirmed the astonishing age of the find: 10,000 years old. That made a pumpkin-like squash and its seeds (called *pepita* in Spanish) the first domesticated plant in the New World. Earliest farming in the Americas traces to around the same time that agriculture dawned in the Fertile Crescent and central China.

Pepitas are still popular in Mexico and Latin America as a snack and ingredient, ground into mole sauces, for example. Nutty-flavored pumpkin seed oil is widely enjoyed in central European countries as a dressing for potato or bean salads.

Choose and Use
Look for unsalted pumpkin seeds, raw or roasted. To roast them straight from the pumpkin, rinse off any flesh and let them dry thoroughly if you can. Then toss them with a little olive oil and your favorite seasoning—sea salt, garlic, cayenne

GIVES YOU
Protein
Monounsaturated and
  polyunsaturated fats
Vitamin E
Vitamin K
Zinc
Magnesium
Copper
Manganese
Iron
Phosphorus)
Phytonutrients
  (phenolic acids
  and phytosterols
  [lignans])

pepper, paprika, cumin. Roast in a 400-degree oven for at least 20 minutes, tossing occasionally. For crispier seeds, start by boiling them for 10 minutes in lightly salted water or bake longer at a lower temperature. Note that butternut squash seeds can be roasted in the same fashion.

For Your Health

Pumpkin seeds have about as much protein as almonds. Though short on fiber and rather high in calories due to their fat content, most of the fat is polyunsaturated, which, especially when they replace saturated fats in the diet, may protect healthy brain functioning and stave off type 2 diabetes, heart disease, and macular degeneration.

Pumpkin seeds are a good source of zinc, with a small handful providing a fifth of the recommended daily intake of this mineral. Zinc is critical to healthy immune functioning, and deficiencies have been linked to pneumonia in the elderly and diarrhea among children in the developing world.

Pumpkin seeds also contain various forms of vitamin E, including gamma-tocopherol, which may protect cells from oxidation and inflammation.

For Our Planet

Probably the most sustainable way to consume pumpkin seeds is to support a local farmer by buying a fresh pumpkin from August through early winter—and let the gourd do double duty as ornament and food. Though most of the canned pumpkin in the U.S. is grown in Illinois, packaged pumpkin seeds may well be imported. For more on winter squash seeds, see pages 96–99.

✦ TAKE AWAY

Roast pumpkin seeds yourself or purchase unsalted ones.

PAIRINGS ✦ AUTUMN TRAIL MIX

A special Halloween time treat is toasted pumpkin seeds eaten simply out of hand. These tasty, crunchy seeds can also be thrown onto a salad or combined with a selection of other nuts and dried fruits for an autumn-themed trail mix.

SALMON

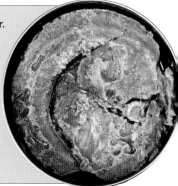

There's something almost mythical about the life cycle of salmon. They hatch in inland freshwater streams and rivers. There the tiny fry mature into smolts ready to take on salt water before they head for the open ocean. Salmon reach maturity at sea, then return to their very place of beginning with an unerring homing device thought to involve both light sensing and smell. It is thought that geomagnetic imprinting plays a role. They spawn in these natal waters, and quickly die. Some salmon cover astounding distances in their journeys. One chinook salmon was tagged in the Aleutian Islands of the Pacific Ocean and recovered a year later in Idaho's Salmon River, having traveled some 3,500 miles.

For millions of years, these returning silver-colored fish have fed the land and its creatures with nutrients from the sea. The earliest evidence of people eating salmon comes from caves on the north coast of Spain and dates back as far as 16,000 years. Salmon bones some 7,000 years old have been recovered at a site on the Columbia River in Oregon.

PREP TIP ✦ CANNED SALMON

Many people think of canned salmon as an inferior food, or overlook it altogether. In fact it's highly nutritious and environmentally sound. Canned pink or sockeye salmon, which is labeled red salmon, is affordable and available on grocery shelves everywhere. It makes a wonderful sandwich melt. Toss it with a little mayonnaise, spoon it onto whole-grain bread topped with a thin slice of cheese, and put it under the broiler for a minute or two. Red salmon is canned with skin and bones cooked so they melt in your mouth, a highly bioaccessible source of magnesium, selenium, and calcium. Form it into patties with bread crumbs, mayonnaise, and mustard; broil for about ten minutes for a cheap, heart-healthy, protein-rich meal.

GIVES YOU

Protein
Niacin
Vitamin B12
Vitamin B6
Riboflavin
Vitamin D
Thiamine
Selenium
Phosphorus
Polyunsaturated fats

Choose and Use

Salmon is so rich and flavorful that common preparation methods tend to be light and healthy. Steaks can be pan-fried in a little olive oil, slow roasted, or grilled. Fillets are lovely poached, steamed in a foil pouch with lemon and garlic, fried in the skillet, or broiled.

For Your Health

On the question of protein quality and quantity, this silken, orange-fleshed fish stacks up well against beef. On the question of healthy fats? Salmon wins, hands down.

Salmon is one of the most bountiful sources of omega-3 fatty acids, polyunsaturated fats that may reduce a person's risk of heart disease, sudden cardiac death, stroke, and even arthritis and Alzheimer's disease. The particular omega-3s found in fish are especially beneficial. A review published in 2006 concluded that eating one or two weekly servings of fish, especially fatty fish like salmon that are high in marine omega-3s, reduces a person's chances of cardiac death by more than a third.

There are many possible mechanisms for this effect. The properties of omega-3s include effects on blood lipids called triglycerides, blood pressure, blood clotting, and heart rhythm.

For Our Planet

Go for wild Pacific salmon if possible—king (or Chinook), sockeye (red), coho (silver), or pink (also called humpback)—and avoid farmed Atlantic salmon.

+ TAKE AWAY

Salmon provides a wealth of fatty acids essential for cardiovascular health.

Lake trout and Arctic char are in the same family as salmon, have similarly lustrous pink flesh, and like salmon are rich in protein and omega-3 fatty acids. They're also environmentally responsible choices, for the most part. According to the Monterey Bay Aquarium, spotted seatrout wild-caught in Florida and Louisiana is a "best choice" from the standpoint of sustainability. It is advised, however, to limit consumption due to elevated mercury levels. Arctic char, generally farmed in closed, recirculating systems, is a "best choice" for marine sustainability.

Pacific salmon are plentiful in waters off Alaska, Washington, and Oregon and are harvested in relatively sustainable ways. These were generally ranked as environmentally friendly choices as of 2013. But make sure to check these guides regularly; they change as fishing and aquaculture practices evolve.

The Atlantic salmon, which before the 19th century spawned in nearly every river of the American Northeast, now hangs on in small numbers at fewer than a dozen sites. Dams blocking major river systems and destruction of spawning habitat by development and agriculture are largely to blame.

Today, almost all Atlantic salmon sold in the U.S. is farm-raised, and most of it is imported from Canada, Norway, Chile, or the U.K. Unfortunately, farming has not been an eco-friendly alternative. Raised in pens in the ocean, millions of fish escape each year and can spread disease or breed with wild fish, perhaps making wild salmon populations less hardy. Salmon farms also release organic and chemical wastes into the ocean.

Though coho salmon farmed in inland tanks in the U.S. are an exception—and the industry is working to improve its methods—major environmental groups currently discourage the purchase of imported farmed salmon.

SESAME SEED

This tiny seed used for its oil and as a food was likely domesticated in the Indus Valley of northwestern India by 2500 B.C., spreading west to Mesopotamia by 2000 B.C. Still further west in ancient Egypt, the pharaoh Tutankhamun was entombed in 1323 B.C. with a variety of seeds, including sesame. An alabaster lamp in the shape of a lotus flower held traces of sesame oil.

   The plant is an annual that stands a few feet high, with narrow deep-green leaves and a pale yellow trumpet-shaped flower. The sesame seed and its oil are common in Asian, Middle Eastern, African, and Indian dishes. Europeans and Americans favor the seed as a crunchy addition to bread and its crusts.

Choose and Use

Breads sprinkled with sesame seeds make a tasty, nutty complete protein, as does the popular Middle Eastern sesame paste tahini mixed with mashed chickpeas in hummus. The ancients used sesame seeds as a condiment mixed with herbs and salt to give flavor to foods. Tahini combined with olive oil, lemon juice, and spices makes a delightfully refreshing salad dressing. And sesame

GIVES YOU

Protein
Dietary fiber
Thiamine
Niacin
Vitamin B6
Monounsaturated and
   polyunsaturated fats
Copper
Manganese
Calcium
Magnesium
Iron
Phosphorus
Zinc
Phytonutrients
   (phytosterols
   [lignans])

oil is great for stir-frying in a piping-hot wok, as it has a high smoke point. Sesame seeds come in a variety of colors, including brown, red, and black; darker seeds tend to have a stronger nut flavor and contain pigments with antioxidant properties. The antioxidants in sesame oil make it unusually slow to spoil.

For Your Health

An ounce of sesame seeds has almost five grams of protein and a sixth of your daily fiber. It is a powerhouse of minerals, providing more than a quarter of the daily requirement for calcium and nearly as much phosphorus, both important for building strong bones. Sesame seeds also provide ample supplies of zinc, critical to the immune system; antioxidants selenium and copper, which help the body absorb iron; and potassium and magnesium, which, when present in sufficient quantities in the diet, have been associated with lower blood pressure.

A good source of both mono- and polyunsaturated fats, sesame seeds are also replete with phytosterols, plant steroids that are similar to cholesterol and can block its absorption in the intestine. Consuming lots of phytosterol-dense foods has been shown to lower blood cholesterol. There's some evidence to suggest that phytosterols may also help prevent some forms of cancer.

For Our Planet

In the U.S., sesame growing occurs mostly in the Southwest, but the country imports more sesame than it grows. India and Guatemala are the top two sources. The drought-tolerant plant does well in poor climatic conditions and is an important cash crop in Nigeria, Sudan, and Ethiopia.

✦ TAKE AWAY

Sesame seeds add minerals and a tasty crunch to your dishes.

PREP TIP ✦ **TOASTING**

Sesame seeds are a favorite when it comes to Pan-Asian cooking. Toasting really brings out their flavor, and it's simple in a hot pan on the stovetop. Black and white sesame seeds create a pretty crust for seared fish like tuna.

SMALL SILVER FISH: ANCHOVY, HERRING, MACKEREL, SARDINE

Anchovy, herring, mackerel, and sardine each comprise a number of species. The U.S. Food and Drug Administration lists 19 species that may be sold as anchovy, and 13 for which the marketing label "sardine" is permitted.

All these fish swim in schools near the surface of the ocean, and, at least when they are small, feed on plankton while themselves providing nourishment to sea birds, marine mammals, and larger fish.

People have enjoyed these fatty, protein-rich fish for thousands of years, inventing methods for smoking, pickling, fermenting, and packaging them to protect against rapid spoilage, a problem because of their highly unsaturated, very long chain fatty acid content.

Ancient Greeks and Romans used small fatty fish such as anchovies in a sauce called *garum,* salting them and allowing them to ferment in the sun for weeks or months. The fish paste itself fed the poor, whereas the liquid it exuded went to the upper classes.

"Kippers," the split and cold-smoked herring dish, was developed in the 19th century and is beloved by the English.

CONSIDER ✦ CHOOSE CANNED

Sardines, anchovies, and the like can be found fresh at your fishmonger's counter, but far easier is finding them on supermarket shelves. Inexpensive, they're a great ingredient to keep on hand in the pantry and are a sustainable choice because they are low on the food chain.

PREP TIP ✦ **PAIR WITH AROMATICS**

Most people have little experience with silver fishes, such as anchovies, other than as part of a classic Caesar salad or an occasional pizza topping. Pairing anchovies and other richly flavored, oily fish with fresh, crisp vegetables like fennel or celery provides balance and texture. For a special hors d'oeuvre or light lunch, serve on whole grain crackers or crispbread.

✦ TAKE AWAY

Try canned fish on crackers for a heart-healthy snack.

During the Napoleonic wars of the early 19th century, the French government offered a prize for a method of food preservation it could use to supply soldiers in the field; this resulted in canning, and, by 1820, the first canned sardines. Canned sardines became enormously popular among Americans during World War I, leading to the rise and eventual fall of Cannery Row, a concentration of sardine canneries in Monterey, California, made famous by John Steinbeck's 1945 novel by the same name. Scientists now believe naturally occurring climatic fluctuations may have contributed to the collapse of the Monterey sardine fishery, long attributed to overfishing.

Choose and Use

With the occasional exception of mackerel and herring, these fish generally come to us heavily salted and canned or jarred in oil. Rinsing in water will somewhat reduce sodium content. Though all oil packaging boosts calories, many of these small fish are packaged in olive oil or other unsaturated fats, which are often heart-healthy monounsaturates. As with tuna, water-packed alternatives are usually available; some prefer their more delicate consistency. If you're fortunate enough to find any of these small, oily fish fresh, try grilling or lightly pan frying them; canned are delicious on crackers or in Mediterranean pasta and salad dishes.

For Your Health

Like the prized salmon and trout, these humbler oily fish are rich in omega-3 fatty acids, the polyunsaturated fats that may reduce a person's risk of heart disease, sudden cardiac death, stroke, arthritis, Alzheimer's disease, and age-related macular degeneration. Herring and mackerel also provide some mono-unsaturated fats, which lower blood cholesterol among other health benefits.

A 2013 study following 2,700 people age 65 and older over 16 years found that those with the highest blood levels of marine omega-3s (levels attainable by eating about five ounces of

GIVES YOU

Protein
Polyunsaturated fats
Vitamin D
Niacin
Vitamin B12
Vitamin B6
Riboflavin
Selenium
Magnesium
Phosphorus
Calcium
Iron

Puttanesca is common in Italy, a simple variation on tomato sauce featuring chopped anchovies and black olives. It's also a great way to boost the nutrition of pasta and get healthful omega-3s into finicky palates: your kids probably won't notice, and you'll enjoy the additional richness and flavor.

anchovy or herring a week) lived, on average, more than two years longer than those with lower levels.

Eating the soft bones of small mackerel, anchovies, and sardines also provides a concentrated source of calcium. Sardines, meanwhile, are an excellent source of vitamin D, needed to help the bones absorb calcium. Most people living in the northern hemisphere are deficient in vitamin D due to inadequate sun exposure; individuals who are older or obese are especially at risk.

For Our Planet

These little fish occupy the bottom of the food chain, feeding on tiny organisms and bits of algae. That makes them a more environmentally efficient source of food energy than larger fish. Indeed small oily fish are frequent ingredients in the fishmeal fed to livestock as well as farmed fish; it takes more than three pounds of these wild ocean fish to produce a single pound of

farm-raised salmon—a concerning drawback of salmon aquaculture.

Fish lower on the food chain are also less likely to contain dangerous levels of mercury than larger fish such as tuna, due to their short lifespans and the fact that they don't eat other fish whose flesh may contain the pollutant. The larger king mackerel is an important exception; the U.S. Food and Drug Administration (FDA) advises pregnant and nursing women and young children to avoid it, although moderate consumption is fine for healthy adults.

It's also a good idea to check the Monterey Bay Aquarium or another seafood sustainability guide for up-to-date information on vulnerable fisheries. As of 2013, Monterey Bay advised avoiding sardines from the Mediterranean (Atlantic sardines) because of overfishing.

SOYBEAN

Some scientists are questioning the long-held theory that the Chinese alone domesticated the soybean some three thousand years ago. Analyses of charred remains from China, Japan, and Korea suggest that the small wild legume may have been eaten in China as long as nine thousand years ago, and domesticated there perhaps 5,000 years ago. Larger, domesticated types of soybean appear in Japan around the same time, and in Korea about 2,000 years later; it's possible people in these locations domesticated soybeans independently from the Chinese.

In any event, this nutritious legume has formed the basis of traditional foods prepared in these Asian societies for over a thousand years, including soy sauce (made from fermented soybeans), miso (a fermented soybean paste), and tofu (made from soymilk much as cheese is produced from animal milk).

Choose and Use

Texturized soy protein, the ingredient in many "fake" meats, retains much of the original soybean's fiber and other nutrients, as do roasted soy nuts and edamame, the soybean harvested and eaten while still green. Plain soybeans, dry or canned, can be used as you would any beans, in burritos, salads, soups, or stews, for example.

For Your Health

Soybeans get into Western diets in many ways, most often with their oil—which accounts for nearly 80 percent of edible oil consumed in the U.S. Soy protein, which goes into all sorts of processed foods, soy-based frozen desserts, nutrition bars, and (rehydrated into texturized soy protein) meat extenders and substitutes.

PREP TIP ✦ EDAMAME

Edamame is a Japanese favorite, common in sushi restaurants. Grab a bag of soybeans from the freezer and steam briefly, then serve in a bowl lightly salted for a different kind of snack.

Taken whole—cooked like any other legume—the soybean provides protein comparable to that of an egg, with lots of fiber (40 percent of suggested daily intake in a cup), and plenty of iron. Its oil, quite low in saturated fat, is more than 50 percent linoleic acid, a polyunsaturated fat that lowers cholesterol when replacing unhealthy fats in the diet.

A great deal of research has focused on possible benefits from soy isoflavones, a type of flavonoid that binds (weakly) to estrogen receptors and thus has been proposed as a possible mechanism important in the prevention of heart disease, osteoporosis, and cancers of the breast, uterus, and prostate. However, a 2006 research review by an American Heart Association scientific committee concluded that the cardiovascular benefit of soy protein or isoflavones is "minimal at best," and evidence for benefits in bone loss and cancer is meager. On the other hand, the committee endorsed the notion that, because of their fiber, protein, favorable fat profile, and vitamins and minerals, soy products are a heart-healthy replacement for animal products high in saturated fat. For more on tofu, see pages 216–217.

For Our Planet

In the U.S., about 90 percent of the soybean crop consists of the "Roundup Ready" variety, genetically modified to survive applications of the commonly used weed killer. This has increased yields and cut down on the need for deep plowing with heavy equipment, which, proponents argue, maintains soil. But genetically modified crops are highly controversial, not least because of concerns about how they will affect the surrounding ecosystem. A study published in 2012 found that, rather than reducing the overall use of herbicides as claimed, Roundup Ready crops led to the development of herbicide-resistant weeds—something that also occurs with non-genetically modified crops—which actually led to increased herbicide use.

GIVES YOU

Protein
Dietary fiber
Polyunsaturated fats
Vitamin K
Riboflavin
Folate
Vitamin B6
Thiamine
Manganese
Iron
Phosphorus
Magnesium
Copper
Potassium
Selenium
Calcium
Zinc
Phytonutrients
    (flavonoids,
    phytosterols)

TOFU

The first step in making tofu is to cook ground soybeans in water, then strain out the fibrous solids. To the resulting soy milk the preparer adds a coagulant that causes the milk to separate into liquid whey and firmer lumps called curds. Pressed into cakes, these curds make the smooth, mild food popular in many Asian countries, especially China and Japan.

Tofu probably originated in ancient China well before its earliest documentation in A.D. 950. People may have stumbled on the process accidentally, perhaps by adding unrefined salt to a soybean stew or allowing it to coagulate under the influence of lactic-acid bacteria. Or maybe they learned the technique from migrating Mongolian herders, who had experience making a fermented-milk product.

Choose and Use

The harder the tofu, the more fat, calories, and protein it contains. Tofu processed with calcium sulfate as a coagulant will provide more calcium.

Tofu is a very versatile food that takes up cooking flavors. Silken tofu adds protein to smoothies and a creamy mayonnaise-like texture to sandwich spreads, salad dressings, pasta sauces, and sweet puddings; it's great chunked in soup, too. Firm or extra-firm tofu is excellent sautéed, stir-fried, or marinated and grilled; try it in a sandwich.

A light and zesty Japanese summertime dish is cubed silken tofu topped with fresh ginger, soy sauce, scallions, and other flavorings.

For Your Health

Though lower in fiber than other soy products, tofu offers ample quantities of protein as well as calcium, a real plus, especially for people who avoid dairy foods.

GIVES YOU

Protein
Manganese
Calcium
Iron
Phosphorus
Polyunsaturated fats
Phytonutrients
    (flavonoids)

Miso, an ancient Japanese food, is a thick paste made by fermenting soybeans with salt and a special fungus. It's used as a flavoring for the familiar miso soup, as well as meat, fish, and tofu dishes, Miso has protein, fiber, and minerals (including calcium) but is also very high in sodium. Tempeh looks a bit like tofu, but it's made with whole soybeans instead of soymilk, contains more protein and fiber than tofu, and has a stronger, "meatier" texture. It comes from Indonesia, and is made by fermenting soybeans with fungus. You can slice or crumble tempeh and use it as a meat substitute in just about any dish, from burgers to stir-fries.

Some claims about the benefits of soy protein—that it offers important protection against heart disease and may prevent a host of cancers—have not been established unequivocally, according to a 2006 review by the American Heart Association. On the other hand, studies show that eating soy protein modestly improves cholesterol levels, so replacing saturated-fat-laden animal proteins such as cheese and meat with soy foods like tofu is likely to be a healthy change, for both you and the planet. A 2008 review concludes that soy protein also appears to slow bone loss in postmenopausal women.

For Our Planet

Eating plant-based proteins almost always has a gentler impact on the natural world than consuming animal products, and tofu is no exception. It's a cruelty-free, resource-efficient food whose production requires no animal feed and only a fraction of the water (about 244 gallons per pound) required to produce the same amount of chicken (about 815 gallons). The waste pulp of the soybean is often fed to animals.

TUNA

With its powerful tail and sleek body, the tuna plies the world's open oceans, a predator built for speed. Tuna spines discovered in a cave in East Timor, an island south of Indonesia, represent the earliest evidence of humans eating tuna, and indeed of advanced fishing techniques, since to harvest the meaty fish requires taking to the sea. The find dates to 42,000 years ago.

There are 15 species of tuna, a subgroup of the mackerel family, but 4 species make up the bulk of those caught for food: skipjack (roughly 60 percent of the catch), yellowfin (24 percent), bigeye (10 percent), and albacore (5 percent). The highly prized bluefin tuna fishery has been drastically overexploited and is subject to international quotas.

GIVES YOU

Protein
Thiamine
Niacin
Vitamin B6
Vitamin B12
Vitamin D
Selenium
Phosphorous
Potassium
Magnesium
Polyunsaturated fats

Choose and Use

Long-lived tuna tend to absorb mercury, the pollutant generated by industrial activities that settles into the ocean. For that reason, the U.S. Environmental Protection Agency (EPA) advises childbearing women and young children to limit consumption of "white" albacore tuna (which is higher in mercury) to six ounces a week, and canned "light" tuna to two meals (12 ounces) per week. Albacore (the only species canned as white tuna) along with bluefin tuna (found most often in sushi) are the species highest in omega-3 fatty acids. Frozen or fresh tuna steaks are most often yellowfin.

For Your Health

Tuna is a great protein source that's also high in healthy fish oil, with albacore tuna being comparable to some salmon species in marine omega-3 fatty acids. This type of polyunsaturated fat, population studies suggest, lowers the risk for heart disease, stroke, heart arrhythmias, as well as arthritis and Alzheimer's

✦ TAKE AWAY

Tuna is high in essential fatty acids, but it also absorbs mercury, so enjoy it in moderation.

disease. Polyunsaturated fat is especially important in fetal development during pregnancy for brain and eye health. Some types of tuna are rich in potassium and magnesium, both important for maintaining healthy blood pressure and heart rhythm. A three-ounce serving of canned white (albacore) tuna offers 80 percent of a day's recommended intake of selenium, an antioxidant mineral that's vital to immune functioning and possibly cancer prevention.

For Our Planet

Tuna presents even the most environmentally responsible consumer with a confusing picture. Whether or not a particular tuna product can be considered sustainably caught depends on the species of tuna, how it was caught, and where. For example, most environmental groups caution against the use of the purse seine with a "fish aggregating device" (a large net similar to a bag with a drawstring encloses schools attracted by a floating object) as well as the longline (a very extensive line set at intervals with baited hooks) because of unacceptably high bycatch; these methods may snag and kill other fish, sharks, dolphins, sea birds, and sea turtles.

The Monterey Bay Aquarium discourages eating the massively overfished bluefin tuna in any context. Meanwhile, there are six stocks of albacore tuna in the world's oceans; most albacore are

---

PAIRINGS
✦
TUNA NIÇOISE

Tuna Niçoise is a popular salad in France and includes tuna, black olives, hard-cooked egg, green beans, and potatoes with Dijon or anchovy dressing. The traditional dish uses canned tuna, an economical choice that works perfectly for this dinner salad; a special version might substitute a seared tuna steak.

CONSIDER ✦ CHOOSING CANNED TUNA

Convenient and nutritious, no pantry should be without canned tuna. Selecting the best choice for you and the planet begins by reading the labels. Choose cans with no added sodium, which your body doesn't need. "Oil-packed" tuna can provide additional flavor, and most are healthy unsaturates, but "water-packed" is lower in calories. And don't forget to consult a sustainable seafood guide.

harvested from the Pacific, but one stock—North Atlantic albacore—is overfished, and its products are best avoided.

Here's the rub: At the fishmonger or in the grocery aisle, you usually cannot discover the provenance of a particular tuna product. Canned "chunk light" tuna is mostly skipjack, but how was it caught? Where did that *particular* albacore (steak or canned) come from—and was it harvested by minimal-bycatch pole and line?

The only practical approach is to go with marketers that have vetted their seafood sources. Find a fishmonger you trust. Or look online for products certified by the Marine Stewardship Council. Greenpeace endorses boutique brands like Wild Planet, as well as Safeway's "Safeway Select" canned tuna, caught by purse seine without fish aggregating devices, and Whole Foods "365" brand tuna, caught by pole and line.

TURKEY

Several native species of turkey inhabited the Americas in the millennia before Columbus arrived on New World shores. Scientists believe the Aztecs of Mexico were the first to domesticate turkey. New research suggests this same domesticated turkey may have reached Mayan people in Guatemala by 2,000 years ago, and that the Anasazi of the U.S. Southwest domesticated their own turkey around 200 B.C.—not for food, but for feathers to use in rituals and to adorn blankets and robes. The Wampanoag, who took part in a harvest festival with the pilgrims of Massachusetts in 1621 (commemorated today as Thanksgiving) hunted but did not keep turkeys.

Choose and Use

When watching saturated fat and calories, skip the skin. Ground turkey breast made into patties with seasonings makes a tasty and nutritious, planet-friendlier alternative to beef burgers. Like other poultry, turkey carries bacteria such as *Salmonella* that can cause food poisoning; safe handling means washing hands, surfaces, and utensils after contact with raw turkey, and cooking it thoroughly to kill any bacteria.

For Your Health

Turkey is a lean, low-calorie protein source—with a whole lot less saturated fat than pork and beef.

It's also comparatively high in iron and potassium, especially the dark meat. Like other meats, turkey is a good source of B-complex vitamins, which help the body produce energy from food and support normal nerve functioning.

For Our Planet

The Environmental Working Group lists turkey as a "good" meat choice, based on associated greenhouse gas emissions.

GIVES YOU

Protein
Niacin
Vitamin B6
Riboflavin)
Potassium
Selenium
Phosphorus
Zinc
Iron

✦ TAKE AWAY

Turkey is a naturally lean meat, but remove the fatty skin.

Ground beef is a common ingredient in dishes ranging from hamburgers and tacos to stews and casseroles. Any recipe that calls for beef can easily swap in turkey or chicken with similar results. While not the exact same flavor as beef, the seasonings and spices used in your recipe will no doubt keep your tastebuds happy. Selecting poultry over beef is a greener choice given the lower amount of resources needed to produce it.

But in conventional husbandry, the birds are often raised in enormous, densely packed barns and given antibiotics routinely to accelerate growth and control infection; this can promote the development of antibiotic-resistant germs. Bred for quick-growing and very large breasts, the Broad-Breasted White turkey sold by nearly all commercial producers cannot mate naturally and often ends up painfully overweight and lame.

There are also a lot of smaller-scale turkey farms in the U.S., including a few farms that raise heritage breeds like the Bourbon Red or Narragansett; these are more expensive than grocery-store turkeys, but in taste tests they win hands-down. Other good options are organic and/or free-range or "pasture-raised" turkeys; they're more humanely treated than conventionally raised birds and may be leaner and healthier, too.

WALNUT

People probably first began to cultivate the walnut tree in the Caucasus 7,000 years ago. It's likely they gathered them even earlier in the nut tree's native range from the Balkans to the Himalayas. Enjoyed along with fruit after a meal, the large, protein-rich walnut was a favorite of the ancient Romans, and it spread throughout the empire. Whole walnuts lay on a table in the Temple of Isis at Pompei when the town was destroyed by the eruption of Mount Vesuvius in A.D. 79.

Though the peanut (which is actually a legume, not a tree nut) accounts for more than half of Americans' overall nut consumption today, the walnut's chewy texture and slightly bitter flavor make it the most popular nut for baking.

GIVES YOU

Protein
Dietary fiber
Vitamin E
Vitamin B6
Folate
Thiamine
Manganese
Copper
Magnesium
Phosphorus
Iron
Zinc
Monounsaturated and
    polyunsaturated fats
Phytonutrients (phenolic
    acids, flavonoids,
    phytosterols)

Choose and Use

Walnuts are extremely versatile, suited to savory and sweet foods alike. Sprinkle them into oatmeal, on salads—try spinach and spring greens, fruit such as pear, and a little blue cheese—or sauté them into pasta, rice, or cooked vegetables. They give breads and pastries a nutritional lift and heartier flavor. When looking to snack, watch out for products that have added sodium.

For Your Health

Among nuts, walnuts are uniquely high in phytonutrients. A 2007 study reviewing the chemical composition of ten nuts found they are number one in total phenols, a class of phytonutrients that includes phenolic acids and flavonoids, and ranked second in antioxidant capacity.

In a 2009 review of 13 small trials, researchers concluded that diets enriched with walnuts lowered total and "bad" low-density lipoprotein (LDL) cholesterol. Other small studies of walnut-enriched diets have shown reduced markers of inflammation, lower blood pressure, and improved function of the lining of blood vessels (which helps regulate blood pressure and clotting). And a 2013 study following 135,000 women over 10 years found those who ate the most walnuts lowered the risk of type 2 diabetes.

A little goes a long way, though; like all nuts, they are energy-dense and just an ounce of walnuts packs more than 180 calories.

For Our Planet

The U.S. is the second-largest grower of walnuts in the world, after China, and the world's biggest exporter. The vast bulk of this crop is grown in California, on thousands of farms averaging about 50 acres in size. Young trees don't bear for several years, but they typically live 75 years. Cash crops such as corn are sometimes grown between the tree rows while a walnut grove matures. Walnut trees put down very deep roots that help them survive drought and retain soil. The very hard hulls of the walnut are used commercially in various products, including plastics and glues, abrasive cleaners, and insulation.

PAIRINGS
✦
WALNUT PAIRINGS

As with other nuts, toasting brings out the flavor of walnuts. Their slightly bitter taste pairs well with rich cheeses and are a terrific addition to green salads including citrus or berries; a vinaigrette made using walnut oil is the perfect dressing.

WHITE FISH: HAKE, HADDOCK, HALIBUT, FLOUNDER, COD, SOLE, POLLACK

Whereas oily fish are pelagic—they swim in the open water column—white fish are often demersal species, meaning they live near the sea floor where it's dark and food is relatively scarce. They eat mollusks, crustaceans, small fish, worms, and sea squirts.

The oil in white fish is concentrated in the liver. This tiny organ is dense with nutrients; indeed, discovery of the properties of cod liver oil in the 1930s led to the conquest of rickets, a severe vitamin D deficiency. However, processing the fish for food removes the liver, leaving flesh that is very lean and rather delicate of flavor.

By around A.D. 1000, the seagoing Vikings fished for cod from their longships, establishing an early international trade in cod, salted and dried for long-distance travel, between the Nordic countries and western Europe.

CONSIDER ✦ CHOOSING FISH

How is a person to know what to make for dinner considering the wide variety of fish at the seafood counter? While there are some minor differences in flavor and texture, the similarities make them equally good choices when it comes to simple seafood suppers. Chatting with your fishmonger about which is fish is freshest and in season is a good place to start. You'll also want to consult a sustainable seafood guide to understand which choices are the greenest.

PREP TIP ✦ SLOW ROAST

Many people are intimidated by cooking fish, but it's actually one of the simplest things you can prepare for dinner. Like other animal proteins, however, fish can dry out and become tough and flavorless if overcooked. A sure-proof way to ensure perfectly cooked and moist fish is by slow roasting at low heat for 30 to 45 minutes. (Time varies by thickness.)

GIVES YOU

Protein
Niacin
Vitamin B6
Vitamin B12
Vitamin D
Phosphorus
Selenium
Magnesium

Choose and Use

Rounder fish such as cod may be cut into steaks (across the bone), which grill nicely. Flat fish such as sole and flounders you'll find in fillets. These tender cuts do better with gentle treatments such as steaming (or baking in foil), poaching, broiling, or pan-frying. Halibut, cod, and pollack are fairly firm. Flounder and sole are delicate and easily overcooked; the fish is done as soon as it turns opaque throughout, about 10 minutes for each inch of thickness.

In general, any of these mild white fishes can be substituted for another. Cod is the traditional basis for the not-so-healthy, deep-fried fish and chips, but any white fish can be coated in egg, seasoning, and flour or cornmeal and pan-fried for a somewhat healthier approach that locks in flavor and moisture. Marinating

also helps keep these mild fish juicy, although some people find their subtle flavor is best accented with just a drizzle of olive oil or a little garlic, some herbs, and a squeeze of lemon.

For Your Health

The American Heart Association recommends eating at least two servings of fish—preferably fatty fish—each week, and that's largely due to the benefits of fish oil to the heart.

White fish are very low in oil, so they're much lower in omega-3 fatty acids than oily fish such as salmon or herring. Even so, the fat they do contain is largely healthy. And as a lean, low-calorie, low-sodium source of protein, white fish are an eminently healthy food in their own right.

White fish are particularly good sources of B-complex vitamins. Deficiencies of B6 and B12 are not uncommon among the elderly and heavy drinkers, among other groups. These vitamins are important regulators of homocysteine, a marker

✦ TAKE AWAY

These mild fishes taste divine with seasoning— olive oil, lemon, pepper, and parsley.

for cardiovascular disease; they help the body metabolize food for energy and are vital to normal nerve function and the production of hemoglobin (a red protein that carries oxygen in the blood).

For Our Planet

Whether a white fish is sustainable depends on the particular species and how and where it's harvested. The Monterey Bay Aquarium's Seafood Watch program lists Pacific flat fish such as sole, flounder, and halibut as "good alternatives"—meaning there are concerns, but the negative environmental impacts associated are less extensive than those for items on the "avoid" list.

Cod and pollack are more problematic. According to Seafood Watch, most Atlantic cod available in the U.S. comes from well-managed fisheries of Iceland and the northeast Arctic; but only a small proportion of these cod are caught with hook and line, a technique with minimal environmental impact. Some cod fisheries are depleted by overfishing, and both cod and pollack are often gathered by bottom trawlers that scrape the ocean floor, destroying precious habitat.

The simplest approach may be to shop grocery chains with sustainable-seafood policies. Greenpeace conducts an annual CATO (Carting Away the Oceans) study, ranking major supermarket chains on their concern for sustainable seafood. See the most recent report at www.greenpeace.org/seafood.

YOGURT

Early yogurt making has left little trace in the archaeological record. One theory about the origins of this tangy fermented food holds that, some 7,000 years ago, goat herders of Central Asia learned the process after noticing that milk carried in skins thickened and soured into an edible and longer-lasting food. The bacteria required to make yogurt might have come from plants or from the animal-skin sacs. The food then moved across Iran to Turkey ("yogurt" is a Turkish word whose root means "to condense") and the Balkans, as well as south to India.

The Nobel prize–winning Russian microbiologist Ilya Mechnikov first popularized yogurt as a health food in 1908 with a paper attributing the astonishing longevity of Bulgarian peasants to benign bacteria in yogurt that crowded out disease-causing germs.

Choose and Use

Greek-style yogurts tend to be significantly higher in protein and lower in sugar, but also higher in saturated fat. Choose non- or low-fat varieties of any yogurt (low-fat dairy consumption may be associated with reductions in blood pressure). Also check labels for sugar and calories, as they vary dramatically by flavor and type of yogurt.

Mixing yogurt with oats or other grains and fruit is a familiar favorite, but try cooking with it, too—in dips, salad dressings, sauces for savory dishes, and soups.

For Your Health

Yogurt's felicitous effects on the bowel are related to its "friendly" bacteria—two organisms specifically approved for this use by the U.S. Food and Drug Administration (FDA),

GIVES YOU

Protein
Calcium
Phosphorus)
Riboflavin
Vitamin B12
Probiotics

✦ TAKE AWAY

Enjoy yogurt's plentiful probiotics, but avoid flavored yogurts high in fat and sugar.

Fruit yogurt may sound healthy, but often, fruity additives contribute little nutritionally, while turning yogurt into a confection along the lines of ice cream or pudding. Select nonfat to retain the nutrients while keep the calorie and sugar at bay. And for a healthier dessert alternative, add chopped fruit or berries of your choice and drizzle with a bit of honey or agave.

Lactobacillus bulgaris and *Streptococcus thermophiles*. They convert milk sugars to lactic acid. Sometimes manufacturers add other bacteria such as *Lactobacillus acidophilus* for enhanced "probiotic" effect, establishing helpful organisms that will out-compete pathogenic bacteria in the digestive tract.

Research on probiotics is evolving, but studies have shown that consuming live-bacteria yogurts can help ease digestive troubles associated with irritable bowel syndrome, and stem the diarrhea that can result from taking antibiotics. Plain, low-fat yogurt tops the list of calcium-rich foods, which makes it a great snack for children age 9 to 13, teenage girls, middle-aged women, and the elderly, all at risk for inadequate intake of the bone-building mineral.

For Our Planet

Nonorganic yogurt raises all the environmental and animal-welfare issues associated with the conventional dairy industry. Animals are often treated with antibiotics, as well as growth hor-mones that increase their milk production but raise the animals' risk of lameness and painful udder infections. Dairy cattle pro-duce methane, an important greenhouse gas, and waste ponds associated with large concentrated feeding operations can pol-lute the air with ammonia.

WHOLE GRAINS

Beginning some 12,000 years ago, during the Neolithic agricultural revolution, humans learned to cultivate the cereals that grew naturally in their environments—wheat in the Near East, rice in China, maize in Central and South America, sorghum in Africa—and settled down in the first permanent villages to reap their increasingly ample harvests. As agriculture emerged and spread around the globe, cereal grains took up a central place in the human diet.

The ability to produce large quantities of carbohydrate-rich food led to population explosions, which in turn gave rise to more complex and stratified societies. But scientists believe that early farmers may actually have been less healthy than their hunter-gatherer predecessors. Reliance on a few staples—principally cereal grains—meant nutritional gaps, intermittent famine, and, eventually, smaller bodies, weaker bones and teeth, and shorter lives.

Today, cereal grains are still the very stuff of life for humanity, with eight cereals—wheat, maize, rice, barley, sorghum, oats, rye, and millet—accounting for more than half the calories and about half the protein consumed around the world. Without these staples, the planet would never have come to support seven billion human beings; deprived of grains today, many would starve. The cereal grains provide energy in the form of carbohydrates, some protein, and unsaturated fats; they fortify the body with B-complex vitamins, minerals, fiber, and an array of phytonutrients that may have anti-inflammatory and other salubrious effects. Cutting out grains to avoid carbohydrates or gluten (to which a growing number of people are sensitive, although frank celiac disease is relatively rare) doesn't necessarily yield a healthier diet, and often requires careful planning to provide fiber and other valuable phytonutrients grains provide.

Grain Values

Grains don't give the body everything it needs, of course. For example, they tend to lack vitamins A and C (ascorbic acid), calcium, and some of the essential amino acids that together make a nutritionally "complete" protein. (Quinoa is a notable example of a grain that includes all the essential amino acids humans need, which is partly why the United Nations named 2013 the International Year of Quinoa.) In some parts of the developing world, reliance on a cereal-based diet leads to iron or zinc deficiency. Unlike other cereals, corn contains a form of niacin (a metabolite of nicotine also called vitamin B3) that's not absorbable;

some Africans whose diets are dominated by this staple suffer from the skin sores, diarrhea, and mental impairment of pellagra, a deficiency disease 18th-century Europeans called corn sickness.

While over-reliance on a single cheap staple can lead to nutritional deficiencies, an additional problem is that oftentimes grains have been processed to remove coarse outer layers containing the valuable germ and bran—and along with them much of the food's nutritional value.

Grain Components

Until the 19th century, when the Industrial Revolution brought mechanization to the milling process, most people ate whole grains—whole wheat, brown rice, whole rye, and barley. But people soon came to prefer the soft texture and mild flavor of refined grain products, in part because they came to see "brown bread" and other traditional whole-grain foods as the province of a countrified lower class.

A cereal grain has three basic components. Enclosing the kernel are protective bran layers, which contain fiber, minerals, vitamins, and phytonutrients. Inside, at the base of the seed, is the germ. This is the plant's embryo, ready to sprout under the right conditions; it's replete with vitamins, unsaturated fats, and phytonutrients. Nestled beside the germ, accounting for most of the kernel's bulk, is the endosperm; this is the germ's starchy food source, and it's full of carbohydrates, along with protein and a small quantity of vitamins and minerals.

Refined grains are processed to eliminate most or all of the bran and germ, leaving only the carbohydrate-rich yet relatively nutrient-poor endosperm. This provides energy but is low in nutritional quality. In response to outbreaks of pellagra and other problems related to malnutrition, in the 1940s the U.S. government required refined grain products to be enriched with iron as well as B-complex vitamins niacin, riboflavin, and niacin; folate was added in the 1990s after studies showed that the babies of pregnant women who consume plenty of this B-complex vitamin are less likely to be born with spina bifida and other neural tube defects.

But even enriched white wheat flour has 25 percent less protein than whole wheat flour, as well as lower levels of vitamin E, some B-complex vitamins, and the minerals magnesium, manganese, potassium, and zinc. White flour contains less than one-quarter of the fiber of whole-wheat flour.

Healthy Whole Grains

The bottom line: Despite the current dietary fads focused on the low-grain diets of the Paleolithic period, people who eat diets high in whole grains tend to have lower rates of largely preventable diseases such as heart disease, stroke, type 2 diabetes, and perhaps colorectal cancer. The fiber in whole grains helps the digestive system function well and also helps people eating a plant-based diet maintain a healthy weight.

A survey in 2000 by the market-research firm NDP Group suggests people are eating more whole grains, but they still account for only 11 percent of grains consumed, indicating a persistent and marked preference for refined-grain breads, pastas, rice, and baked goods.

Part of the problem is that it takes some investigation to figure out just which foods really are whole grain. Breakfast accounts for

When you eat whole grains, you minimize waste by using the entire food source.

well over half the whole grains Americans eat, when shopping for cereals, check for the word "whole"—as in the whole wheat that is the principal ingredient in Wheaties, and the whole oats that go into Cheerios. Some will include multiple whole grains, with added bran.

The whole-grain contents of breads can be particularly obscured. "Enriched wheat flour" means white flour—and you'll find it even in many breads and snacks that contain some whole grain and are advertised as such. "Multigrain" means only that more than one grain is included; they may not be whole grains, so read the ingredient list for the word "whole." Color is not a very helpful indicator either; traditional pumpernickel bread is made with course whole-grain rye flour (called rye meal), but many commercial versions contain plenty of refined flour, wheat gluten to make it fluffier, and colorants to achieve the dark hue that comes from coarser flour and slow baking. Look for the label "100 percent whole grain."

Planet-Friendly Choices

To achieve a diet that's nutritious and enjoyable often means marrying healthy mainstays with dishes that provide a bit of novelty and variety. This certainly holds true for grains. If you enjoy a bowl of oatmeal every morning, you might sit down to a whole-wheat roll—or perhaps a side of quinoa—at dinner. For most people, an adjustment to the nuttier and more complex flavors of whole grains can be acquired with repeated exposure and delectable dishes.

Most likely, you'll eventually come to prefer the taste and texture of whole grains—and your health will thank you for it. You will be making a planet-friendly choice too. Though animal products are far more resource intensive than plant foods generally, grains such as wheat and rice do demand a great deal of land and especially water. But by eating whole grains you are minimizing waste by using the entire food source. In addition, the nutrients that we lose by processing grains must then be added through another dietary source, thus requiring yet more resources to keep us healthy when we eat processed rather than whole grains.

AMARANTH

Amaranth grains are nestled in feathery crimson, purple, or gold flower clusters that adorn the tops of six-foot stalks. Not technically a cereal—the plant belongs to a different family than wheat and barley—amaranth has been consumed like a grain for thousands of years by Native American peoples, from the southeastern U.S. to South America. The Aztecs prized it as a staple food and the basis for religious ceremonies. After the Spanish conquest in 1521, Cortés and his people evangelized the Aztecs—and banned amaranth. Today, people in various parts of the world—from Mexico, to India and Nepal, to Greece—eat the seeds or greens of amaranth.

Choose and Use

Amaranth flour and seeds are available in health food and specialty grocery stores and are becoming increasingly available in super-markets. Cook the seeds in water like rice, and combine them with fresh vegetables, tofu, and savory herbs, or go sweet with a break-fast porridge loaded with raisins and nuts for a rice-like pudding. Amaranth seed can also be popped in a hot, dry pan, like popcorn. The flour is a common ingredient in gluten-free breads and cakes.

✦ TAKE AWAY

This protein-rich whole grain is vegan-friendly and gluten-free.

PREP TIP ✦ **PORRIDGE TO POPPED**

Amaranth is a highly versatile ingredient in the kitchen. The small grain absorbs water easily and thus makes an excellent gluten-free thickener substitute for wheat flour when making sauces. It also creates a fine hot cereal on a cold winter's morning. Amaranth can also be popped for a crunchy alternative to popcorn and, when combined with other flours, it provides great texture in gluten-free baking.

If you're going gluten-free, amaranth is a whole grain you'll want to meet. Not only does it have the highest protein content of any gluten-free grain, it has more protein than wheat. It's also a powerhouse when it comes to the minerals iron, calcium, and magnesium. Importantly, it also contains more lysine than other gluten-free grains, an amino acid many grains lack.

GIVES YOU

Protein
Dietary fiber
Manganese
Magnesium
Phosphorus
Iron
Copper
Selenium
Calcium
Pyridoxine (vitamin B6)
Folate
Zinc
Phytonutrients
  (phytosterols)

For Your Health

Amaranth has about as much protein as oats, and more than wheat, rice, or cornmeal. Unlike the protein in most grains, amaranth protein contains the essential amino acid lysine. Its high lysine content makes it a great addition to vegan diets, replacing the animal products that are the main source of lysine for most people. And its protein is gluten free, a plus for those with an intolerance or allergy. In addition to being high in cholesterol-lowering soluble fiber, amaranth is rich in phytosterols, plant compounds that resemble cholesterol and block its absorption into the bloodstream.

For Our Planet

No more than a few thousand acres of amaranth grow in the Midwest and Great Plains. A relative of pigweed, the plant is naturally drought and weed resistant. According to the Thomas Jefferson Agricultural Institute, the key cost in producing this grain is trucking it to one of the three main food companies that buy amaranth for redistribution or use in products.

BARLEY

Some 10,000 years ago, in the area of modern-day Jordan and Israel, the world's first farmers learned to sow this spiky grass for the nutrient-rich seeds clustered at its head. Archaeologists believe a second, independent domestication may have occurred about a thousand miles to the east. Over the next several millennia, the cereal spread along with agriculture itself into Europe. Today barley is grown around the world, and it enters the human diet mainly by way of animal feed and beer, the latter a tradition that reaches back several thousand years to the ancient Sumerians of Mesopotamia.

GIVES YOU

Dietary fiber
Protein
Manganese
Magnesium (if hulled)
Iron
Niacin (vitamin B3)
Riboflavin (vitamin B2)
Thiamine (vitamin B1)

PAIRINGS ✦ BEEF UP YOUR SOUP

Most people know barley from adding it to soups, and that's a great place to use it. A chewy grain that won't dissolve in your stock, barley adds texture and fiber that make soup a meal. It also makes a hearty pilaf when combined with mushrooms, onions, and sage.

Choose and Use

Terrific in soups and stews or Middle Eastern–style salads, barley is cooked in water much like rice. It can be soaked to reduce cooking time. Barley bread is a dense, nutty accompaniment to tomatoes, olives, onions, and feta cheese. Or spread it with honey, jam, or protein-rich nut butter. It is an excellent substitute for beef in vegetarian chili.

For Your Health

The headline on barley: plenty of fiber (as long as it's pearled, not hulled). Ounce for ounce it has more fiber than just about any other whole grain. Dietary fiber, and in particular complex sugars called beta-glucans that are especially prevalent in barley fiber, are soluble fibers that help lower cholesterol by attaching to bile acids in the intestine and sweeping them out with waste. The resulting dearth of bile acids stimulates the liver to make more; to do that, it must draw down the bloodstream's supply of cholesterol, a component of bile acids. Published in 2010, a review of 11 randomized, controlled, clinical trials found that consuming barley and beta-glucans derived from the grain reduces cholesterol significantly

Based on this and other research, the U.S. Food and Drug Administration (FDA) allows whole-grain barley to carry a label saying it may play a role in reducing risk for heart disease.

For Our Planet

Barley is an adaptable, "high-residue" crop that helps prevent soil erosion and retain moisture. Most of the U.S. crop goes to malt (a key ingredient in beer) and livestock feed. Barley acreage has declined in recent years as farmers devote more land to high-priced corn—in growing demand for ethanol production—although commodity prices fluctuate, and corn is no different.

FOOD SCIENCE
✦
PEARLED OR HULLED

Barley is usually either "pearled" or "hulled," referring to the degree to which the grain has been processed. Not a "whole grain," pearled barley is polished and has most of its bran layer removed; hulled retains all of the fiber and nutrients and is the better choice for your body.

BROWN RICE

Prehistoric hunter-gatherers of Central China gathered rice grains growing wild in flood plains and rain-filled puddles. By 4,600 B.C. the very long transition to full-scale rice cultivation was well advanced. Today, 90 percent of rice is still grown in Asia, and many people worldwide depend on polished white rice as a staple food.

"Brown" rice describes not a particular variety of rice but a minimally processed form of rice considered whole grain in which only the husk has been milled away. For white rice, milling also removes the inner bran layers and tiny germ (from which a sprout would arise), leaving only the starchy endosperm (in the life cycle of the plant, the germ's food).

Choose and Use

You can choose brown rice whether you're eating sticky rice in sushi, a fluffy Basmati rice in an Indian dish, or a medium-grained rice in a Tex-Mex burrito. Cook rice in a heavy pot to avoid burning; no need to add oil or salt. The oil in its bran makes brown rice go bad faster than white, but refrigeration can extend its six-month shelf life.

For Your Health

Though enrichment of white rice restores thiamine and niacin stripped away in milling, and adds iron and folate, brown rice is

GIVES YOU

Dietary fiber
Manganese
Selenium
Magnesium
Niacin
Thiamine
Pantothenic acid
   (vitamin B5)
Pyridoxine

PREP TIP ✦ **A BETTER-FOR-YOU RICE PUDDING**

Leftover brown rice makes a rich but healthy pudding when combined with almond or coconut milk: simply boil on the stovetop and simmer until thickened. Season with cinnamon and vanilla for a tasty dessert. Fresh berries, golden raisins, or toasted almonds provide a further flavor boost.

still a better source of fiber and minerals, especially manganese. Some lab studies suggest rice bran or the oil in rice bran can reduce LDL cholesterol and blood pressure, both risk factors for heart disease. A study published in 2010 looked at women in the large Nurses' Health Study and found that eating two or more servings of brown rice per week was associated with a lower risk of type 2 diabetes—whereas eating at least five servings a week of white rice boosted risk. That may be related to how fiber slows the absorption of sugars.

For Our Planet

Microbes feeding on organic matter submerged in flooded rice fields emit methane—an important heat-trapping greenhouse gas 21 times more potent than carbon dioxide. In fact, rice production accounts for about a fifth of human-generated methane. But farmers in both China (where rice production is a top source of methane) and the U.S. (where landfills and livestock operations are top sources) have made big improvements in the last decades by draining paddies mid-season—good news for the environment.

✦ TAKE AWAY

Introduce brown rice to your diet for greater fiber and nutritional value than highly processed white rice.

BUCKWHEAT

Buckwheat is a rather diminutive green plant with heart-shaped leaves. A profusion of delicate white flowers conceals the course, three-sided brown seeds we mill into flour for pancakes and soba noodles, or roast and cook for kasha. Not a cereal botanically speaking, buckwheat has nevertheless been consumed as a grain for thousands of years. It was first domesticated in southwest China around 6000 B.C., then carried by Buddhist monks to other Asian countries and spread through trade routes to the Middle East and on to Europe. Buckwheat (kasha) became an important food in eastern Europe; Russia and Poland are still major producers today, although second to China.

   In the U.S., buckwheat is a minor crop, grown primarily for human food; when U.S. production peaked around the time of the Civil War it was a common livestock and poultry feed.

Choose and Use
Ground with its bran layers, buckwheat flour is a hearty, robustly flavored, high-fiber addition to griddle cakes, crepes, and baked goods, usually in combination with other grains because of its strong flavor. Toasting buckwheat groats (hulled grain kernels) before cooking in water or stock enhances their flavor and texture. Or you may buy them already roasted (often labeled

✦ TAKE AWAY

Enjoy buckwheat's lively flavor in flour or other dishes—this grain also supports probiotic health.

FOOD SCIENCE ✦ IT'S NOT WHEAT

Buckwheat is in no way related botanically to wheat, though it was given the name due to its similar properties. Technically a seed, most people recognize gluten-free buckwheat as a popular pancake ingredient in America. Buckwheat noodles are quite common in Japanese and Korean cuisine.

PREP TIP
✦
GIVE YOUR BAKED GOODS A HEALTHY BOOST

Cooked buckwheat groats make a fine hot cereal, and buckwheat flour is a popular ingredient in desserts and pancakes. Popular in Russia, buckwheat pancakes are known as blinis. Swapping out some of your white flour for buckwheat flour will provide more vitamins, minerals, and fiber, and is a good way to make your desserts just a little bit better for you. Buckwheat also produces a flavorful honey.

GIVES YOU

Dietary fiber
Protein
Copper
Magnesium
Potassium
Niacin
Pantothenic acid
Phytonutrients
  (flavonoids)

as kasha). Join them with mushrooms and onions, and add to bowtie pasta for a traditional eastern European dish—or create a hot breakfast cereal with fruit and a touch of honey.

For Your Health

Buckwheat is high in protein and relatively high in the essential amino acid lysine, lacking in most plant foods. It's high in both insoluble and soluble fiber, which together help regulate cholesterol and blood glucose, as well as maintain a healthy bowel, in part by providing fuel for "friendly" bacteria (probiotics) that crowd out pathogens. Buckwheat protein may also have an unusual ability to attach to cholesterol, limiting its absorption into the bloodstream. Buckwheat is the only grain that contains a phytochemical called rutin; in laboratory studies this flavonoid has demonstrated activity against blood clumping and inflammation. Buckwheat is gluten-free.

For Our Planet

Buckwheat grows quickly and thrives in poor soil. It's sometimes used as a cover crop to crowd out weeds and retain moisture and soil between cash-crop plantings. It can then be plowed under as a natural fertilizer (so-called green manure) and be allowed to decompose, thereby releasing its stored nutrients into the soil to feed the next crop.

OATS

Early human foragers ate wild oats, but evidence of deliberate cultivation dates only to about four thousand years ago in central Europe; the grain head of the domesticated oat did not shatter and disperse, making it easier to harvest.

Choose and Use

Oats are one of the few grains typically eaten whole. In rolled oats, the groats, or hulled kernels, are simply flattened by heavy rollers and steamed. Thus they retain their full nutritional value: the inedible husk is removed but the bran and germ remain. Steel-cut oats have basically the same nutritional profile as whole rolled oats. Oat flour used to make breads and other baked goods also incorporates the whole grain. Everyday breakfast doesn't get much healthier than a classic porridge made from oats and the addition of dried or fresh fruit and nuts with nonfat milk—or almond, soy, and rice milks are also delicious. This makes for a hearty meal that will stabilize blood sugar and keep you feeling full throughout the morning.

For Your Health

When it comes to protein, whole oats pack both quantity—the highest of any cereal (not counting quinoa)—and quality, offering a well-balanced amino acid profile resembling that of soy, peas, and other legumes. Rice protein has a similar makeup but

GIVES YOU

Dietary fiber
Protein
Pantothenic acid
Thiamin
Manganese
Magnesium
Phosphorus
Zinc
Iron
Unsaturated fat
Phytonutrients
   (avenanthramides)

PREP TIP ✦ HOT BREAKFAST IN FIVE MINUTES

While many grains can be made into porridge, oatmeal is a classic that kids and adults have been enjoying for centuries. Steel cut oats have more "bite" than rolled oats, but whole rolled oats have just as much nutrition and cook in a fraction of the time. Combining oats with water and a touch of cinnamon makes a quick, healthy, and inexpensive breakfast that's especially delightful in colder months.

PAIRINGS
◆
BEYOND BREAKFAST: OAT GROATS

For years rice has been the popular favorite when it comes to an easy side dish. Today, many other grains are coming into their own as alternatives to keep dinner interesting. Oat groats have an almost nutty texture that are cooked similarly to rice and can be added to salads, made into pilafs, or served on their own to add healthy variety to meal time.

is low in quantity. (Both are gluten free, though some oat products in stores may be contaminated with gluten.)

Oats are high in soluble fiber, notably beta-glucan, that's especially helpful in lowering cholesterol; their polyunsaturated fats also reduce cholesterol levels. Research on the cholesterol-lowering effects of oats is solid enough that the U.S. Food and Drug Administration (FDA) and American Heart Association endorse a health claim for oats and oat products.

Oats are the sole source of a phytonutrient class called avenanthramides. Though it's not well understood, lab studies have shown antioxidant, anti-inflammatory, and anti-itch properties.

For Our Planet

Oats grow quickly and retain nutrients and moisture in soil, so farmers sometimes grow them to nourish or protect other crops. Though the U.S. is still a major producer, total acreage has been in decline since the 1920s, partly due to decreased need for horse feed.

QUINOA

Quinoa (pronounced KEEN-wah) is not a true cereal grain, but the dense, nutritious seeds clustered at the head of the goosefoot plant, a relative of beets, spinach, and chard. It originates from South America, and indeed was both a staple and a sacred food—the mother grain—of the Incas. Seduced by its delicate flavor and impressive nutrient profile, Americans have created growing demand for quinoa in recent years, but it is still grown chiefly in Peru, Bolivia, Ecuador, and Chile.

Choose and Use

Quinoa seeds are coated with a bitter-tasting resin that's usually rinsed off before marketing, but some prefer to rinse it again under cold running water for good measure. It cooks quickly, in about 15 minutes; avoid turning its pleasantly rustic texture to mush by overcooking. Quinoa of any color is excellent with iron-rich sautéed greens, in any kind of soup or stew, and as a nutritious alternative to rice in any dish; it makes a wonderful pilaf. It can also be added to green salads for a boost of protein, flavor, and texture. Mixed with nuts, fruit, and maple syrup, it makes an excellent breakfast as well.

For Your Health

When it comes to protein, quinoa is the mother of all grainlike foods, providing nearly twice the protein of most whole grains,

GIVES YOU

Protein
Dietary fiber
Manganese
Magnesium
Phosphorus
Iron
Calcium
Zinc
Copper
Potassium
Thiamin
Riboflavin
Folate
Vitamin E
Phytonutrients
  (flavonoids)

FOOD SCIENCE ✦ A GLUTEN-FREE GRAIN

Variety is incredibly important when it comes to diet, and there are lots of great grains from which to choose when making dinner. Quinoa's fluffy texture can be enjoyed the same way as rice—in pilafs or as a bed for stir-fry—and it's gluten free.

PREP TIP
✦
QUINOA:
A SUSTAINABLE CROP

Highly sustainable, quinoa has become immensely popular in recent years, and 2013 was called the International Year of Quinoa by the Food and Agriculture Organization of the United Nations. This indigenous and sustainable crop includes all of the essential amino acids, making it a "complete" protein.

and a better-quality protein that includes all the essential amino acids. It is also a richer source of vitamin E than most other grains.

This mild-flavored pseudograin also packs a varied mix of nutrients unusual in grains, including calcium, healthy unsaturated fats, and an array of phytonutrients that may have antioxidant and anti-inflammatory effects.

Though little studied in humans, quinoa fed to rats on a high-fructose diet helped limit the animals' cholesterol and regulate blood glucose. People with celiac disease who add quinoa or oats, or foods made from their flours, to a "standard" gluten-free diet (that limits grains and relies heavily on rice) experience substantially improved intake of protein, iron, calcium, and fiber, according to a celiac specialist dietitian's retrospective review of diet history records that was published in 2009.

For Our Planet

Quinoa's surging popularity has dramatically increased its price both in wealthy nations and in its place of origin. South American growers and their communities reap substantial rewards, but locals are also being priced out of their nutritious staple and are substituting inferior foods such as white rice. The abrupt move to intensive cultivation for export has depleted the soil in some areas.

✦ TAKE AWAY

Add quinoa to your plate for savory flavor that offers nearly double the protein in most grains.

WHOLE WHEAT

Agriculture began with the domestication of wild wheat grasses some 12,000 years ago in the Fertile Crescent. Today wheat is second only to rice as a human food crop, providing the world's population with more than 20 percent of its total calories. A staple for roughly 40 percent of humanity—in Europe, North America, and parts of Asia—wheat is the key ingredient of bread in all its local varieties, as well as pasta, crackers, pastries, breakfast cereals, and noodles.

Choose and Use

Finding whole-grain wheat products can be trickier than it sounds. The label "wheat bread" or "multigrain bread" means next to nothing. Look for the term whole wheat, then check the list of ingredients to see whether whole grains predominate. Wheat-bran cereals may be full of fiber and nutrients, but they can lack some of the nutrients of cereals that also include the whole grain (whole wheat).

GIVES YOU

Dietary fiber
Protein
Iron
Phosphorus
Zinc
Copper
Thiamine
Niacin
Folate
Phytonutrients (lignans)

✦ TAKE AWAY

Ensure that mineral- and nutrient-rich whole grains are truly present in food by carefully reading labels.

A common way to encounter the whole wheat grain itself, known as bulgur, is with tomato, cucumbers, mint, parsley, and olive oil in the Middle Eastern salad called tabouleh. Bulgur has all the healthy pluses of whole grain, and it can be enjoyed much like rice, as a side dish to fish or poultry, in soups, or tossed into salads. It's also a terrific meat substitute in vegetarian chili.

For Your Health

Americans consume plenty of wheat, but it's mostly refined, with the nutritious germ and bran layers milled away. The whole grain includes a host of components that contribute to health, including fiber, minerals, heart-healthy unsaturated fats, and phytonutrients such as lignans, which, by occupying hormone receptors, block hormones that may promote cancer.

Whereas refined-wheat products (like white bread) are a mainstay of diets that contribute to diabetes and other diseases through their deleterious effects on blood glucose and insulin, consumption of whole grains and foods that contain them help lower risk of heart disease and several cancers.

For Our Planet

Though not an especially resource-intensive crop compared with other staple foods, wheat is the most widely grown crop in the world. The big environmental challenge is the sheer demand for this grain, expected to climb 60 percent by 2050 due to population growth and increasing consumption of wheat products in the developing world. This will require increased yields; one controversial approach to meeting the demand is genetically modified wheat, under development by Monsanto and others. Wheat and other grains are most environmentally friendly when planted as part of a rotation of crops that helps to reduce fertilizer and pesticide use as well as to promote soil health and resiliency.

WILD RICE

Like some of the other "grains," wild rice is a wetland seed-bearing grass and not technically a cereal (grain). Native Americans may have gathered it from shallow streams and lakes since prehistoric times. Natives of the Great Lakes region where wild rice grows abundantly—the Ojibwe, Cree, and Menominee ("wild rice people," so named by the Ojibwe)—long enjoyed it as a staple. Today it is still collected from wild stands in Minnesota and other Great Lakes states, although most of the wild rice sold commercially is farmed in California, where the crop was introduced in the 1970s.

Choose and Use

Wild-gathered rice is more expensive than the farm-grown variety, although some find its varying flavor more stimulating to the palate. Both kinds add an earthy taste and texture to casseroles, pilafs, and traditional stuffings. Try it with sautéed mushrooms and onions or on salads of greens or citrus fruits.

For Your Health

Though brown rice is a little higher in fiber, wild rice provides more protein, with somewhat higher levels of lysine and methionine, essential amino acids that are typically lacking in grains. Wild rice is lower in carbohydrates than brown rice, which may

GIVES YOU

Dietary fiber
Protein
Zinc
Copper
Niacin
Riboflavin
Pyridoxine
Folate

CONSIDER ✦ THINK BEYOND HOT

Like some other "grains," wild rice isn't botanically a grain at all. Unique in taste, wild rice is often combined with rice or other grains to provide a balance of flavors. While often served hot as a side dish or poultry dressing, cold or warm rice makes a toothsome salad when tossed with salad greens, herbs, nuts, and fresh fruit. Toasted walnuts and orange segments go especially well.

✦ TAKE AWAY

Treat yourself to wild rice, high in protein and omega-3 fatty acids.

be helpful in stabilizing blood glucose. Very low in total fat overall, wild rice is relatively rich in omega-3 fatty acids, a poly-unsaturated fat that reduces inflammation and may thwart the development of heart disease and ameliorate ailments such as arthritis and depression.

For Our Planet

The development of cultivated "paddy" rice made the food more widely available, drove down its price, and, some argue, relieved pressure on wild strands. But some Native American and environmental groups have been concerned that the development of cultivated varieties robs Ojibwe of their treaty-granted rights to the wild rice and could lead to the contamination of wild strands. Several companies sell wild-grown "lake and river" wild rice, including Ojibwe-owned Native Harvest, whose product is traditionally hand harvested.

CHAPTER FIVE

FATS and OILS

Fat gets a bad rap sometimes, but like protein and carbohydrates, it is a macronutrient essential to life. It is also the most energy-dense of the three, with more than twice the calories: about 9 per gram in fat compared to 4 per gram in protein or carbohydrates. Not only do fats and oils add flavors and textures to a wide range of foods, both savory and sweet, they are also important for preventing disease and staying healthy. Knowing which forms of fat and how much to eat is a key first step; knowing how to choose and use them is equally important.

Chemically speaking, fats and oils are characterized by their component fatty acids, 25 different naturally occurring combinations of carbon, hydrogen, and oxygen atoms. Fatty acids are differentiated by their atomic structures, particularly their "saturation," a term in chemistry referring to whether the fatty acid can absorb more hydrogen or not. An unsaturated fat will bond with more hydrogen molecules; a saturated fat will not.

Both saturated and unsaturated fats occur in nature. Animal fats such as suet, lard, and butter are *saturated fats*. They are solid at room temperature, have a greasy or waxy texture, and spoil more slowly than unsaturated fats.

By contrast, most plant-derived fats are *unsaturated fats*. Concentrated mainly in seeds or nuts, these fats are extracted by pressing or grinding, and they are liquid at room temperature. Unsaturated fats can be either monounsaturated or polyunsaturated, referring to the number of double bonds of hydrogen in the molecule. Double bonds make these oils more perishable and more sensitive to oxygen, heat, and light than saturated fats.

Two important classes of polyunsaturated fatty acids are available only from food: omega-6 and omega-3. Both occur in plant oils—omega-6 particularly in corn, safflower, and sunflower oil—and omega-3 fatty acids also occur in fatty fish like sardines, mackerel, and salmon. Western diets tend to be high in omega-6 fatty acids and low in omega-3 fatty acids. A typical American diet has a 20:1 ratio of omega-6 to omega-3, while some research suggests that a ratio of 3:1 or 4:1 may be better. For that reason, it's a good idea to find ways to increase the omega-3 fatty acid foods on your menu. This chapter will give you ideas how.

Fat in the Diet, Fat in the Body

Everybody knows that fats and oils make food taste good. They add richness, texture, and flavor. They aid in browning and emulsion

(making things creamy), and they make baked goods come out tender and flaky.

Fats do more than taste good, though. Because they take longer to digest than proteins and carbohydrates, fats help us feel full longer. They also stimulate production of a hormone that suppresses the appetite and signals us to stop eating. In terms of sheer survival mechanisms, stored fats represent the body's energy reserves—one pound of body fat provides enough energy for one and a half to two days of normal activity. The problem is, human beings often reserve more energy than we use, resulting in thicker waistlines.

A body's fat requirement varies throughout a person's lifetime. At birth, human breast milk provides a special combination of fatty acids (among other key nutrients), which is why many nutritionists and health professionals advise new mothers that "breast is best." As infants grow, fats help form cell membranes in all the organs. The retina and the central nervous system are mainly composed of fats. The body needs fats to produce growth hormones, sex hormones,

and prostaglandins (hormonelike chemicals that regulate many body processes). Fat deposits protect vital organs and help regulate body temperature. Only when they are eaten with fats can the body can absorb some important fat-soluble vitamins, such as A, D, E, and K.

Body fat is not a simple function of the fat a person eats. The body is relatively efficient in storing dietary fat, but excess calories from carbohydrates and proteins are also converted to fat, leading to weight gain when energy consumed exceeds energy expended. A growing body establishes fat cells at certain key periods, such as infancy and adolescence. Once established, fat cells are permanent, though they may shrink with weight loss or expand with weight gain. Eating habits also begin early in life when children develop taste preferences and habits. Fats have their place in a healthy family's diet—but the right kinds of fats are key.

Those who eat an insufficient amount of fat in their diets can experience depression, heart disease, malnutrition, and other severe physical problems. On the other hand, those who maintain a diet high in certain kinds of fat face increased risks of heart disease, stroke, circulatory disorders, and cancer of the colon and rectum, prostate, breast, uterus, and ovaries.

Cholesterol and Trans Fats

Cholesterol is another fat essential for health. It is present throughout the body, especially in brain, nerve, liver, and blood cells. Of the two types of cholesterol—HDL (for high-density lipoproteins) and LDL (for low-density lipoproteins)—it has become common to speak of of HDL as "good" and LDL as "bad," but both are necessary—in the right proportion. HDLs are large molecules that circulate in the blood,

*Not only are fats essential to good health,
they taste good, too!*

scavenging unused cholesterol and recycling it back to the liver. Smoking, obesity, and a sedentary lifestyle can all lower one's HDL levels, leading to plaque deposits that block the arteries and limit blood flow (known as atherosclerosis). In the typical American diet, increasing vegetable fats and reducing animal fats will lead to a more balanced cholesterol count.

Another type of fat—trans fats, or trans fatty acids—forms naturally in the guts of some ruminant animals (cows and goats, for example) and is found in low amounts in many foods also high in saturated fats, such as milk, cheese, and meat. More significantly, trans fats are a key ingredient in many processed foods, in the form of partially hydrogenated vegetable oil.

Hydrogenation is an industrial process by which hydrogen is added to vegetable oil, transforming liquid oil into solid fat and improving the texture, stability, and shelf life of food made with it. This invention proved a real boon to manufacturers in the early to mid-twentieth century. Margarine, vegetable shortening, and all sorts of snack foods were developed containing partially hydrogenated vegetable oil. We have since learned, though, that of all the fats in the diet, trans fats have the most harmful effect on human health, particularly on blood cholesterol levels and risk of cardiovascular disease—more so than saturated fat or dietary cholesterol.

During the 1990s, studies seeking the causes for a rising incidence of heart disease in the United States identified trans fats as one of the culprits. Public health campaigns to eliminate trans fats from the American diet have since then proven effective, and many manufacturers now proudly claim "no trans fats" on their packaging. Trans fat content in our food has declined by 50 percent since 2005. Laws also limit the amount of trans fats that manufacturers and restaurant chains can use in the foods they offer, and health-conscious consumers avoid any items containing partially hydrogenated oil.

Know Your Fats

It is now well established scientifically that the type of fat a person consumes has a greater impact on that individual's general health than the amount of fat she or he ingests. Indeed, the heart-healthy Mediterranean diet, based on the culinary traditions of countries bordering the Mediterranean Sea, is actually quite high in unsaturated fats, such as those found in olive oil and nuts. The wisest diet choice is not to avoid fats altogether. Not only are fats essential to good health, they taste good, too! Instead, learn which kinds of fats and oils are most beneficial for your body and use that knowledge to shape your menu and adjust your eating habits.

CANOLA OIL

Extracted from the crushed seeds of the rape plant, rapeseed oil—also known as canola oil—was first used as a lamp fuel in Asia and Europe. The word "rape" comes from the Latin *rapum,* meaning turnip. The yellow-blossomed rape plant is related to the turnip, cabbage, mustard, and other members of the Brassicaceae family. Rapeseed oil was originally very high in erucic acid, which can damage cardiac muscle. Considered too toxic for human consumption, it was banned by the FDA in 1956. A new hybrid of rapeseed was later developed with a lower content of erucic acid, labeled Can.O., L-A for "Canadian Oilseed, Low Acid," hence the name "canola oil."

Once a specialty crop in Canada, canola is now a major U.S. cash crop, exported to Japan, Mexico, China, and Pakistan. Most U.S. canola is grown in North Dakota.

Choose and Use

Light yellow in color with a neutral flavor, canola oil is an inexpensive and versatile ingredient that may be used as a cooking or salad oil, when you want to highlight the taste of other ingredients. Canola's high smoking point (the temperature at which it breaks down and begins to burn) makes it a good choice for grilling, stir-frying, or deep-frying foods. This oil turns rancid when stored

GIVES YOU

Vitamin K
Vitamin E
Monounsaturated and polyunsaturated fats
Phytosterols (sitosterol, campesterol)

CONSIDER ✦ BIOFUEL

The global demand for vegetable oils like canola is expanding rapidly, due not only to increasing populations and individual preferences but also to the massive upsurge in growing it for biofuel. Canola's efficiency as a biofuel is unclear, however, and the deforestation that currently occurs to clear land to produce it leads to habitat loss.

PREP TIP
✦
GREAT IN BAKING

Olive oil is lauded for its high mono-unsaturated fat content, particularly oleic acid. But mild-flavored canola oil has almost as much oleic acid, good news for people who don't care for the distinct taste of olive oil. Canola is a great choice for mellower vinaigrettes and marinades. With its healthier nutritional profile, it's also a terrific choice for baking in lieu or soybean or corn oil.

improperly, so keep it in a tightly sealed container away from heat and light. "Cold-pressed" canola oil has a longer shelf life.

For Your Health

Canola oil has the lowest saturated fat content of any oil commonly available in the United States, and it contains omega-3 and omega-6 fatty acids in healthy proportions. In fact, one tablespoon of canola oil contains 100 percent of the daily value of alpha-linolenic acid (ALA), an essential omega-3 fatty acid that the body cannot make and must get from the diet. Sixty percent of the fat in canola oil comes from monounsaturated fats such as oleic acid, which helps lower LDL, or "bad" cholesterol, and increase HDL, or "good" cholesterol, in the blood. Because of this, the FDA allows manufacturers to label canola oil as a food that reduces the risk of heart disease.

For Our Planet

In part because of consumer pressure, farm organizations are actively seeking ways to make rapeseed a sustainable crop. In 2012, the Cargill agricultural company supplied what they claimed to be the first verifiably sustainable rapeseed crop to Unilever, a multinational corporation that plans to source all of its raw materials sustainably by 2020. Unilever uses canola oil to make mayonnaises and margarines, among other food products.

✦ **TAKE AWAY**

Use this golden oil to accentuate flavors and lower your risk of heart disease.

CHOCOLATE

Chocolate is made from beans harvested from the large cacao pods that grow on a tropical tree native to South America. Both the Mayans and the Aztecs believed cocoa beans had magical properties and used them to brew a bitter drink called *xocolatl*, the probable origin of the word "chocolate." In 1502, Columbus brought cocoa pods back from the New World, and by the 17th century sweetened chocolate was a fashionable drink throughout Europe.

Cocoa beans are fermented, dried, roasted, and cracked, to separate the nib or central part of the cocoa bean, from the shell. The nibs are ground to extract a natural vegetable fat called cocoa butter, leaving a thick brown paste, which is further refined to produce cocoa powder and varieties of solid chocolate that include dark, semisweet, sweet, and milk chocolate.

Choose and Use
Supermarkets stock a mouth-watering array of domestic and imported chocolate containing varying percentages of cocoa solids and flavored with everything from mint to bacon—proof that the art of chocolate making is flourishing. Cocoa powder is used in beverages and baking (Dutch-processed has fewer flavonols, since the alkali process destroys some of the

FOOD SCIENCE ✦ WHITE CHOCOLATE

Unlike traditional brown-colored chocolate, whether milk, dark, or semisweet, white chocolate does not contain the dark-colored solids of the cacao bean. It does contain cocoa butter, however (as well as sugar and milk), which accounts for its mild chocolaty flavor and pale ivory color.

PAIRINGS
✦
FAIR TRADE CHOCOLATE

Cacao is often grown by farmers who do not receive just wages for their work, and reports have indicated child slavery is not uncommon. When satisfying your craving, look for the "Fair Trade Certified" label, which ensures your purchase supports farmers who receive a fair price, invest in their land, and do not employ child or slave labor.

GIVES YOU

DARK CHOCOLATE, 70-85 PERCENT COCOA SOLIDS:

Manganese
Copper
Iron
Magnesium
Dietary fiber
Phosphorus
Zinc
Potassium
Monounsaturated fats
Phytonutrients
    (flavonoids)

antioxidants). Solid chocolate may be eaten as is, or melted and incorporated into desserts. Chocolate has an incredible depth of flavor, since cacao features over 400 distinct smells (roses have 14). Tightly wrapped chocolate will keep for months in a cool, dry place.

For Your Health

The darker the chocolate, the greater its concentration of flavonol antioxidants, which can lower blood pressure and reduce the risk of heart disease. Consuming dark chocolate daily has been proven to reduce stress hormones in people with high anxiety levels. A good source of minerals such as manganese, copper, and iron, chocolate is also very high in saturated fats and when eaten in excess contributes extra calories and sugar to the diet. Choose dark rather than milk chocolate, and enjoy it in small quantities.

For Our Planet

To make sure your chocolate is sustainably sourced, purchase chocolate labeled "Rainforest Alliance Certified." This guarantees the cocoa is shade-grown, using practices that have a minimal impact on the rain forest and which conserve the habitat of native plant and animal species. This certification also ensures that cocoa farmers and laborers have decent working conditions.

FLAXSEED: GROUND AND OIL

Humans have had an enduring relationship with the flax plant, which they named *Linum usitatissimum,* or "of maximum usefulness." For tens of thousands of years, flax has been cultivated as a source of food and textiles. Its strong fibers have been spun into sails for our ships, strings for our bows, and clothing and armor for our bodies. Graced with light blue, bell-shaped flowers, the flax plant is the source of linen fabric and produces golden or brown seeds used primarily today as a dietary supplement, and to produce linseed oil, an industrial lubricant.

Choose and Use

Flaxseed and oil can be found in natural food stores and in many supermarkets. Cooking does not diminish the omega-3 in flaxseed, so it may be baked into muffins and breads without losing this fatty acid. The seeds have a mild, nutty flavor. Grinding just before use, in a coffee or nut grinder, preserves their nutritional benefits. Sprinkle ground seeds on salads, yogurt, or breakfast cereals, or on ice cream or other desserts. Flaxseed can also be sprouted and used in salads and sandwiches. Some people experience bloating or flatulence when they first introduce this high-fiber food into their diet. Drinking more water should help such gastrointestinal symptoms abate over time.

   Flaxseed oil is most often used as a dietary supplement. Practically flavorless, it may be added to protein shakes or other beverages or taken in capsule form. However, the whole seeds offer more complete nutrition, though the omega-3s it provides are not the long-chain EPA and DHA most critical for human health.

For Your Health

Flaxseed has a unique nutritional profile. The seeds and oil are remarkably rich sources of omega-3 fatty acids, which can help

GIVES YOU

GROUND FLAXSEED:
Monounsaturated and
   polyunsaturated fats
Manganese
Vitamin B1
Dietary fiber
Magnesium
Tryptophan
Phosphorus
Copper
Phytonutrients (lignans)

FLAXSEED OIL:
Monounsaturated and
   polyunsaturated fats
Vitamin E

PREP TIP
✦
A NUTTY ADDITION

Flaxseeds have become a favorite among those looking to increase their intake of omega-3s. This small seed can be purchased raw or toasted and can be added to many different foods for texture with its mildly nutty flavor. Try as a topping for yogurt, sprinkle a handful on a salad, or add to cooked cereals to boost your intake of heart- and brain-healthy fats.

balance the omega-6 in Western diets, due primarily to the high corn content of many processed foods. Flaxseed is also the number-one source of phytonutrients called lignans, important antioxidants that may prevent precancerous cellular changes and reduce the growth of hormone-related cancers. Finally, flaxseed contains mucilage gums that support the health of the intestinal tract. Flaxseed oil lacks some of the nutrients found in the seeds and must be refrigerated, whether in capsule or liquid form, to preserve its benefits.

For Our Planet

Flax earns high marks for sustainability, in part because the entire plant can be used to make products such as linen cloth, twine, and linseed oil. After the oil is extracted, the remaining meal can be formed into nutritious bars called oilseed cakes and fed to cattle and chickens to create heart-healthier meat.

HEMP OIL

An ancient legend says that the Buddha, founder of Buddhism, survived for six years eating nothing but a single hemp seed each day. Hemp has a unique nutritional profile and has been consumed as a food since ancient times, but today this useful plant is transformed into insulation, auto parts, paper, and even stone.

Most industrial hemp is grown in China. In the United States, this versatile crop still suffers from guilt by association as a result of its relationship to the marijuana plant, and its cultivation is severely restricted. Hemp and pot both belong to the plant genus *Cannabis*, which contains molecular compounds called cannabinoids, including the psychoactive ingredient THC (tetrahydrocannabinol) and an antipsychoactive ingredient called CBD (cannabidiol). Unlike marijuana, hemp is very low in THC and high in CBD, and one cannot get high from smoking or ingesting it.

Choose and Use

Purchase small quantities of raw seeds in bulk or prepackaged, and sprinkle on granola, puddings, or other desserts, or blend into smoothies; toasting brings out their nutty taste, but eating the seeds raw provides the most nutritional benefits. Hemp oil is extracted from hemp seeds by cold-pressing, resulting in oil that ranges in color from off-yellow to dark green. Best used for cold and warm dishes where temperature is kept below the boiling point, hemp oil should not be used for frying. It adds a nice nutty flavor to foods and may be used in salads and baked goods, or taken by the spoonful as a dietary supplement. Store hemp oil in the fridge once the bottle is opened.

GIVES YOU

HEMP SEED (SHELLED):
Polyunsaturated fats
Phytosterols (beta sitosterol, campesterol)
Vitamin E
Protein
Magnesium
Zinc
Iron
Dietary fiber

HEMP OIL:
Polyunsaturated fats
Phytosterols (beta sitosterol, campesterol)
Vitamin E
Protein

For Your Health

One unique benefit of hemp resides in its particular ratio of omega-6 to omega-3 essential fatty acids (3:1), which exceeds the 4:1 ratio recommended for the body's health. Most people consume too few omega-3 fatty acids, and ingesting foods containing whole hemp seeds or hemp oil can help boost your intake. Hemp provides all of the essential amino acids that the body requires. The phytosterols in hemp also help lower LDL cholesterol by blocking the absorption of cholesterol into the intestines.

For Our Planet

Hemp is an environmentally friendly crop that requires few pesticides and no herbicides. It stabilizes and enriches the soil in which it grows. Sustainable hemp is currently grown on farms in Canada, Europe, and China.

In contrast to flax with its high omega-3 content, hemp contains a broad profile of all the essential fatty acids. Crushed hemp seeds taste remarkably like crushed nuts; consider adding a handful to baked goods or porridge; store in the refrigerator to prolong shelf life. Choosing hemp products is an investment in this sustainable crop.

✦ TAKE AWAY

Use hemp oil to provide your body with all the essential amino acids it needs.

OLIVE OIL

One of the most ancient foods on Earth and a symbol of peace and wisdom, olives were cultivated before the invention of written language. Plucked straight from the tree, olives are inedible to humans and must be brined before they are fit for consumption. Originally the ripened fruit was pressed to extract oil for lamps and cooking, as well as cosmetic and ceremonial uses. Spanish missionaries planted the first olive trees in California, where most domestic olive oil is now produced. Imported olive oil may come from Greece, Italy, France, and Spain and varies widely in flavor and color, depending on the region of origin and the condition of the crop.

Choose and Use

Extra-virgin olive oil (EVOO), which derives from the first cold pressing of the olives, varies in color from straw yellow to bright green and has a flavor that ranges from peppery to fruity. Save the more expensive EVOO for use on salads and for drizzling over grilled vegetables; its low smoke point (the temperature at which it begins to burn and smoke) makes it less than ideal for high-heat cooking, though it can be used in faster-cooking dishes. Unlike flavor-filled extra-virgin and virgin olive oil, "pure" olive oil and "light" olive oil have a neutral taste and higher smoke point preferable to some palates and suitable for cooking and baking. Replacing the butter and cream in mashed potatoes with olive oil increases this healthy fat in your diet. Olive oil tastes best when used within two months of purchase but will last up to two years if stored in a cool, dark place. It turns cloudy and solidifies when refrigerated, but it will clarify and liquefy at room temperature.

GIVES YOU

Monounsaturated and polyunsaturated fats
Vitamin E
Vitamin K
Phytonutrients
Phytosterols (tyrosolesters)

PAIRINGS
✦
DRIZZLE AWAY

A cornerstone of Mediterranean cuisine, olive oil's flavor differs by variety, from mild and light to fruity or peppery. A staple in cooking, a drizzle adds a burst of richness and flavor to dishes likes soups, savory tarts, salads, and beyond. It's also great for dipping with a crusty loaf of bread—and more healthful than butter.

For Your Health

Olive oil is a staple of the Mediterranean diet, widely regarded as one of the healthiest in the world. Olive oil has been intensively studied, and research has linked it to weight loss, digestive and bone health, and improved cognitive function, especially in older adults. A review of the existing science, conducted at the University of Athens in 2011, concluded that a high intake of olive oil was associated with lowered odds of having any type of cancer. Nine different categories of polyphenols present in olive oil function in the body as both antioxidants and anti-inflammatory nutrients.

For Our Planet

Drought-tolerant olives require 50 to 75 percent less water than other crops, meaning fewer resources are used in their production. However, waste and residue are particularly high in olive oil production. In 2013, the development of software that calculates the carbon footprint of olive oil production processes will help olive oil businesses assess their environmental impact.

SAFFLOWER OIL

This ancient crop, related to the sunflower and native to the mountains of southwest Asia and Ethiopia, has been prized by various cultures as a medicinal plant and cultivated for its yellow, orange, and red thistle-like flowers, which have been used as a textile dye. Garlands made from safflower blossoms were found in the tomb of the pharaoh Tutankhamun. Now raised almost exclusively as an oilseed plant, most safflower is grown in India.

Choose and Use

This flavorless and colorless oil can be a nutritious yet silent partner in many dishes. Traditionally refined safflower oil is best used cold, whereas high-oleic oil has a high smoking point and may be used for frying foods. Expeller pressing is preferable to chemical processes used to extract oil from saf-flower seeds, which may leave traces of chemicals behind. As with all cooking oils, keep away from heat and light, and seal tightly to prevent oxidation.

GIVES YOU

Vitamin E
Monounsaturated and
   polyunsaturated fats
Phytosterols
   (campesterol,
   stigmasterol,
   beta-sitosterol)

FOOD SCIENCE ✦ PARTIAL HYDROGENATION

Like soybean oil, safflower oil is often used to make margarine by employing "partial hydrogenation." Through this process, the addition of hydrogen molecules to the oil creates a solid, more shelf-stable fat that mimics the look and mouthfeel of saturated fats like butter. The process also results in the creation of trans fats, however, a risk factor for high cholesterol and heart disease. Partially hydrogenated fats are commonly used in processed foods like cookies and crackers. While many foods have removed harmful trans fats, read the ingredients list to avoid purchasing foods with "partially hydrogenated vegetable oil."

Safflower's orange flowers are a cheaper alternative to saffron. Its oil is neutral tasting and rich in monounsaturates, like olive oil. For those who prefer their salad dressings to feature the flavors of bright vinegars, fresh herbs, and spices rather than the oil, safflower is a good choice. An easy vinaigrette includes about one part vinegar to two or three parts oil seasoned with a bit of salt and freshly ground black pepper; garlic, shallot, or herbs provide additional flavor.

✦ TAKE AWAY

Reduce "bad" cholesterol by using safflower oil in your recipes.

For Your Health

Nutritionally similar to sunflower oil, traditional safflower oil has more polyunsaturated fats than any other commonly used cooking oil. A variety high in oleic acid, often used in infant formulas, contains more monounsaturated fats. Some of the latest research into safflower oil has focused on its nutritional benefits for women. For instance, clinical studies in 2009 and 2011 demonstrated that postmenopausal women with type 2 diabetes who added safflower oil to their diets experienced a reduction in abdominal fat, increases in insulin sensitivity and "good" HDL cholesterol, and decreased inflammation. This oil contains heart-healthy phytosterols that may lower LDL cholesterol in the blood.

For Our Planet

Safflower grown in the United States is a high-yield crop that can survive with little or no irrigation, thanks to its deep taproot, and the application of insecticides and pesticides is often unnecessary. The lower water needs and the limited use of fossil fuel–intensive chemicals make this oil one of the most planet friendly.

SUNFLOWER SEEDS AND OIL

One of the only crop species to originate in North America, the sunflower is well named; these plants swivel their golden heads to follow their namesake's passage across the sky each day. Sunflowers thrive in the bright heat of the wind-swept Great Plains, though more are commercially grown in the Dakotas than in the so-called Sunflower State of Kansas. The sunflower's broad face is packed with oily seeds, tucked inside hard shells. Many people enjoy snacking on the roasted kernels, but the seeds are also used for birdfeed and principally as a source of salad and cooking oil.

Choose and Use

Dried or roasted sunflower seeds are sold prepackaged or in bulk. They should look and smell fresh. Both shelled and unshelled are available, but shelling them yourself is a laborious process. Sunflower seeds are often heavily salted, so opt for the unsalted to avoid excess sodium intake. Sprinkle sunflower kernels on salads, or add to hot and cold cereals or baked goods. The seeds may also be ground and used in place of flour for coating meat or fish.

Light yellow to golden in color, sunflower oil has a mild flavor. Due to its relatively high smoke point (450° F) sunflower oil may be used for frying as well as in baked goods and as a neutral-tasting salad oil. Like other oils, it eventually turns rancid if exposed to oxygen, heat, and light.

For Your Health

Of seeds and nuts commonly eaten in the United States, sunflower seeds have the highest phytosterol content. Phytosterols reduce cholesterol levels in the blood, boost the immune system, and help protect against lung, stomach, ovarian, and breast cancer. The vitamin E in these seeds benefits the body in

GIVES YOU

SUNFLOWER SEEDS:
Vitamin E
Manganese
Copper
Tryptophan
Magnesium
Selenium
Vitamin B6
Phosphorus
Folate
Protein
Niacin
Pantothenic Acid
Iron
Potassium
Zinc
Phytosterols
  (beta-sitosterol,
  stigmasterol,
  campesterol)

SUNFLOWER OIL:
Vitamin E
Vitamin K
Monounsaturated and
  polyunsaturated fats

FOOD SCIENCE ✦ REFINED AND UNREFINED

Oils like sunflower can be obtained from their seeds either by crushing them through an expeller press or through chemical extraction; either is safe to eat. Oil may also be "refined" or "unrefined." Unrefined oil is less heat stable and more flavorful, making it a good choice for vinaigrettes or marinades. Refined oil removes many nutrients but can be a safer choice when cooking at high temperatures, like frying.

many ways, such as in building red blood cells and muscle tissue and protecting against heart disease.

Different types of sunflower oil have different fat profiles. Linoleic sunflower oil, the original and most commonly used variety, contains more polyunsaturated fats than high-oleic sunflower oil, which is higher in monounsaturated fats. A third variety, called NuSun, is a mid-oleic oil developed using standard plant-breeding techniques to provide the food industry with a heart-healthier frying oil.

For Our Planet

Sunflowers are drought-resistant, and herbicide use on commercially grown plants declined by 80 percent between 1996 and 2008 as a result of demand from eco-conscious consumers and companies pressuring for more sustainable farming practices. A major market for U.S. sunflowers, Europe enforces strict guidelines about sustainability.

PREP TIP
✦
GOOD FOR FRYING

Sunflower oil is a mild-flavored oil, making it a good choice when a mellow flavor is desired. It would work well in a simple marinade or salad dressing. Like canola, corn, and peanut oil, sunflower oil also has a very high smoke point, making it a good choice for frying food.

The history of beverages begins, naturally enough, with water. This mutable element varies hugely in form and character, It might issue from rivers, springs, or deep wells; fall from the sky as rain; or bubble up clouded with silt or fizzy with suspended gases. It has, until relatively recently, been more appropriately referred to as "waters." Humans, whose earliest ancestors were water-dwelling organisms, still possess bodies consisting of more than two-thirds water.

For millions of years—the vast majority of our evolutionary history—water was the only thing that human beings drank. Our billions of cells require water to function, and this clear, abundant, and calorie-free beverage is more essential to our daily survival than food. Once developing infants no longer require the nutrients present in breast milk, water provides everything we need to replenish the fluids our bodies lose through metabolism, perspiration, respiration, and elimination. So effectively does plain water address these physiological needs that it was not until the birth of agriculture 11,000 years ago that alternative beverages began to be developed.

Bottled versus Tap

At various times and places throughout history, people have lacked access to sources of clean water, as a result of both naturally occurring contaminants and human-created pollution. This problem originally led to the development of beverages that help purify water and thus provide a way to hydrate the body without putting health at risk. In the West, beer brewing and wine making developed, in part, as a way to decontaminate drinking water, as did the practice of brewing tea in the East. Boiling water to create a beverage from infused tea leaves kills waterborne contaminants, resulting in a beverage that is safe to drink. As an added boon, the caffeine present in this hot drink acts as a mild stimulant and provides other health benefits.

Much later, bottling water became another method of insuring its purity. Far from being a recent phenomenon, bottled water in the United States actually predates the American Revolution. Early consumers drank bottled water for health reasons, just as many people do today. By 1856, over 7 million bottles were produced annually at Saratoga Springs, one of the most popular bottling facilities and a natural source of mineral springs, which are purported to have therapeutic properties. In the early twentieth century, when chlorine was regularly added to municipal drinking supplies, bottled water fell from favor, since clean water was readily available from the tap.

In the 1970s, concerns about the growing problem of water pollution led to renewed sales of bottled water. The French mineral water company Perrier launched a million-dollar marketing campaign that made its uniquely shaped green glass bottle a status beverage. In the United States, tap water costs just a fraction of a penny per glass, but since the 1980s bottled water has eclipsed it in popularity. Americans currently drink more bottled water than milk or beer, even though research has shown that bottled is no safer or better tasting than tap water, and may actually contain more contaminants. The economic and environmental costs of bottled water, in terms of waste, energy use, and production of greenhouse gases, have prompted local governments in the United States and Canada to consider banning its sale. Developing nations such as China, Pakistan, and India, where many people lack access to dependable sources of clean water, are now the world's second-largest consumers of bottled water.

Beer, Wine, and Spirits

Besides replenishing bodily fluids and purifying drinking water, beverages have evolved to fulfill a range of human purposes, from the sacred to the medicinal and recreational. Various types of alcoholic beverages have served all of these functions. Nearly every creature on Earth is attracted to the fermentation of yeast and sugar or starch, a natural process that results in ethyl alcohol. Alcoholic beverages have been consumed by virtually every culture in the world throughout most of their recorded history, in part as a health precaution in the absence of clean water sources. The ancient Egyptians brewed beer in their homes on an everyday basis. People in ancient Honduras drank a

Beverages have evolved to fulfill a range of human purposes, from the sacred to the medicinal and recreational.

fermentation of chocolate. Distilled spirits were first introduced during the 12th and 13th centuries. Prior to the Enlightenment, people in western Europe drank weak beer and wine throughout the day.

Imbibing alcoholic beverages to temporarily alter one's state of consciousness is one of the few universal features of human behavior. Over the course of our history, alcoholic beverages have served as a social lubricant and as a means of promoting relaxation. They have provided nutrition and increased the pleasures of eating. Intoxicating beverages have been ingested for their medicinal, antiseptic, and analgesic properties, as well. Alcohol, especially wine, is regarded by some cultures as a gift from God and afforded a prominent place in religion and worship. Alcohol can be misused, however, and chronic overconsumption produces long-term health problems. Certain cultures have periodically banned the consumption of alcohol for religious or public health reasons, such as during the Prohibition era in the United States (1920–1933). The religion of Islam expressly forbids the consumption of alcoholic beverages, as do some branches of Christianity, including Mormonism. However, current research has determined that alcohol in general—not just wine—is heart healthy, and moderate consumption is beneficial for most adults.

Sweet and Fizzy Drinks

An alternative to alcoholic or "hard" beverages, what came to be known as "soft" drinks were first marketed in the 17th century, specifically in France, where a mixture of water and lemon juice sweetened with honey was sold by street vendors who carried tanks on their backs. The invention of methods for artificial carbonation enabled the creation of beverages that imitated gaseous mineral waters that many considered therapeutic. This association of carbonated water with health led to the installation of soda fountains in drugstores, which used pressurized tanks of carbonic acid gas to create fizzy beverages. Pharmacists added tinctures of cocaine, caffeine, and tobacco to these energizing "health" drinks, along with different flavorings and sweeteners. By the time many of these additives were phased out, people had developed an unhealthy thirst for such sugary beverages, which were originally sweetened with glucose in the form of cane and beet sugar. Plentiful and cheap to produce, thanks to U.S. government corn subsidies, high-fructose corn syrup became the major component of most popular soft drinks by the 1990s.

Today, sweetened, carbonated beverages are thought to be a major culprit in the global obesity epidemic. Though research is ongoing, fructose does not seem to trigger the same appetite-suppressing signals as glucose does. Sugars of all kinds contribute excess calories and health risks. New laws seek to limit or ban sugary drinks in some schools.

BEER

Beer dates from at least 6,000 years ago, when the Sumerians began fermenting a low-alcohol beverage from barley. Originally, the drink was consumed as a nutritional supplement: an ancient inscription counsels every good mother to supply her school-age sons with two jars of beer to ensure their healthy development. Beer has long been a working man's drink, a grain beverage that almost anyone could make at home. The builders of the pyramids received some of their payment in unfiltered beer.

Beer consists of four main ingredients: water, malt (germinated grain), hops, and yeast. Almost every culture worldwide has independently developed methods of brewing beer from local ingredients. In the United States, most beers range in alcohol content from 3.2 to 8 percent; anything over 5 percent must be labeled "ale."

GIVES YOU

Niacin
Folate
Vitamin B6
Magnesium
Phosphorus
Potassium
Selenium

✦ TAKE AWAY

Choose from a wide variety of beers to find your favorite, but avoid overconsumption.

Choose and Use

Most supermarkets carry a wide assortment of domestic and imported beers, ranging from lighter beers such as lagers and pilsners, to darker styles such as porters and stouts. These have varying flavors, which pair well with different foods. Recently, craft beers from independent microbreweries have become popular. Unlike wines, most beers do not benefit from aging. Store bottled beer upright in a cool, dark place and refrigerate before serving. Once opened, bottled beer goes "flat," or loses its carbonation within a couple hours.

For Your Health

Most of the nutrients in grain are lost in the brewing process. Beer's proven benefits relate principally to its alcohol content, since moderate daily intake of alcohol has been determined to protect against heart disease, and to lower the risk of stroke and certain types of cancers, including those of the colon, ovary, and prostate. Studies also indicate that drinking beer may help prevent kidney stones, and that the silicon present in beer may increase bone density. However, overconsumption of this high-calorie beverage can contribute to abdominal obesity, aka the aptly named "beer belly," among other health problems. Notably, alcohol (of any kind) at higher intakes is a strong risk factor for breast cancer.

For Our Planet

Major beer producers use a huge amount of water in the brewing process. The carbon footprint of a pint of "suds" varies depending on whether it is bottled or draft, and where the beer is produced and consumed. Cans require far less energy to recycle than glass bottles. The footprint of an imported bottled beer may be three times larger than that of a locally brewed pint of beer on tap, so opting for a draft of local brew is a more sustainable choice.

PREP TIP
✦
BEER DIVERSITY

Though mostly water, beer's primary ingredients include malted cereal grains, yeast, and hops. It is the unique combination of these—Which grain is used? Is the malt light or dark? Is fermentation slow or fast, hot or cold? How much hops? What type of yeast?—that determines a beer's strength, bitterness, and color, from pale ale to nut brown to stout. Recent years have seen a growing interest in artisan beers and microbrews, which are as challenging and interesting to pair with food as wine.

COFFEE

Coffee is a tropical evergreen shrub that grows in mountainous regions between the tropics of Cancer and Capricorn. Roasted coffee beans were first brewed into a beverage on the Arabian Peninsula around A.D. 1000. The practice spread throughout the Arab world in the 15th century as an alternative to drinking alcohol, prohibited under Islamic rule. Some historians argue that we have coffee to thank for the Enlightenment, the dramatic flourishing of Western thought that occurred during the 17th century. The French Revolution first percolated in a coffeehouse, and in these gathering places individuals from different backgrounds came together to socialize and exchange new ideas, under the stimulating influence of this naturally caffeinated beverage. Coffee drinking fueled commerce and became part of the rituals of business, and coffee is currently the second-largest traded commodity after crude oil.

Choose and Use

Beans labeled arabica are usually grown by organic and fair-trade coffee producers. A Fair Trade certification guarantees that the people who grow and pick your coffee beans have been paid a fair price, and that ethical labor practices have been followed. Fair-trade guidelines also require a limit on the use of pesticides and fertilizers in coffee production, and reduced impact on native plant and animal species. Avoid coffee labeled robusta, which is often of inferior quality and grown in environmentally damaging ways. You can purchase preground coffee or buy the beans and grind it yourself for maximum flavor. The finer the grind, the stronger the coffee; dense espresso, typically savored in small amounts, requires a very fine grind. Fresh beans yield the best flavor, so purchase in small amounts and store away from light in a cool, dry place—refrigeration or freezing does it no favors.

GIVES YOU

Riboflavin
Pantothenic acid
Potassium
Manganese
Magnesium
Phytonutrients
   (phenolic acids)

FOOD SCIENCE
✦
CAFFEINE

The myriad health benefits of coffee are due in part to its caffeine. Mildly addictive, the caffeine content varies depending on preparation as well as type and roast. Brewed coffee generally includes 150-200 mg in a 12-ounce serving, about the same amount of caffeine in a 2-ounce espresso shot; instant coffee contains about 100-150 mg.

For Your Health

According to a 2005 study by researchers at the University of Scranton, Pennsylvania, coffee is the top source of powerful phenolic antioxidants in the U.S. diet, studies have shown that moderate coffee intake (two to four cups a day) may reduce the risk of liver cancer and gallbladder disease, improve alertness and concentration, and increase longevity. Caffeine itself is part of the healthful mix coffee provides, although decaf still includes the same range of antioxidants and phytonutrients and avoids potential insomnia and jitters that occur in some people. Good quality decaf tastes just as rich as caffeinated varieties. "Instant" coffees offer equivalent benefits, if not the same flavor, as fresh brewed. Many coffee-based drinks have added sugar and saturated fats, which considerably reduce the health benefits of this beverage.

For Our Planet

The world's thirst for coffee has led to monoculture plantations and severe environmental degradation in regions where this crop is grown. Swaths of rain forest land, essential to the biodiversity of the region and health of the planet, have been slashed and burned to clear land for more coffee plants. The fair trade movement offers economic incentives and training to encourage environmentally sustainable farming methods. Choosing Fair Trade Certified coffee helps support these efforts. Coffee that's certified "shade grown" by the Smithsonian Institution is the most sustainable.

MILK

Cave paintings depicting cows being milked offer proof that animal milk has been part of the human diet for thousands of years. People around the world consume milk from goats, camels, reindeer, llamas, sheep, and water buffalos, but cow's milk is the most popular, especially in the United States. European dairy cows were first brought to North America on Spanish ships during the 15th century. The inventions of two French scientists made the modern dairy industry possible: pasteurization, a high-heat process that kills harmful pathogens, and homogenization, which breaks up milk fats to keep them from separating and rising to the top as cream.

In 1993, the U.S. Food and Drug Administration (FDA) approved the practice of injecting dairy cows with an artificially produced growth hormone (recombinant bovine somatotropin, rBST and abbreviated BST, also known as rBGH), which increases milk production by 25 percent. Whether milk from BST-treated cows should be labeled, and whether BST adversely affects human health, is an ongoing controversy; organic dairy farms often choose to label their products "BST-free." Cow's milk is available in many varieties and can be made into a range of dairy products, including butter, yogurt, sour cream, and—most delicious of all—cheese, which first came about as a means of preserving milk during periods when animals were not lactating.

FOOD SCIENCE ✦ DAIRY ALTERNATIVES

While an excellent source of protein and calcium, the majority of the world's population is lactose intolerant. A wide array of non-dairy beverages is available, including soy, almond, rice, and coconut to name a few. Fortified alternatives often provide similar nutrition to cow's milk and have a lower environmental impact.

GIVES YOU

100 PERCENT
GRASS-FED COW'S MILK:

Iodine
Vitamin D
Calcium
Riboflavin
Phosphorus
Vitamin B12
Protein
Selenium
fatty acids
Magnesium
Phosphorus
Zinc
Potassium
Pantothenic acid
Vitamin A
Phytonutrients
   (carotenoids,
   isoflavones)

Choose and Use

The healthiest milk is from cows that have been pastured and grass-fed, so choose this whenever it is available. As a beverage, low-fat milk is most popular, but nonfat (skim) milk is a better choice for limiting saturated fat and saving a few calories. Used judiciously in cooking, whole milk, half-and-half,

and cream add richness to soups and sauces. Ultrapasteurized boxed milk, popular in Europe and increasingly in the United States, can be stored without refrigeration. Foods rich in oxalate and phytates, which occur naturally in foods like spinach, berries, and grains, can inhibit calcium absorption somewhat, but there is no need to limit these foods if you are eating a varied diet with adequate calcium.

For Your Health

Fortified with vitamins A and D, U.S. cow's milk is a natural source of bone-strengthening calcium among a large set of vitamins, minerals, and phytonutrients. Conjugated linoleic acid (CLA) in milk has been associated with many health benefits, mostly in animal research, including immune system support and reduced body fat. Milk from grass-fed cows contains from two to five times as much CLA as milk from cows fed on hay and grain, as well as a higher content of omega-3 fatty acids. It also features a more balanced fat composition, with less of the saturated fatty acid often associated with heart disease.

✦ TAKE AWAY

Choose nonfat milk or dairy alternatives for a rich source of calcium and other nutrients.

A growing interest in minimally processed foods has led to a surge in raw milk consumption. Raw milk is more likely to contain potentially fatal pathogens, and children are particularly vulnerable due to their developing immune systems. Do your health a favor by sticking to pasteurized milk.

For Our Planet

The 100,000 farms that constitute the U.S. dairy industry currently account for 2 percent of total greenhouse gas emissions due to methane-producing cows. In 2013, the U.S. Department of Agriculture and American dairy producers renewed an agreement to reduce emissions by 25 percent and increase the sustainability of the dairy industry in the years to come. Environmental scientists stress the importance of smaller herd sizes and the value of grass in making milk a more earth-friendly beverage.

SPIRITS

The production of spirits, or distilled alcoholic beverages, depends upon fermentation. Organic (meaning, carbon-containing) materials containing carbohydrates naturally decompose, or ferment. When the ethyl alcohol produced by this process is heated, and the resulting vapor is condensed, the distilled condensation has a high alcohol content. The two ingredients essential to fermentation, carbohydrates and yeast, occur everywhere; as a result, civilizations all over the world have developed their own forms of alcoholic beverages.

The earliest spirits were made from grapes and honey, but eventually people used corn, rice, barley, and even potatoes to produce distilled "hard" alcohol. From the beginning, distilled spirits have served many purposes, from recreational to medical. Brandy made from distilled wine and rum from sugarcane molasses helped placate sailors during long sea voyages during the age of exploration from the 15th to the early 17th century. Grog, a mixture of rum, water, and lemon or lime juice, was a compulsory beverage for British sailors in the late 18th century. The vitamin C in the citrus helped reduce the incidence of scurvy. Today, spirits such as vodka (Russia), ouzo (Greece), tequila (Mexico), and scotch (Scotland) are all infused with deep cultural associations related to their countries of origin.

Choose and Use

Hard alcohol production is subject to many controls. Made from the blue agave plant, all tequila is imported from Mexico. Also strictly regulated, whiskey is made from fermented grain mash and aged in wooden casks. Different varieties of whisky, such as Scotch and bourbon, are produced in specific geographic locations (Scotland and Kentucky, respectively)

PAIRINGS
✦
SIPPING SPIRITS

Similar to tasting wine, sipping spirits is an art that includes examining the color, observing the liquid drip down the sides of the glass after a swirl (its "legs"), breathing in the aroma, and taking a small sip that rolls around your tongue. Most importantly? Enjoy.

and are subject to different processes and ingredients. Gin and vodka are among the most popular types of clear spirits; vodka is neutral in flavor, whereas the taste of gin comes from juniper berries and can vary greatly depending on the herbs and other ingredients used in its production. Firmly capped and stored in a cool, dark place, spirits keep indefinitely. Hard liquor has a far higher alcohol content than beer or wine and should be enjoyed sparingly. Spirits may be savored on their own or mixed with other components in a cocktail. Rum and sweet liqueurs are also popular flavorings in desserts.

For Your Health
The health benefits of moderate drinking are well documented: alcohol can help prevent heart attacks and strokes and raise "good" high-density lipoprotein (HDL) cholesterol levels. Per ounce, distilled spirits have more calories than beer or wine, so moderation is key. Generally, equivalent alcohol doses are obtained from 1.5 ounces of liquor, 12 ounces of beer, and 5 ounces of wine. The number of calories in hard alcohol is correlated with its "proof" (200 proof is 100 percent alcohol)—the higher the proof, the more calories. Liquor is often blended with fruit juices and other types of alcohol, so the final calorie count for a single cocktail can be substantial. Mixing water, soda, or tonic water with spirits is a lower-calorie choice.

For Our Planet
The distillation process uses large amounts of water and energy, though some producers now convert waste products into fuel. On the whole, the alcoholic beverage industry sets fewer sustainability goals than other industries, but the sustainable spirit movement is gaining ground. Seek out micro-distilleries in your area, and investigate producers that get high marks for sustainable practices.

GIVES YOU
Certain varieties of hard liquor contain trace amounts of vitamins and minerals. However, since these amounts are very small and alcohol should only be consumed in limited amounts, spirits offer virtually no known nutritional benefits beyond their alcohol content.

TEAS AND INFUSIONS: GREEN, BLACK, HERBAL

After water, tea is the second most popular drink in the world. Both green and black teas are made from the glossy leaves and leaf buds of a shrub called Camellia sinensis, related to the ornamental camellia and native to India and China. While botanically identical, black tea is prepared from fermented tea leaves and contains more caffeine and tannins than unfermented green tea.

Tea became a daily drink in China around the third century B.C., and several centuries later the Chinese introduced it to Japan. Made with boiled water, tea provided a sanitary beverage in places with dubious water quality. Preparing and drinking matcha, or powdered green tea, became a highly ritualized ceremony in Japanese culture. Trade relations with China introduced tea to the Europeans in the 17th century. This stimulating beverage has been credited with fueling the Industrial Revolution by keeping the laboring classes, who formerly drank weak beer throughout the day, more alert at their tasks.

PREP TIP ✦ STEEPING

In some parts of the world, drinking tea is a daily ritual. Critical to a splendid cup of tea or herbal infusion, steeping is an important step that differs by variety; whether the leaves were loose or prepackaged also matters. To steep the perfect cup, follow the instructions carefully. If you're planning on making iced tea, you'll want to brew a stronger pot to allow for the diluting effect when the ice melts.

Choose and Use

Available loose or in bags, tea tastes good both hot and cold, served plain or with lemon and lightly sweetened with sugar or honey. Home-brewed teas are healthier than bottled, which often contain added calories and sugar and excess packaging. From delicate Darjeeling from India to England's Earl Grey, there are thousands of varieties; experiment to find a tea you love.

For Your Health

Green tea has a higher concentration of certain flavonoids than black tea. The most abundant is a catechin called epigallocatechin-3-gallate (EGCG), believed to be responsible for most of green tea's antioxidant and anticancer properties. These include the prevention of atherosclerosis and hypertension; protection against pediatric brain tumors, and geriatric cognitive decline, Alzheimer's, and Parkinson's disease; improved weight loss and bone density; and prevention of prostate, ovarian, and many other cancers. A 2006 study published in the Journal of the American Medical Association showed that drinking green tea lowers one's risk of death from all causes, especially cardiovascular disease. Results of this study were more pronounced in women than in men.

Black tea can reduce the risk of stroke, and its antibacterial qualities guard against cavities and gum disease. Flavonoids remain in decaffeinated teas, so feel free to switch to decaf later in the day. Herbal teas have been less studied, but health claims are likely in concert with their food source, potential benefits ranging from aiding digestion to promoting lactation.

For Our Planet

Tea farming raises a number of social and environmental issues. Acreage devoted to tea cultivation limits regional biodiversity and contributes to soil erosion and water pollution. Purchasing Fair Trade Certified and organically grown tea helps make this a more sustainable beverage. Compost your old tea bags and used leaves; loose tea requires less packaging than tea in bags.

GIVES YOU

HERBAL:
Health benefits depend upon the substance being infused, but they have lower concentrations of antioxidants than black or green tea. Most are caffeine-free, but beware that some commercially produced teas are black or green tea flavored with herbs and contain caffeine.

GREEN:
Phytonutrients
(flavonoids,
phenolic acids)
catechins for both
Fluoride

BLACK:
Phytonutrients
(flavonoids,
phenolic acids)

WATER

Water is an essential nutrient, the basis of all life on Earth, and no civilization has survived without prioritizing this precious resource. On a planet covered with oceans, freshwater accounts for just 3 percent of the Earth's water supply, and two-thirds of it is frozen in glaciers or otherwise inaccessible. The available freshwater is unevenly distributed around the planet, and much is polluted or unsustainably managed. Agriculture soaks up 70 percent of the world's freshwater use, but 60 percent of this is wasted due to leaky and inefficient irrigation systems. At current rates of overconsumption, our freshwater reserves are being depleted twice as fast as the growing global population rate. By 2025, diminishing water supplies will likely impact two-thirds of the Earth's peoples and pit the needs of communities against industry, rich against poor, state against state, and nation against nation. We have yet to reach a global consensus about how to conserve and manage the world's water supply. However, people everywhere agree that water scarcity represents one of the greatest challenges of this century.

CONSIDER ✦ DESERT AGRICULTURE

Essential for human life, water is also fundamental to a country's economic stability given its critical role in food production. Many countries with arid regions or deserts face water shortages that threaten food security. An increase in severe weather due to climate change further strains this precious natural resource.

GIVES YOU

Drinking water collected from aquifers, lakes, and rivers contains a range of minerals, including calcium and magnesium, present in varying quantities, depending on the source and location. Water contains no protein, carbohydrates, fat, or fiber.

Choose and Use

Approximately half the bottled water sold in the United States comes from municipal water supplies. Those concerned about water quality should know that bottled water may actually contain more contaminants than tap water. Whereas 90 percent of U.S. tap water must meet strict Environmental Protection Agency (EPA) regulations for water quality, the bottled water industry is largely unmonitored. It takes about three liters of water to create one liter of bottled water: Fill up a BPA-free reusable bottle from your tap to conserve precious water resources and keep plastic bottles out of the landfill. Install a filter on your faucet if contaminants are a concern where you live. Approximately 15 percent of Americans rely on private wells for their drinking water, which are not subject to EPA standards.

Water from the tap should be your go-to beverage of choice to meet your nutritional needs, but there's little evidence to support the oft-repeated dictum to drink eight glasses of water a day. Among healthy individuals, it's best to listen to your body: when you're thirsty, drink. Downing a tall glass of water 30

✦ TAKE AWAY

Satisfy your thirst with tap water for a sustainable drink filled with nutrients.

minutes before a meal can help with weight loss, since you will feel full and may eat less. However, drinking a lot of water during meals may interfere with the digestive process. About eighty percent of one's daily water requirements come from beverages like water, coffee, tea, and juice and the rest from food.

Sports drinks such as Gatorade have been developed to help athletes to quickly rehydrate and replace electrolytes and carbohydrates, as well as the potassium and sodium lost through sweating. Recently, coconut water has been touted as "nature's sports drink." This healthy and low-calorie beverage includes vitamins, minerals, and antioxidants and can help correct a potassium deficiency. However, those who exercise strenuously require the additional sodium that most traditional sports drinks contain. Markets sell many premixed flavorings for water, in liquid and powder form. Water may also be "enhanced" with various vitamins, minerals, and even caffeine, but many of these drinks contain additional calories. Pure, clean water is best enjoyed in its natural state, or with a wedge of lemon, a slice of cucumber, or a sprig of mint.

For Your Health

Water is essential to health. All our bodily functions depend upon water. Among its myriad benefits, it helps maintain blood pressure, improves mental performance, eliminates toxins from our bodies in conjunction with the liver, increases athletic performance, and aids in digestion. Water provides the most nutrients with the least amount of calories. Since the 1950s, fluoride has been added to drinking water in many U.S. municipalities to protect against tooth decay. Fluoridation is considered one of the top 10 public health achievements of the 20th century, although some claim that adding fluoride, a naturally occurring element in soil and water, is harmful to our health. Most developed nations do not fluoridate their water, and voters in some cities have rejected fluoridation.

For Our Planet

Bottling water uses energy and creates waste. Boxed water may soon replace bottled as a more environmentally friendly alternative, but filling up a reusable container with tap water is still the most sustainable option. In 2010, federal policies were established to help promote sustainability in the U.S. water infrastructure, requiring the government to partner with state and local agencies to ensure a clean, safe, and plentiful water supply.

FOOD SCIENCE
✦
BOTTLED WATER

While convenient, drinking bottled water is not the greenest choice: it takes about 3 liters of water to create 1 liter of bottled water. Research has shown that most tap water is just as tasty as bottled so assuming your water is safe, using your tap is the top choice for the planet. It's best to bring your own reusable bottle that can be refilled when on the road.

WINE

The roots of winemaking reach back many thousands of years into human history. A biblical story has Noah landing on Mt. Ararat after the flood and immediately planting grapevines. This alcoholic beverage may be even older than beer, as evidenced by stains inside vessels dating from the Neolithic period (8500–4000 B.C.). From early on, wine was employed in religious ceremonies, and better-tasting wines were reserved for the elite social classes.

The naturally fermented juice of grapes, wine is easier to make than beer but more difficult to store. A true art and science of winemaking had to wait until the mass production of glass bottles in the 19th century. Until recently, only a limited number of regions were known for winemaking. Today, vineyards producing excellent wines exist throughout the world.

✦ TAKE AWAY

Enjoy wine in moderate amounts to help prevent heart disease.

GIVES YOU

RED WINE:

Phytonutrients
(stilbene, flavonoids,
phenolic acid,
resveratrol)
Manganese
Iron
Magnesium
Phosphorus
Potassium

Choose and Use

Most modern supermarkets stock a wide range of red, white,
rosé, sparkling, and dessert (sweet) wines. A wine merchant can
offer suggestions about which varieties best complement certain foods. The best advice, though, is be guided by your own
tastes. It is far better to enjoy yourself than to fret over choosing
the right combination of wine and food. Store unopened wine
in a cool, dark place. Bottled wine should be kept on its side
to prevent the cork from drying out. Some wines must be aged

FOOD SCIENCE ✦ FERMENTATION

Grape juice becomes wine through fermentation, in which added yeasts reacts
with sugars from the grapes to create alcohol (specifically, ethyl alcohol).
Temperature, speed, oxygen, and the container used for fermentation all
impact the nature and character of the wine. The same grape can produce
drastically different wines depending on how it's fermented, as anyone who's
compared a California chardonnay, produced in oak barrels, with a French
Chablis (also the chardonnay grape), produced in stainless steel casks.

for a few years under proper conditions to achieve their full potential; however, many don't age well and are best consumed soon after purchase. Red wines are usually best served at cooler room temperatures (roughly 60 degrees). White wines should be refrigerated before serving and stored in the fridge after opening. Wines intended for use in cooking should be good enough to drink.

PREP TIP ✦ WINE PAIRING

Classic advice on pairing wine with food was overly simple: white wine with seafood or vegetables, red wine with beef, and either with poultry depending on preparation. There is considerable variation among red and white wines, however, and finding the best match to your particular dish can be a challenge. If you're not an expert, many agree to just drink what you enjoy.

Terroir comes from the French word terre, meaning "land" or "earth." Generally referring to climate, geography, and geology of a particular place, it's a term used to characterize differences among wines. Even within the same variety of grape, the smell, taste, and color of wine varies markedly due to terroir—as well as the style and specific ingredients of the winemaker.

For Your Health

A polyphenol called resveratrol present in red wine may help repair blood vessels, prevent blood clots, and reduce "bad" low-density lipoprotein (LDL) cholesterol, although most research is in animal models consuming very high doses. Resveratrol resides in the grape skins, which give wine its red color. The skins also contain many of the bioflavonoids and phenols from which wine's health benefits derive, which is why purple grape juice shares some of its health properties. Research shows that moderate consumption of alcohol helps prevent heart disease; resveratrol may provide additional benefit, but wines of all varieties and colors are beneficial due to their alcohol content.

For Our Planet

Wine is shipped all over the world, but the largest component of its carbon footprint is packaging (predominantly glass bottles and corks), which accounts for 46 percent of wine's total carbon emissions. Wine grapes tend to grow in marginal-quality farmland, thus making good economic use of low-yield land. Grapevines are tough plants that don't necessarily require pesticides or fertilizers to thrive. In fact, vines grown in mediocre soil that lacks water produce smaller grapes. A higher skin-to-juice ratio is desirable for wine grapes, since most flavor components are concentrated in the skin. Composting the pressed skins and seeds back into the vineyard preserves the terroir—the unique character of a place that distinguishes the wine's flavor.

✦ TAKE AWAY

Wine, especially red, may offer more than a pleasing meal accompaniment.

SEASONINGS

A BRIEF HISTORY OF SPICES

Added to foods to intensify or improve their flavors, seasonings include herbs and spices as well as condiments. They have been considered important enough to wage wars over, and the human desire for them has proved stronger than our fear of the unknown. The demand for spices, in particular, has fueled great voyages of discovery, carved out intercontinental trade routes, and sparked armed conflicts. Spices have commanded astronomical prices, and they have been regarded as valuable enough to serve as currency at various times in history: cumin seeds were accepted as tithe, and people have paid their rent in peppercorns.

The story of spices typically begins in the Eastern Hemisphere, but in the Americas the Aztecs, Mayans, and Incas used seasonings as well. Besides enlivening bland or tainted foods, spices were valued in early cultures for their medicinal properties. They were used as antidotes for poisons and to cure disease and prevent illness. Ancient people invested certain spices with magical properties and used them in religious ceremonies to commemorate major life events such as births, marriages, and deaths.

The Role of Seasonings in Health

Today seasonings are still highly valued, less expensive, and available in supermarkets, specialty stores, or online. Used extensively to enhance the flavor of many processed foods, salt is an example of a seasoning that is cheap and plentiful today, but which was once one of the most valuable commodities on earth. Unlike other seasonings, salt is essential for human health, but our current craving for it far surpasses our body's daily requirement of this mineral. Introducing a wider range of herbs and spices into the foods we prepare may help wean our palates away from salt and help us limit our sodium intake. Many consumers think of herbs and spices as a means to add a bit of color, flavor, or heat to a dish without adding salt, fat, or calories; however, some seasonings have antioxidant levels that rival those of fruits and vegetables when regularly added to the diet. Current scientific research often bears out ancient beliefs and traditional medical practices, such as those in Ayurvedic and Chinese medicine, about the health benefits of herbs and spices.

The New American Palate

The increasing diversity of the North American population has led to a growing demand for a wider array of seasonings. Latinos now represent the largest-growing immigrant group, followed by Asians, bringing with them a taste for the flavors of home. The United States is the world's largest spice importer and consumer. Most supermarkets now devote an extensive amount of shelf space to "ethnic" ingredients from different world cultures, and seasonings once considered exotic have become commonplace. Half of the spices shipped to the U.S. come from India, Mexico, Indonesia, Canada, and China. Fresh herbs rarely travel well, but their seeds do. Herbs native to one global region become immigrants, too, taking root in new corners of the world, lending their flavors to local cuisines. Finally, a growing interest in healthy eating and "natural" methods of disease prevention have inspired many to learn about the nutritional benefits of seasonings.

BASIL

Highly fragrant basil is rich in bone-building vitamin K. The herb contains an array of volatile oils that help protect against unwanted bacterial growth, making this a beneficial additive to uncooked foods. The flavonoids present in basil help protect cell structures as well as chromosomes from radiation and oxygen-based damage. Best tasting when fresh, basil leaves should be added at the end of the cooking process to preserve their flavor. This summertime plant will flourish in a sunny windowsill garden, and growing your own means you can avoid buying it packaged in plastic. An abundance of basil can be made into traditional pesto, with the addition of ground pine nuts, garlic, Parmesan cheese and olive oil. During summer's bounty, make some extra and freeze to enjoy during winter months.

BLACK PEPPER

Found on every table in the country, pepper was once used as currency, and a man's wealth was measured by his supply of it. Black, green, and white peppercorns, which are ground to make pepper, are the fruit of the same tropical vine (though pink peppercorns are not) and reflect different stages of development and processing methods. Black pepper stimulates the taste buds and signals the stomach to secrete hydrochloric acid, which promotes digestion. It contains manganese, vitamin K, and iron, and works as a carminitive to help prevent the formation of intestinal gas. Green peppercorns are most likely to be found preserved in a pickle brine and are used in a quite different way from black or white pepper. The world's first sustainable black pepper was produced in Indonesia in 2013. The Rainforest Alliance Certified black peppercorns are grown in a manner that promotes biodiversity and reduces the use of pesticides and chemicals.

CAYENNE PEPPER

CILANTRO

Cayenne pepper is a spicy, orange-red powder made from a tropical chili pepper belonging to the Capsicum genus. Its warm color signals the presence of beta-carotene, an anti-oxidant that the body converts into vitamin A. Capsaicin, the volatile oil that gives cayenne pepper its heat, is widely used as a topical treatment for pain relief. Cayenne also has been shown to have cardiovascular benefits. Cultures where large quantities of chili peppers are consumed experience lower rates of heart attack and stroke. Cayenne has also proven effective in ulcer prevention. Surveys have shown that Chinese patients suffer from three times more gastric ulcers than Indians and Malaysians, who regularly consume chili peppers. Cayenne pepper also rapidly drains congested nasal passages by stimulating mucus membranes. International efforts to make spice production less damaging to biodiversity may soon result in sustainable cayenne pepper.

This ancient spice, mentioned in the Old Testament, is known by two names. Its fresh green leaves are called cilantro; the seeds of the plant (available whole or ground into powder) are known as coriander, and neither tastes like the other. Cilantro has a strong flavor (some say soapy) well suited to highly seasoned foods common in Indian and Mexican cuisine. Rich in beneficial phytonutrients, cilantro leaves are sometimes confused with those of Italian flat-leaf parsley. They belong to the same plant family but are not at all similar in flavor. When incorporated into uncooked foods, such as salsas, cilantro acts as a natural antibacterial to kill salmonella. Coriander seeds have a mild, aromatic character and are used in pickling and curry blends. Guidelines established by the Sustainable Spice Initiative (SSI) will soon be extended to coriander/cilantro, along with the other culinary spices recognized by the European Spice Association (ESA).

CINNAMON

CUMIN

Cinnamon is made from the inner bark of a tropical evergreen tree. Harvested when pliable, it is dried and ground to form the powdered spice sold in stores, or left in rolled tubes called quills and packaged as "sticks." Cinnamon's healing properties come from essential oils found in the bark and include preventing the growth of unwanted pathogens in food, limiting unwanted blood clotting, and reducing blood sugar levels in individuals with type 2 diabetes. The scent of cinnamon alone has been shown to boost brain functioning. Of more than one hundred varieties, the most commonly available types are Ceylon and Chinese cinnamon. Wonderful in many sweet baked goods, cinnamon is also often used in savory North African and Middle Eastern dishes, adding warmth and depth. Like bamboo, cinnamon is an inherently sustainable crop, which grows naturally without the aid of agrochemicals. The first Rainforest Alliance Certified cinnamon became available in 2013.

Native to Egypt, cumin was very popular in Europe during the Middle Ages and is used today in many Middle Eastern, Indian, and Mexican dishes. Available as both "seeds" and in powdered form, this aromatic spice is made from the fruit of a plant in the parsley family. The amber variety is most common, but white and black cumin seeds may also be found in specialty markets. Rich in iron, cumin blends well with curries and in chili. Traditionally, cumin seeds have long been recognized as a digestive aid, a belief supported by recent studies indicating that this spice stimulates digestive enzymes in the pancreas. Ground cumin will keep in a cool, dark place for six months. Whole seeds stay fresh twice as long. Sustainable Spice Initiative (SSI) guidelines will help ensure that this spice will be produced more sustainably in the future.

DILL

GINGER

Mentioned in the Bible as well as in ancient Egyptian writings, dill has long been valued for its curative properties. Both the leaves and seeds are used as seasoning, though the seeds have a stronger flavor. Dill, especially the seed, is a good source of calcium, which helps prevent bone loss. Monoterpenes in this herb's oils make dill a "chemoprotective" food, which can help neutralize certain carcinogens. Flavonoids in this plant also provide beneficial components. Dill's wispy green leaves are frequent additions to Russian and Scandinavian foods. Fresh is superior to dried in flavor. Dill seeds can soothe the stomach after meals, so keep a small dish on the table. Organic dill is widely available, and this plant may be easily grown in a kitchen herb garden.

Ginger root is the underground rhizome of the ginger plant. This versatile spice has an aromatic and spicy flavor well suited to both sweet and savory dishes. Ginger is especially popular in Asian dishes, where it is often paired with garlic. As a home health remedy, ginger has long been used to relieve the symptoms of motion sickness and nausea, but clinical studies have proven inconclusive. The root also contains anti-inflammatory compounds called gingerols, which can diminish the pain and swelling associated with arthritis. Fresh ginger must be refrigerated; unpeeled, it should keep for three weeks. The light brown skin is usually removed with a paring knife before grating or chopping the flesh. Powdered ginger root is often added to baked goods. Organizations such as Sustainable Harvest International are encouraging more farmers in countries such as Belize to produce sustainable, organically grown ginger.

MINT

Mint is an ancient herb, long prized for its culinary and medicinal properties. Many varieties exist, including peppermint and spearmint, and its cooling, aromatic flavor may be used to enhance both sweet and savory dishes. Peppermint oil has been shown to soothe the digestive system, relieving indigestion and the symptoms of irritable bowel syndrome, although it may negatively affect people with heartburn or gastroesophageal reflux disease (GERD). A 2010 study of antioxidants in 3,100 foods, beverages, and seasonings placed peppermint at the top of the list of culinary herbs for its antioxidant content. Mint leaves are also infused into an aromatic herbal tea, a traditional beverage prepared to welcome guests in the Middle East. Fresh mint leaves have a vibrant green color. Refrigerated, they will keep for several days, wrapped in a dampened paper towel inside a loosely closed plastic bag. Mint will thrive in a kitchen garden; growing your own reduces packaging waste.

MUSTARD

The mustard plant is a member of the mighty *Brassicaceae* family, which includes broccoli, cabbage, and Brussels sprouts. Like its cruciferous relations, mustard contains certain beneficial phytonutrients called glucosinolates that may help guard against gastrointestinal (specifically, colorectal) and possibly lung cancers. Mustard seeds are sold whole, ground into powder, or processed with other ingredients and spices into a yellow or brown paste called "prepared mustard." Mustard seeds are available in colors ranging from white and yellow to brown and black, with varying degrees of spiciness. Mixing mustard powder with water prompts an enzymatic reaction that enhances the heat and pungent flavor of this popular spice, creating a homemade version of the familiar supermarket condiment. Guidelines established by the Sustainable Spice Initiative (SSI) will help make sustainable mustard seed available in the future.

OREGANO

PARSLEY

An aromatic herb with gray-green oval leaves often featured in Mediterranean cooking, oregano was little known in the United States until after World War I, when American GIs returning from Italy brought word of it back home with them. Derived from the Greek meaning "mountain joy," oregano is native to northern Europe, where this plant is sometimes called wild marjoram, to distinguish it from its cousin, sweet marjoram. The volatile oils thymol and carvacrol, both antibacterials, are present in oregano, and oregano oil can help fight MRSA (strains of antibiotic-resistant bacteria) and staph infections. Italian, Greek, or Mexican varieties of this herb taste delicious with tomato-based Italian dishes; many recipes call for dried, but fresh oregano offers greater health benefits though more must be used to impart the same flavor. Sonoran oregano, grown and harvested by the Seri Indians, is a sustainable crop.

Once relegated to mere garnish status on American plates, fresh parsley is rich in vitamins K, C, and A and lends its bright, grassy flavor to various foods. Originally used as a medicine in ancient cultures, the herb contains volatile oils and flavonoids, both highly beneficial to human health. The two most commonly available varieties are curly parsley and the milder flavored flat-leaf Italian type. Immerse stems in a jar of water and store in the fridge, loosely covered with a plastic bag; fresh parsley will keep for quite awhile this way, if you refresh the water every few days. Fresh is best; this herb loses its flavor quickly when dried. Plant parsley in a sunny windowbox, and you'll always have fresh leaves at hand.

ROSEMARY

SAGE

This flowering evergreen shrub is native to the Mediterranean, where it has been prized since ancient times for both culinary and medicinal uses. Recent studies suggest that smelling rosemary improves long-term memory and brain function, which may explain why, in ancient Greece, students wore rosemary sprigs in their hair while studying for exams. As is true of many herbs, fresh rosemary is superior to dried. Most recipes use the plant's narrow, gray-green leaves, which are easily stripped from the stems. This herb's assertive flavor pairs well with lamb and other meats, as well as chicken and fish. You can grow your own rosemary, or choose organically grown using sustainable farming methods.

Long revered for its culinary and medicinal properties, the name of this herb derives from the Latin word *slavere*, meaning "to be saved." The lance-shaped, silvery green leaves of the sage plant are an excellent memory enhancer; a British study conducted in 2003 demonstrated that essential oil from sage may enhance memory in healthy young adults. The dried root of certain varieties of this herb contains active compounds similar to pharmaceuticals developed to treat Alzheimer's disease. Sage is also a source of beneficial flavonoids, phenolic acids, and enzymes with antioxidant and anti-inflammatory properties. Fresh sage leaves will keep for a few days in the refrigerator; dried sage leaves are also used to lend depth of flavor to soups and stews. Growing your own sage keeps those plastic herb packages out of the landfill.

THYME

TURMERIC

Native to southern Europe and the Mediterranean, this delicate-looking herb has a penetrating flavor and was historically associated with bravery. Widely used in cooking, thyme also has a long history as a treatment for respiratory problems and is a good source of vitamin K for bone health. Thymol, the primary volatile oil in thyme, helps protect cellular membranes. The oils in thyme have been shown to limit microbial growth, so adding fresh thyme to a vinaigrette may help reduce any bacteria on salad greens. Fresh thyme and dried thyme are both widely available. Fresh thyme should be added to food toward the end of the cooking process, since heat causes a loss of flavor. Dried thyme can be added at the beginning. Thyme is a hardy plant that grows easily worldwide without the use of pesticides.

The root of a tropical plant related to ginger, this rhizome has multiple uses: as a textile dye, a spice, and a healing remedy. Ballpark mustard gets its bright yellow color from turmeric, and the spice lends its warm and bitter flavor to curry powder. Turmeric is an ancient spice native to Indonesia and southern India, used in traditional Ayurvedic and Chinese medicine. Turmeric's vivid color comes from curcumin, an antioxidant that may inhibit the growth of cancer cells by helping the body destroy mutated cancer cells. Many Indian recipes season cauliflower with powdered turmeric, a combination that may prevent prostate cancer and limit the spread of established cancers. The combination of turmeric and onions may afford protection against colorectal cancers. Sustainable turmeric cultivation can double a farmer's profit—an excellent incentive for sustainable production.

ABOUT THE AUTHORS

P. K. Newby, Sc.D., M.P.H.

Nutrition scientist, educator, food writer, and speaker, P. K. Newby has studied diet, chronic diseases, and sustainable eating for more than 15 years. She teaches in the Gastronomy, Culinary Arts, and Wine Studies program at Boston University and the program in Sustainability and Environmental Management at Harvard Extension School. She holds a doctorate from Harvard University's School of Public Health and master's degrees in public health and human nutrition from Columbia University. Newby shares sound science and fabulous cooking on her blog, *The Nutrition Doctor Is in the Kitchen: Where Science Is Sexy and Healthy Eating Is Spectacular.*

Barton Seaver

Chef, author, speaker, and National Geographic Fellow Barton Seaver is host of the National Geographic Web series Cook-Wise and is the director of the Healthy and Sustainable Food Program at the Center for Health and the Global Environment at the Harvard School of Public Health. A graduate of the Culinary Institute of America, he was named *Esquire* magazine's 2009 "Chef of the Year." In 2012 he was named by Secretary of State Hillary Clinton to the United States Culinary Ambassador Corps. He is the author of *For Cod & Country* and *Where There's Smoke: Simple, Sustainable, Delicious Grilling,* both published by Sterling Epicure.

CONTRIBUTING WRITERS

Monique Vescia
VEGETABLES | FATS AND OILS | BEVERAGES | SEASONINGS

Monique Vescia is a writer, dedicated home cook, and avid follower of foodie blogs. She has written on a range of subjects, including health, earth science, photography, and social networking. She lives in Seattle, one of the epicenters of the farm-to-table movement, with her husband and son, and raises bees in her backyard.

Katharine Greider
FRUITS | PROTEINS | WHOLE GRAINS

Katharine Greider is a freelance writer living in New York City. Her work has appeared in dozens of national and local publications. She is the author of two books, most recently *The Archaeology of Home: An Epic Set on a Thousand Square Feet of the Lower East Side* (PublicAffairs, 2011).

ILLUSTRATIONS CREDITS

ILLUSTRATIONS CREDITS

INDEX

NATIONAL GEOGRAPHIC
FOODS FOR HEALTH

Published by the National Geographic Society

John M. Fahey, *Chairman of the Board and Chief Executive Officer*

Declan Moore, *Executive Vice President; President, Publishing and Travel*

Melina Gerosa Bellows, *Executive Vice President; Chief Creative Officer, Books, Kids, and Family*

Prepared by the Book Division

Hector Sierra, *Senior Vice President and General Manager*

Janet Goldstein, *Senior Vice President and Editorial Director*

Jonathan Halling, *Design Director, Books and Children's Publishing*

Marianne R. Koszorus, *Design Director, Books*

Susan Tyler Hitchcock, *Senior Editor*

R. Gary Colbert, *Production Director*

Jennifer A. Thornton, *Director of Managing Editorial*

Susan S. Blair, *Director of Photography*

Meredith C. Wilcox, *Director, Administration and Rights Clearance*

Staff for This Book

Gail Spilsbury, *Project Editor*

Sanaa Akkach, *Art Director*

Uliana Bazar, *Illustrations Editor*

Grassroots Graphics, *Design and Production*

Marshall Kiker, *Associate Managing Editor*

Lisa A. Walker, *Production Manager*

Galen Young, *Rights Clearance Specialist*

Kate Olsen, *Production Design Assistant*

Erin Greenhalgh, *Editorial Intern*

Susan Nguyen, *Editorial Intern*

Developed and produced by Print Matters, Inc. (www.printmattersinc.com)

Production Services

Phillip L. Schlosser, *Senior Vice President*

Chris Brown, *Vice President, NG Book Manufacturing*

George Bounelis, *Vice President, Production Services*

Nicole Elliott, *Manager*

Rachel Faulise, *Manager*

Robert L. Barr, *Manager*

The National Geographic Society is one of the world's largest nonprofit scientific and educational organizations. Its mission is to inspire people to care about the planet. Founded in 1888, the Society is member supported and offers a community for members to get closer to explorers, connect with other members, and help make a difference. The Society reaches more than 450 million people worldwide each month through *National Geographic* and other magazines; National Geographic Channel; television documentaries; music; radio; films; books; DVDs; maps; exhibitions; live events; school publishing programs; interactive media; and merchandise. National Geographic has funded more than 10,000 scientific research, conservation, and exploration projects and supports an education program promoting geographic literacy. For more information, visit www.nationalgeographic.com.

National Geographic Society
1145 17th Street N.W.
Washington, D.C. 20036-4688 U.S.A.

For information about special discounts for bulk purchases, please contact National Geographic Books Special Sales: ngspecsales@ngs.org

For rights or permissions inquiries, please contact National Geographic Books Subsidiary Rights: ngbookrights@ngs.org

First paperback printing 2014

The Library of Congress has cataloged the hardcover edition as follows:
National Geographic Foods for health: choose and use the very best foods for your family and our planet / contributions by Barton Seaver and P.K. Newby.
  p.cm.
 Includes index.
 ISBN 978-1-4262-1332-8 (hardcover : alk. paper) -- ISBN 978-1-4262-1333-5 (hardcover (deluxe) : alk. paper)
 1. Food. 2. Nutrition. 3. Functional foods. 4. Health promotion. 5. Consumer education.
 TX353.C6224 2013
 641.3--dc23
                                    2013026965

ISBN 978-1-4262-1332-8
ISBN 978-1-4262-1333-5 (deluxe)
ISBN 978-1-4262-1275-8 (paperback)

Printed in China

14/RRDS/1

SHAPE (AND FUEL!) YOUR FUTURE

with National Geographic Books

These essential resources provide the tips, advice, remedies, and recipes you need to be and stay healthy.

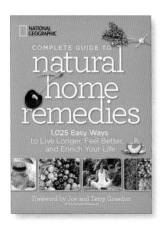

Packed with the power of nature and the ease of finding remedies on hand, this book combines the authority of science with age-old folklore and tried-and-true cures.

Tieraona Low Dog, M.D., integrative physician and expert in natural medicine, shares her favorite remedies and recipes to help you find milder, more natural ways to get well.

A guide to healing foods and home remedies reported to and verified by Joe and Terry Graedon, this book contains as much information as a voluminous encyclopedia, yet it's quick, easy, inviting, and fun to read!

Join Barton Seaver—master chef and National Geographic Explorer—on a year-round culinary adventure. With fascinating sidebars, profiles on real people, and cool facts, this book will have kids ruling the kitchen in no time!

FOR KIDS!

AVAILABLE WHEREVER BOOKS AND EBOOKS ARE SOLD

nationalgeographic.com/books

NATIONAL GEOGRAPHIC

Like us on Facebook: Nat Geo Books

Follow us on Twitter: @NatGeoBooks

LYMPHEDEMA

Books published by the American Cancer Society

A Breast Cancer Journey: Your Personal Guidebook, Second Edition

American Cancer Society Consumers Guide to Cancer Drugs, Second Edition, Wilkes and Ades

American Cancer Society's Complementary and Alternative Cancer Methods Handbook

American Cancer Society's Complete Guide to Colorectal Cancer, Levin et al.

American Cancer Society's Complete Guide to Prostate Cancer, Bostwick et al.

American Cancer Society's Guide to Pain Control: Understanding and Managing Cancer Pain, Revised Edition

Angels & Monsters: A child's eye view of cancer, Murray and Howard

Because...Someone I Love Has Cancer: Kids' Activity Book

Cancer in the Family: Helping Children Cope with a Parent's Illness, Heiney et al.

Cancer: What Causes It, What Doesn't

Caregiving: A Step-By-Step Resource for Caring for the Person with Cancer at Home, Revised Edition, Houts and Bucher

Coming to Terms with Cancer: A Glossary of Cancer-Related Terms, Laughlin

Couples Confronting Cancer: Keeping Your Relationship Strong, Fincannon and Bruss

Crossing Divides: A Couple's Story of Cancer, Hope, and Hiking Montana's Continental Divide, Bischke

Eating Well, Staying Well During and After Cancer, Bloch et al.

Good for You! Reducing Your Risk of Developing Cancer

Healthy Me: A Read-along Coloring & Activity Book, Hawthorne (illustrated by Blyth)

Informed Decisions: The Complete Book of Cancer Diagnosis, Treatment, and Recovery, Second Edition, Eyre, Lange, and Morris

Kicking Butts: Quit Smoking and Take Charge of Your Health

Our Mom Has Cancer, Ackermann and Ackermann

When the Focus Is on Care: Palliative Care and Cancer, Foley et al.

Also by the American Cancer Society

American Cancer Society's Healthy Eating Cookbook: A celebration of food, friends, and healthy living, Third Edition

Celebrate! Healthy Entertaining for Any Occasion

Kids' First Cookbook: Delicious-Nutritious Treats to Make Yourself!

LYMPHEDEMA

Understanding and Managing Lymphedema After Cancer Treatment

From the Experts
at the American
Cancer Society

Foreword by
SAM DONALDSON

Published by
American Cancer Society
Health Promotions
1599 Clifton Road NE
Atlanta, Georgia 30329, USA

Printed in the United States of America
Designed by Shock Design, Inc., Atlanta, Georgia

5 4 3 2 1   05 06 07 08 09

Library of Congress Cataloging-in-Publication Data

Lymphedema : understanding and managing lymphedema after cancer
    treatment : from the experts at the American Cancer Society ; fore-
    word by Sam Donaldson.
        p. cm.
    1. Lymphedema--Popular works.   2. Cancer--Treatment--Complica-
    tions--Popular works.   I. American Cancer Society.
    RC646.3.L966 2006
    616.4'2--dc22

                                                        2005018837

A NOTE TO THE READER

The information contained in this book is not intended as medical advice and should
not be relied upon as a substitute for talking with your doctor. This information may
not address all possible actions, treatments, medications, precautions, side effects, or
interactions. All matters regarding your health require the supervision of a medical
doctor or appropriate health care professional who is familiar with your medical needs.
For more information, contact your American Cancer Society at 800-ACS-2345 or
http://www.cancer.org.

Brief Contents

ADVISORY PANEL AND MEDICAL REVIEW

Terri Ades, APRN-BC, MS, AOCN, director of cancer information, Health Promotions, American Cancer Society, Atlanta, GA

Jane M. Armer, PhD, RN, associate professor, Sinclair School of Nursing; director of nursing research, Ellis Fischel Cancer Center, University of Missouri-Columbia, Columbia, MO

Andrea Cheville, MD, director of cancer rehabilitation, assistant professor of rehabilitation medicine, Abramson Family Cancer Research Institute, University of Pennsylvania, Philadelphia, PA

Joseph L. Feldman, MD, head of the division of physical medicine and rehabilitation, Evanston Northwestern Healthcare, Evanston, IL

Meg Hull PhD, RN, regulatory nurse coordinator, Research and Data Management, Greenebaum Cancer Center, Baltimore, MD

Christine Miaskowski, PhD, professor and chair, Department of Physiological Nursing, University of California-San Francisco School of Nursing, San Francisco, CA

Jeanne A. Petrek, MD, FACS, director of the surgical program, Evelyn H. Lauder Breast Center, Memorial Sloan-Kettering Cancer Center, New York, NY

Robert Smith, PhD, director of cancer screening, Cancer Control Science, American Cancer Society, Atlanta, GA

Bonnie Teschendorf, PhD, director of quality of life science, Cancer Control Science, American Cancer Society, Atlanta, GA

ADDITIONAL REVIEW

Scott Bischke, MS, caregiver for person with lymphedema, Bozeman, MT

Ted Gansler, MD, director of medical content, Health Promotions, American Cancer Society, Atlanta, GA

Kate Gibson, MS, person with lymphedema, Bozeman, MT

Kathy Windmoeller, MEd, EdS, person with lymphedema, Columbia, MO

EDITOR
Amy Brittain

MANAGING EDITOR
Gianna Marsella, MA

BOOK PUBLISHING MANAGER
Candace Magee

DIRECTOR, BOOK PUBLISHING
Len Boswell

STRATEGIC DIRECTOR, CONTENT
Chuck Westbrook

We would like to give special thanks to those who generously shared their personal experiences with lymphedema for use in this book.

CONTENTS

FOREWORD

SAM DONALDSON, ABC NEWS CORRESPONDENT

Most people haven't heard of lymphedema. Until 1995 I hadn't heard of it either. But after I had lymph node surgery for malignant melanoma I noticed swelling in my leg and doctors diagnosed me with lymphedema. Then my mother-in-law developed swelling in her arm after breast cancer surgery to her underarm lymph nodes. After fighting cancer, we both faced a new challenge: lymphedema.

Photograph ©ABC Photography Archives

Some cancer treatment affects the lymph system by disrupting lymph flow. This backup of fluid is called lymphedema. Lymphedema can cause swelling and other complications, and it can affect your overall health, your daily life, and your self- image, especially if it is severe.

Lymphedema can be treated but not cured. I'm lucky in that I can control my mild lymphedema by wearing a compression garment. If I don't wear it, I feel like I'm hauling around a vat of Jell-O on my leg. So every morning for the past 10 years I've put on a thick compression stocking that stretches from my toes to my groin. It prevents my leg from swelling and allows me to go about my daily life more comfortably.

Our understanding of lymphedema and the best ways to treat it are still evolving. Developments like compression garments have drastically improved how well people with lymphedema can function. As more attention is brought to the issue, treatment strategies will only improve. But we need to discover more—how to prevent lymphedema and how to cure it if it does occur.

It's important to support biomedical research into how we can cure and eradicate devastating illnesses. Increased awareness and funding for research are the keys to finding the answers we need. Because lymphedema has affected my family, medical research in this area is a personal priority. And we have reason to be optimistic. As more and more organizations and individuals push for lymphedema advancements and share knowledge, we open the door to breakthroughs and discovery that may change the way we think about lymphedema.

Through *Lymphedema: Understanding and Managing Lymphedema After Cancer Treatment*, the American Cancer Society focuses much-needed attention on this often-ignored condition. This book explains how you can work with health care professionals to obtain high-quality lymphedema care and explores how to cope with the physical and emotional challenges lymphedema can present. Whether you are at risk for or affected by lymphedema, this book provides the information and support you need.

Having lymphedema doesn't have to mean not doing the things you want to do, either personally or professionally. Lymphedema can be managed if you understand your risks, take proper precautions, and receive treatment from knowledgeable and qualified professionals. This outstanding resource from the experts at the American Cancer Society can help you do just that.

PREFACE

RUTH MCCORKLE, PhD, FAAN
The Florence S. Wald Professor of Nursing
Director, Center for Excellence in Chronic Illness Care
Yale University School of Nursing

Lifesaving treatments for cancer sometimes involve side effects that can disrupt patients' quality of life. One of these potential side effects is lymphedema. But despite the seriousness of lymphedema, it has long been neglected and ignored.

My personal experience with lymphedema began about eight months after I completed adjuvant chemotherapy and radiation following a lumpectomy and axillary node dissection for breast cancer. Lymphedema developed gradually; I could no longer wear a ring on my affected hand, my watchband was too tight, and I couldn't button my blouse at the wrist. My oncologist dismissed my symptoms. When I persisted in voicing my distress about what he diagnosed as "mild" lymphedema, I was referred to a hospital-based physical therapist to establish an exercise program. I was simply told to return if my symptoms became worse. I was discouraged and felt as though no one was listening.

Fortunately the timing of these events coincided with the annual Oncology Nursing Congress, where I found helpful information on lymphedema and was referred to a physical therapist in my local community who specialized in lymphedema. The therapist and I established a plan of care that included 10 weeks of structured care and self care. Within one month my arm was noticeably improved. My treatment over the following year included a comprehensive approach: a daily exercise regimen with stretching; arm bandaging; and a compression sleeve. Active participation in a support group with other women with lymphedema also helped me. I incorporated these management strategies into my daily routine for years. I continue to wear my compression sleeve during the day.

Prevention is an essential part of follow-up care. But while at-risk people can incorporate risk-reduction measures into their daily lives, even the most watchful person has no guarantee that lymphedema will not occur. In spite of my vigilance to protect my arm, twelve years later I had an episode that caught me unprepared. When I suddenly felt miserable and developed a fever with chills, I soon realized I had full-blown cellulitis. After a trip to the emergency room and three days of intravenous antibiotics in the hospital, I was discharged with a referral to a local lymphedema clinic. After daily compression bandages and manual lymph drainage, my arm returned to its pre-surgery size. The culprit had been a thin sliver from my son's pinewood derby car that I had removed, dismissed, and forgotten.

The American Cancer Society is dedicated to enhancing the quality of life of people confronting a cancer diagnosis and undergoing treatment. The creation of this book reflects a major evolution in the attitudes of health professionals about lymphedema diagnosis and management. *Lymphedema: Understanding and Managing Lymphedema After Cancer Treatment* is a much-needed educational guide that informs patients and family members about lymphedema, how to reduce the chances of developing it, and how to manage it if it occurs. While lymphedema treatment has improved in recent years, only heightened awareness will help lower individuals' risk of developing the chronic condition in the first place. This book should be recommended for all people whose cancer treatment puts them at risk for lymphedema.

My lymphedema has taught me how important it is to be responsible for my own health and to work in partnership with my health care providers to maintain it. Patients may increasingly be the ones to alert health professionals that symptoms are occurring. Armed with the knowledge that lymphedema can be managed, a person with lymphedema can advocate for him- or herself. But the important message of this book is *lymphedema can be managed.*

The 1990s helped us recognize that measures now exist to effectively treat lymphedema. Now we must ensure that clinicians and patients work together to prevent, manage, and minimize the debilitating effects of this condition.

INTRODUCTION

I f you have been diagnosed with cancer, you probably talked with your health care team about the potential side effects of cancer treatments. But you may not have been told that you could eventually experience discomfort or swelling in your arm or leg after cancer treatment, and you may have been puzzled, shocked, and alarmed if these symptoms did develop. You may not even have known that your cancer treatment put you at risk for a condition called lymphedema.

Lymphedema is the buildup of lymph fluid in the body. Lymph fluid is made up of protein, salts, water, and white blood cells and flows through the lymph system, an important part of your body's circulatory system.

The focus of this book is secondary lymphedema, which is caused by external factors (such as cancer treatment) that disrupt lymph drainage. Another type of lymphedema—one that is not explored in depth in this text—is called primary lymphedema, in which a person is born with factors that lead to the development of lymphedema.

This book is a good place to start building your understanding of lymphedema and taking control of what is happening to your body. Whether you are concerned and don't know how to prevent the condition from developing, are confused or upset about what is happening to your body, want to know how best to treat the effects you're experiencing, or are seeking additional support and understanding, this book will provide the information you need.

Lymphedema Is Not Your Fault

You are not to blame for your lymphedema. The factors that can put you at risk, such as cancer treatment, are out of your control. Experts can't predict which people at risk will develop lymphedema, nor can they explain why some people eventually get lymphedema and others do not.

Experts have many things to learn about lymphedema, but we know this: when lymphedema occurs, it is not the fault of the person who develops it.

Who Is at Risk for Lymphedema?

A person with decreased lymph system drainage (see chapter 1) may be at risk for developing lymphedema. Anyone undergoing the surgical removal of lymph nodes or other surgery or radiation that affects the lymph nodes or lymph vessels is at risk. People treated for cancers of the breast, prostate, or uterus, or for lymphoma or melanoma, are most likely to undergo treatment that puts them at risk. Other people at risk for lymphedema include those whose cancer has spread to the lymph system.

Some people without cancer may also be at risk for developing lymphedema, including those who have been injured or sustained trauma to the body that damaged their lymph system. A worm called filaria causes over 100 million cases of lymphedema worldwide, but this parasite is rare in developed countries.

The Challenges of Lymphedema

Lymphedema is a chronic condition, which means it can be a lifelong challenge. It can be managed, but it is not curable. Although research may one day allow for lymphedema *prevention*, we do not yet know how to absolutely prevent lymphedema in an at-risk individual. Therefore the focus for at-risk people is currently on *risk reduction*.

There are many unknowns related to lymphedema, and education and additional study are urgently needed.

The Need for Increased Awareness

People who know they are at risk for lymphedema can take measures that may help prevent its onset. Therefore it is essential that people who are at risk, such as those who undergo cancer treatment affecting the lymph nodes, understand the risk factors for lymphedema and what they can do to reduce the likelihood that they will have lymphedema.

Although awareness of lymphedema is increasing, the condition is not widely understood or discussed. As a result, some medical professionals may not be fully informed about lymphedema risk, diagnosis, or treatment. If you have lymphedema, you may have already realized this the hard way—by encountering doctors or nurses unfamiliar with the condition you cope with each day.

Health care team members may not fully understand the condition and may downplay the impact lymphedema has on a person's life. But lymphedema is not only "a little swelling," and it shouldn't be ignored. It is a big deal to those it affects: it can have a major effect on a person's health, body image and self-confidence, and quality of life.

Further Study Is Essential

Although doctors have been aware of the condition for a long time, in comparison to other side effects of cancer treatment, lymphedema has not been widely researched. Lymphedema may take years to appear and often begins with symptoms that can't be seen. These factors complicate doctors' ability to study the condition. Additional lymphedema research could help the medical community discover how best to help both those at risk and those who already have lymphedema.

Most of the research that has been done has focused on the largest population with lymphedema: women who have been treated for breast cancer. When these women develop lymphedema, it typically affects the upper extremities. This leaves people who have lymphedema in the lower extremities or other body areas without a lot of information about the differences in their condition. We'll discuss lymphedema of the upper and lower extremities in this book, as well as lymphedema in other areas of the body.

In an effort to encourage further research and education, the National Lymphedema Network (NLN) is gathering and evaluating lymphedema-related information. If you have lymphedema or are at risk for the condition, you can help by filling out a short questionnaire at http://www.lymphnet.org; click on the "Questionnaire" link. You may also print the questionnaire and return it to NLN (see the *Resources* section in the back of this book for NLN contact information).

Care Standards and Language Are Becoming More Uniform

Much of the support for and study of lymphedema have evolved in just the past few decades. Because the field is young, standards have not yet become universally adopted. Universal standards are needed for:

- **vocabulary:** Various health care professionals who care for those with the condition typically use a limited but consistent set of lymphedema-related terms. Until recently different vocabulary may have been used to refer to aspects of lymphedema and treatment.
- **treatment standards:** Universal standards may not be formally embraced, but experts generally agree that the current recommended and standard treatment is complete decongestive therapy (CDT; see chapter 6).

- **system of grading lymphedema:** Experts lack a universally recognized system that allows them to clinically evaluate how advanced lymphedema is, how to gauge progress, and how to adapt treatment to responses.

Coping with Lymphedema

Lymphedema is a complication of some types of cancer and cancer treatments and, when swelling or skin changes occur, it is a visible side effect. It can be an outward sign of the past; people may find that their lymphedema symptoms remind them of their cancer. A swollen arm, hand, leg, or foot is likely to be more visible than the effects of a person's radiation or surgery. But lymphedema is not just a change in the appearance of a limb. It can affect many facets of a person's life:

- overall health
- medical care
- emotions
- self-image
- relationships and intimacy
- job-related, insurance, and financial issues

Throughout this book we explore the practical concerns related to lymphedema risk, precautions, and care, and offer detailed information to help guide you through day-to-day decisions and challenges.

Your Role in Your Care

Doctors caring for people treated for cancer may not address ways of reducing lymphedema risk or talk to patients about precautions. Unlike some types of cancer, lymphedema is not deadly. As a result, doctors may focus on preventing cancer recurrence rather than trying to reduce the risk of lymphedema. Many medical professionals are not aware of issues surrounding lymphedema

The person who has had cancer treatment is often responsible for discovering what there is to know about risk reduction and management options. If your health care team is not familiar with how to reduce the risk of lymphedema or is not experienced in treating it if it occurs, the job of gathering information about lymphedema and securing care may fall to you. If you develop lymphedema, you will play an essential role in the management of your condition.

How This Book Can Help

This book describes what lymphedema is, steps you can take that may lower your risk of triggering lymphedema, symptoms to be aware of, and the treatment options that exist if you do develop lymphedema.

The American Cancer Society developed this book with experts in the fields of lymphedema care and research to address the many important issues related to lymphedema. The book was created with a team of nurses, doctors, and lymphedema care specialists, as well as the input of people coping with lymphedema.

The book addresses many common concerns about lymphedema and provides available answers to the many questions you may have. Some of the topics in this book were shaped by questions posed to the American Cancer Society by people concerned or wondering about an aspect of lymphedema. In hopes of helping others and letting readers know they are not alone, the text also includes some personal experiences shared by people affected by lymphedema.

The chapters in this book will help you explore issues you may face and educate you about your options. Being informed and empowered to make knowledgeable decisions about your care will help you better understand and meet the challenge of lymphedema.

Talk to your health care team about any questions you may have; if your doctor or nurses are not familiar with lymphedema, you may want to share with them what you learn from this book. Rely on health care professionals who are experienced in lymphedema diagnosis and care if at all possible. We encourage you to actively seek the information you need.

It is not possible to predict who will get lymphedema, but recognizing it early and starting treatment promptly is the best way to manage it. Let *Lymphedema: Understanding and Managing Lymphedema After Cancer Treatment* be a resource to you. Take things one step at a time and find what works best for you.

How This Book Is Organized

You may find it most helpful to read the chapters in consecutive order, considering each phase from beginning to end and anticipating future issues. Or you may want to read only the section (or sections) most applicable to your current experience.

Section I explains the lymph system, how lymphedema develops, and common symptoms.

Section II focuses on who is at risk and offers specific precautions that might protect against developing lymphedema.

Section III explains how lymphedema is diagnosed and how a person with suspicious symptoms often plays an essential role in diagnosis.

Section IV guides you through preparing for treatment and setting goals, explores treatment options, and offers helpful details about self care. It explains the roles of therapists and how to find them, and addresses practical concerns such as the cost of treatment, insurance, and other health care resources.

Section V explores the potential changes caused by lymphedema, including body changes and effects on home and work life. It outlines support options and suggests how to handle others' curiosity.

Section VI focuses on exciting research that may pave the way for new developments in understanding, preventing, diagnosing, and caring for lymphedema.

The overviews that introduce each section include a personal story from someone affected by lymphedema, as well as a list of related questions you may have (answers can be found within the section that follows).

The *Resources* section in the back of the book lists includes a directory of American Cancer Society resources, lymphedema organizations, and patient and family services. The *Glossary* offers definitions of terms you are likely to encounter as you learn about lymphedema.

About the American Cancer Society

Represented in more than 3,400 communities throughout the country and Puerto Rico, the American Cancer Society is a nonprofit health organization dedicated to eliminating cancer as a major health problem. This book is just one example of the many ways the Society seeks to fulfill its mission of saving lives and diminishing suffering from cancer through research, education, advocacy, and service. A specific goal for the year 2015 is improving the quality of life of cancer survivors.

The American Cancer Society is the largest private source of cancer research dollars in the United States. Founded in 1913 by 10 physicians and 5 concerned members of the community, the organization now has over 2 million volunteers. Most offer their time free of charge to the American Cancer Society to work to conquer cancer and improve the lives of those affected by it.

We invite you to contact the American Cancer Society (800-ACS-2345 or http://www.cancer.org) to learn more about what we can do for you.

ᴧ What is lymphedema? What causes it?

ᴧ I'm not sure what the lymph system does. How can it cause so many problems if it gets damaged?

ᴧ Where can lymphedema develop?

ᴧ What symptoms should I be on the lookout for? Is swelling the first symptom?

ᴧ How will I know if I have lymphedema?

ᴧ Does lymphedema hurt?

ᴧ How long does lymphedema last? Will it go away, or will I have it forever?

MAZO'S STORY ✒
Coping with Lymphedema

PUSHING FOR PROPER ATTENTION

I discovered I had lymphedema treatment six months after my mastectomy. My initial thought was "Why wasn't the fact that I could get lymphedema stressed?" No doctors or nurses had mentioned the possibility.

I didn't have any tightness or other odd sensations before the swelling. I've always had a small wrist, and when I suddenly couldn't get my watch to close I immediately called the doctor's office. I explained my situation to the receptionist, who told me "You just have lymphedema and you'll probably be referred to a clinic for therapy." It took approximately six weeks of demanding to finally get someone to schedule me for lymphedema therapy.

TREATMENT IS IMPORTANT

I considered compression bandaging and massage therapy somewhat effective for my swollen arm but ultimately stopped maintenance. After my arm, hand, and fingers swelled up again, I began to see the benefits of maintaining therapy. Now I massage my arm and use my compression devices. During the day I religiously wear a compression sleeve and glove. If you have lymphedema, be sure to massage, exercise, and wear your compression garment daily.

RELYING ON SUPPORT

My family has provided tremendous emotional support. My husband and daughter also helped with bandaging and lift heavy items for me.

My two sisters and I are each other's support systems. My eldest sister, a nurse, had treatment for breast cancer and discovered only after inquiring that she'd had lymph nodes cut in a recent surgery. I wish I'd been advised not to ever lift heavy items after my mastectomy and radiation treatments, and I warned her never to lift anything remotely heavy. My youngest sister was just recently diagnosed with the telltale signs of breast cancer and just underwent a lumpectomy with benign results.

My coworkers help out by lifting the 200-pound boxes of copy paper at work. Since it involves my unaffected arm, I still engage in recreational bowling.

EXPLAINING LYMPHEDEMA

Sometimes people do stare and ask questions. However, if a person is sincere or genuinely curious, I take time and explain that I've had surgery (mastectomy) with follow-up radiation treatments that resulted in my permanently bloated arm and hand condition (lymphedema). I look at it as an opportunity to educate the masses about lymphedema.

—MAZO
lymphedema of the arm
following breast cancer treatment

CHAPTER ONE

WHAT IS LYMPHEDEMA?

Lymphedema is a condition that involves a buildup of fluid in the body. "Lymph" is an almost colorless fluid and "edema" means a buildup of fluid in body tissues. Some cancer treatments can put a person at risk for lymphedema, which can occur immediately after cancer treatment or many years later.

Lymphedema is not a life-threatening condition. It usually affects the arm or leg but may affect any body part. Symptoms may be so mild that a person only notices that his arm or leg feels heavy or tight. But if left untreated for a long time, lymphedema can cause progressively worse swelling and other complications.

Throughout this book we explore ways to protect against and effectively manage lymphedema. Although few studies have focused on preventing lymphedema, some precautions seem to help protect against lymphedema development in people who are at risk.

To understand lymphedema, it helps to understand what the lymphatic (or lymph) system is and how it works, as well as types of lymphedema and potential symptoms.

The Lymph System

The circulatory system is a network of veins, arteries, and capillaries that moves blood through the body to the heart, the lungs, and out into

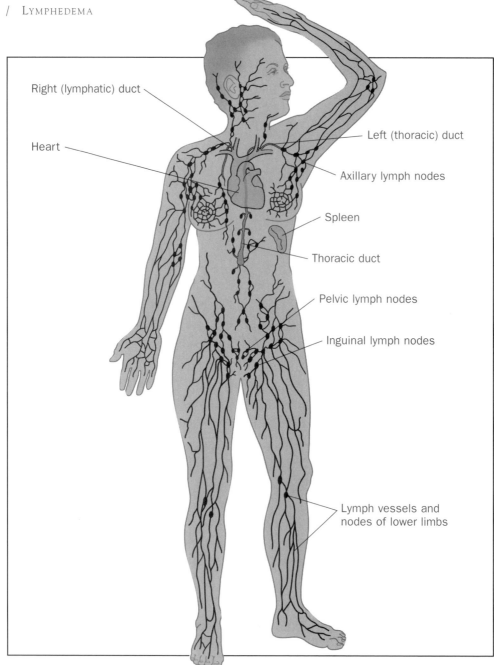

Right (lymphatic) duct

Heart

Left (thoracic) duct

Axillary lymph nodes

Spleen

Thoracic duct

Pelvic lymph nodes

Inguinal lymph nodes

Lymph vessels and
nodes of lower limbs

Figure 1.1 The lymph system
This illustration of the female lymph system shows important elements of the lymph system, including the lymph vessels that transport lymph, lymph nodes that drain and filter lymph, and ducts that drain lymph into the bloodstream. Axillary (underarm) lymph nodes are most likely to be affected by breast cancer treatment.

the body again. A corresponding system called the lymph system drains and transports lymph fluid throughout the body by means of a system of lymph vessels.

The circulatory system pumps blood away from the heart through arteries and capillaries. As blood flows through the body, plasma (the fluid portion of the blood) exits the porous capillaries and leaves the bloodstream. Once the plasma leaves the capillary it becomes interstitial fluid, the fluid that surrounds cells and supplies them with what they need to function, including dissolved nutrients, gases, water, and proteins. This fluid also receives the waste products from cell metabolism, which is removed by the lymph and blood vessels.

Blood continues to circulate through the body and is pumped back to the heart through the veins. But a small amount of excess fluid and protein is left behind in body tissues.

This excess fluid is moved out of the tissues and back into the bloodstream by the lymph system. Within the lymph vessels are valves and muscles that help move the fluid in one direction through the body, toward the heart. Unlike the circulatory system, which has its own pump (the heart) to move blood throughout the body, it is the contraction of smooth muscle (involuntary or automatic muscle) in the walls of the lymph vessels that push lymph fluid toward the heart. The movement of the diaphragm (the muscle under the lungs that contracts when you breathe), muscle contractions, stretching the skin, the pulsing of the arteries, and pressure from outside the body also aid lymph flow.

As it circulates, lymph fluid passes through lymph nodes clustered along the lymph vessels. The spleen, thymus, and bone marrow are also part of the lymph system, however, these structures are not involved in lymphedema.

As it maintains a balance of fluid in the body, the main jobs of the lymph system are to:

- **drain** lymph fluid
- **transport** lymph fluid
- **filter** bacteria, viruses, dying cells, and inorganic particles from lymph fluid
- **remove** excess lymph fluid

Lymph Fluid

Ninety percent of the fluid that surrounds cells (the interstitial fluid) is transported by veins; the lymph system moves the rest. The thin, permeable walls of the wide lymph vessels allow interstitial fluid and its large protein molecules to enter. Once in

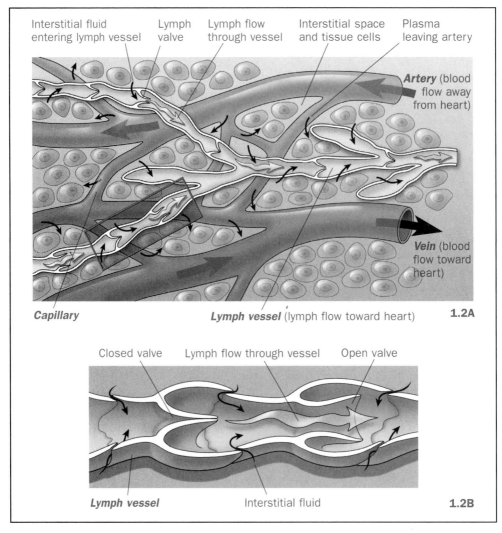

Figure 1.2A and 1.2B Lymph vessels and valves

Figure A shows the constant flow of fluid in the body through lymph vessels, arteries, and veins. Fluid that surrounds cells is called interstitial fluid; once it enters a lymph vessel it is called lymph fluid (or simply lymph). Valves in the lymph vessels keep lymph flowing toward the heart. Figure B shows an area of lymph vessel and valves in more detail.

the lymph vessels, the fluid is called lymph fluid and is transported to the lymph nodes for eventual return to the bloodstream. The lymph system moves one to two quarts of lymph fluid a day from the body back into the bloodstream.

Lymph fluid (also simply called lymph) is an almost clear liquid made up of protein, salts, and water, and, like the blood, it also contains white blood cells. Through transporting lymph, the lymph system plays a role in immune surveillance. Bacteria, fungi, and other potentially harmful substances are transported within lymph to the lymph nodes. In the lymph nodes these substances are presented to immune system cells, which mount a response to protect the body.

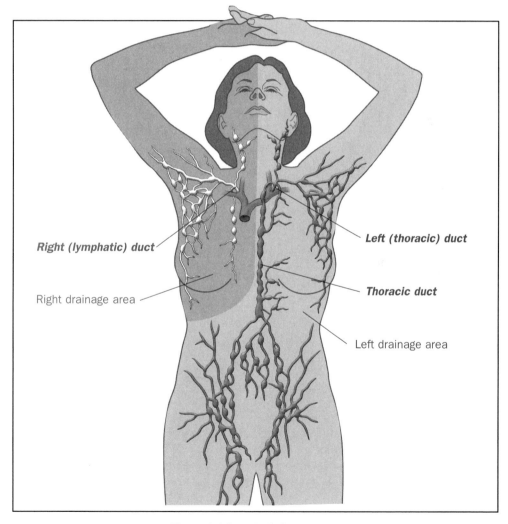

Figure 1.3 Lymph drainage areas
Three-quarters of lymph in the body is drained by the thoracic duct (on the left side of the body), while the remaining one-fourth is drained by the lymphatic duct (on the right side).

Lymph Vessels, Ducts, and Drainage

Some lymph vessels are located very close to the skin surface, while others are farther under the skin in the deeper fatty tissues. Lymph vessels converge in the neck to form two large lymph vessels called ducts. Like watersheds on the earth, which drain rainwater back into a body of water, the ducts collect the fluid from specific drainage regions of the body and send it back into the blood near the heart. The left duct, the thoracic duct, drains the majority of the body's lymph, collecting fluid from the left side of the body as well as the right leg and the lower right area of the abdomen. The right duct, the lymphatic duct, collects the rest of the body's lymph. Lymph is returned to the bloodstream through large veins just under the collarbone. Damage to a portion of the lymph system can cause lymphedema in the area of the body it drains.

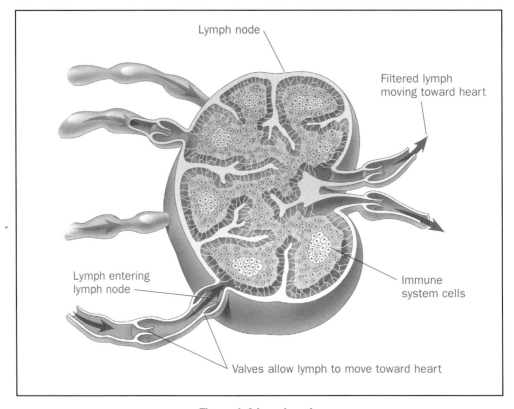

Figure 1.4 Lymph node
This illustration of a lymph node shows the flow of lymph and the valves that allow lymph into and out of the node, toward the heart. (Not to scale.)

Lymph Nodes

As lymph fluid travels through the body toward the heart, it passes through small, bean-shaped structures called lymph nodes (also called lymph glands). Lymph nodes filter lymph and remove substances such as dead cells, bacteria, and viruses that could be dangerous to the body. (These substances are destroyed by white blood cells, which digest them into harmless substances.) Trapping these toxins prevents them from circulating through the bloodstream when the lymph fluid is returned to the blood. The other job of lymph nodes is to produce lymphocytes, infection-fighting white blood cells.

The 500 to 1500 lymph nodes in the body are mainly located in groups along lymph vessels in the neck, groin, arm, leg, and other areas of the body, including the head, abdomen, pelvis, and chest (see figure 1.1). Groups of lymph nodes in each region of the body are named for the area they drain. Some are close to the skin, while others are deeper in the body around major lymph vessels. Lymph node sizes vary throughout the body; they may be as small as a sesame seed or as large as a grape, or approximately one-fifth centimeter to one inch. Lymph nodes under the arms, called axillary lymph nodes, are most commonly affected by surgery and treatment for breast cancer. Treatment that impairs lymph nodes in the neck could potentially cause lymphedema in the head and neck, and surgery to the inguinal lymph nodes in the groin can cause lymphedema swelling in the leg.

"Deep" lymph nodes surround large blood vessels in the abdomen, pelvis, and chest. However, you might be able to feel the lymph nodes in your neck, groin, and under your arm; these nodes are located in clusters near the skin. They are especially easy to locate when you are sick because they may swell as they filter harmful cells and produce white blood cells to fight infection.

What Happens When Lymphedema Develops? ·

Lymphedema is an excess of fluid and protein caused by impaired lymph flow from the tissues. It occurs when the amount of fluid in the affected body area exceeds the lymph system's ability to drain it. Any blockage in or damage to lymph nodes and vessels makes it harder for the lymph system to remove fluid from distant areas. If the non-damaged portion of the lymph system cannot remove enough of the fluid in that part of the body, the extra, protein-rich fluid builds up and causes lymphedema.

In people who are treated for cancer, a damaged lymph system is most likely to have been caused by surgical lymph node removal or by radiation therapy. Surgery or radiation may change the way lymph fluid flows within the area that was treated.

Lymph fluid can bypass a lymph node, but if a node has been removed and scar tissue has developed around it, lymph fluid may become trapped.

Damage to the lymph system interferes with the lymph system's ability to isolate invading bacteria or other harmful substances and may allow infection to develop without detection by the immune system.

When May Lymphedema Develop and How Long Will It Last?

The onset of lymphedema is often subtle and unpredictable. Lymphedema usually develops slowly over time, causing a feeling of tightness or heaviness before swelling develops. It may occur immediately after treatment or much later. Lymphedema most often occurs in the first 2 or 3 years after treatment but has been reported to have developed as many as 30 years after treatment.

Secondary Lymphedema

Secondary lymphedema is the most common type of lymphedema and the type focused on throughout this book (referred to elsewhere in the text simply as "lymphedema"). It may be caused by a blockage or interruption in the lymph system, usually at the lymph nodes under the arm or in the groin area. Secondary lymphedema typically develops slowly over time and is long-term, or chronic. (However, it may develop rapidly if triggered by infection, inflammation, or trauma.) As noted, it may show up many months or even years after cancer treatment, and symptoms such as swelling can range from mild to severe.

People who have many lymph nodes removed and/or radiation therapy may have an increased risk of developing lymphedema, but doctors still do not fully understand why some patients are more likely to have problems with fluid buildup than others.

Other Types of Lymphedema

This book concentrates on secondary lymphedema, which is caused by external factors (such as cancer treatment) that interrupt or disrupt a healthy lymph system. But there are other types of lymphedema as well.

Primary Lymphedema

In primary lymphedema, a person is born with genes that predispose him to developing lymphedema. Primary lymphedema is a rare condition, affecting 1 in 6,000 people in the United States. It develops because lymph nodes or vessels are missing or abnormal and do not work the way they should. This type of inherited lymphedema can affect all four limbs and other body areas, but typically occurs in the legs.

The severity of lymphedema's effects varies from person to person and depends upon many factors, including the extent of scarring from surgery or radiation.

Possible Symptoms and Complications

The potential symptoms of lymphedema and the complications that can accompany it emphasize why it is so important to prevent the condition when possible, diagnose existing lymphedema early, and treat it aggressively.

Impaired lymph movement, known as lymphostasis, is a precursor to lymphedema that doesn't cause visible symptoms. Lymphedema begins before visible changes like swelling develop. Lymphedema is considered "subclinical" before it causes any observable signs.

Over time lymphedema does create noticeable effects. Swelling develops as the first and most visible outward symptom, often in the arm, leg, or trunk area. Lymphedema symptoms may be called a symptom "cluster" since a person with lymphedema may experience some or all of them at one time. Early symptoms may include:

- **a full, tight, or achy feeling in the limb**
- **a swollen limb** on the side of the body where cancer was treated
- **decreased flexibility** in the limb
- **visible skin changes,** such as tautness or pitting (skin that remains indented after being pressed)

A person with swelling in the arm or leg does not necessarily have lymphedema. Talk to a doctor if you notice any suspicious

"Temporary" Lymphedema

While this book focuses on long-term, or chronic, lymphedema, a few cases of lymphedema are temporary. For example, about 1 in 20 women whose lymph nodes were affected by breast cancer treatment develop temporary lymphedema, also called transient or acute lymphedema. Temporary lymphedema may develop as soon as a few days after treatment or six to eight weeks later. It generally lasts less than six months, and most people have it for only a few weeks. This type of lymphedema is usually mild; the skin "pits" (indents) when pressed, but the skin does not harden. The affected area may look red and feel hot. Treatment includes elevating the affected limb and using medicines to reduce inflammation.

Some doctors consider this temporary swelling simply "edema" since factors other than the lymph system are usually involved. A person treated for cancer may be at risk for developing temporary edema if, for example, a vein is blocked by a blood clot or by inflamed tissue.

symptoms, and consider seeking out a doctor experienced in the management of lymph system conditions.

A Full or Tight Feeling

About 50 percent of people with mild lymphedema have a full, tight, or achy feeling in their affected limb. This is typically the first clue a person has that lymphedema is developing. These vague symptoms can't be seen or examined by a doctor, but a person might feel that things aren't quite right in the affected arm, leg, or other body area.

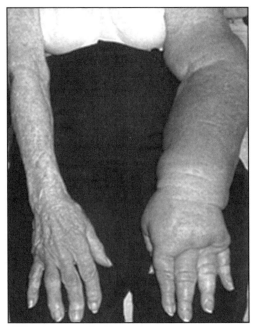

Figure 1.5 Lymphedema of the arm
The photo above shows severe swelling in a woman's left arm from lymphedema. Reprinted from http://www.acols.com/before.html by permission of the Academy of Lymphatic Studies.

Swelling

Swelling is the most visible sign of lymphedema. If lymphedema progresses for months without treatment, lymph vessels expand and allow more fluid to remain in body tissues. Lymph vessel valves become dilated and fail to direct lymph toward the heart, allowing fluid buildup and swelling.

Swelling from lymphedema most often occurs in the arms or legs, but it can occur in any organ or area, including the breast, neck, trunk, genitals, or face, depending on the location of the damage to the lymph system. If lymphedema develops because of breast cancer or its treatment, for example, the condition can affect the area around the breast, underarm, shoulder blade, and the arm on the side of surgery. If lymphedema develops because of cancer in or cancer treatment to the abdomen, a person may have swelling of the abdomen, genitals, or one or both legs.

Upper extremity lymphedema may affect the area from a person's wrist to the underarm, the outside area of the elbow, or only the hand. Lower-extremity lymphedema usually affects the foot (but may not affect a person's toes) and leg or the genitals and buttocks.

Swelling in the hand or arm can make it difficult to perform the tasks of daily living or work. Uncontrolled swelling in the leg or foot can make it difficult to simply walk. When a limb becomes especially swollen, it is heavier (which puts stress on muscles around it). Treatment can be effective in reducing swelling and restoring a person's ability to move and function as before. (See chapter 6 for more information about treatment for lymphedema.)

You may wonder why fluid cannot simply be drained from the body with a needle. Fluid is built up throughout the tissues, so trying to remove fluid this way would be like trying to use a needle to extract liquid from a wet sponge—not very effective.

Lymphedema results in one type of fluid buildup. But fluid buildup and swelling in the body may occur because of other reasons, including allergic reactions, kidney failure, heart conditions, blood clots, liver conditions, or burns. These conditions produce swelling on both sides of the body rather than in one arm or leg. It is important to see your doctor and have a physical examination to determine the cause of any significant swelling.

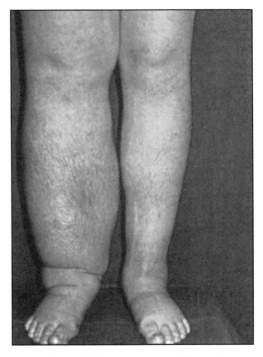

Figure 1.6 Lymphedema of the leg
The photo above shows severe swelling in a man's right leg from lymphedema. Reprinted from http://www.acols.com/before.html by permission of the Academy of Lymphatic Studies.

Changes in Skin Condition

The goal of lymphedema treatment and management is to prevent the condition from progressing to the point of causing problems such as skin changes. Most patients with mild lymphedema do not develop skin changes. With the exception of pitting, the skin changes described below are generally associated with lymphedema that has progressed and worsened.

A person with stage I, II, or III lymphedema may have "peau d'orange" skin changes, in which skin resembles the skin of an orange (swollen so that hair follicles look like little dimples).

Pitting

Especially in early stages of lymphedema, skin over the affected body area easily "pits"—that is, if it is pressed, the skin indents and stays indented. The tissue remains supple, and fluid causing the swelling can be moved elsewhere in the body (through manual lymph drainage, or MLD; see chapter 6). You may first notice indentations in your skin from tight shirt cuffs, watch bands, or jewelry, or you may notice dents after resting your arms or legs on an irregular surface—the edge of a counter or coffee table, for example. Pitting is usually present even in advanced lymphedema, but as skin and tissue beneath it become more stiff more pressure may be required to make the skin pit.

Stiff, Hard Skin

If lymphedema is not treated, the skin over the area affected by lymphedema eventually becomes stiff. This stiffness occurs because protein and other debris aren't removed, but stay put instead, encouraging white blood cells and inflammatory cells to collect in the area where the stagnant protein is concentrated. This stagnation produces low-grade inflammation and the deposit of collagen fibers (structural proteins in the skin), which causes fibrosis, or hardened skin and tissue. Fibrosis further blocks the flow of lymph under the skin surface. In advanced lymphedema, skin may become thick, hard, callused, or bumpy.

Easily Damaged Skin

In advanced lymphedema skin tissue may weaken and be more susceptible to wounds, especially over bony areas such as elbows or knees. It's a good idea to check your skin each day, especially under compression bandaging or garments where skin may rub.

Skin Breakdown

Occasionally lymphedema is so severe that skin over the affected area allows fluid to leak from the skin. Lymphedema rarely progresses so rapidly that lymph fluid is leaking from the skin when a person is diagnosed. However, either malignant lymphedema (lymphedema caused by pressure on lymph vessels, lymph nodes, or both from a malignant, or cancerous, tumor) or cellulitis (inflammation or infection of the skin and underlying tissues) can cause skin breakdown to happen relatively quickly.

Pain or Tingling

Lymphedema itself does not usually cause pain. However, a person with advanced lymphedema may experience considerable pain beneath the skin, which may be due to pressure on or stretching of nerves as a limb expands or as fluid accumulates.

Treating lymphedema or infection should help resolve the pain. Nonsteroidal anti-inflammatory drugs (NSAIDs; for example, aspirin or ibuprofen) can help relieve muscle pain that may result from holding the body in a different or awkward position due to changes in a limb or heaviness in a limb that puts stress on the supporting muscles.

Pain Not Due to Lymphedema

Lymphedema may cause areas of pain if you have an infection. However, it never causes bone pain, problems with nerve function, or loss of movement. If you are experiencing any of these symptoms, tell your doctor. She will do more testing to determine the cause. Because nerves under the arm can be injured during underarm lymph node surgery, you may have numbness, tingling, or nerve pain below the armpit and along the inner arm to your elbow. This is not caused by lymphedema.

Painful tendon conditions (such as tennis elbow [inflamed tendons in the elbow], swimmer's shoulder [tendons trapped in the shoulder], or swollen tendons in the hand, wrist, or forearm) may also be associated with lymphedema. These problems can be caused by changes in the way you move because your limb weighs more and is larger than before. The inflammation that accompanies these conditions can trigger or worsen lymphedema, so it's important to diagnose and treat them right away.

Infection

The lymph system is important to the body's defense against infection. The nature of lymphedema means that part of the lymph system has difficulty moving fluid, bacteria, and cellular waste out of the affected area of the body. The stagnant bacteria may flourish and lead to infection.

Lymphedema impairs the lymph system's ability to isolate and remove bacteria, which delays the immune system's response in recognizing and fighting it. For this reason an infection can progress rapidly before the immune system responds. (The immune systems of lymphedema patients function normally in other areas of their body and are not globally impaired like those of people on chemotherapy. Chemotherapy weakens the entire immune system for a time.)

Cellulitis, an infection of the skin and soft tissue beneath it, is caused by bacteria that enters the body through broken or cracked skin. It may develop in a person with lymphedema because stagnant lymph fluid slows the immune system's ability to mount an effective and timely response. Cellulitis causes the skin over the infection to be red and hot. Treatment is straightforward if cellulitis is diagnosed early. Your doctor will treat cellulitis with antibiotics, preventing the spread of infection.

Lymphangitis is an inflammation of one or more lymph vessels usually caused by infection; it may cause swelling and tenderness.

Fungal infections like athlete's foot may occur between the toes of a person with lymphedema of the foot when fungus is allowed to multiply quickly and cause infection.

Possible Infection: When to Call the Doctor

Potentially dangerous infections such as blood poisoning may occur if lymphedema and its effects aren't addressed. The symptoms below could signal an infection and may require antibiotics. Call your health care team right away if:

- any part of **your affected limb feels hot, painful, is red, or becomes more swollen**
- you develop a **temperature over 100.5 degrees F** or shaking chills that are not related to a cold or flu

Appropriate antibiotics will reduce swelling and skin discoloration caused by infection.

Fatigue

Some people with lymphedema report fatigue that interferes with daily activities, including work or home tasks. Fatigue may decrease your motivation to spend time with others, to be physically active, and to be intimate with a partner. The causes of such fatigue have not been well studied and may not be directly linked to lymphedema, but to factors such as body weight, activity levels, coping with a chronic condition, or cancer treatment side effects, for example. Getting adequate rest and sleep, setting priorities, reducing stress, eating a healthy diet, and staying fit can help you cope. Fatigue may also be a result of cancer treatment or another condition; talk to your doctor about your fatigue, when it began, and how long it has persisted.

Rare Lymph Vessel Tumors

Dangerous tumors of the lymph vessels are an extremely rare complication of advanced, long-term, usually lower extremity lymphedema. The cause of these rare tumors is unknown. When they occur, typically 10 or more years following cancer treatment, signs such as raised bruise-like blue-red bumps on the skin appear.

 I didn't learn about lymphedema until recently, and my doctor doesn't know much about it either. Do many people have this condition?

 Who gets lymphedema and why?

 I had cancer treatment years ago. Am I at risk for lymphedema now?

 Is there anything I can do to protect against triggering lymphedema?

 Have any of the risk-reduction suggestions I hear about been proven effective? Which measures are most likely to prevent triggering lymphedema?

 Do I need to change my whole life to reduce my risk of triggering lymphedema?

 I have lymphedema; was it caused by something I did or didn't do?

 If my doctor doesn't know about lymphedema, how can I explain what it is and get the help I need?

 I read that exercise and repetitive motion could possibly trigger lymphedema. I thought exercise was good for me. What should I do?

 My friends say flying in a plane could bring on lymphedema swelling. Is that true? What can I do if I plan to travel by air?

KATE'S STORY ∾
Coping with Lymphedema

LYMPHEDEMA AND AN ACTIVE LIFESTYLE

I first noticed that my legs looked bigger one day while bicycling after treatment for recurrent cervical cancer. When my legs continued to swell day by day, my husband, Scott, and I learned about lymphedema through my oncologist. Once diagnosed with lymphedema, I was afraid it would be a threat to my fitness and active lifestyle—all my life I had loved backpacking, bicycling, skiing, and running.

My husband Scott and I both went to "training" and learned proper massage—manual lymph drainage (MLD)—techniques to manage my lymphedema. The massage worked! Once we felt more confident about keeping my lymphedema under control, we planned an 800-mile hike along the Continental Divide Trail of Montana. It was something we would have done before, and I didn't want cancer or lymphedema to stop me from doing the things I love.

I fended off the swelling by wearing compression stockings, soaking my legs in cold streams and lakes, elevating my legs during breaks, and doing regular massages on myself and with the help of Scott.

We enjoyed the walk through wilderness so much that we continued hiking down the trail in the following years, completing Wyoming, Colorado, and New Mexico. I am so thankful that I can manage my lymphedema self-sufficiently and that my husband and I can continue to live the active lifestyle that means so much to us.

—KATE
lymphedema of the legs
following cervical cancer treatment

CHAPTER TWO

WHO IS AT RISK FOR LYMPHEDEMA?

Lymphedema can occur in men or women. It can develop after surgery or radiation for any type of cancer that affects the lymph nodes or lymph drainage, but it most often occurs after treatment for breast cancer, pelvic cancers such as prostate or uterine cancer, lymphoma, or melanoma (a form of skin cancer).

Patients who have many lymph nodes removed *and* radiation therapy to the lymph nodes have a higher risk of developing lymphedema than those who only have lymph nodes surgically removed (so that they may be examined under a microscope to see if cancer has spread).

The risk for lymphedema remains throughout a person's life. Unfortunately it is impossible to predict who will and will not develop the condition.

The Difference between Causes, Risk Factors, and Triggers

It is important to recognize the differences between a cause, a risk factor, and a trigger for the development of lymphedema. The *cause* of all secondary lymphedema is trauma to the lymph system. A person with a *risk factor* such as prior surgery or radiation to the lymph nodes is susceptible to lymphedema, but will not necessarily develop it. A *trigger* is what stimulates lymphedema to develop in an at-risk person.

Causes of lymphedema are explored in chapter 1. In this chapter, we discuss risk factors and triggers. Later in the book we look at precautions that may help protect against lymphedema and how to be aware of changes in your body so you can identify lymphedema early.

How Common Is Lymphedema?

It is difficult to pinpoint how many people suffer from lymphedema because:

- there isn't a standard method of diagnosing the condition
- it affects upper extremities and lower extremities at different rates
- cases develop at different rates after initial lymph system damage
- potential lymphedema causes (such as surgery or radiation that involves the lymph nodes) don't lead to lymphedema in everyone
- cases being diagnosed now reflect older treatment methods, not recent methods designed to minimize effects on lymph nodes, such as sentinel node biopsies (see page 23)

However, judging by even the lowest suggested estimates, lymphedema affects hundreds of thousands of people in the United States.

Lymphedema in the Arms

The majority of the lymphedema cases diagnosed in the United States are a result of breast cancer treatment. Generally between 15 to 20 percent of women who have standard lymph node removal to treat breast cancer will develop lymphedema of the arm (but estimates range from 10 percent to over 50 percent). This is approximately 1 in 5 of the 2 million breast cancer survivors in the United States, or about 400,000 women. Changes in surgical techniques (such as removing smaller samples of lymph nodes for analysis) have made lymphedema somewhat less common following breast cancer treatment. Still, lymphedema is a health concern for many women.

Lymphedema in the Legs

It's difficult to estimate how often lymphedema of the legs occurs. Estimates of the number of people with lymphedema following treatment for reproductive cancers, genital cancers, and melanomas of the legs range from 0 to 60 to 80 percent.

One complicating factor is that a definition of the changes that constitute lymphedema hasn't been officially established for lower extremity lymphedema, and measurement methods aren't in place. Another challenge is that cancer treatment that affects deep pelvic lymph nodes (as with gynecological, bladder, colon, or prostate cancers) often affects both legs, so pinpointing an increase in leg size is difficult.

Lymphedema in Other Areas of the Body

Existing methods of measuring lymphedema-related swelling do not allow for measurements of non-limb swelling; therefore it is impossible to pinpoint how common lymphedema is in other areas of the body. Available estimates of lymphedema of the genitals range from 2 to 5 percent. Information is not available for how commonly lymphedema of the head and neck or trunk occurs.

More Lymphedema Cases Detected *and* Prevented

Diagnosed cases of lymphedema may be increasing even as methods of reducing the incidence of lymphedema are successfully preventing the condition. For example, even conservative surgery such as lumpectomy (removal of only the tumor and a surrounding margin of normal breast tissue) and sentinel lymph node biopsy (see page 23), which could reduce lymphedema risk, continue to be accompanied by radiation treatment, which may increase risk. Other reasons for increased incidence are explained here.

Lymphedema Appears Months or Years after Treatment

Although extensive lymph node sampling and biopsy is becoming less widespread, it was used for many years to diagnose and treat cancer. These procedures increase lymphedema risk. Current, less invasive surgical procedures could prevent some future cases of lymphedema. But because there is a delay in lymphedema onset, people developing the condition now may reflect the vigorous lymph node examination or radiation treatment to the lymph system used in years past. It will take years to see the impact of less invasive treatments on the number of lymphedema cases that develop.

Awareness and Diagnosis Are Increasing

Both patients and doctors are becoming more aware of what lymphedema is, so more cases are accurately diagnosed. More people with lymphedema recognize that prompt and appropriate care can help alleviate symptoms. Therefore these people may be more likely to seek treatment rather than languishing without proper care.

People Are Living Longer after Cancer Treatment

Treatment advancements are helping more people to live long lives after cancer. The same health-preserving surgery or radiation that can extend a patient's survival puts her at risk for lymphedema by allowing more years in her lifetime for the condition to develop.

What Are the Risk Factors for Lymphedema?

As explained in chapter 1, lymphedema results from an overload in the amount of fluid, proteins, and other substances in the body tissues. When lymphedema develops, it is because for some reason lymph is not traveling freely from the affected body area as it should, either because of a blockage in or damage to the lymph system.

Changes in the lymph system may be due to:

- **surgery:** During surgery for some cancers (or for other conditions), lymph nodes and any lymph vessels intertwined with the nodes may be cut or removed. Having many lymph nodes removed from under the arm, in the groin, or in the pelvis increases the risk of lymphedema.
- **radiation therapy:** Because it may damage the lymph nodes and create scar tissue that constricts lymph vessels, radiation treatment under the arm or in the groin, pelvis, or neck can affect the flow of lymph fluid, putting a patient at increased risk for lymphedema.
- **infection:** An infection that has spread to the lymph nodes may block the passage of lymph fluid through the nodes and lead to a buildup of lymph. Infections can also damage the lymph vessels just under the skin.
- **tumor growth:** Tumors that have invaded an area of the lymph system can affect its functioning and may cause lymphedema.
- **other health conditions or injury:** Certain health conditions (infections or blood vessel conditions, for example) or severe trauma to the body that injures the lymph system may impair lymph flow in the same way that cancer treatment, infection, or invading cancer can.

Surgery

The lymph system may be directly impaired by surgery or affected by scar tissue that forms after surgery. A lymph node *biopsy* involves surgically removing a lymph node and examining the tissue under a microscope to detect or rule out the presence of cancer.

Sentinel Lymph Node Biopsy May Reduce Lymphedema Risk

Because the main side effect of removing lymph nodes is the development of lymphedema, doctors have tried to develop new ways of determining if cancer has spread to lymph nodes without removing all of them. Procedures such as the sentinel lymph node biopsy (also called sentinel node biopsy) should reduce the number of people who develop lymphedema. As this is a relatively new procedure, long-term data about how risk is affected is not yet available, but few cases of lymphedema have been reported following sentinel lymph node biopsy.

In a sentinel node biopsy, a radioactive substance and a blue dye are injected into the area around the tumor. The surgeon finds and removes the "sentinel node(s)"—the first lymph node or nodes into which these substances accumulate—by using a handheld Geiger counter and looking for a lymph node colored by the blue dye (the usual color of lymph nodes is pinkish tan). The sentinel node is the lymph node most likely to contain cancer cells because it is connected to lymph vessels that surround the tumor. Once it has been removed, the node is examined under a microscope by a pathologist, a doctor who specializes in laboratory tests to diagnose diseases.

If the sentinel node contains cancer, the surgeon removes more lymph nodes in the area. If the sentinel node is cancer-free, full lymph node surgery is avoided. This careful process is likely to reduce the risk of lymphedema.

This limited sampling of lymph nodes is not appropriate for some patients. For example, if a woman with breast cancer has multiple underarm lymph nodes that are enlarged and very firm in consistency (indicating they contain large deposits of cancer), a traditional lymph node dissection will probably be done rather than sentinel lymph node biopsy.

Removing multiple lymph nodes for examination is called a lymph node *dissection*. The removal of lymph nodes directly impacts the lymph system.

The vast majority of people diagnosed with lymphedema are women who have been treated for breast cancer. Women who have a mastectomy (surgery to remove all or part of the breast and sometimes other tissue) and most women who undergo removal of even part of the breast (as in a lumpectomy) also have some lymph nodes removed. Patients with melanoma may also be treated with surgery and lymph node removal, as can those treated for ovarian, cervical, vulvar, head and neck, prostate, testicular, bladder, or colon cancer.

Lymph Node Removal

The goal of surgery may be either to remove a tumor located near or invading the lymph system (see *Tumor Growth*, below), or to remove and examine lymph nodes to determine if cancer has spread from the original cancer site.

If cancer is present, cancer cells may spread through the lymph system toward other areas of the body. Lymph nodes, in their role as part of the body's defense system, will likely have filtered out and captured some cancer cells. A surgeon may therefore remove some lymph nodes near a tumor to find out if cancer is present in the lymph nodes and if it may have spread beyond them. Some lymph vessels that carry fluid from the arms or legs to the rest of the body may also be removed because they are intertwined with the lymph nodes.

Other Surgery That Disrupts the Lymph System

Hernia surgery, bypass surgery (surgery involving the heart, arteries, or blood vessels), or knee, neck, or abdominal surgery may in rare cases disrupt the lymph system. Likewise, knee replacement, hip replacement, or vein harvesting procedures (which may be used during heart surgery) may possibly injure the lymph system and lead to lymphedema. However, this is rare because these kinds of surgery do not affect the lymph drainage basins (also called lymph node beds; a lymph basin or bed is the group of lymph nodes that drain a region of the body), for example in the groin or under the arms.

Radiation

Radiation treatment can shrink lymph nodes, cause scarring in the lymph system, or impede the flow of lymph fluid—all of which put a patient at increased risk for lymphedema. Women with breast cancer may receive radiation to the breast and underarm lymph nodes. People affected by cancer affecting the groin area or advanced cancer that has spread to the groin may receive radiation treatment that damages lymph nodes in the groin.

Tumor Growth

Although it is rare, benign or malignant (cancerous) tumors that have spread to lymph nodes in the neck, chest, underarm, pelvis, or abdomen may block the passage of lymph fluid through the nodes and lead to a buildup of lymph. Growing tumors that put pressure on the lymph vessels or the large lymph duct in the chest may also obstruct the flow of lymph.

Injury

An injury to the body may affect the lymph system in the same way surgery disrupts lymph vessels or nodes. A break in the lymph system or scar tissue resulting from damage to or near the lymph system can slow or block lymph flow.

Additional Factors That May Increase Risk

Other factors may add to a person's risk of developing lymphedema. Those who have had surgery, radiation therapy, tumor growth, or other injury that has affected the lymph system may be at increased risk for lymphedema if they also have one or more of the risk factors listed in the following sections.

Infection

Local infections can harm tissues directly, encourage the development of fibrosis (scar-like tissue), and play a role in the development of lymphedema. An infection that has spread to the lymph nodes can slow or stop lymph from flowing through lymph nodes. Even a minor infection can cause the body to send more blood and fluid to the infected area, contributing to the buildup of solid debris and triggering or worsening lymphedema.

Age Is Not a Likely Risk Factor

Age may contribute to an overall weakening of the lymph system. An older person's lymph system does not push fluid through the body as forcefully as that of a younger person. Because of this, researchers have studied the possibility that age might be a lymphedema risk factor. However, no evidence clearly indicates that a person who is older when her lymph system is damaged is more likely to develop lymphedema. Any higher rates of lymphedema in older people that do in fact exist could be related to (1) the high number of lymphedema cases in women with breast cancer and (2) the fact that over 75 percent of breast cancer cases are diagnosed (and treated in ways that may increase lymphedema risk) in women over 50. Also, older women may have been treated some time ago with methods that increased their risk more than current treatment methods might.

In an unfortunate cycle, once lymphedema has developed, it weakens or stops the filtering of bacteria, increasing the likelihood of an infection. (See chapter 6 for information about treatment for infection.)

Blood Vessel Conditions

Experts aren't sure how much slowed or blocked blood flow in the veins may contribute to lymphedema swelling. We do know that there are only two pathways for the removal of fluid from tissue: veins and the lymph system. Therefore, if veins are moving blood more slowly than is normal or if they are blocked, the lymph system has to work harder to regulate fluid in that area of the body. This restricted flow through the veins could therefore potentially contribute to the start of lymphedema and swelling, especially in the legs. Thus it's important to treat blood clot conditions quickly to avoid chronically overloading and damaging the lymph system.

Immobility

Lymph is pushed through the body by muscle contractions and involuntary movements such as breathing. Immobility (for example, if a person is on bed rest) can lead to a buildup of lymph. Moving an at-risk arm or leg as you are able is important. If you are confined to bed, talk to your doctor about exercises you may be able to do to keep lymph moving.

Obesity and Weight Gain

Some studies have shown that obesity contributes to the development of lymphedema. Women who are more severely overweight seem more likely to have severe lymphedema. However, a more important risk factor for lymphedema than weight itself may be weight *gain* after cancer treatment. A person who was obese when she was diagnosed with cancer and remained obese may not have the increased risk of someone who gained significant weight in the years since her diagnosis.

Body Mass Index

Calculating body mass index (BMI) is a way to help doctors evaluate if a person is at a healthful weight. Obesity is defined as a body mass index of over 30. However, factors other than BMI should also be considered when judging how much someone should weigh, so BMI measurements should be used only as a guide.

You can calculate your BMI by going to the American Cancer Society Web site, http://www.cancer.org, and searching for BMI or by using this equation:

BMI = (your weight in pounds × 700) ÷ (your height in inches, squared)

Talk to your doctor about your results; he understands your full health history and can put your BMI into context.

Maintaining a Healthy Weight

Maintaining a healthy weight may help prevent lymphedema from developing. And even minor weight loss can help reduce the swelling caused by lymphedema and help your health in numerous other ways. About one-third of cancer deaths are related to poor diet and not enough physical activity, and being overweight or obese is also a risk factor for heart disease and diabetes. People who maintain a healthy body weight live longer, on average, than those who do not. (See also *Be Physically Active* in chapter 3.)

Ask about Lymphedema Risk before Cancer Treatment

If you have not yet undergone cancer treatment, it is important to talk to your medical team beforehand about the possibility of lymphedema. Talk to your doctor about lymphedema risk and any ways to minimize that risk without compromising cancer treatment.

CHAPTER THREE

CAN PRECAUTIONS LOWER THE RISK OF TRIGGERING LYMPHEDEMA?

Lymphedema occurs only after a series of events and factors raise a person's risk, opening the door for its development. As you know, cancer treatment is the factor that most commonly raises the risk of lymphedema, and undergoing therapy to treat cancer is necessary to preserve a person's health.

Although certain precautions might help prevent lymphedema symptoms, sometimes lymphedema develops despite these preventative measures. No one can point to a person's actions as the reason why lymphedema occurred. There may be existing differences in some people's lymph systems that put them at increased risk for lymphedema development; the lymph anatomy has not been thoroughly studied for this possibility.

Lymphedema most commonly occurs in the limbs, but it may affect any area of the body impacted by a damaged lymph system. The general protective measures offered in this chapter and throughout the book may be applied not only to an at-risk arm, leg, hand, or foot, but to the trunk, genitals, or head and neck.

Suggested Precautions

Although much remains unproven about how to protect against triggering lymphedema, many experts recommend that people who are at risk follow the basic guidelines listed within this chapter, which may lower the risk of developing lymphedema or delay its onset. Other factors such as your health history and current health status can affect your risk and your doctor's recommendations for self care, weight maintenance, and exercise. Because each person's situation is unique, check with your doctor and your lymphedema therapist, if you have one, to find out which recommendations may be best for you.

Use Common Sense When Proof Is Lacking

Because no scientific studies have proven that lymphedema can be prevented, the recommendations offered by lymphedema experts and explored in this chapter are often based on common sense, observations, or current beliefs rather than evidence. Despite this lack of hard data, experts emphasize the importance of taking precautions that might avoid triggering lymphedema because there is no known cure for the condition once it develops.

Until more research is done, the best method of protection may be keeping in mind the suggestions here and modifying your potential risk as you can to protect your body. But you don't have to drastically change your lifestyle or avoid your regular activities. This isn't recommended, nor has it been proven to prevent lymphedema from developing.

For example, a 20-year study of women with lymphedema after breast cancer treatment tracked their former and present "high-risk" occupations and hobbies. Prior to the study, women who were cooks were thought to be at high risk for lymphedema because of the potential for burns and women who were gardeners, veterinarians, and florists were also thought to be high risk because of the risk of scratches. However, the group of "high-risk" occupations and hobbies were studied and were not clearly associated with lymphedema.

In general, people at risk are believed to reduce their chances of triggering lymphedema by (1) not stimulating the body to produce more lymph than the body can transport from that area and (2) not blocking the flow of lymph. Avoiding injury, caring properly for the skin, and exercising as directed help achieve these goals.

Protecting against potential trauma to the lymph system and infections in affected limbs are logical ways a person might help prevent lymphedema.

Be Physically Active

Your doctor may recommend special exercises as part of your lymphedema treatment. But many people with lymphedema wonder how walking, running, playing sports, or otherwise being physically active may affect their lymphedema.

It isn't known exactly how exercise affects the body of a person with a compromised lymph system. Vigorous exercise increases blood flow, which increases the amount of fluid entering the body area being exercised—most often the arms and legs. Increasing muscle metabolism also increases the production of solid debris. Some people fear that repetitive, extended exercise may therefore trigger lymphedema by overloading the local lymph system. However, many experts feel that in general, people at risk for or diagnosed with lymphedema benefit from being moderately physically active and following the precautions described in this section.

Physical activity not only helps reduce weight (which can help reduce risk, see chapter 2); it directly affects lymph flow. Muscle contractions squeeze body tissues and help move lymph through the body. Therefore physical activity, which involves many muscle movements, is good for a *normal* lymph system because it helps lymph keep flowing. Moderate physical activity is thought to also benefit an impaired lymph system. The deep breathing and movement of the diaphragm required in aerobic exercise encourages lymph to move out of the limbs and toward the heart.

You will need to weigh the potential benefits and risks of physical activity. Your body's response will depend in part upon the condition of your lymph system, how intensely you exercise, what activity you choose, and your fitness level.

Avoid Straining or Weakening Muscles

It is important to use your limb for normal everyday activities so you retain your strength. However, using muscles more intensely (as when you lift a heavy box) or for a longer period of time (as when you vacuum) than you are accustomed to can cause muscles to be "overloaded" or stressed. But experts do not thoroughly understand how "overload" works or how it may affect lymphedema. Any risk of triggering lymphedema through brief, intense muscle activity probably depends in part upon your muscle strength, size, and your aerobic fitness level.

Protecting an at-risk or affected arm or leg from all physical activity will weaken it over time. This may make it more vulnerable to overload during lower levels of activity and susceptible to lymphedema swelling.

Overuse that could result in injury has been associated with the onset of lymphedema in some people. Therefore you may want to follow these suggestions and talk to your doctor or physical therapist about physical activity recommendations that may be most appropriate for you:

- **Do not protect your arm or leg from regular movement; maintain your normal activity level.**
- **Exercise regularly but try not to over-tire your limb.** Ask your doctor or physical therapist about being fitted for a compression sleeve or stocking to wear during strenuous activities (see below).
- **If your arm or leg starts to ache, rest and elevate it.**
- **Use your unaffected arm or both arms to carry heavy items** such as groceries, handbags, or children.

Special Physical Activity Precautions

The benefits of exercise are generally thought to outweigh the risks for a person at risk for triggering lymphedema. The precautions in the sections that follow here may help you stay fit and protect your body.

Keep in mind that some types of exercise you enjoy may allow you to be vigorously active without directly involving an at-risk area of the body; for example, cycling works the legs significantly more than the arms (although it does increase blood flow in the body and therefore increases lymph flow to some extent). Gripping handlebars, dumbbells, or other exercise equipment uses muscles in the arm, and doing so for extended periods when you are not used to it could potentially overload your arm muscles.

CONSULT YOUR DOCTOR

Talk to your doctor about recommended types of exercise before you begin them. She will take into account how severe your lymphedema is, how it has progressed, how well your joints work, and your muscle strength, among other factors.

WEAR A COMPRESSION GARMENT

Ask your doctor about being professionally fitted for a compression sleeve or stocking (see chapter 6) to wear while walking or exercising. Sleeves must be professionally fitted so they are not too loose (which won't help control swelling) or too tight (which could trigger swelling by constricting at either end).

BEGIN GRADUALLY

If you are approved for activity by your doctor, are at risk, and have a properly fitted compression garment, begin a low-intensity exercise routine gently and for short periods. Be aware of which muscle groups you use during each exercise. Alternate muscle groups and take frequent rests so as not to overload your arm or leg. If you have any pain after exercise, tone down your level of activity next time and take it gradually. Lifting only light (three- to four-pound) weights or swimming slowly may be a good way to begin.

CONSIDER CONSULTING A PHYSICAL THERAPIST OR PHYSIATRIST

A physical therapist is a health professional who recommends exercises and other methods to restore or maintain the body's strength, mobility, and function, and a physiatrist is a doctor who specializes in rehabilitation medicine. These experts can provide guidance and develop a personalized exercise routine appropriate for your situation.

Everyone is different. Blanket recommendations don't take into account your specific situation and health status. You may have to wait and see if a level of physical activity causes swelling to begin or worsen. Carefully monitor the size of your at-risk arm or leg for any changes (see chapter 4 for more detail about monitoring your condition).

Repetitive Motion

Repetitive motions, according to some anecdotal reports and limited study, may trigger lymphedema. With any physical activity, lymph and blood flow through the body are increased (and could worsen the effects of a blocked area of the lymph system). Another potentially complicating factor is the possibility of muscle "overload" mentioned earlier.

However, experts are not sure if repetitive motion contributes to the development of lymphedema. There have been no large-scale studies linking repetitive motion (or other forms of physical activity) to either protecting a person from or triggering lymphedema.

If you were at risk for lymphedema and had an assembly line job doing the same strenuous, repetitive motion for eight hours a day, you might be advised to carefully monitor your at-risk body area for any changes. But in general, repetitive motions, even vacuuming, might be better rather than worse for people at risk for triggering lymphedema of the arms, and walking is encouraged for those at risk for lymphedema of the legs. (The pounding involved in jogging adds stress to the body and encourages more vigorous blood and lymph flow, but it has not been proven to trigger lymphedema.) Wearing an appropriate compression garment helps reduce the risk of triggering swelling and is critical for someone with lymphedema.

A limited and often-mentioned study of women at risk for lymphedema following breast cancer treatment who participated regularly in rowing—vigorous and repetitive upper-body conditioning—showed little to no change in arm circumference after weeks of strenuous and repetitive upper body workouts. The study participants gradually and incrementally increased their activity. More research is needed to clearly establish how repetitive motion may affect the lymph system in someone at risk for or diagnosed with lymphedema.

Try to Avoid Infection

Your body responds to infection by making extra fluid to fight the infection. This extra fluid in a compromised portion of the lymph system can overload it and trigger lymphedema in an at-risk person. Therefore good hygiene and careful skin care may reduce the risk of triggering lymphedema by helping you avoid infections.

Following the suggestions here will help you care for your at-risk limb and prevent infection, especially on the side of the body where you received treatment. The number of suggestions listed below may be discouraging at first. It takes time to adjust to changes and it is normal to sometimes feel frustrated about making changes in everyday habits. Your doctor, lymphedema therapist, or both can help you determine which measures are most important and relevant for your situation.

Maintain Clean and Soft Skin

Keep skin clean and soft to avoid cracks that could potentially let germs into the body:

- **Keep the affected limb clean.** Wash twice daily if you get dirty or perspire. Avoid vigorous scrubbing and dry your leg or arm thoroughly. Moisturize afterward.
- **Keep your hands, feet, and cuticles soft and moist** by regularly applying low pH moisturizing lotion or cream.

Avoid Cuts, Bites, or Pinpricks

Be careful to prevent breaks in the skin to avoid creating entry points for infection:

- **Use an electric shaver** for removing underarm and leg hair; it may be less likely to break the skin than a straight razor.
- **Prevent insect bites.** If necessary, cover your body with lightweight clothing or use an insect repellent when outdoors. Applying antihistamine cream may help if you are stung by a mosquito. If you are stung by a bee in the

affected limb, clean and elevate the leg or arm, apply antihistamine cream and ice, and contact your health care provider if it becomes infected.

- **Cut nails straight across.** See a podiatrist (a doctor who specializes in treating foot conditions) as needed to prevent ingrown toenails and infections.
- **Push cuticles back gently with a cuticle stick** rather than cutting them with scissors, or simply leave them as is.
- **Watch for early signs of infection.** Call your doctor right away if you develop a rash, red blotches, swelling, hot skin, tenderness, or fever.

If your arm is affected:

- **Try to have blood draws, IVs, and injections in an unaffected limb** if possible. Having a blood draw in an affected limb will not necessarily result in the development of lymphedema, but *may* trigger it (possibly because of the constriction of the tourniquet involved, although it is brief). Request that flu shots and vaccinations be given in an unaffected arm or in the hip. Avoid injections in the buttock if the leg on that side of the body is at risk for lymphedema.
- **Wear protective gloves** when doing household chores involving chemical cleansers or steel wool, gardening or yard work, and perhaps while cooking or washing dishes (to prevent cuts from knives or other sharp edges).
- **Wear a thimble** when sewing to avoid needle and pinpricks.
- **Keep pets' claws trimmed** to avoid scratches.

If your leg is affected:

- **Wear appropriate shoes.** Wear well-fitting, closed-toe shoes instead of sandals. Going barefoot increases the risk of cuts and stubbed toes.
- **Keep your feet clean and dry.** Wear cotton socks.

Care for Injuries

If you do develop a break in the skin, tend to it right away, keeping it clean and safely covered:

- **Clean and protect any skin openings** caused by cuts, abrasions, insect bites, hangnails, or torn cuticles. Wash with soap and water, use an over-the-counter antibacterial cream on any openings, then cover with a sterile bandage.
- **Use sterile gauze to wrap injuries** rather than tape; do not wrap tightly.
- **Apply cool (not cold) water to burns** for 15 minutes, then wash with soap and water and apply a clean, dry dressing.

Prevent Burns

Like infections, burns can cause the body to make extra fluid that may build up and cause swelling in an at-risk person. Try to avoid burns:

- **Protect your limb from sunburn.** Use sunscreen that is labeled SPF 15 or higher and try to stay out of the sun during the hottest part of the day. Adding a hat, an umbrella, lightweight, long-sleeved clothing, and long pants helps prevent sunburn as well.
- **Avoid activities that irritate or chap the skin.**
- **Avoid extreme hot or cold.** Don't expose the body area affected by lymphedema to ice packs, heating pads, hot tubs, and saunas. Drastic temperature changes can cause the body to send more blood to the hot or cold area of the body to regulate temperatures. Heat increases blood flow, which leads to increased lymph flow; chilling causes shivering, which increases blood and lymph flow.
- **Avoid testing water temperature with your affected limb.** Your affected leg or arm may not detect temperatures as well as it did in the past. Test bath water temperatures with an unaffected limb.

If your arm may be affected:

- **Avoid burns from frying oil and steam.** Cover the pan when frying and be careful when removing the lid from a boiling pot or microwaved dish. Use caution when draining hot foods.
- **Use oven mitts when cooking.**

Try to Avoid Constriction or Pressure

In the lymph system of a person without lymphedema, fluid moves in and out of the lymph system, blood vessels, and tissues somewhat like water traveling through a sieve. But constriction or squeezing of the arm or leg may increase the pressure in nearby blood vessels, which may increase fluid and swelling in the area (like water building up behind a dam). Some people have associated constriction with the onset of lymphedema. Try to also be careful when traveling:

- **Wear a compression garment** when you travel by air to avoid a drastic change in pressure. Ask your doctor or therapist about being fitted for a garment.

If your arm may be affected:

- **Do not wear tight jewelry, clothing, or gloves** and consider avoiding wearing jewelry (including rings, bracelets, and watches) altogether on the limb at risk for lymphedema.

- **Avoid using shoulder straps** on an at-risk arm when carrying briefcases or purses.
- **Avoid having your blood pressure taken on the affected limb** since the cuff constricts the arm.
- Women should **wear a loose-fitting bra** so the straps do not dig into the shoulder of the at-risk arm. If you are using a prosthesis (breast form) following a mastectomy, use a lightweight prosthesis rather than a heavier one.

If your leg may be affected:
- **Avoid wearing tight elastic bands** such as those on socks, stockings, or undergarments.
- **Do not cross your legs** while sitting.
- **Avoid sitting or standing in one position** for more than 30 minutes. Movement allows muscles to pump and enhance lymph flow.

Make Sure Health Care Professionals Know about Your Risk

Let each new doctor or nurse who cares for you know that you are at risk for lymphedema. If possible, you may want to avoid having your blood pressure taken or a blood sample drawn in a way that might constrict an at-risk limb and trigger lymphedema (see *Try to Avoid Constriction or Pressure* on the facing page). A health care professional may be able to successfully treat you *and* avoid triggering your lymphedema, but only if aware of your risk.

Keep in mind, however, that it's likely more important to protect against infection and breaking the skin through burns, cuts, hangnails, or biting your nails than to avoid a health care professional's drawing blood (which involves a brief period of constriction and a sterile needle).

Carry Information about Your Risk

You may want to carry brief, clearly stated information about your lymphedema risk in your wallet along with your identification or health insurance card. However, keep in mind that an emergency health care worker will rightfully focus on preserving life through necessary measures rather than pausing to note lymphedema risk.

Some at-risk people choose to purchase and wear a wristband, bracelet, or necklace referring to a wallet card with information about risk. A MedicAlert or other similar bracelet or necklace or the National Lymphedema Network's (NLN) Lymphedema Alert bracelets and necklaces (http://www.lymphnet.org/bracelet.html) can spell out

Air Travel and Lymphedema

Lymphedema onset has been associated with air travel. This potential trigger may be due to a combination of factors, which are listed below. Precautions that may reduce the risk of triggering lymphedema are also listed.

Factor that May Increase Risk	How to Reduce Risk
Changes in pressure. The pressure at flying altitude is lower than that on the ground and can allow fluids to gather in the limbs.	• Talk to your doctor about a professionally fitted compression garment. • Wear your compression garment when traveling by air (put it on before you leave home and remove it when you arrive at your destination).
Sitting still. Staying seated and still slows lymph movement and may allow fluid to build up in the arms or legs.	• Get up, stretch your legs, and walk up and down the aisle every hour during the flight. • Consider taking advantage of short "airline yoga" guides available on some airlines. • Lift the arms, stretch the shoulders, gently twist the abdomen, and flex the arms and legs. • Deep abdominal breathing moves the diaphragm and helps lymph flow.
Lifting and carrying luggage. Lifting and carrying heavy baggage can put the muscles at risk of being overloaded and causing swelling.	• Pack lightly if you can. • Consider checking baggage rather than lifting heavy bags to and from the overhead compartment. • Ask for help lifting and carrying bags if necessary.
Dehydration. The air in a plane is dry and can dehydrate the body. Lymph is protein-rich, and protein molecules draw in and hold water, which can cause or worsen swelling.	• Drink non-alcoholic beverages such as water and fruit juices before and during the flight. • Alcohol contributes to dehydration, so consider drinking little or no alcohol before and during the flight. • Avoid salty snacks.

Air Travel and Lymphedema *(continued)*

One frequently cited potential factor is air pressure. A person without lymphedema may not be able to get his shoes on after a long flight because the lower air pressure allows blood to pool and make the foot swell; lowered air pressure may allow some of the same pooling in the lymph system.

However, at an altitude of 37,000 feet, the cabin air pressure is roughly the same as that of an altitude of 5,000 to 8,000 feet above sea level. You would expect that if air pressure in airplanes triggered lymphedema, living in or traveling to areas of the United States at these altitudes would also be likely to bring on lymphedema. Yet higher rates of lymphedema have not been reported in areas of high elevation.

Ask your doctor if you should consider wearing a professionally fitted compression sleeve or stocking when flying if you fly frequently or for long flights. A well-fitted compression garment may help prevent swelling by providing external support. Make sure to wear a new compression garment before travel to ensure that it fits properly. (See chapter 6 for more information about compression garments.)

your risk. Note that wearing constricting jewelry such as a bracelet that is too tight is *not* recommended for a person at risk for or affected by lymphedema.

A notice of your arm risk might read: "I am at risk for lymphedema. Please draw blood, take blood pressure, give an IV or any other injection in my _____ (*right or left—whichever is unaffected*) arm." Sign this notice and ask that the information be prominently entered into your medical chart. (Note that health care professionals rarely take such measures on the leg rather than the arm because of the risk of blood clots in the leg veins.)

If You Are In the Hospital

If you are in the hospital you will have numerous health care professionals caring for you and you may not be able to tell them all about your lymphedema risk. You may want a notice of your risk posted at the head or foot of your bed and ask your loved ones to share your risk with your health care providers. Before having surgery you may want to ask your surgeon to talk to your doctor or your lymphedema therapist to clarify the potential impact of surgery and request he take action, if possible, to minimize further disruption of your lymph system.

If You Are Undergoing Chemotherapy or Radiation

If you are undergoing intravenous chemotherapy, you will be receiving many injections. If your arm is at risk, talk to your doctor about injecting the other arm or inserting a vascular access device (VAD) into the chest or arm for injections. Drugs can then be given directly into the VAD or through an intravenous line (IV) connected to the VAD when you go in for chemotherapy.

Chemotherapy temporarily weakens your immune system and increases your chance of developing an infection, bruising, or bleeding. Examine your skin regularly for problems, alert your doctor to any redness or potential infection, and keep your skin clean to reduce the risk of lymphedema.

If you are undergoing radiation, care for your affected skin gently with antibiotic ointment and avoid extensive exposure to sunlight and harsh conditions such as chlorinated water in a pool or hot tub.

While precautions may help people avoid triggering lymphedema, some people may follow precautions precisely and still develop the condition. One of the first symptoms of lymphedema may be a feeling of tightness around the arm, hand, leg, or foot on the side of the body that was treated for cancer. Chapter 4 explores why monitoring your body and potential lymphedema symptoms can help lead to prompt diagnosis, and the importance of evaluating suspicious symptoms right away. If you do develop lymphedema, effective treatment exists to help manage the condition.

❧ How can I tell if I have symptoms of lymphedema?

❧ How can I remain aware of changes in my own arm or leg?

❧ Things don't feel quite right and I think I might have lymphedema. How can I explain to my doctor why I'm concerned?

❧ If I have swelling, can my doctor examine me and tell me if it's lymphedema right away?

❧ What does my weight have to do with lymphedema?

❧ My doctor measured my leg with a tape measure and says I have lymphedema. Is this all that is needed to diagnose lymphedema?

❧ What kind of information could I share to help my doctor evaluate me for lymphedema?

BILL'S STORY ✑
Coping with Lymphedema

WHAT I WISH I'D KNOWN

I had surgery on my left shoulder five years ago for skin cancer (squamous cell carcinoma), then surgery to remove lymph nodes under my arms the following year. I wish that someone had told me that lymphedema was a possible treatment outcome. If someone did tell me, it wasn't emphasized. So lymphedema came as a surprise.

TREATMENT HELPED DRAMATICALLY

My surgeon referred me to lymphedema therapists, who have given me most of my information about lymphedema. Therapy reduced the swelling so my affected arm is fairly close to the size of my right arm. I had manual lymph drainage (MLD) at therapy and did some at home, which wasn't as effective. Now I wear a compression garment that helps maintain the progress we made. I've gone back to therapy for MLD to get the swelling down before ordering a new sleeve.

My wife helps pull my compression sleeve all the way up, but I can get it on pretty well myself using a plastic donning aid. When I sleep I wear a special padded sleeve, which I think looks like an arm protector for dog training. It's great; it gives relief from wearing the sleeve all day.

HOW LYMPHEDEMA HAS CHANGED THINGS

I like to do a lot of landscaping work in the backyard and it's been curtailed significantly because of a combination of discomfort, loss of strength, and limits in my range of motion. I still have some swelling. It's difficult to get a button-down shirt over that arm, so I don't wear that kind of shirt, and I'm self-conscious about wearing short-sleeved shirts. But having lymphedema in my left arm rather than my right, dominant arm was a blessing.

WHEN PEOPLE ASK QUESTIONS

What calls people's attention to the lymphedema more than the swelling is the compression sleeve. Sometimes people ask what's wrong with my arm, and I just explain what lymphedema is. Most of the time they haven't heard of it, and they just say "oh" and that's the end of that.

KEEPING PERSPECTIVE

Lymphedema isn't a pleasant experience. It's bothersome, but after a while it became part of my body and I just coped with it. Try to give it time and get a good-fitting compression garment and eventually lymphedema will become a smaller part of your life.

—BILL
lymphedema of the arm
following surgery on lymph nodes

CHAPTER FOUR

EARLY DIAGNOSIS IS ESSENTIAL

Careful monitoring and follow up after cancer treatment can help diagnose lymphedema early, which may prevent severe lymphedema-related complications and allow for less intensive management options. Early diagnosis may also allow for more successful treatment and improved outcomes.

Lymphedema that is not promptly treated can delay wound healing and increase the likelihood of infections. A buildup of lymph fluid in the tissues can also lead to discomfort, swelling, and skin changes.

In this chapter we explore the challenges of diagnosing lymphedema. We also describe how health care providers determine if lymphedema is present and why early detection is essential in stopping the progression of lymphedema.

The Challenge of Diagnosing Lymphedema

A delayed diagnosis can limit options for early, more effective treatment. Several factors complicate the diagnosis of lymphedema—and can frustrate those in need of prompt attention:

- Criteria for diagnosing lymphedema are not universally recognized.
- It is difficult to precisely evaluate the symptoms of lymphedema; evaluation requires expertise and can involve specialized equipment.

- Many health care professionals are not educated about lymphedema.

You are the one most likely to notice changes in your own body. Stay aware, and bring any suspicious symptoms to the attention of your doctor.

Your Role in Diagnosing Lymphedema

If you are at risk, it is important to be aware of potential symptoms of lymphedema. One of the first symptoms a person with lymphedema may experience is a feeling of tightness in the at-risk limb. Your clothes may feel snug or your fingers may be swollen and your rings feel tight. Promptly report to a doctor or nurse any tightness, skin changes, or swelling that could indicate early lymphedema. Also report any limb injury or infection, however minor it may seem, which could trigger lymphedema.

Note that in some cases swelling may be caused by cancer recurrence, so it is doubly important to see your doctor if you develop what seem to be lymphedema-related symptoms.

Being Aware and Examining Your Body

If you notice any of the symptoms listed in chapter 1 that last for one to two weeks— or any worrisome body changes or other side effects, including weight loss, weakness, numbness, tingling, or pain—call your health care provider. Don't wait for a scheduled follow-up visit. Your doctor can determine if any changes may be due to lymphedema or to cancer, treatment, or another health condition.

Although the methods suggested below don't precisely measure limb size and condition, following them regularly may help you notice any changes in your limb size or skin condition. They only apply to evaluating arms or legs, not other body areas:

Examining Your Body for Changes
- **If your arm is at risk, trace your finger along your triceps,** the muscles on the back of your upper arm. Note if there is any change in or fullness of the tissue covering the muscle.
- **If your leg is at risk, pinch the skin over the toes** or above the balls of both feet. Is one side thicker, rubbery, or more difficult to pick up? It may be easiest to notice changes in your feet.

You may want to briefly examine your at-risk body area each day for changes or potential signs of lymphedema and look at your body in front of a mirror. Tell your doctor if you notice any changes:

- **Examine the symmetry of bony areas**—your knees, ankles, elbows, or wrists. Does each leg or arm "match"? Lymphedema commonly causes soft tissue accumulation in bony areas, and the following measures will highlight any difference in symmetry:

  (1) Look at your arms or legs from the front and sides while holding them as straight as possible.

  (2) Examine your:
      - arms when holding them straight out to the side, then with your elbows bent 90 degrees in front of you and your fingers pointed to the ceiling
      - knees when you are sitting and your legs are bent 90 degrees. If your leg is at risk, is the area behind the ankle (near the Achilles tendon) puffy? Are the indents behind the side of the ankle swollen?

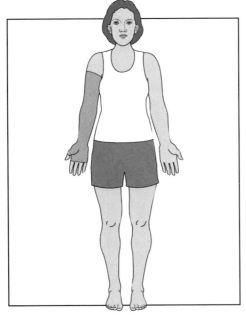

Figure 4.1
Look at your arms or legs from the front when they are as straight as possible.

Figure 4.2
Look at your arms or legs from the side when they are as straight as possible.

(3) Look at your arms with your fingers pointing toward you in the mirror, then with your elbows bent and palms on your shoulders.

- **Note how prominent veins and tendons are** on each of your arms or legs. Are you able to trace veins along the inside of your forearms? On the back of the hand and near the knuckles? What about on the top of the foot?
- **Measure your arm or leg** regularly in the same two places. Measuring at bony places such as the elbow, wrist, ankle, or knee may be easiest. (See page 53 for more about how health care providers measure limbs as part of diagnosis.)

Being an Active Participant in Follow-Up Doctor's Visits

After cancer treatment, you will probably have follow-up appointments with your doctor every three or four months for two to three years and once or twice a year after that. Follow-up care is primarily aimed at allowing doctors to check whether your

Figure 4.3
Examine your arms when holding them straight out to the side.

Figure 4.4
Examine your arms with your arms to the side and elbows bent 90 degrees, fingers pointed up.

cancer has returned or spread. But follow-up appointments can also allow your health care provider to spot treatment side effects or complications—such as lymphedema—that develop immediately or long after treatment is finished.

At each follow-up visit, tell your health care provider about any pain, new or changing symptoms, or physical problems that affect your daily activities. At any visit with a new doctor or nurse, make sure to share your cancer history, cancer type, and details about treatment you received. These factors may affect your care. Share information about any prior surgeries and especially lymph node removal, including the number of nodes removed and whether you had radiation therapy. Voice your concerns about blood pressure cuffs or blood draws and the risk of triggering lymphedema.

If you are not confident that you can correctly provide information about your cancer and treatment, ask your oncologist for a short summary of your cancer history, including cancer diagnosis, stage, and procedures done to diagnose and treat cancer. Provide copies of your cancer history to doctors, massage therapists, and other health care team members who care for you.

Figure 4.5
Look at your arms when your fingers are pointing toward you in the mirror.

Figure 4.6
Look at your arms with your arms in front of you, elbows bent, and palms on your shoulders.

How Lymphedema Is Diagnosed

There is not a set of specific criteria universally used to diagnose lymphedema. However, the presence of certain symptoms helps a health care team rule out other conditions and potentially establish a lymphedema diagnosis.

To evaluate you for lymphedema, doctors (1) review your medical history and health status and (2) physically examine your body. After discussing your health status, your health care provider will look at your at-risk or affected limb and examine it for visible signs. A physical evaluation for lymphedema should include:

- a general examination
- determination of weight and ideal healthy weight
- measurements of the arms or legs
- evaluation of symptoms and changes in sensation in the affected body part
- measurement of protein levels in the blood to help rule out nutrition-related fluid retention and swelling, through what is called an albumin (protein) test

If your health care provider is not experienced in diagnosing lymphedema, you may want to ask for a referral to a professional with experience in diagnosing lymphedema. Contact the National Lymphedema Network (NLN; 800-541-3259; http://www.lymphnet.org) for a list of doctors who have lymphology as a sub-specialty.

You may want to use the information in the remainder of this chapter to guide your discussion with your doctor. If your doctor doesn't pursue the methods here, bring them up and ask about them. Doctors should be receptive to talking through their diagnosis methods.

Reviewing Medical History and Health Status

In attempting to diagnose or rule out lymphedema, doctors will review your medical records, including lab and diagnostic tests, if they are available. To create a complete picture of your medical history, a health care provider will ask questions related to potential causes, triggers, and the progression of lymphedema, as well as any prior history of or treatment for lymphedema. Your doctors may also ask you about any weight changes in the past year, how often you exercise, allergies, and medications you are taking, both prescription and nonprescription (such as dietary supplements).

Certain health conditions may cause lymphedema-like symptoms, contribute to lymphedema, or affect lymphedema treatment options. Therefore if you experience any of the effects listed in this section, your doctor will want to find out if you have other medical conditions, including diabetes, kidney disease, high blood pressure, heart conditions, deep vein thrombosis (a blood clot that usually occurs in the deep veins of the lower leg), or chronic venous insufficiency (poor blood circulation from the legs to the heart). Some signs that could seem to indicate lymphedema could actually be related to cancer or another condition that impairs lymph circulation. Someone with heart or respiratory problems, for example, may have swelling that is not lymphedema. Using lymphedema treatment methods on swelling caused by other conditions may cause serious complications. See your doctor promptly to determine the cause of any changes in your health status and determine how best to manage them.

Assessing General Health

A person's general health and body systems may affect lymphedema and vice versa. During the general exam, your health care provider will take your blood pressure, pulse, and respiratory rate. He may also assess your range of motion, strength, and fine motor skills, which may be negatively affected by the effects of lymphedema.

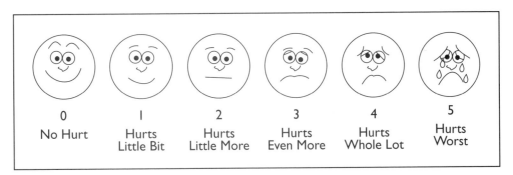

| 0 | 1 | 2 | 3 | 4 | 5 |
| No Hurt | Hurts Little Bit | Hurts Little More | Hurts Even More | Hurts Whole Lot | Hurts Worst |

Figure 4.7 Wong-Baker FACES Pain Rating Scale

This is a common type of pain rating scale that is easy to understand and generally allows a person to provide an accurate measure of his or her pain. You may use it to evaluate how factors or activities increase or alleviate your pain or to gauge whether medication or treatment is relieving pain. If you are keeping records of daily activities or lymphedema management strategies and what helps or hurts, including simple line drawings of these faces may help you compare your comfort levels on different days and better understand pain patterns. From Wong DL, Hockenberry-Eaton M, Wilson D, Winkelstein ML, Schwartz P: *Wong's Essentials of Pediatric Nursing*, ed. 6, St. Louis, 2001, p.1301. Copyrighted by Mosby, Inc. Reprinted by permission.

Lymphedema Questionnaire

If you suspect you have lymphedema, your doctor will likely ask you many of the questions below. As you prepare for your visit, you may want to jot down your answers to these questions and think through your symptoms, their progression, and their effects on your quality of life. You may want to offer your answers to your doctor as a reference. Insert any detail you feel is relevant to share, and also write down any questions you have for your doctor in preparation for your appointment.

Your cancer history

1. What type of cancer were you treated for? _____

2. What type of treatment(s) did you receive? How long ago did you have treatment? ____

   _____

3. Have you had lymph nodes removed? How many, and from what area of the body were they removed? _____

Other potential causes or triggers

1. Have you sustained even minor injury (including burns, bites or stings, or broken skin) to your abdomen, arms, or legs? _____

2. Did you have an infection before your symptoms developed? _____

3. Have you been immobile for a time (for example, using a wheelchair)? If so, for how long? _____

4. Have you traveled to a developing country (where filaria—worms that can enter the body following a bite by an infected insect and disrupt the lymph system—are present)? _____

Changes in the limb

1. Have you noticed feelings of tightening or heaviness in your arm or leg? If so, approximately how long ago did they begin? _____

2. Have you had a hard time fitting your leg or arm into sleeves or pant legs? _____

3. Do rings, watches, bracelets, pants, socks, or shoes fit more tightly than usual, although you have not gained weight? _____

4. Have you felt weakness, pain, or aching in your limb? _____

5. Have you felt tingling or numbness in your limb? _____

6. Have you noticed redness, swelling, or signs of infection in your limb? _____

Lymphedema Questionnaire *(continued)*

Skin changes

1. Does your skin look shiny, have fewer folds, and feel stiff or taut, or does your skin indent when pressed and stay indented? _____

2. Have you experienced skin changes in your affected limb, such as weeping or oozing fluid? _____

Potential triggers and progression of symptoms

1. Have you experienced any similar symptoms before? If so, did you receive treatment for them? What type of treatment? _____

_____

2. How do your symptoms change with body position or activity? Have any specific factors seemed to bring on or worsen them? _____

3. How have your symptoms changed over time? _____

Effects on your daily life

1. Is your dominant arm affected? _____

2. Do you have decreased flexibility or range of motion in your hand, elbow, wrist, fingers, leg, knee, ankle, or toes? _____

3. Have you had trouble sleeping because of discomfort in your arm or leg? _____

My questions to ask

1. _____

2. _____

3. _____

Assessing Any Pain

Some people with lymphedema experience discomfort or pain. If you are in pain, your health care team will likely run additional tests to figure out the cause, whether lymphedema or another health issue. (See chapter 6 for various ways of relieving pain caused by lymphedema.)

A pain scale may help you explain your level of pain and how it fluctuates according to certain activities or other factors. Consider the following questions as you evaluate any pain you are experiencing, and share the answers with your doctor:

- How long have you experienced pain?
- Did you have pain or other symptoms before you showed signs of lymphedema?
- Where do you feel the most intense pain? Does it radiate out from that area?
- Is your pain constant?
- What makes the pain worse? What makes it better?
- How does activity affect your pain?
- Does pain vary with the degree of swelling in your affected body part?
- Does pain subside after a night of sleep and worsen through the day? Or is the opposite true?
- How would you describe your pain (for example, achy, throbbing, stabbing, shocking, or burning)?
- How would you rate your pain on a scale of 0 to 10?

Evaluating Healthy Weight: Body Mass Index

During a physical exam, health care providers note your height, how much you weigh, and your body mass index (BMI). Obesity and weight gain can contribute to the development of lymphedema, so a doctor may recommend that you focus on eating healthfully, as well as being physically active, as appropriate. (See chapter 2 for information about body mass index, physical activity, and lymphedema.)

Identifying External Stress on the Lymph System

The doctor may also weigh your breast prosthesis if you have one and make note of the locations, lengths, and widths of any scars. Scars from surgery can obstruct lymph flow when scar tissue hardens and attaches to underlying structures (physical therapists can help break up some of the restriction caused by scarring).

Doctors may also look for indications of constriction—such as marks from tight bra straps, socks, watches, rings, or bracelets—to determine if tight clothes or jewelry may be triggering lymphedema.

Evaluating the Risk of Potential Cancer Recurrence

Your doctor may request your pathology report because information such as the location and number of lymph nodes surgically removed or potentially damaged by radiation may help her evaluate the risk that cancer recurrence is causing lymphedema. Tell your health care provider if you are in pain or having range-of-motion problems, weakness, burning or prickling, or numbness.

Evaluating Sensations of Fullness or Tightness

Diagnosing lymphedema before swelling occurs allows for the most effective management. Lymphedema that causes a feeling of fullness or tightness but does not yet cause swelling (stage 0 lymphedema; see page 59) should be monitored. Although this stage of lymphedema does not usually require active treatment, taking certain precautions can help prevent it from worsening and causing more serious complications (see chapter 3).

Tell your doctor as accurately as you can when the feeling began, how persistent it is, and if anything about the sensation has changed over time. Keeping written records of the dates you notice changes and descriptions of what you experience may help your doctor better understand your health status and help plan for potential future treatments.

Evaluating Skin Condition

In diagnosing or ruling out lymphedema, your health care provider will look at your limb and skin condition and note any visible skin changes such as altered texture, firmness, color, temperature, and any breaks in the skin.

Keep in mind that there is no standard language used to discuss the appearance of the skin, but your doctor will note anything not typical and anything that differs from conditions in other areas of your body. He will specifically look for skin that pits (indents when pressed), fibrotic (hard or scar-like) areas, any lymphoceles (firm areas of swelling due to lymph buildup) close enough to the skin to be felt, breaks in the skin, or infection. Remember, you are the best source of information on skin changes; be prepared to tell your doctor about any changes you have noticed since your last visit.

Measuring and Comparing Limb Size

One way doctors diagnose lymphedema is by comparing a person's limbs and identifying a difference in size. This is currently done by measuring either each limb's (1) circumference (the distance around the limb) at the same point or (2) volume (the amount of space it takes up). Neither method is considered both consistent and accessible enough to be standard.

Limb size may vary in a person; a right-handed person may naturally have a larger right arm than left, even if her left arm is affected by mild lymphedema. Limb size may change over time because of factors such as changes in your activities, the effects of cancer treatment, and weight loss or gain.

These methods of measuring are not useful in evaluating lymphedema swelling that occurs in both limbs or in other areas of the body, such as the trunk; a system has not yet been developed to measure non-limb lymphedema swelling.

Keep in mind that some people may experience other symptoms of lymphedema (such as a feeling of heaviness in the affected limb) without showing a large difference in limb volume. Therefore health care providers will take into account your other lymphedema-related symptoms as they evaluate your limb size and potential lymphedema.

Limb Circumference

Measuring both arms or legs at several corresponding points and noting any difference in size is the most widely used method of diagnosing lymphedema. Some doctors use a tape measure to measure around the swollen limb and the unaffected limb in several places. This technique is sometimes called the comparative circumferential measurement method (CCMM). A size difference of one to two centimeters (less than one-half inch to approximately three-fourths of an inch) or more between limbs is commonly considered a sign of lymphedema and may help a health care provider diagnose lymphedema.

Measurements made over time, including any measurements made before cancer treatment, are most helpful. However, a person's arm or leg is not often measured before treatment, so this comparison is not always possible. Having an ongoing record of limb size can also help assess changes in limb size over time—for example, to gauge improvement after treatment or swelling that is worsening.

This method is easy, requires only a tape measure and calculator, and involves a simple comparison with the unaffected limb. Immediate results help the doctor provide a diagnosis on the spot. However, as noted earlier, limb size may vary in a person, and there are a few other challenges with using this method to help diagnose lymphedema:

- **Measurements may vary** when different doctors and nurses are measuring and even when the same person measures a patient at different times. The amount of tension that should be used on the tape isn't standard. For example, if held too tightly, the tape constricts the limb and indicates a smaller measurement than is accurate.

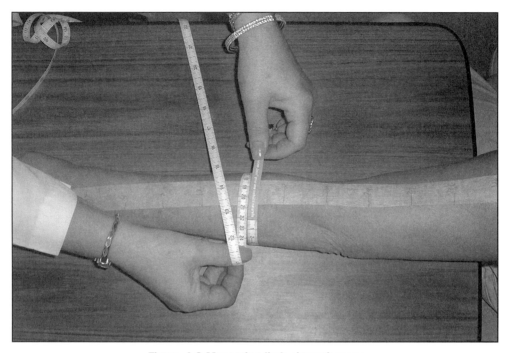

Figure 4.8 Measuring limb circumference
A nurse uses a tape measure to determine the distance around the arm of a patient with lymphedema. Applying special paper tape with measurements marked on it (shown running down the arm) during each visit and measuring at a specific line ensures that the same place on the arm is evaluated each time. Copyright 2005. From "The problem of post-breast cancer lymphedema: Impact and measurement issues" by Jane M. Armer. Nursing Perspectives. *Cancer Investigation* 2005 (1): 76–83. Reproduced by permission of Taylor & Francis Group LLC., http://www.taylorandfrancis.com.

- **There is no standard difference that constitutes lymphedema.** A difference of two centimeters would be drastic in someone with slender arms and hard to determine in someone with larger arms (although calculating the percent of change can help avoid this potential complication).
- **Minimal lymphedema may exist without creating a measurable difference** in limb size. Report any symptom of persistent tightness in your arm, hand, foot, or leg as soon as possible so it can be evaluated by a doctor.

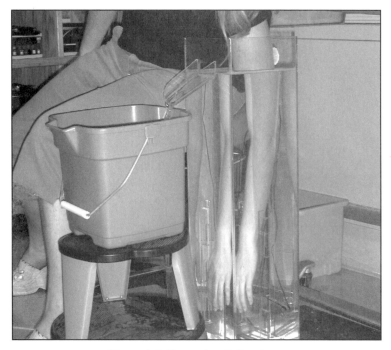

Figure 4.9 Measuring limb volume

A woman with lymphedema submerges her arm in water so doctors can determine its volume. Her arm must be submerged to the same point in the same amount of water each visit so measurements will accurately reflect changes in volume. Copyright 2005. From "The problem of post-breast cancer lymphedema: Impact and measurement issues" by Jane M. Armer. Nursing Perspectives. *Cancer Investigation* 2005 (1):76–83. Reproduced by permission of Taylor & Francis Group LLC., http://www.taylorandfrancis.com.

Limb Volume

Measuring by water displacement is more accurate than using a tape measure to determine the circumference of a limb, but doctors report common disparities in volume measurements. Measuring limbs this way is awkward and requires special, bulky (although not expensive) equipment, as well as training. Water displacement measurements don't provide information about specific areas of swelling or the shape of the swollen limb, and should not be used if the person with lymphedema has open wounds. For these reasons water displacement is not the primary method used to measure limbs.

The method involves submerging each arm or leg in a cylinder of water and noting the difference in how much the water level rises for each side of the body. The arm or leg must be submerged to exactly the same point each time, and the person must remain still and stable. Experts have not determined how much volume constitutes a significant difference, although some consider a difference of 200 ml (milliliters) important.

Perometry uses infra-red lasers (a kind of radiation similar to that used in heat lamps) to estimate the volume of an area of the body, such as a leg affected by lymphedema. However, equipment is expensive, so the test is not widely available. Further study is needed into how useful it is and how it can best be used. Perometry might be more useful for assessing lymphedema of the arm or leg and less helpful in cases of lymphedema of the trunk or head and neck.

Imaging Tests

The study of a person's health history and a physical examination usually provide the information necessary for a diagnosis of lymphedema. Imaging tests (methods that produce pictures of internal body structures) may help support diagnosis but are not definitive ways of diagnosing lymphedema. Some health care teams may use them to rule out other potential health issues. These tests may be expensive; talk to your doctor and insurance company about whether a recommended imaging test is covered under your plan, and understand beforehand what the goal of the test is and how results may affect your treatment options.

LYMPHOSCINTIGRAPHY

Lymphoscintigraphy involves injecting a radioactive substance and dye into the body so lymph flow can be seen and measured. There are no consistent standards set for interpreting the results. The test does not currently produce reliable information about the rate of lymph flow. It is very expensive, and someone with lymphedema may have "normal" results. Some lymphedema therapists may be hopeful that lympho-scintigraphy will allow them to view open lymph pathways and see where to redirect lymph, but most lymph care professionals do not feel the test provides enough detail to be useful for this purpose.

MAGNETIC RESONANCE IMAGING (MRI) AND COMPUTED TOMOGRAPHY (CT)

An MRI is a method of taking pictures of the inside of the body. Instead of using x-rays, MRI uses powerful magnetic fields to produce images. A computed tomography, or CT scan, also called a CAT scan, is an imaging test in which many x-rays of an area of the body are taken from different angles. The images are combined by a computer to produce cross-sectional images of the inside of the body. MRI and CT scan images can be made clearer through the use of a contrast material, such as a dye given into a vein or by mouth.

MRI and CT scans can identify tissue swelling but are mainly used to look for an obstruction like a tumor that could contribute to swelling. MRI and CT scans may therefore be useful in evaluating a person's risk of cancer recurrence or to rule out other causes of swelling, but neither test is used to diagnose lymphedema.

DOPPLER ULTRASOUND

An ultrasound is an imaging method in which high-frequency sound waves are used to outline a part of the body. The sound wave echoes are picked up and displayed on a television screen. A Doppler ultrasound shows the flow of blood through the body and can identify or rule out problems in the veins. For example, a Doppler ultrasound of the arm or leg affected by lymphedema and the surrounding lymph area can show if a blood clot in a blood vessel may be causing lymphedema-like swelling that is not actually lymphedema. Doppler ultrasound cannot, however, be used to directly view normal or constricted lymph flow or to diagnose lymphedema.

Lymphedema Stages or Grades

Staging or grading systems are numbers or letters assigned to sets of physical signs ranging from mild to increasingly severe. A health care provider may rely on staging or grading systems during diagnosis to describe the severity of lymphedema. Determining the grade or stage of your lymphedema can help guide treatment decisions and other care recommendations.

However, lymphedema staging and grading information is not yet standard. Health care providers, professional organizations, and other groups may rely on different systems of staging or grading. The existence of multiple systems may add to the confusion about how to talk about and categorize lymphedema. A standard staging system could improve doctors' ability to establish appropriate care for patients and could help advance the study of lymphedema by allowing the comparison of people at the same stages.

Many experts consider only three stages in evaluating lymphedema and omit the stage that doesn't involve outward signs that can be evaluated by a doctor. But an increasing number of health care professionals include the important pre-symptomatic stage, where lymphedema can be best managed, which makes for a four-stage system.

Within each stage lymphedema may be classified further, depending on how swollen the limb is:

- mild (less than a 20 percent increase in volume)
- moderate (a 20 to 40 percent increase)
- severe (over a 40 percent increase)

International Society of Lymphology Staging System

Swelling alone is not a reliable indicator of lymphedema severity. The four-stage (stages 0 through III) system of staging described below provides detail about skin condition and swelling to help more accurately categorize cases of lymphedema that occur in the limbs.

Stage 0   **No swelling or pitting** of the skin, but a person with mild, "subclinical" lymphedema may have a **feeling of heaviness in the limb** due to fluid buildup. This stage may be present for months or years before pitting, swelling, or stage I, II, or III symptoms appear.

Stage I   Stage I lymphedema **may be reversed** by elevating or compressing the limb. It is the first stage when visible symptoms occur, and may be **called "pitting" lymphedema** because a fingertip pressed into swollen limb tissue forms an indent or pit. The **arm or leg is usually not swollen in the morning** when a person wakes up, but progresses throughout the day.

Stage II   Stage II lymphedema involves **increased swelling**, which is not reduced by elevating the limb. **The skin pits**. In stage II, the **tissue is hardened** and thickened. A person with stage II lymphedema is at increased risk for infection of the tissues, such as cellulitis.

Stage III   In Stage III lymphedema the skin is affected in the deeper dermis layer, and **skin hardness and swelling are not reversible without treatment**. Typically the **affected limb is swollen and large**. The skin may thicken. Harmful bacteria thrive rather than being moved through the lymph system and may cause **skin inflammation, thickness, and toughening. Lymph may leak through damaged skin.**

Grading System for Non-Limb Lymphedema

The National Cancer Institute provides a system grading non-limb lymphedema from normal to severe. The four grades listed on the next page provide a basic method of evaluating lymphedema of the head, neck, trunk, and genitals. Current circumference and volume measurement systems do not allow for more detailed evaluation of swelling that occurs in these body areas.

Lymphedema of the Head and Neck

Stage 0   Swelling is local and doesn't affect regular functioning.

Stage I   Swelling is local and affects regular functioning.

Stage II   General swelling in the face or neck affects regular functioning (for example, it may make it more difficult for a person to turn her head or open and close her mouth).

Stage III Swelling is severe and may accompany ulcers on the skin or brain swelling; the ability to eat is severely affected.

Lymphedema of the Trunk and Genitals

Stage 0   Swelling is present or bony areas are not very easily seen beneath the swollen tissue. There may be pitting of the skin.

Stage I   Because of swelling, bony areas are very difficult to identify and natural folds of the skin aren't apparent. Swelling has changed the shape of the affected body area.

Stage II   Lymph fluid weeps through the skin. Swelling interferes with daily functioning. Swelling has drastically changed the shape of the affected body area.

Stage III Lymphedema is disabling and dramatically interferes with functioning.

Limitations of the System

Ideally a staging system could include independent evaluations of skin, tissue, and size to more accurately pinpoint lymphedema severity. The system does not yet allow for this level of detail.

Stages or grades only reflect the physical state of an arm or leg affected by lymphedema, not how it functions or how much discomfort it causes. Those with lymphedema in other body areas may be able to help doctors pinpoint the severity of their lymphedema by answering questions about symptoms and any changes in their ability to do daily tasks. A health care provider uses the various methods of testing outlined in this chapter to evaluate the functioning of the lymph system in more detail and to develop additional observations that can help in making treatment plans.

- I heard that simply keeping my arm or leg elevated will make lymphedema go away. Do I need to think about other treatments too?

- Neither my family doctor nor my oncologist seem to have any knowledge of lymphedema. Are there lymphedema specialists I can consult for a second opinion?

- I've heard about different schools that train "certified" lymphedema therapists. What does this mean, and should I focus on therapists from one school over another?

- How do I find a qualified therapist and treatment center?

- What are my treatment options? Do I need to pursue all of my therapist's treatment recommendations? What happens if I don't?

- What can I expect from treatment? Is it going to make my swelling disappear? Will my lymphedema be gone for good?

- How long do I need to receive active treatment? Can I do some of this at home?

- Can't I just use a first-aid Ace-type bandage to wrap my limb instead of the kind my therapist uses?

- How can I stay active without making my lymphedema worse?

- I've heard about surgery for lymphedema. How successful is it?

- I'm having some discomfort and slight pain. Is this normal? Should I tell my doctor about it?

- I'm not sure my insurance covers treatment. How do I find out? What are my options if it doesn't?

- Are there any resources to help me with the cost of treatment and equipment?

BARBARA'S STORY ❧
Coping with Lymphedema

BEING ALERT TO SYMPTOMS OF LYMPHEDEMA

When I was growing up, many women who had had breast cancer treatment and mastectomies—which were a big secret—also wore long sleeves, disguising the swelling in their arms. So I was aware early on that an enlarged arm could be associated with breast cancer treatment but had never heard a name for the condition.

At the hospital where I had a lumpectomy and radiation, breast cancer patients received pamphlets instructing us in lymphedema precautions, had sessions with physical therapists, and attended a presentation by a woman living with lymphedema. However, I have a dozen friends treated elsewhere who were not even told about lymphedema.

TAKING PRECAUTIONS

I was pretty good about taking the easy precautions that didn't come up every day. I didn't go into hot tubs, for example, and I wore gloves for gardening. After a long business flight or picking up my grandchildren a lot I would often feel an achy, leaden heaviness in my arm. I simply elevated it. But five years ago, not long after I celebrated the 10-year anniversary of my lumpectomy, I tried to put on my favorite bracelet and couldn't get it closed.

LOCATING TREATMENT WAS A CHALLENGE

But my HMO, surgeon, gynecologist, and internist didn't know how to advise me about finding treatment. So I sat in my living room and called about 40 different physical therapists out of the phone book. Many of them thought treating lymphedema consisted solely of hooking you up to a compression pump. Some therapists who clearly didn't know what lymphedema was assured me they could treat it, which was quite alarming. Finally I learned about a center dedicated to treating lymphedema that was not far from work. I went every weekday for four weeks and I return every six months to be measured and get replacement gloves and sleeves.

MAINTAINING PROGRESS

I wear the custom-made compression sleeve and glove prescribed for me, and I perform my lymphedema exercise program daily. I am careful to avoid any infection in my arm or hand—I use a special oven mitt to prevent burns and have prescription antibiotic cream for injuries. My arm is essentially within a centimeter of the size I had reduced it to with active treatment.

—BARBARA
lymphedema of the arm
following breast cancer treatment

CHAPTER FIVE

PREPARING FOR TREATMENT AND SETTING GOALS

Although there is currently no cure for lymphedema and it can be a long-term condition, *it can be successfully managed.* Effective treatments exist to reduce swelling and prevent swelling from getting worse, as well as limit the risk of infection—a common and problematic complication of lymphedema. Specially trained lymphedema therapists develop treatment plans, administer treatment, train you to care for your lymphedema at home, and track progress.

This chapter and the following chapter are closely linked; this chapter addresses factors to keep in mind before treatment and the next chapter outlines lymphedema treatment options that may be successful—as well as those you may hear about that may be ineffective or potentially harmful.

Prompt Treatment Is Important

Seeking and getting treatment early, before lymphedema has progressed, may allow a shorter course of active treatment to control mild, moderate, or severe lymphedema.

Early stage (stage I, for example; see chapter 4) lymphedema may be relieved by elevating the affected limb and keeping skin soft. Compression sleeves can also control swelling in early stages of lymphedema.

If lymphedema progresses, the affected limb may become hot and red and the skin may be hard and stiff. If left untreated, lymphedema can lead to lymphangitis (infection, caused when bacteria is allowed thrive in stagnant lymph), disfigurement, and debilitation or weakening of the arm.

Tell your doctor before beginning lymphedema treatment. She will want to make sure you have no health conditions that could affect your lymphedema treatment plan or be negatively affected by treatment.

Treat Underlying Conditions First

Your lymphedema treatment plan will depend upon the cause of your lymphedema. Because swelling may be caused by other health conditions, lymphedema treatment may be affected by other conditions, and because lymphedema treatment could exacerbate other problems, your health care provider will identify and address any other existing health issues before you begin lymphedema treatment.

Deep venous thrombosis (DVT; blood clots in the legs), heart disease, liver or kidney conditions, and other disorders may cause limb swelling and should be treated independently from the lymphedema. Talk to your doctor about DVT. If it is an active concern, lymphedema treatment should be postponed until the DVT is resolved. Massage of the lymph system is not recommended for people suffering from blood clots. Massage could stimulate blood clots to move toward the heart, which could be life threatening.

Infections

If you have lymphedema and also have an infection in the lymph system, your infection must be treated before lymphedema itself is managed. If infection develops, all ongoing lymphedema treatments, including massage and compression, will be stopped until your doctor prescribes an appropriate antibiotic (a medicine used to kill bacteria that cause disease) such as penicillin. You may resume lymphedema treatment while treating the infection to prevent your lymphedema from getting worse and reduce the risk of another infection.

Communicating with Your Lymphedema Therapist

It is the health care professional's job to make you feel comfortable with the information you're getting and to be sure you understand the condition and the treatment options available to you. Don't be afraid to take notes and ask for exact explanations you can review after your appointment. If you don't understand information related to your care, ask that it be repeated, rephrased, or explained. You might say, "I'm having trouble understanding what you said—would you mind telling me again, and could you put it another way?" It may also be useful to repeat what was said and ask for confirmation: "Let me see if I have it right. You're saying that…"

If you are researching options, show the therapist that you are an educated patient and that you want him to be a supportive partner. Don't feel embarrassed to ask questions. Prepare a list ahead of time, and when you meet with him, ask the most important questions first.

Tell your lymphedema therapist about your concerns so he can help you find a solution. Only you know what you're feeling. Therapists cannot help you meet your needs if you don't make them known.

Your Role in Your Treatment

Treatment for lymphedema isn't passive. You will need to participate in treating and managing your lymphedema. In fact, you are *the* most important factor in the successful management of lymphedema. Self care (care you provide for your own lymphedema) is essential. After active treatment, you will need top commit yourself to reducing your symptoms by taking daily precautions—for example, caring for your skin and applying compression bandaging. It's important to follow through with treatment and your self-care treatment measures to prevent lymphedema from progressing.

Setting Treatment Goals

Talk with your lymphedema care specialist about treatment goals, including (1) the tasks and time demands that will be required of you during treatment and (2) realistic expectations for treatment outcomes. Treatment goals will depend on the severity of your lymphedema and any other health conditions you may have, as well as your ability and willingness to adhere to treatment recommendations, such as bandaging your limb.

Your Independent Care Goals

Insert the details of your self care, as determined by you and your care specialist. Make sure you understand the details of your expected role in treatment so you can correctly follow recommendations and achieve positive results.

Skin care _____
_____
_____

Bandaging _____
_____
_____

Self massage _____
_____
_____

Therapeutic exercise_____
_____
_____

Special precautions _____
_____
_____

Other care _____
_____
_____

Plans for assistance if unable to care for myself as outlined here _____
_____
_____
_____

Daily Life and Home Factors That May Affect Treatment

The self-care methods that are most effective in managing lymphedema can be a challenge; they may be time-consuming and difficult to complete without the help of another person. Personal factors may affect your ability to travel to a care facility and bandage or exercise at home.

You may want to consider the issues below and discuss them with your lymphedema specialist to ensure that she understands the specifics of your life and lifestyle. She may be able to suggest potential solutions to anticipated challenges. Note that community services such as home health care, day services, housekeeping, home delivery of prepared meals, transportation, senior center programs, and others may be available to you.

HOME LIFE

- Do you live with others or alone?
- Do you work full-time or part-time? At home or in an office? What types of activities are involved (for example, extensive typing, lifting boxes, or standing for long periods)?
- Do you have physical limitations, such as difficulty reaching, moving around, completing household chores, driving, or bathing or dressing?
- Do you currently receive any help (from a friend, family member, other caregiver, or community service) with personal care, physical therapy, or transportation?

OBTAINING HELP FROM OTHERS IF NECESSARY

- **Travel:** Do you have a friend or family member who could help you travel to treatment if needed?
- **Bandaging and skin care:** Do you have a friend or family member who could help you regularly bandage your affected limb or help you care for your skin if needed? Do you have someone to call on if that helper is unable to help you?
- **Massage:** Do you have a friend or family member willing to be trained by a professional to provide special lymphedema massage on your affected limb?
- **Exercise:** Do you have a friend or family member who could help you regularly exercise your affected limb if needed?

Treatment Goals

Although it's difficult to precisely measure treatment results, tracking changes in your condition and ability to do daily tasks can help you stay motivated and help you and your lymphedema therapist customize your treatment.

Talk to your therapist about realistic goals and areas in which you can expect marked improvement. This simplified sheet is a starting point. Your therapist can help tailor your treatment and goals to your specific situation. Remember that many factors can affect your results.

You may want to copy this worksheet so you may record your revised symptom conditions and goals on a new sheet as you make progress.

	Current Status	Treatment Specifics and Goal
Limb circumference or volume (cm or ml)		
Range of motion (as measured by your therapist)		
Skin condition (note any problems and details)		
• Skin breaks		
• Texture		
• Pitting		
• Swelling		
• Other		
Quality of Life (consider things you are currently unable to do, have difficulty doing, or feel self-conscious doing)		

By the time active treatment is over, I would like to be able to:

General Physical Activity and Lymphedema

You read in chapter 3 that physical activity for people with lymphedema is a complex issue. Many experts recommend exercising with certain precautions. Being physically active can improve a person's endurance, flexibility, and body composition and alleviate stress, depression, and fatigue. It's also important in maintaining a healthy weight, and as noted in chapter 3, weight gain is a potential trigger for lymphedema.

Before doing any strenuous exercise, such as weightlifting, running, cross-country skiing, or playing tennis, talk with your doctor, nurse, or physical therapist about your specific goals and limitations so that you can decide what level of activity is right for you. When you do exercise, wear a properly fitted compression garment and try not to tire out the affected arm or leg.

Treatment Assessment

There is no standard method of assessing how well a treatment works on lymphedema. Ideally a health care provider would be able to accurately measure the volume of the affected limb or other affected body area before treatment begins, at regular intervals during treatment, and after treatment is finished. She could also assess the precise status of your skin and would be able to evaluate the status of your lymph system. But there are currently no objective ways to determine an improvement in lymphedema. Your doctor, lymphedema therapist, and you may together make a judgment of how well treatment is working and whether to alter treatment recommendations such as compression or exercises, for example. In making these judgments, consider changes in limb size, skin condition, and lymphedema's effect on your quality of life.

When to Stop Treatment

In some cases a change in your health during lymphedema could indicate that you have another condition that should be treated. Talk to your doctor about any sudden changes or problems; he may want to examine you before suggesting that you continue treatment. You may need to stop treatment for lymphedema if:

- you experience a **dramatic increase in swelling**
- you have an **infection** that is not being treated

- you show **complications from existing blood vessel conditions** or are taking blood thinners and show signs of problems such as numbness or pain (ask your doctor which symptoms to be alert for) during treatment; if so, stop treatment immediately and talk to your doctor
- you experience **pain**; see your doctor to evaluate the cause of pain before continuing treatment

Notify your therapist about discomfort, numbness, pain, or other problems you experience during complete decongestive therapy (CDT). He may be able to make adjustments to resolve problems.

If you have advanced cancer, talk to your health care provider and caregiver about how lymphedema treatment and its results affect your quality of life and whether you wish to continue. Your lymphedema therapist may be able to provide treatment at a pace that suits you or train your caregiver to help you with treatment at home. Consider how you feel. Continuing treatment may feel like an overwhelming thought, or it may allow you to be comfortable, retain your range of motion (the extent to which a joint can go through normal movements), and feel in control your body.

CHAPTER SIX

TREATMENT OPTIONS

With proper treatment and self care, even a person with advanced lymphedema should see noticeable improvement in limb size and quality of life. Keep in mind that lymphedema may be triggered inadvertently, and lymphedema symptom flare-ups may occur without an apparent cause. This is not your fault. If flare-ups do occur, remember that treatment can help get swelling and other symptoms back under control.

Which Treatment Is Most Effective?

Experts lack concrete data about the effectiveness of various treatment options. This is in part because experts do not yet have the ability to comprehensively evaluate how well treatment methods work on different areas of the body. As of this writing, two studies are seeking to establish the effectiveness of complete decongestive therapy (CDT) and one of its components, manual lymph drainage (MLD). These studies may provide more concrete data. (See chapter 9 for information.)

There have been many large case series (studies reporting on a collection of patients who received similar treatment) of the effectiveness of lymphedema treatment but few controlled trials (studies in which a new treatment is compared to a standard treatment).

Current evidence supports the treatment's effectiveness and many experts consider CDT (see below) to be the international standard of lymphedema care. Other treatment options, such as surgery (see page 98), are not widely recommended.

Developing Your Treatment Plan

Treatment for lymphedema is typically prescribed by a doctor and should be administered by an experienced professional or team of professionals with specialized training and expertise in lymphedema care. A treatment plan should be specifically tailored to your particular situation and health status. It should detail how often you should be treated, recommended exercises, and specific treatments, which we discuss in this chapter.

Appropriate treatment depends upon the severity of your lymphedema. A trained massage, physical, or occupational therapist may help create the best treatment plan for mild lymphedema; trained and highly experienced lymphedema therapists can care for severe lymphedema with more elaborate treatment. A physical or occupational therapist should assess functioning and range of motion and can treat or help manage any limitations.

Experts generally consider a combination of specific treatments (together, called complete decongestive therapy or CDT) to be the standard of care for people with lymphedema. A lymphedema therapist can offer treatments such as massage and compression that are appropriate for your body and health status and train you in special exercises and skin care regimens you can pursue at home.

Combination Therapy: Complete Decongestive Therapy (CDT)

Lymphedema treatment may include a combination of elements such as:

- **special massage (manual lymph drainage):** stimulating the absorption of lymph and the transportation of stagnant lymph to areas where the lymph system is working properly
- **compression:** keeping the affected limb in bandages or specially fitted garments to prevent swelling, provide external support, and maximize the effects of the muscles pumping lymph through the body

- **exercise:** stimulating the lymph system with activity that stimulates the lymph vessels and, when compression is used, creates fluctuating pressure within the affected limb
- **skin care:** keeping the skin very clean to prevent germs and moisturized to avoid cracking

The combination of these four elements is sometimes known as complete decongestive therapy (CDT). Variations on this combined technique have also been called complex decongestive therapy or combined decongestive therapy (CDT), complex physical therapy (CPT), and complete decongestive physiotherapy (CDP).

How Long Does Treatment Last?

Combination treatment for lymphedema includes two phases: active treatment aimed at reducing swelling as much as possible and a maintenance regimen to keep the swelling down and enhance functioning.

The active treatment phase designed to reduce arm or leg swelling includes pursuing each of the four CDT treatment components daily. Active treatment may involve one treatment visit a day and may last two to six weeks for those with lymphedema of the arm and four to over twelve weeks for those with lymphedema of the leg. (Inpatient lymphedema clinics often treat patients twice a day.) If transportation or travel distance is a challenge, therapy may take place three days a week or on another schedule as determined by you and your lymphedema specialist, although the effectiveness of a treatment schedule of fewer than five days a week has not been established.

During active treatment, treatment bandages are worn 22 or 23 hours a day. Maintenance involves using garments during the day rather than bandages and using elevation (see page 84), massage, exercise, and nighttime bandaging indefinitely, as appropriate.

CDT treatment requires patience and commitment. If you adhere to treatment recommendations, you don't have other complicating health conditions, and your lymphedema responds well to treatment, you may see improvement within a few weeks. It isn't possible to speed up the CDT treatment process of helping the lymph system reroute fluids and keep swelling down. However, reapplying bandages every 12 hours may help.

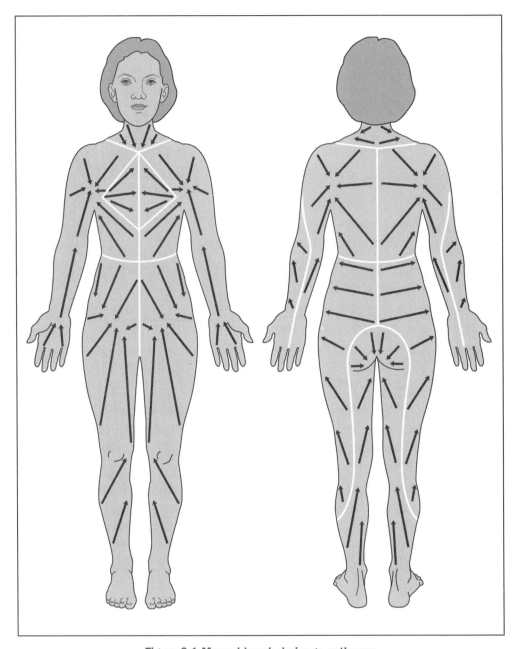

Figure 6.1 Manual lymph drainage pathways

These simplified figures indicate the direction in which manual lymph drainage (MLD) massage strokes help encourage lymph flow and reduce swelling in different areas of the body. Specially trained therapists provide MLD and can train you or a loved one or caregiver to do MLD at home.

Massage/Manual Lymph Drainage (MLD)

Manual lymph drainage, also called MLD, is a set of special massage techniques used to treat lymphedema. It involves using very light pressure to move fluid from the end of the arm or leg toward the abdomen. A version of the method has been used to treat lymphedema for over 100 years. MLD helps alleviate blockage in a lymph drainage area by rerouting lymph to working lymph channels and promotes the movement of lymph toward the nodes.

A trained MLD therapist uses a flat hand to lightly stretch the skin in both a parallel and a perpendicular direction to the lymph vessels to encourage the vessels to stretch. Rather than using long strokes along the skin as one would in traditional massage, the therapist works without slipping the hand along the surface of arm or leg. She works in small areas to slowly and gently push lymph toward a functioning area of the lymph system.

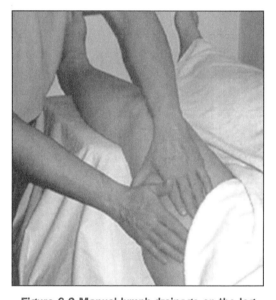

The person receiving treatment typically lies on his back, stomach, or side. The MLD therapist begins at the center of the body (for example, at the neck for upper body lymphedema) to clear lymph centrally, then moves to clear unaffected lymph node basins, and lastly moves to the affected area. The therapist first moves lymph from the affected areas nearest the newly cleared area in the trunk and gradually works on the affected areas farthest from the trunk. Therapy will typically include the neck, back, and the functioning underarm or groin lymph nodes, then focuses on the nonfunctioning area of the lymph system.

Figure 6.2 Manual lymph drainage on the leg
A therapist trained in manual lymph drainage (MLD) applies light strokes to the leg of a person with lymphedema to gently push lymph toward a functioning part of the lymph system. Reprinted from http://www. nortonschool.com/mldcdtcourse.html by permission of the Norton School of Lymphatic Therapy.

Beginning the 30- to 90-minute massage treatments when lymphedema is in early stages allows for the most success because the tissues and skin are still elastic and easily manipulated. However, if lymphedema has progressed and fibrous (tough or hard) or scar-like tissue has developed, it is more difficult to affect lymph drainage. Treatment will still be effective, although it may take time.

Treatment from someone unfamiliar with lymphedema—for example, a massage therapist with no training in MLD—might cause damage. MLD involves specialized techniques and a light touch (unless therapists are attempting to break down fibrosis). Vigorous massage—sometimes known as therapeutic massage—may be too aggressive and may harm the lymph vessels and aggravate lymphedema.

Self Care and MLD

You and a partner or caregiver can learn manual lymphatic drainage from a trained professional and may use this technique at home during the maintenance period of your treatment. The National Lymphedema Network (NLN) sells videos outlining daily self-care measures including manual lymph drainage for upper and lower extremities, as well as bandaging and skin care. Careful instruction will help you apply the correct pressure and strokes. Report any increase in swelling or lack of progress in reducing swelling. If you aren't seeing a reduction, talk to your lymphedema therapist. He may recommend that you receive MLD or other treatment from a trained specialist instead of—or along with—self massage for more dramatic results.

Treatment plans also incorporate compression, discussed below, and exercise, discussed on page 84.

Compression

Compression is an essential element of CDT. When lymphedema develops, the tissues in the affected limb may lose their elasticity. Compression both helps reduce swelling and encourages the stagnant lymph in the limb to move out of the area and into functioning lymph passageways. The pressure on the outside of the limb decreases the internal pressure in the lymph system.

Although compression has been used to treat lymphedema for years, a set of accepted guidelines does not exist regarding optimal amounts of pressure, treatment duration, and which type of compression is most effective. Your lymphedema therapist will evaluate the severity of your lymphedema and affected body area and will determine a compression strategy most appropriate for you.

Compression Bandages (Wrapping)

Compression bandaging can provide enormous benefit by reducing swelling, pain, and the feeling of heaviness in the limb. It is an essential aspect of successful CDT.

Bandages used for people with lymphedema of the limb are commonly applied in layers on the foot or hand and up the limb. Lymphedema of other areas, such as the chest or genitals, requires special wrapping. Bandages exert pressure that encourages the flow of lymph toward the heart. Ultimately waste products in lymph are removed by the body through the kidneys. Useful proteins in lymph can be recycled.

Many therapists will encourage patients to increase fluid intake after MLD and/or bandaging. Even if fluid intake not encouraged, patients may urinate more than usual after treatment.

The special "short-stretch" bandages used to treat lymphedema swelling conform to changing limb sizes. Ace-style ("long-stretch") bandages should not be used, as they can produce a tourniquet effect. Bandages may be the most useful compression method of returning a limb to its original shape because they allow customized padding to be wrapped beneath them to focus on specific areas. They may be used for 2 to 4 weeks, or for over 10 weeks for lower extremity lymphedema.

During active treatment, short-stretch bandages are applied to your affected limb immediately after MLD and are kept on until the next day, when you shower and attend another MLD session. Wearing the bandages for as long as possible will help reduce your limb volume.

Incorrectly applied compression bandages can be ineffective or even harmful. Bandages should be applied by trained health care professionals, who can teach you or a loved one how to properly bandage your limb.

Compression bandaging and underlying padding can be bulky and may feel cumbersome at first. Bandaging on the foot may require that you wear a larger or wider shoe size (talk to your therapist about shoe brands that might work best). But most people adjust and ultimately cope well with the bandages. Getting used to the appearance of the wrapped limb may be the most difficult aspect of the treatment.

Short-stretch bandage brands include Rosidal K, Comprilan, and LoPress. Your therapist can advise you about which types and brands of finger or toe bandages and padding may be most appropriate for your situation, as well as cotton bandaging or gauze if a layer will be applied beneath other bandages to protect your skin.

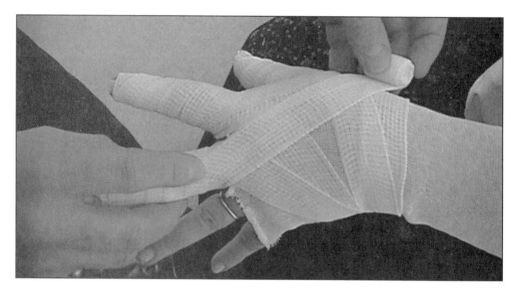

Figure 6.3A Compression bandaging of the hand

This photo shows how an overlapping layer of cotton padding is applied beneath bandages to help prevent swelling in a hand affected by lymphedema. Reprinted by permission of the Norton School of Lymphatic Therapy.

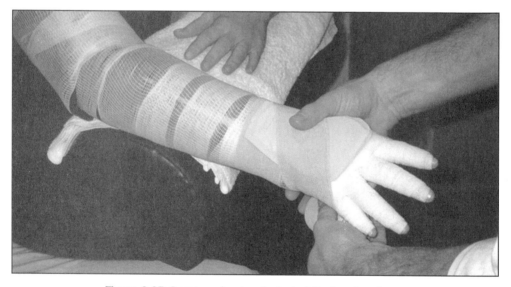

Figure 6.3B Compression bandaging of the hand and arm

The photo above shows special padding placed over the hand and wrist area to customize an area of compression, and bandages being applied over it. Reprinted by permission of the Norton School of Lymphatic Therapy.

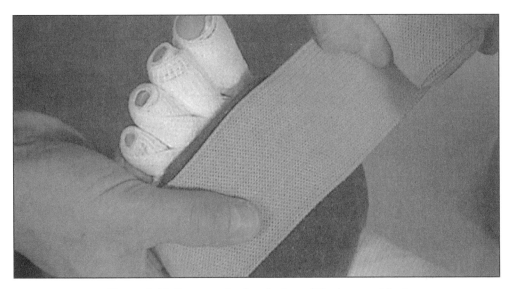

Figure 6.4A Compression bandaging of the toes and foot

Customized padding allows therapists to apply more compression to certain areas. Here, padding is placed beneath short-stretch bandages on the top of the foot to control swelling. Reprinted by permission of the Norton School of Lymphatic Therapy.

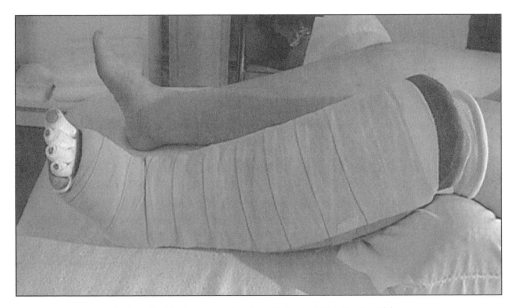

Figure 6.4B Compression bandaging of the foot and leg

This photo shows a leg wrapped with compression bandages to control swelling to the knee. Reprinted by permission of the Norton School of Lymphatic Therapy.

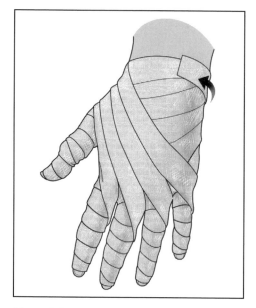

Figure 6.5A Bandaging of the fingers and hand

These drawings show how the overlapping pattern of cotton padding and overlying bandages covers the fingers, hand, and arm to apply pressure to the limb and stop it from swelling. A lymphedema therapist can show you and a loved one or caregiver how to bandage your affected body area to control lymphedema swelling.

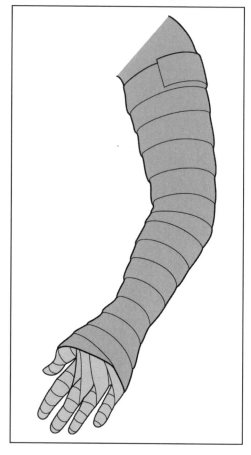

Figure 6.5B Bandaging of the hand and arm

SELF CARE AND BANDAGING

You can learn from a trained specialist how to bandage your own limb (with help from a family member or other helper, as necessary). Practicing with your lymphedema specialist will ensure that you can correctly apply bandages. Like any other skill, bandaging correctly will get easier as you practice. Seeing the positive treatment results from bandaging your own limb may help you feel more in control of your body.

Keep in mind that swelling may be affected by climate, weight, and daily activity. If you do not consistently wear bandages, you will probably eventually see increased swelling; going back to the bandaging regimen recommended by your specialist will help control swelling.

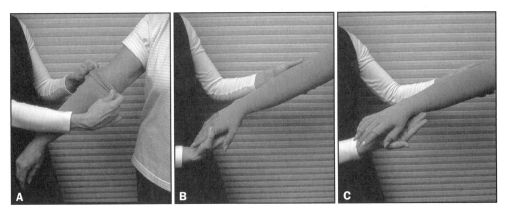

Figure 6.6 Compression sleeves

Photo A shows a compression sleeve being pulled on. (Donning aids can help you pull your sleeve on without another person.) Photo B shows a sleeve with a gauntlet piece and photo C shows a sleeve with a glove piece. Your doctor or lymphedema therapist will determine which type of sleeve is most appropriate for you. Photographer: David Calicchio, copyright 2001. Reprinted by permission of Reflections Boutique, Ted Mann Family Resource Center at UCLA.

Compression Garments

Compression garments are prescription custom-fitted or standard-size sleeves or stockings that apply controlled pressure around the area affected by lymphedema. Like compression bandages, they are designed to stimulate lymph flow. More pressure is exerted against the hand or foot and less is applied farther up the limb. A person with lymphedema of the genitals may wear a garment that looks similar to the fitted bike shorts worn by professional cyclists but is specially designed to provide lymphedema support.

Compression garments should be fitted by a health care professional who is experienced in sizing them. Because compression garments are specially fitted and do not accommodate changing limb sizes, they are most helpful during the maintenance period of treatment, *after* bandages have reduced the swelling in an arm or leg. Compression garments may then be used indefinitely to maintain limb size and shape and prevent swelling. Because they will stretch to allow for some swelling, they should only be worn during the day (bandages are used to control swelling during the night).

Compression garments come in different sizes and apply different levels of pressure. They should completely cover the area of swelling so they don't constrict along the edge.

Compression sleeves for lymphedema of the arm fit securely from the armpit to the wrist, and a gauntlet piece or a separate compression glove extends over the hand to help avoid swelling in the hand, where the sleeve ends. One-piece sleeves are available but are less popular because the hand piece can't be removed for work or other activity.

For lower extremity lymphedema, compression stockings exert low or moderate pressure and either cover the leg from the foot up to just below the knee or cover the full leg up to the groin to prevent fluid accumulation in the upper thigh. Your lymphedema therapist should be able to advise you about the best garment for treating your lymphedema.

If you are wearing a compression garment regularly, it will last three to six months before it loses its ability to compress properly. After a few months, see an experienced health care practitioner to evaluate the status of your compression garment.

Brands include Jobst, Juzo, Sigvaris, Medi/Mediven, Gottfried, Barton-Carey, and Bio-Concepts.

SELF CARE AND COMPRESSION

The best way to control lymphedema-related swelling is to wear a compression garment during the day and bandage the limb at night. It is especially important to wear a sleeve or stocking during physical activity and air travel.

If this routine feels overwhelming, don't abandon it without first talking to your health care team about potential modifications likely to minimize increases in swelling. It may be possible to wear a garment each day while you are active but modify nighttime bandage wear, for example. The goal of compression—and of all lymphedema treatment—is to allow you to achieve your lymphedema treatment goals, pursue your daily activities, and maintain your quality of life.

Talk to your lymphedema therapist and review manufacturers' instructions for laundering and caring for the garment—it may need to be washed daily and air dried. Garments should not be placed in a dryer or in the sun. Some people choose to buy two identical garments and wear them on alternate days.

Regularly examine your body where the garment begins and ends and around your inner ankle or inner elbow for any redness, irritation, or swelling. This could indicate that the garment doesn't fit properly. No garment should fit too tightly or so loosely that you see gaps.

Alert your doctor if you have any numbness or tingling in the hand or foot while wearing the garment. Also, when visiting the doctor for follow-up appointments, make sure to bring your garment along with information such as the manufacturer, make,

How Much Pressure Is Enough?

Different classes of compression garments are available. Your doctor may suggest that you try a low compression garment and evaluate its effectiveness before graduating to a higher compression. Most people with lymphedema of the arm will need compression sleeves that exert at least 20 to 30 mm Hg (millimeters of mercury) of pressure; people with lower extremity lymphedema conditions generally need stockings with at least 30 to 40 mm Hg of pressure. If you are at risk for lymphedema and your doctor has approved a compression garment (for example, during air travel), she will generally recommend a sleeve of 20 to 30 mm Hg or less or a stocking of 30 to 40 mm Hg or less.

Garment Class	Pressure mm HG*	Used for
I	20–30	• Mild lymphedema of the arm • Reducing the risk of triggering lymphedema of the arm when traveling by air
II	30–40	• Mild to moderate lymphedema of the arm • Mild lymphedema of the leg • Reducing the risk of triggering lymphedema of the leg when traveling by air
III	40–50	• Severe lymphedema of the arm • Moderate lymphedema of the leg
IV	>50	• Severe lymphedema of the leg

*The abbreviation mm HG stands for millimeters (mm) of mercury (HG) and is a standard commonly used to measure pressure.

compression level, size, and age of your compression garment. Keep the box and bring it with you; the labels in your garment will probably fade.

Compression Pumps

The value of pneumatic (air pressure–driven) compression pumps has not been clearly established. Although they have been the mainstay of lymphedema treatment for many years, many health professionals do not support their use, noting that they may be ineffective and may even exacerbate swelling. People with certain co-existing health conditions, such as heart conditions or blood clots in the veins, should not use pumps.

A compression pump is connected to a cuff that encircles the arm or leg and provides intermittent pressure. Sequential pumps apply pressure in a series of chambers along the limb rather than applying pressure to the whole limb at once. The pump inflates and deflates the cuff on a timed schedule to apply pressure and encourage lymph to move. It inflates first at the hand and then up the arm. Each section stays inflated as new sections are inflated. This inflation pattern is thought to reproduce the natural pressure and flow of the lymph system.

Pumps are used with the aim of removing excess lymph fluid from a limb and thereby reducing swelling. They do not remove protein from body tissues, however, which may allow lymphedema to progress. Pumps may only push fluid to where the cuff or sleeve ends. After the use of a pump, lymphedema has been reported in nearby areas of the body that were unaffected before pump treatment, including the trunk or genitalia. Pain and bruising are also potential complications.

Too much pressure can rupture lymph vessels, so a trained specialist should regulate any use of a compression pump and cuff.

Exercises

Exercises can increase lymph flow and help the body absorb proteins, which helps reduce lymphedema, but an exercise program should be undertaken gradually, created by a therapist experienced in lymphedema and treatment, and supervised by your doctor.

Elevating Your Arm or Leg

Although some people find that taking time to lie with an arm or leg raised interrupts the flow of daily activities, elevation may help reduce early stage lymphedema.

To benefit from elevation, prop up the affected arm or leg above the level of your heart for 45 minutes two or three times a day while lying down. Put your arm on pillows so your hand is higher than your wrist and your elbow is slightly higher than your shoulder; prop up your leg so your foot is higher than your ankle and your knee is slightly higher than your hip.

It is not clear exactly how elevation may help reduce swelling, but it may reduce the pressure in blocked lymph vessels. After swelling has been reduced by elevation, a compression sleeve or stocking can help maintain the size of the limb.

Exercise therapy for lymphedema will vary according to your health status, physical ability, and needs, but it typically includes:

- **remedial exercises** such as flexing and curling the hand, arm, foot, or leg to encourage lymph to flow through the limb
- **stretching** to maintain or restore range of motion and flexibility, reduce fibrosis, and increase lymph flow
- **aerobic activity** to encourage lymph flow through muscle contraction, increased heart rate and blood flow, and the movement of the diaphragm
- **strength training** to protect muscles from fatigue, which stimulates the production of lymph

Trained therapists will help outline the frequency, duration, and level of difficulty appropriate for you; recommendations are tailored to many facets of your individual health status and prior activity level. It is important to bandage your affected limb or wear a compression garment during exercise; see below for more information about self care.

You may experience problems with range of motion in your arm, hand, leg, or ankle—usually because of factors not directly related to lymphedema. Talk to your doctor about exercises that can help increase your range of motion and strengthen your muscles.

Self Care and Exercise

You should generally bandage your affected limb or wear a compression garment during exercise. Regularly examine your at-risk body area for any increased swelling, especially if you gradually exercise at more vigorous levels.

Use your affected limb as you normally do; for your arm, this includes combing your hair, bathing, dressing, and eating; for your leg, this means walking and climbing stairs. Follow through with lymphedema exercise recommendations.

Specific Exercises for Lymphedema

People with lymphedema of either the arm or leg may begin with the following remedial exercises and stretches, repeating each 10 times. Breathe deeply during all exercises. Before beginning, talk to your therapist about the best exercises for your situation, if you should repeat more or fewer times than recommended here, and how many times a day you should do your recommended exercises.

LYMPHEDEMA STRETCHES

- **Take 5 deep breaths**; movement of the diaphragm stimulates the flow of lymph.
- **Roll your head** slowly down to the chest and over so you are looking to the side; hold for a moment. Repeat on the other side.
- **Let your head gently drop** to one side to stretch your neck; hold for a moment. Repeat on the other side.
- **Shrug your shoulders.** Lift your shoulders as you inhale and drop them and stretch them down as you exhale.
- **Roll your shoulders.** Pull shoulders gently back, down, forward, and up in a smooth circle.

EXERCISES FOR LYMPHEDEMA OF THE ARM

For lymphedema of the arms, repeat each 10 times.

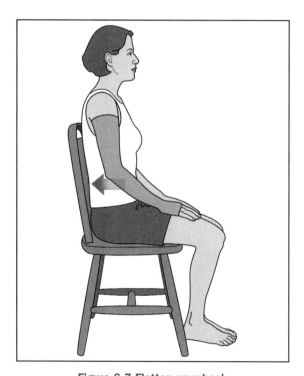

Figure 6.7 Flatten your back
While seated, flatten your lower back and push back with your abdominal muscles against a chair, or while lying down with knees bent press against the floor. Hold for 5 seconds while exhaling.

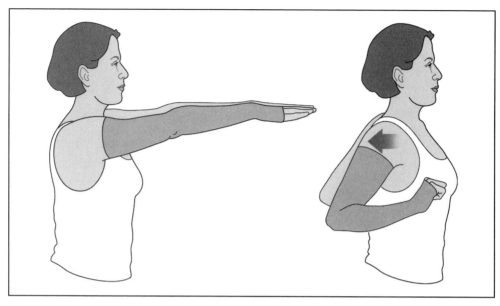

6.8 Rowing

Reach forward with both arms, then pull your arms back as though you're pinching something between your shoulder blades. Hold for 5 seconds.

6.9 Prayer

Press your hands against each other in front of your chest with elbows bent (in a prayer-like position). Hold for 5 seconds while exhaling.

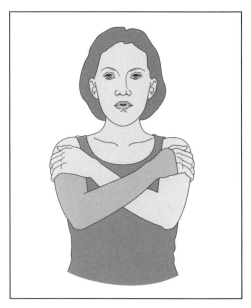

6.10 Climbing a ladder

Reach one hand up and pull one hand to the chest so that one arm is fully extended and one is close to the body; hold for a moment, then reverse.

6.11 Hug yourself

Stretch your arms out to the side, then hug them to the opposite shoulder. Hold for 5 seconds.

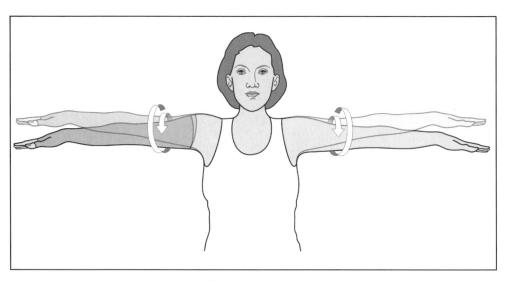

6.12 Arm circles

Stretch your arms straight out to each side and make small circles in the air, rotating your shoulders.

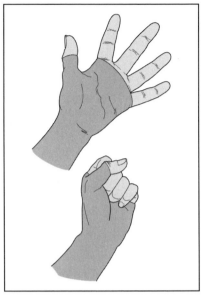

6.13 Wrist rotation
Flex your wrists, push them forward, then rotate them in circles.

6.14 Fist
Flex your fingers, then close them into a fist.

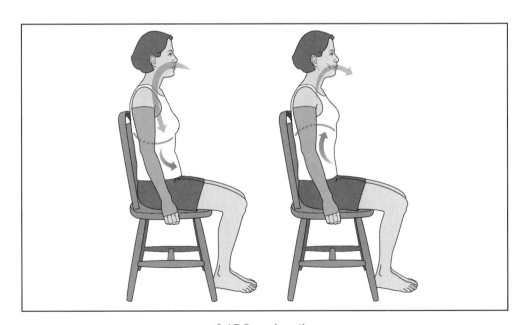

6.15 Deep breaths
Take 5 deep breaths; movement of the diaphragm stimulates the flow of lymph.

EXERCISES FOR LYMPHEDEMA OF THE LEGS

Lie on the floor with your knees bent to begin. Repeat each 10 times. (You may sit or stand—as shown in the figures—for some of the exercises if you prefer.)

6.16 Half stomach crunch

Exhale and bring your shoulders off the floor, tightening your abdominal muscles. Inhale and lower. (If you have osteoporosis, talk to your doctor before doing this exercise.)

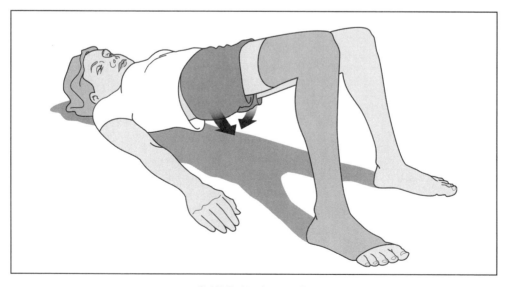

6.17 Buttock crunch

Raise your buttocks and squeeze gently together. Hold for 2 seconds.

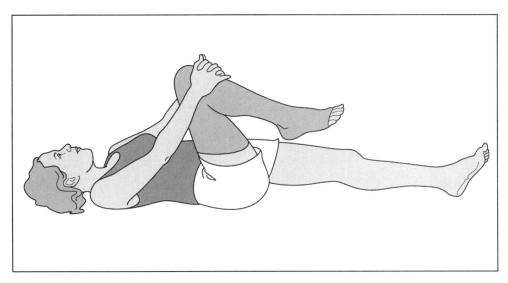

6.18 Climbing stairs

Pull one knee to your chest, then extend as though you're climbing stairs; repeat with the other knee.

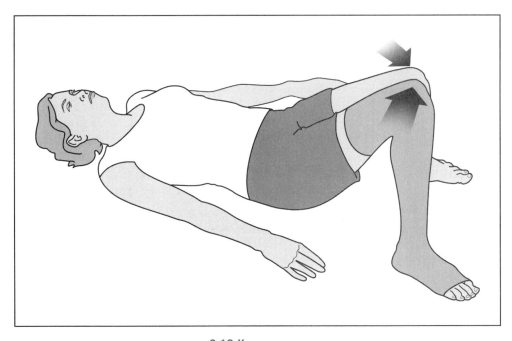

6.19 Knee squeeze

Squeeze your knees gently together. Hold for 2 seconds.

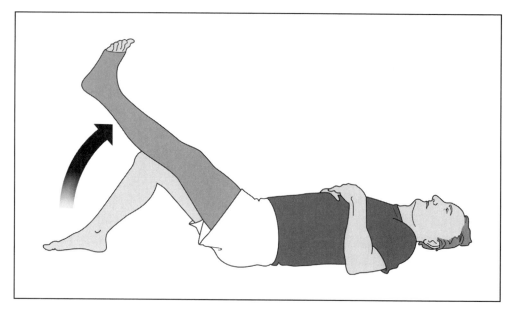

6.20 Leg lift
Lift one foot until your leg is straight. Hold for 2 seconds. Repeat on the other side.

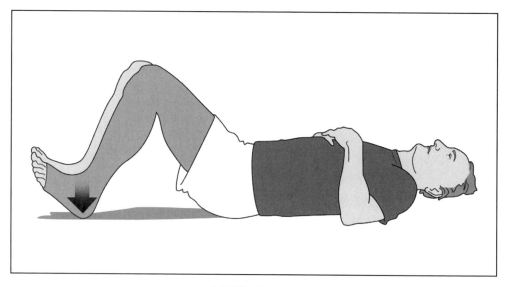

6.21 Heel press
Press your heels gently into the floor to exaggerate the bend in your knees. Hold for 2 seconds. (Alternatively, lie on your stomach and point your toes, then bend your knees and bring flexed ankles close to your buttocks.)

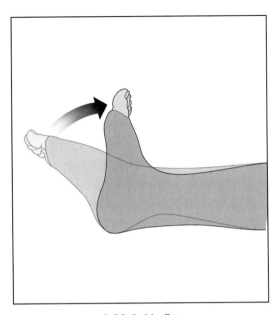

6.22 Ankle flex

Lift your foot and flex your ankle. Repeat on the other side.

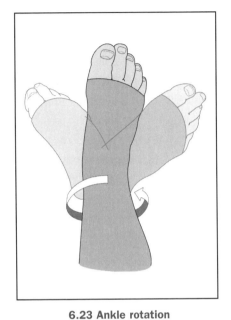

6.23 Ankle rotation

Lift your foot to rotate your ankle. Repeat on the other side.

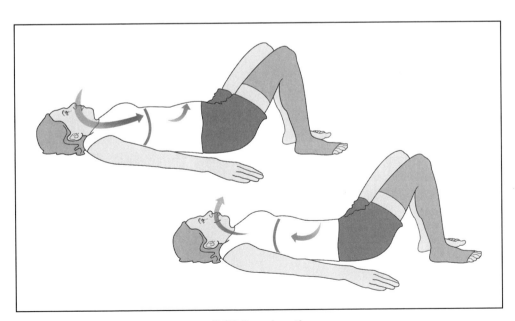

6.24 Deep breaths

Take 5 deep breaths; movement of the diaphragm stimulates the flow of lymph.

Skin Care

As noted in chapter 1, infections are a common complication of lymphedema, so cleaning, moisturizing, and protecting your skin is important. You may use the same skin care routine you used to help *prevent* infection and the triggering of lymphedema (see page 25 of chapter 2) to *maintain* generally healthy skin and prevent infection.

Self Care and Skin Care

Examine your skin regularly for any problems, and keep skin clean and moisturized through the following measures:

- **Monitor your skin** daily for damage or breaks in skin, especially under compression bandaging or garments where skin may rub and become raw. The skin in an area of the body affected by lymphedema may damage easily. Devices are available that may help you get compression garments or bandages over a bandaged wound. Ask your health care provider about "donning aids."

- **Moisturize your skin** as directed by your health care team. Focus on pH-neutral lotions and oil-based soaps to soften stiff, dry skin and to help prevent it from cracking and thus allowing bacteria to enter the body. Low pH lotions will also slow or prevent the growth of bacteria.

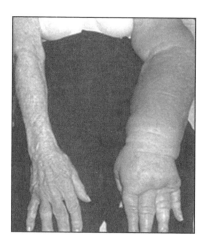 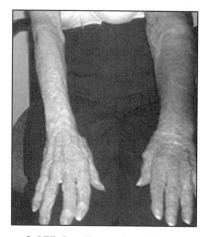

Figure 6.25A Lymphedema of the arm   **Figure 6.25B Swelling reduced through CDT**

Photo A shows severe swelling in a woman's left arm from lymphedema. Photo B shows significantly reduced swelling after complete decongestive therapy (CDT). Reprinted from http://www.acols.com/before.html by permission of the Academy of Lymphatic Studies.

- **Maintain clean skin** and care promptly for wounds. This is essential to stopping infection from developing. If you have lymphedema, your skin may not heal properly when injuries do occur; talk to your doctor about measures that specifically protect against infection, such as using lotions that stop or slow the growth of bacteria.

Drug Therapy

Drugs have not been shown to be effective in treating lymphedema itself, but certain medications may help alleviate any discomfort, infection, or other side effects associated with lymphedema. You may also hear about other medications that are purported by some to help people with lymphedema. Although these are not recommended, we offer information about them as well so you will be informed.

Antibiotics Can Help Fight Infection

Infections that accompany lymphedema may be treated with antibiotics, and skin care may rely upon antibacterial treatments (see the top of this page). If you have recurrent cellulitis infections, you may be advised to use antibiotic ointment even when your skin isn't infected to help prevent cellulitis from developing.

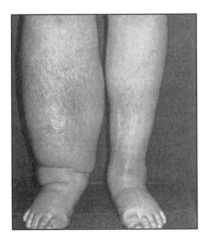
Figure 6.26A Lymphedema of the leg

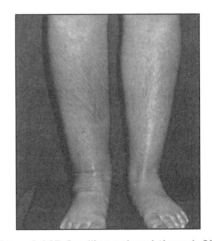
Figure 6.26B Swelling reduced through CDT

Photo A shows severe swelling in a man's right leg from lymphedema. Photo B reflects how much swelling was reduced by complete decongestive therapy (CDT). Reprinted from http://www.acols.com/before.html by permission of the Academy of Lymphatic Studies.

Diuretics Are Not Effective for Lymphedema

Lymphedema is caused by an overload of lymph fluid and proteins, not too much sodium. Therefore diuretics, which flush the body of excess water and salt (through urination), do not help manage lymphedema. They may, however, help reduce swelling due to causes other than lymph system problems, which might happen along with lymphedema, especially in someone with advanced cancer (cancer that has spread from its original site).

Benzopyrones Are Not Proven to Be Effective

Benzopyrones are dietary supplements, which in the United States are regulated as foods rather than medicines. They are not subject to the same review process and safety checks as medicines.

Benzopyrones include the drugs bioflavonoids and coumarin (which should not be confused with warfarin [Coumadin], a prescription blood thinner). Proponents believe that benzopyrones indirectly remove protein lying stagnant in the lymphatic limb and thereby reduce the formation of fibrosis, slowly reducing lymphedema swelling. Studies of benzopyrones in lymphedema treatment are generally incomplete and therefore not reliable, and while some of these studies have shown a benefit, the literature is mixed. Therefore benzopyrones are not considered beneficial for those with lymphedema.

Bioflavonoids, which occur in fruits and vegetables, have not been shown to successfully treat lymphedema. And although coumarin, which was once used in the U.S. as a flavoring agent, is marketed in several foreign countries, the Food and Drug Administration (FDA) banned coumarin from being used in American foods and medications in the 1950s. High doses of coumarin may cause liver damage.

Butchers Broom and Selenium Are Not Proven to Be Effective

Supplements such as butchers broom (*Ruscus aculeatus*) and selenium, an antioxidant, have been tested very little as treatment for lymphedema. While one or two small clinical trials may indicate a decrease in lymphedema-related swelling of the arm, head, or neck after one of these dietary supplements is taken, additional study is needed to confirm any benefit.

The U.S. government does not require dietary supplement manufacturers to undergo testing to prove supplements are effective or even safe. Therefore the risks and benefits associated with many of these mixtures have not been studied and are not known.

If you are using a supplement of any kind, tell your doctors so they may evaluate any risk or benefit to your health. Bring any information you have found to your doctor's attention so you can discuss it together.

A trusted source such as the Memorial Sloan-Kettering Cancer Center's Herbs and Botanical Information Web site (http://www.mskcc.org/aboutherbs) provides reliable information about supplements' effectiveness, potential problems, and interactions.

Pain Management

Swelling can stretch tissues, put pressure on nerves, or cause scar tissue to form and limit range of motion—all of which can cause pain. Skin problems can cause pain as well (these should be treated with antibiotics; see page 95). The most effective way of reducing pain is by treating lymphedema and reducing swelling. Pain relievers and relaxation techniques may help until lymphedema swelling is reduced.

Be open with your health care team about pain you are experiencing, and mention any factors that worsen pain or help alleviate it. (See also *Assessing Any Pain* on page 51 of chapter 4.)

Medicines to Reduce Pain

Medications used to relieve pain, called analgesics, act on various parts of the nervous system to temporarily relieve pain. Aspirin, ibuprofen, and acetaminophen are mild nonprescription pain relievers often used to relieve minor pain. If pain gets worse, your doctor will most likely prescribe more potent medications and can adjust dosages and frequency to help relieve your pain.

Complementary Methods and Coping with Pain

Complementary methods are used to complement, or add to, conventional treatments. Talk to your doctor or therapist about complementary methods that may be appropriate for your situation. Complementary methods such as relaxation techniques, yoga, guided imagery, deep breathing, biofeedback, and meditation can be used along with more traditional active therapy and help many people reduce and cope with pain.

Complementary techniques rely heavily on the ability of the mind to influence responses to pain. Your mind can have a strong positive or negative influence on the way you cope with pain. Because of this potentially powerful mind and body connection, you may want to consider the use of complementary techniques as part of a comprehensive effort to control pain.

Surgery

Different surgical techniques have been used in an attempt to treat lymphedema, but none has thus far been proven to provide better overall results than CDT. In addition, surgery involves potential risk, complications, and cost, and may further damage the lymph

Self-Care Steps and Changes in Symptoms

Work with your therapist to come up with a specific plan for your role in your care. Talk about how often you should pursue self-care steps, and mark down what you do on each day so you and your therapist can more easily track progress and measures that affect your lymphedema.

Weekly Self Care Calendar

Week of _____, _____
month and date   year

	Sunday	Monday	Tuesday
Skin care			
Bandaging			
Self massage			
Therapeutic exercise			
Special precautions			
Other self care			
Assistance			
Special Factors to Note (vigorous exercise, injury, signs of infection)			

system or exacerbate lymphedema. It should only considered in very select cases (such as removing excess skin after swelling is reduced) after CDT therapy has been pursued.

Surgical treatment may attempt to either (1) improve lymph drainage or (2) debulk (remove swollen tissue). Surgery is a method aimed at *managing* rare cases of lymphedema, *but it does not "cure" lymphedema.* Surgery may cause complications such

This calendar may be copied to help you track your care efforts and outcomes. Write down the details of the measures you take each day and results (for example, in swelling, skin changes, or mobility).

During active treatment, your specialist will likely keep a clinical chart somewhat like this to keep track of the treatment methods pursued during therapy appointments and their results.

Wednesday	Thursday	Friday	Saturday

as infection, may leave swollen areas, causes scarring, and necessitates wearing compression garments afterward.

Here are some types of surgery you may hear about:

- **Microsurgery** is a method of surgically creating new lymph channels to try to improve lymph flow, but this surgery may make lymphedema worse. One method involves connecting blood vessels to one another to create new lymphatic channels.
- **Connecting blood vessels to lymph vessels or nodes** to help lymph flow has been tried in a limited number of patients, but swelling returned in most cases.
- **Debulking procedures** involve surgically removing swollen tissue from beneath the skin. Liposuction removes fat from under the skin to reduce the size of an area. These surgeries may end up making lymphedema worse.

Maintaining a Healthy Weight

In chapter 3 we explored risk factors for lymphedema, including gaining weight or being extremely overweight. Maintaining a healthy weight is also important to your lymphedema treatment plan. If you are overweight, any weight loss helps manage lymphedema and improves your overall health in many other ways.

If your body mass index is higher than recommended (you can find out how to calculate it on page 26 of chapter 3), you may want to consider working with a registered dietitian to plan a healthful weight loss program as part of your lymphedema treatment plan. A dietitian is an expert in food and diet who has at least a bachelor's degree and has passed a national competency exam. (For more information about dietitians or for a referral, contact the American Dietetic Association 800-366-1655; http://www.eatright.org.) Your doctor should also be involved in any plans for weight loss.

Complete decongestive therapy allows many people with lymphedema to manage their conditions with success. Its development has made enormous differences in the lives of those with lymphedema. Further research may open the door for new treatment methods. For information about studies of lymphedema treatment options, as well as research into prevention and other important lymphedema-related issues, see chapter 9.

CHAPTER SEVEN

PRACTICAL CONCERNS
Therapists, Treatment Centers, Cost, and Insurance

B ecause active lymphedema treatment and lymphedema therapists are not available in every town, you may need to be proactive to find high-quality lymphedema therapy. Treatment can be expensive, and you'll probably have questions about how to pay for it or ensure that your health insurance covers as much possible. You can become informed by seeking out information about options, asking questions of health care professionals and others with lymphedema, and in short giving yourself a crash course in finding and securing effective treatment.

This chapter details practical issues related to lymphedema treatment, insurance issues, and cost, as well as resources to explore if you cannot work due to active treatment or the effects of lymphedema.

Lymphedema Therapists and Treatment Centers

If you have no other health conditions such as deep vein thrombosis (DVT) that rule out active treatment, you may seek care for lymphedema from a lymphedema therapist.

Lymphedema treatment centers and therapists focus on providing complete decongestive therapy (CDT; see chapter 6) for people with lymphedema. However, therapists' experience and training are not standard, and the additional services provided by an independent therapist and a treatment center are likely to vary. Learn as much as you can about the treatment resources available to you so you can make informed decisions about your care.

Lymphedema Therapists

Well over 1,000 therapists in the United States have been certified in CDT (see *Standards for Training and Experience* on the facing page). A lymphedema therapist may be a licensed doctor, nurse, occupational therapist (OT), physical therapist (PT), OT or PT assistant, or may be licensed or certified in massage therapy. She may have learned about lymphedema care during training for her position. However, a lymphedema therapist typically also undergoes many hours of additional training focused on lymphedema treatment and care. Some therapists are trained in and provide only manual lymph drainage (MLD).

Therapists may work independently or through a lymphedema treatment center. An independent lymphedema therapist or team of therapists overseeing your care should pursue all four elements of complete decongestive therapy (CDT), including special massage, compression, exercises, and skin care (see chapter 6 for more information). A therapist should also be certified in fitting compression garments or be able to refer you to a certified garment fitter.

Lymphedema Treatment Centers

A lymphedema treatment center may provide all aspects of CDT treatment and may also provide follow-up care, including ongoing assessments of your progress and evaluations of your lymphedema. A center may employ a network of specialists who are available to answer questions and address concerns. The specialists and services may include:

- **a supervising doctor**
- **a nurse** who may help manage symptoms, educate patients, and provide therapy

- **a lymphedema therapist** or set of therapists who together provide CDT and train you in self care
- **a specialist certified in fitting compression garments** and instructing patients in bandaging, or referrals to a certified professional
- **support group services**
- **a physical therapist or occupational therapist** (a professional who helps people who have been injured or have a health condition adjust to new methods of completing daily tasks)
- **a licensed podiatrist** (a medical professional who specializes in foot conditions)

Standards for Training and Experience

The United States does not have national standards for lymphedema treatment, therapist training, or therapist accreditation. Lymphedema therapists may attend programs of different course content, length, and hands-on experience. A certificate from a training program therefore only acknowledges participation in a course and does not indicate that specific criteria have been met.

Various Training Schools for Lymphedema Therapists

Lymphedema training schools typically focus on CDT, although they may emphasize certain aspects of this combination treatment. Some focus on the use of padding or MLD, for example. Others use pumps. The potential benefits of particular schools haven't been rigorously studied. The most effective way to manage lymphedema is to seek treatment from an experienced and well-trained therapist who provides CDT and its major elements.

How to Find Certified Therapists and Treatment Centers

Unfortunately, certified therapists and treatment centers are not found in every town, and it may take some initiative and research on your part to find local treatment options. The resources and lists provided by the organizations below do not represent all treatment centers or therapists working in the United States, but they may be helpful starting points. Consult the groups listed here for more information about how their lists are compiled. The resources listed in this chapter are provided for information purposes only and do not constitute recommendations by the American Cancer Society.

Lymphology Association of North America Certification

The Lymphology Association of North America (LANA; http://www.clt-lana.org) is a nonprofit group made up of professionals experienced in lymphedema care. One of the group's goals is to set national voluntary certification standards for lymphedema therapists, and to that end LANA has set its own minimum requirements for certification. A therapist eligible to take the exam must have a current medical license (see http://www.clt-lana.org/faq.html for more detail) or be a licensed or certified massage therapist. Eligible therapists must have completed an additional 135 hours of lymphedema training consisting of hands-on work and coursework. After training they spend one year providing lymphedema care before taking the exam. LANA lists LANA-certified therapists on its Web site (http://www.clt-lana.org/therapists/grads.html) and can provide more detail about the certification requirements they promote.

Commission on Cancer Hospital Lymphedema Programs

Although not focused only on lymphedema treatment, the Commission on Cancer (CoC; http://www.facs.org; 312-202-5085) of the American College of Surgeons recognizes hospitals and health care facilities that have cancer programs offering high-quality cancer care. CoC approval is given only to those facilities that have committed to provide the best in cancer diagnosis and treatment, including lymphedema treatment.

According to the American College of Surgeons, receiving care at a CoC-approved cancer program hospital or facility ensures that you will receive:

- quality care close to home
- comprehensive care offering a range of state-of-the-art services and equipment
- a multispecialty team approach to coordinate the best treatment options available
- access to cancer-related information, education, and support
- ongoing monitoring and improvement of care

You may search online for Commission on Cancer hospitals that provide specific cancer care services, such as lymphedema care, through the American Cancer Society (call 800-ACS-2345 or go to the Web site http://www.cancer.org/asp/search/ftc/ftc_global.asp?navToScreen=ftc_1). Supply your location information, and toward the bottom of the page, under "Rehabilitation Services," choose "Lymphedema Program."

Questions to Ask about Lymphedema Centers

If considering a lymphedema treatment center, you may want to start by asking a treatment center representative the questions below:

1. Is your center certified? If so, by which organization?
2. Does your center include specialists such as:
   - a supervising doctor?
   - a nurse who may help manage symptoms, educate patients, and provide therapy?
   - a specialist certified in fitting compression garments and instructing patients in bandaging (or, alternatively, referrals to a certified professional)?
   - support group services?
   - physical or occupational therapists to guide me in all aspects of CDT (massage, skin care, exercise, and compression)?
   - a licensed podiatrist?
3. How often will my lymphedema be evaluated?
4. Do you provide follow-up services after active treatment is over? If so, do you have a set schedule for follow up?
5. Is there someone I can call if I have concerns or difficulties when I am at home? What is that person's name and number, and what hours is he available?

The National Lymphedema Network

The National Lymphedema Network (NLN; http://www.lymphnet.org; 800-541-3259) is a nonprofit group that offers lymphedema information, a patient referral service, support, and a newsletter. In its resource guide (http://www.lymphnet.org/resource.html), the NLN lists only training programs and therapists that meet NLN-established standards and pay a fee to be listed. This means some qualified programs and therapists will not be shown. Listed treatment centers must have a lymphedema therapist on staff who meets NLN criteria. Contact the NLN for more detail about the certification requirements, training, and certified treatment resources they promote.

Choosing a Lymphedema Therapist and Treatment Center

When making decisions about lymphedema treatment, you will want to ask questions, do research, and weigh factors. This process may be familiar to you from your experience deciding on a cancer treatment. Consider the factors that helped you choose your cancer treatment team; experience, training, success rates, comprehensiveness of care, and your rapport with treatment specialists will all affect your decision.

Questions to Ask When Interviewing a Lymphedema Therapist

Background and Training

You will also want to ask questions of the individual therapist(s):

1. Do you have a license as a doctor, in nursing, occupational therapy, or physical therapy, or certification in massage therapy? Where did you receive your degree or massage therapy experience? In what state are you licensed?
2. Can you tell me about your lymphedema training? How many hours of lymphedema training have you had? (LANA recommends 135 or more.)
3. Have you been certified? If so, by which organization?

Treatment and Experience

1. What can you tell me about your treatment methods? Do you have any literature that will help explain your methods or philosophy of treatment?
2. How long have you been providing lymphedema treatment?
3. How many people have you treated? How many are you currently treating? Could you provide referrals from former patients?
4. Do you provide treatment and guidance that includes all four areas of CDT (massage, skin care, exercise, and compression)? If not, do you provide referrals to other experts?

Care and Self Care

1. Will I be trained in self care for each aspect of CDT?
2. How often will I have treatment and how long will each session last? Are there any alternate treatment schedules if I am traveling a long distance to receive treatment?
3. May I bring a family member or friend with me to learn bandaging and other techniques as necessary?

Outcomes, Fees, and Contact Information

1. Based on my health status and current lymphedema status, what type of results could I expect from treatment in terms of size reduction, skin condition improvement, range of motion, or strength?
2. Will I need a written prescription from my doctor for care? If so, how long will the prescription be valid?
3. What are the treatment fees? Are the treatments you provide typically covered by insurance? Can anyone on site help me submit requests to my insurance company?
4. What sort of prices should I expect to pay for compression bandages, compression garments, and other necessary equipment?
5. What are your office hours? Can you be contacted outside of those hours? If so, how?

Treatment quality and prices may vary; make sure to ask about payment and check with your insurance company about what your policy covers before you begin treatment.

Cost

Lymphedema treatment can be expensive. Effective treatment includes an active treatment phase, which may last a few weeks or months, and a management phase, which may last indefinitely. The various aspects of care involve the time and cost of trained lymphedema specialists, regularly replaced compression bandages and compression garments, and your own training in exercise and self care. Potential care needs and current cost estimates include:

- compression garments: up to $1,000 each; 2 recommended every 6 months
- compression bandages: $120 to $400; replaced every 6 months
- complete decongestive therapy (CDT): $1,500 to $4,000 for a 4- to 6-week course of intensive daily therapy
- manual lymph drainage (MLD): $80 to $100 an hour as needed; many patients pay out of pocket for one session a month

Antibiotics may also be necessary, as may hospital admittance and treatment for side effects such as cellulitis. CDT costs depend upon therapists' rates and how long treatment lasts. Repeated treatment may be recommended to maintain progress or if you have symptom flare-ups. You may need CDT approximately every other year, but after the first course of CDT costs typically drop as you require less direction and play a more active role in your treatment.

Paying Out of Pocket

Unfortunately, people with lymphedema must often decide if they are able and willing to pay out of pocket for treatment. With costs so high, many people in need of treatment may not have this option.

Consider speaking to a lymphedema treatment center or lymphedema therapist about the possibility of stretching payments over a period—a year, for example—rather than paying a lump sum.

Grants and Scholarships

Grants and scholarships may be available to help you pay for supplies, treatment, or both. Ask your doctor, medical director, or lymphedema therapist for information, or contact the organizations below to find out about potential aid. Some hospitals may offer grants to help pay for treatment; ask about any options for assistance.

Companies that manufacture lymphedema bandages or garments may offer some financial assistance. Juzo offers six scholarship vouchers of up to $1,000 to people with lymphedema each year. Patients can use the $1,000 for treatment or bandages. Juzo provides a custom garment (or two standard garments) free of charge to each scholarship recipient. For more information or an application, call 800-222-4999 or go online to http://www.juzousa.com/dealer.

Community-based Komen Affiliates may offer grants through the Susan G. Komen Breast Councer Foundation for lymphedema treatment and care. To find your local affiliate and search for lymphedema-related grant opportunities, contact the Susan G. Komen Breast Cancer Foundation (800-IM-AWARE; 800-462-9273; or go to http://www.komen.org and search for "community-based grants").

Insurance Challenges

If you have health insurance, you will want to find out which aspects of lymphedema care are covered. Out-of-pocket costs vary considerably across insurance carriers. While many insurance companies will pay for limited lymphedema treatment, they may not cover all costs, such as co-payments or the cost of two compression garments and bandages, which generally require replacement at least every six months. If you have insurance and your insurance company does cover care and supplies, it may have a cap on the amount it will pay each year.

Like many aspects of lymphedema awareness, any efforts you put toward arguing your case for coverage may also help increase awareness and the likelihood that others who need treatment will eventually be fully covered. Working to secure coverage for your own treatment may therefore serve others as well.

You may want to consider contacting your state and congressional representatives to ask that lymphedema treatment and compression garments and bandages be covered by insurance. In an inspiring example, lymphedema treatment and equipment is now covered by Virginia law because of patients and advocates who brought attention to the issue and delegates who took action in that state.

Approval May Take Time

An insurance company may submit your coverage request to a medical review team. The team's review may require additional information from you. You may need to follow up to make sure that a need for information isn't holding up the process. The review may also take time—possibly months.

Insurance May Not Cover Care

Check with your insurance company about criteria for coverage of various aspects of lymphedema therapy. Unfortunately, some insurance companies do not cover lymphedema treatment and supplies. However, it may be possible to educate your insurance company or emphasize your need for care by enlisting the help of a health care professional and sharing your experience.

Lack of coverage is in part linked to the scarcity of lymphedema research that exists. Case studies and anecdotal evidence suggest CDT treatment is helpful in treating the condition, but few clinical trials have proven the value of either combined treatment or its individual elements (see chapter 9 for information about studies in this area). Therefore insurance companies may consider CDT experimental and deny coverage.

Insurance companies may have specific requirements for coverage. For example, they may require that a licensed medical doctor, nurse, physical therapist, or occupational therapist provide treatment. Lymphedema therapists do not always fall under one of these categories, as in the case of massage therapists trained to provide lymphedema treatment.

Garments and bandages need regular replacement. Therefore most insurance providers do not consider bandages and garments "durable medical equipment" like wheelchairs and walkers and thus do not cover their use. However, you may be able to explain your need and gain coverage—for example, by attaching a prescription with a detailed claim that describes the compression garment or bandages and their use.

Keep Detailed Records

As you pursue coverage and seek reimbursement for treatment, document your claims by keeping copies of letters of medical necessity, bills, receipts, requests for sick leave, and correspondence with insurance companies. Write down the times and dates you speak with someone at the company and the person's name, along with any information you receive verbally. Don't be afraid to ask to receive information about coverage in writing.

Questions to Ask about Insurance and Costs

You may want to pose the questions below to your insurance agent as you evaluate your insurance options. Call the toll-free number on your insurance card and note the date of your call, the information you receive, and the name of the person you speak to.

Your State Insurance Commissioner's office (a number should be located in your local phone book under "State Government") may also be able to provide information about coverage and claims.

Insurance

1. Is lymphedema treatment that is provided by a lymphedema treatment center or health care center covered by insurance? Is treatment that is provided by an individual therapist covered? Is the therapist required to have a special degree, certificate, or training?
2. Do you have a list of participating lymphedema specialists? Do you cover any specialists who are not listed in your provider directory?
3. Are the following lymphedema treatments covered?:
   - manual lymphatic drainage
   - skin care and related products and training
   - training in exercises from a physical or occupational therapist
   - the purchase and regular replacement of compression bandages and garments
   - follow-up visits to a lymphedema treatment center or health care center
4. Are there any limits on the number of visits, duration of treatment, or costs covered?
5. Is there a toll-free number I can call for insurance information? Is it important to speak to the same person each time I call?
6. Who should I call to find out if a specific procedure is covered?
7. How can I appeal for additional coverage if I need it?

Costs

1. How much will I pay in copayments?
2. What else will I pay for out of pocket? Is there a maximum amount covered?
3. Are programs available to help me with the costs of traveling to and from treatment centers?
4. How might the government help me? How extensive is specific coverage?
5. Do I qualify for any special benefits?
6. Can I claim any of these expenses on my taxes?

Submit Detailed Claims

A doctor or helpful therapist at your treatment center may be your best ally if you encounter challenges in obtaining insurance coverage. Submit claims with literature documenting the value of lymphedema treatment, bandages, or garments. Speak with your doctor about providing support for your claim, such as a letter of medical necessity, and ask him about articles from medical journals and other documentation that may support your case. He may have experience submitting claims and be able to share helpful strategies.

You might want to include your own detailed summary of how lymphedema has affected your functioning and how any treatment you may have already received has improved your condition. Include specifics about what happens to your affected limb and your quality of life when you do not receive treatment.

If Coverage Is Denied

If your claim is denied, ask for help:

- Ask if your doctor, medical director, or another staff member has experience in filing lymphedema-related insurance claims.
- Consult staff at the treatment claims office at your center for advice.
- Ask your doctor to write a letter of medical necessity, explaining the need for long-term treatment and regular replacement of compression garments, for example.

Sometimes the insurance company denies claims based on specific language in the policy. To figure out if the denial is due to an interpretation of the policy, ask the company for the specific language that supports the denial of coverage. To find out what the appeal process is, call your insurance company.

The Appeal Process

To find out about your insurance company's appeal process, contact them directly. The National Lymphedema Network offers a sample insurance appeal letter you may fill out and ask a doctor at your lymphedema treatment center to sign and send if you have been denied coverage for compression garments or bandages (http://www.lymphnet.org/insuranceletter.html).

Insurance Coverage for Women Treated for Breast Cancer

On October 21, 1998, the Women's Health and Cancer Rights Act (WHCRA) was signed into law. The provision requires all health plans that cover mastectomy to provide for coverage of prosthetic devices and reconstructive surgery after a mastectomy, including addressing physical complications such as lymphedema. All group health plans—along with their insurance companies or health maintenance organizations (HMOs) that provide coverage for medical and surgical benefits with respect to a mastectomy—are subject to the requirements of WHCRA. Small businesses may not be required to provide this level of coverage. Larger companies may require deductibles and co-insurance.

Because the WHCRA doesn't specify Medicare codes for lymphedema coverage, it might help to know Medicare codes and share them with your doctor: 457.0 (lymphedema post-mastectomy, partial lumpectomy), 457.1 (primary lymphedema, other)—however, these may change, so you'll want to confirm them.

If you have questions or concerns about the complex law, contact the Department of Labor (866-444-3272; http://www.dol.gov). You can also call your health plan directly (a number should be listed on your insurance card) with questions or call your State Insurance Commissioner's office (a number should be listed in your local phone book under "State Government").

Health Care Resources and Insurance Options

If you do not have insurance or are unsure of your coverage, you may find the information and health care resources below helpful. Coverage may vary from state to state and will depend on your unique health status and qualifications; consult the groups below for more information.

If you are without insurance and are exploring your options, consider the following:

- An **independent broker** may be able to help you locate a reasonable benefit package. Group insurance is usually preferable to individual insurance.
- You may have access to **group insurance through your employer** if you are employed by a large company. The best type of plan is a "guaranteed issue" insurance plan, one in which employees are eligible for benefits regardless of health history.
- Explore whether there are **health maintenance organizations (HMOs)** or health care service plans in your community. Coverage can be quite comprehensive through these plans. Many offer one period of open enrollment each year during which applicants are accepted regardless of health history.

- If you have been working for 60 days or more, you should be able to keep your medical insurance through the Consolidated Omnibus Budget Reconciliation Act (**COBRA**). Your employer should be able to tell you, in writing, about your COBRA option. If you have questions, contact the U.S. Department of Labor's Employee Benefits Security Administration (866-444-3272; http://www.dol.gov/ ebsa/faqs/faq_consumer_cobra.html).
- Determine whether you can apply for **group insurance** through fraternal or professional organizations (such as those for retired persons, teachers, social workers, realtors, etc.). Look for a "guaranteed issue" plan.
- If you are currently employed, don't leave your job until you have explored insurance conversion options through your current plan. Many group plans have a clause for **conversion** to individual plans, although premiums may be considerably higher. These individual plans usually must be applied for within 30 days of termination.

Be aware of differences in coverage. Ask insurance carriers specifically about lymphedema coverage, coverage of pre-existing conditions, choice of physicians, protections against cancellations, and increases in premiums. Ask what the deductibles are. (The deductible is how much you need to pay before insurance picks up the costs of your care.) Keep in mind that higher deductibles sometimes accompany better comprehensive coverage.

Medicare

Medicare is federal health insurance for people who are at least 65 years old or who have been permanently disabled and/or have had a Social Security disability benefit for 24 months. Medicare provides basic health coverage, but it doesn't pay all of your medical expenses.

Medicare is divided into two parts. Part A pays for hospital care, home health care, hospice care, and care in Medicare-certified nursing facilities. It is free. Part B covers diagnostic studies, doctor services, durable medical equipment used at home, and ambulance transportation.

HMOs that have contracts with the Medicare program must provide all hospital and medical benefits covered by Medicare. However, you must usually obtain services from the HMO network of health care providers. If you have questions about Medicare, contact Medicare (800-MEDICARE; 800-633-4227; http://www.medicare.gov) or the U.S. Social Security Administration (800-772-1213; http://www.ssa.gov).

Medicare Coverage of Lymphedema Care

Medicare does not cover CDT. Although the value of compression pumps has not been proven and pumps may actually worsen swelling (see chapter 6 for more information), compression pumps have been covered by Medicare since 1986, with certain limitations. Medicare section 60-16 (confirm, as this may change over time) requires that a lymphedema patient undergo four weeks of other therapy without showing improvement before using an approved type of pump. "Other therapy" may include bandaging or a compression garment, exercise, and elevation, which aren't covered by Medicare, and MLD isn't mentioned.

Although Medicare does not cover compression garments (unless you have a venous stasis ulcer, a sore on your leg caused by impaired blood flow), for a woman with a diagnosis of lymphedema after mastectomy, Medigap insurance may cover a portion of a compression garment after Medicare denial. This coverage is offered through the Women's Health and Cancer Rights Act (see page 112).

Medicaid

Medicaid is another government program that covers the cost of medical care. To receive Medicaid, your income and assets must be below a certain level, which varies from state to state. Not all health providers take Medicaid. Some examples of groups eligible for Medicaid are low-income families with children, Supplemental Security Income (SSI) recipients, and pregnant women whose income is below the family poverty level. Medicare beneficiaries who have low income and limited resources may receive help paying for their out-of-pocket medical expenses from their state Medicaid program. For more information, contact your state Medicaid office (877-267-2323; for local numbers, look in the phone book or go to http://www.cms.hhs.gov/medicaid/statemap.asp).

Medigap

If you are on Medicare, you may be able to add more coverage with a Medigap policy or a Medicare HMO. There are 10 Medigap policies offered in all but 3 of the 50 states (Massachusetts, Minnesota, and Wisconsin). The plans are standardized and identified by letters A through J. Insurance carriers offer different plans, so check with them for details of coverage. (For basic information, call 800-633-4227 for "Medigap Policies, The Basics," publication 10209, or go to http://www.medicare.gov and search for "Medigap policies".)

Medical Assistance

Medical assistance programs are available for those with incomes under government-defined levels. The scope of these programs varies from state to state but may provide money for expenses, such as prescription medicines. A treatment center social worker or case manager should have information on these local programs. Check into the renewal requirements as you investigate this option so that you'll be prepared if quarterly renewal is required.

Hill-Burton Free or Low-Cost Medical Care

Facilities designated as Hill-Burton centers are required to provide a specified amount of services to people who are unable to pay. If your income is less than twice the United States Department of Health and Human Services Poverty Guidelines, you may qualify for free or reduced medical care. Hill-Burton facilities include hospitals, nursing homes, and outpatient clinics. To find a Hill-Burton facility in your area, call 800-638-0742 or go to http://www.hrsa.gov/osp/dfcr/ (click on "Obtaining Free Care"). At your first visit, request the facility's individual notice, which will describe whether you will qualify for this type of care and will outline the care provided.

Veterans' Benefits

If you are a veteran, you may qualify for benefits from the government. The Department of Veterans Affairs (VA) operates nationwide programs of health care, financial assistance, burial assistance and national cemeteries. However, veterans' benefits are changing and the number of veterans' medical facilities is declining. To get the most accurate information, contact the VA benefits office (800-827-1000; http://www.va.gov).

Options for the Hard-to-Insure: Risk Pools

A number of states currently sell comprehensive health insurance to state residents with serious medical conditions who can't find a company to insure them. These state programs, sometimes called "risk pools," serve people who have pre-existing health conditions and are often denied private health insurance or have difficulty finding affordable coverage. The Health Insurance Portability and Accountability Act of 1996 (HIPAA) provides nationwide standards and a guarantee of access to health insurance coverage in the individual market.

Contact your state department of insurance to find out if such programs are available in your state (call directory assistance in your state capitol for contact information for your state department of insurance).

Help If You Are Unable to Work

If lymphedema is not diagnosed and treated early, it may cause you physical discomfort or result in disability. The effects of lymphedema may make it difficult for you to lift things, grip objects with an affected arm, or walk. For some people with lymphedema, these changes limit their work duties or make it impossible for them to work. In chapter 8 we explore coping with changes in daily life, setting limits, and sharing responsibility. In the final sections of this chapter we focus on protecting your rights and finding assistance if you are unable to work.

Social Security Disability Programs

If you are unable to work at all, a Social Security disability program may provide assistance. Contact the Social Security office to find out if you meet their definition of "disabled" and if you qualify for one of two programs, listed here (800-772-1213; http://www.ssa.gov/disability/):

- Supplemental Security Income (SSI) is a Social Security program that provides monthly checks to the elderly, the blind, and people with disabilities who are in need. SSI qualification typically also qualifies a person for food stamps and Medicaid (to help pay doctor and hospital bills).
- Social Security Disability Insurance pays benefits to you and certain members of your family if you are "insured," meaning that you worked long enough to qualify and paid Social Security taxes.

The Americans with Disabilities Act (ADA)

The Americans with Disabilities Act (ADA) is designed to protect the workplace rights of those who are disabled and receiving medical treatment for serious illnesses. The ADA prohibits discriminating against someone unable to pursue a "major life activity" (such as work duties) based on a health condition. Additionally, many states have their own laws prohibiting discrimination. It's important to know what is covered under the ADA when considering your particular situation.

- For information regarding your rights under the ADA, contact the U.S. Department of Justice (800-514-0301; http://www.ada.gov).
- For information about job accommodations, contact the U.S. Department of Labor's Office of Disability Employment Policy's Job Accommodation Network (800-526-7234; http://www.jan.wvu.edu).
- If you want to file a complaint against an employer for discrimination based on a disability or for more information, contact the U.S. Equal Employment Opportunity Commission (EEOC; 800-669-4000; 800-669-6820 (TTY); http://www.eeoc.gov) within 180 days of the alleged discrimination (or up to 300 days, depending on state and local laws).
- You may also consult an employment discrimination attorney.

Before bringing a claim under the ADA, it is important to note that often you may have to forgo rights and benefits under other laws such as Social Security Disability, which requires that an employee be totally disabled. You cannot be totally disabled to qualify as a disabled person under the ADA.

Family Medical Leave Act (FMLA)

The Family Medical Leave Act (FMLA) allows employees to balance their work and family life by taking reasonable unpaid leave for medical reasons. FMLA is an important law for the immediate family members of anyone with a chronic illness, including lymphedema. It would apply to active lymphedema treatment rather than ongoing self care. The FMLA grants up to 12 weeks of medical leave to eligible employees and preserves health coverage. FMLA does not, however, require employers to provide the family member a salary while away from work. For more information, contact the U.S. Department of Labor (866-4-USA-DOL; http://www.dol.gov/dol/allcfr/ESA/Title_29/Part_825/toc.htm).

You know by now that coping with lymphedema can involve time and energy. Your efforts to learn about each aspect of lymphedema care will be rewarded by your ability to understand and manage the condition. People who are informed are most likely to secure high-quality care and training in self care. By learning about your options for care and coverage and thinking through the practical aspects of obtaining high-quality care, you are opening the door for the best possible treatment outcomes.

- Can I live a normal life with lymphedema? What challenges might I face?

- I feel like my arm or leg has a life of its own. Will I ever feel in control of my body again?

- What can I do if I'm depressed about my lymphedema?

- Since I developed lymphedema I haven't felt like leaving the house as much, and I don't want even my loved ones to see my arm or leg. Is this ever going to change?

- I can't fit into the clothes I used to wear. What can I do?

- I don't feel very sexy right now, although I miss being intimate with my partner. How can I explain how I'm feeling and get through this challenge?

- I'm too tired to be as active as I used to be, and I'm just not able to do everything I did before lymphedema developed. What can I do?

- What can I tell my friends and loved ones about how lymphedema affects my life? What if they are uncomfortable facing my lymphedema?

- I'm not able to follow through with my duties at work. What can I do?

- Some people look at my arm or leg or ask, "What's wrong with you?" Why are they so insensitive? What can I say to them?

- A friend or family member wants to help. How can I get others involved so we can work as a team?

- I feel like the only one in the world with lymphedema. Where can I find other people like me to talk to?

SCOTT'S STORY ❧
Coping with Lymphedema

SUPPORTING A PARTNER WITH LYMPHEDEMA

Watching my wife Kate go through cancer—discovery, treatment, recovery—shattered my heart. I often felt helpless, as if nothing I could do would mend her pain. But eventually I realized that even in those lowest moments—and we had many—there was something I could do: I could love Kate and let her know that she would never be alone.

Happily, Kate recovered from recurrent cervical cancer after multiple years of treatment, including surgeries to remove tumors and lymph nodes, radiation, and chemotherapy. Sadly, however, we soon found that her legs swelled uncomfortably due to treatment. I watched her cry in sadness over the thought that she'd survived cancer only to lose the active lifestyle of running, hiking, and skiing she enjoyed so much.

But much as she had struggled to overcome her cancer, Kate vowed that she would not let lymphedema control her life. She learned all she could about lymphedema—its cause, risks, and manageability. I tried to help in the research each step of the way. Soon we learned about compression stockings and we both took training for proper lymphedema massage.

Manual lymphatic drainage (MLD) proved to be the greatest key in controlling Kate's lymphedema. It helped us return to our more "normal" life. We biked and ran. And we took on a three-month backpacking trip across Montana (recorded in the American Cancer Society book Crossing Divides: A Couple's Story of Cancer, Hope, and Hiking Montana's Continental Divide*). Each night I massaged Kate's legs. Some days were (and are) frustrating, but our control was such that over a five-year period we backpacked about 3,000 miles from Canada to Mexico along the Continental Divide!*

I believe caregivers should know two things about lymphedema: it can be treated, and their love and support helps enable their partner's return to well-being.

—SCOTT
caregiver for Kate, lymphedema of the legs
following cervical cancer treatment

CHAPTER EIGHT

COPING WITH LYMPHEDEMA

Lymphedema is a physical condition that not only poses important practical challenges, it may also have profound effects on your emotions and your attitude. As you face a future with lymphedema you may feel frustrated, upset, and overwhelmed at times. In this chapter we explore potential emotional reactions to having lymphedema, body changes, and changes in your activity level, as well as how you may face new challenges through practical methods of coping. Not all of the issues or strategies explored here will apply to you. Focus on the sections that feel relevant to you and your unique situation.

Coping Strategies

Accepting challenges and problems and then managing and attempting to overcome them is what is meant by "coping." Effective coping often includes a combination of: recognizing the way you best face challenges, acknowledging your feelings, taking action, communicating your needs, and finding support that works for you. Thinking through your options will help you move forward and determine how to best handle your situation at each new step.

Consider How You Have Coped Before

Relying on problem-solving and coping skills can help people adapt to stressful situations, such as facing lymphedema. Try to recall what may have helped you through difficult times before. Consider how you have gained control and found strength and peace in the past—for example, when you faced cancer. The strategies that worked for you then may be helpful again now.

As with other challenges you have faced in your life, it will take time for you to adjust to having lymphedema. Try to remain flexible in adapting to changes and considering alternatives. But keep in mind that everyone copes in a different way. Your feelings and ways of coping aren't right or wrong. They are simply yours.

Assessing Health-Related Web Sites

Many Web sites offer helpful, legitimate health-related information. But some Web sites present myths as facts, suggest unproven methods as miraculous cures, or offer opinions rather than scientific evidence. Sometimes it can be hard to tell the difference. The Health Summit Working Group, supported by a grant from the Agency for Health Care Policy and Research (a part of the U.S. Department of Health and Human Services), established a set of seven criteria for assessing the quality of health-related information on the Internet. Consider the following:

1. **Is the site credible?** The most reliable sources of health information are major organizations, such as the American Cancer Society, government agencies, hospitals, or universities, whose information is reviewed by noted experts and updated frequently. If the author is listed, are credentials included? Is the information current? Does the site indicate how the information is reviewed for accuracy? For example, does the information undergo a peer review process? (This means that reviewers who are professional equals of the author evaluate content.)

2. **Is information accurate and based on scientific data?** Less reliable information will be supported by assumptions, anecdotal reports (stories), and personal experiences. Many larger institutions will list references from scientific journals that support the information provided. A disclaimer should indicate that the content is intended for information and not as medical advice. Information on the Internet does not replace medical care. Information should be balanced, providing the pros and cons of a subject and options and not just one point of view.

3. **Is the purpose of the Web site clear?** Try to determine if the site is trying to sell a product or service. Sites that are commercially focused may provide biased information. If the site collects information from you, is it clear how this information is to be used?

Become Informed

No matter what challenge you are facing, seeking out information can help you determine your options and alleviate fears about the future. Reading this book is a start; relying upon reputable Web sites is another way to learn about your lymphedema (see *Assessing Health-Related Web Sites* for more information.). Your health care team can also be a terrific source of trustworthy information. Explore resources you have relied upon in the past, such as during your cancer experience.

Do you have the option to access information without providing personal information? Is the information provided appropriate to the purpose stated? If the answer to these questions is no, then you may want to consider other sources of information.

4. **Is it clear when links lead you away from the original site?** Are any links on the Web site appropriate to the subject matter, or are they unrelated? Do links sell products or services?

5. **Is information arranged logically and easy to navigate?** If special browsers are needed to access certain information, the site should provide options to access the information. For example, if the information requires that you have the Adobe reader in order to view material, does the site provide a link to download the Adobe software? Does the site provide a way for you to search the information on the site by entering a keyword or phrase? If it does, is relevant information retrieved?

6. **Is it possible to effectively interact with others?** Most Web sites will offer you the opportunity to provide feedback about their site. If the site provides a chat room, is there a moderator or someone who monitors the chat room? Does the moderator provide his or her credentials and the source of his or her compensation?

7. **What other criteria can help evaluate Web sites?** For additional information on the Health Summit Working Group go to http://www.hitiweb.mitretek.org/hswg. Another tool you may consider using to assess the quality of a Web site is the Health On the Net Foundation (HON; http://www.hon.ch). In order to display the HON logo, participating Web sites agree to abide by an established code of conduct. The HON code does not rate the quality or the information provided by a Web site. It only defines a set of rules designed to make sure the reader always knows the source and the purpose of the information provided by the site.

Ask your doctor, nurse, and lymphedema therapist questions about your situation, your life, and what may happen. Ask them to suggest resources that have helped other people with lymphedema. Some of these may be helpful to you. Check with your doctor before making any changes to your care or treatment plan based on what you have read or heard.

Accept That Some Things Are beyond Your Control

You may be familiar with a version of the serenity prayer, which asks a higher power to "grant me the serenity to accept the things I cannot change; courage to change the things I can; and wisdom to know the difference." An essential step in coping with lymphedema is recognizing that while there are certain things you can control—the attitude with which you face events in your life, for example—there are some things you cannot. Seek to acknowledge the difference between them rather than spending your time and energy worrying about or trying to change things out of your control.

Focus on Your Day-to-Day Needs

Facing a lymphedema diagnosis is not easy. Because currently there is no cure for lymphedema and managing the condition can require frequent investments of your time and energy, you may feel discouraged when you think about your future.

It may help to focus on your daily needs. Consider your lymphedema in terms of small, manageable chunks—"I'll protect against cuts when I'm working in the yard today, and I'll bandage my arm tonight before bed"—rather than in broad, overwhelming terms—"I will be dealing with the frustration of lymphedema for years."

Coping with Feelings

Recognize Your Emotions

As you cope with lymphedema, recognize and accept your feelings about it. Don't feel guilty if you have negative feelings about the situation you're facing. Lymphedema is not life-threatening like cancer, but it is a serious condition that has altered your body and your lifestyle in important ways. It is understandable to have a range of emotions about lymphedema, including:

- **Betrayal:** You may feel betrayed by the medical community, especially if you were unaware of your risk, and you may feel betrayed by your body when you experience skin changes or swelling.

- **Frustration and sadness:** You may be frustrated or sad about changes in your life.
- **Resentment:** You may be resentful of the time it takes to care for your body now.
- **Embarrassment and shame:** You may be embarrassed if others stare at your swollen arm or leg, or when you need to wear loose clothes or two different sizes of shoe.
- **Isolation:** You may feel isolated, as though no one understands what lymphedema is, much less what you're going through as you cope with it.
- **Helplessness or hopelessness:** You may feel helpless or hopeless when you realize there is no cure for this lifelong condition, and sometimes you may want to simply give up trying to manage it.
- **Fear:** You may be afraid that your lymphedema will get worse or that treatment won't work.
- **Anger and outrage:** You may be upset about the negative effects lymphedema has on your body and your freedom, and you may be outraged that more is not being done by researchers and insurance companies to help people with lymphedema.

Don't be hard on yourself if you get down; it is difficult to stay positive all the time. Later in this chapter we discuss enjoying your life and focusing on what is important to you despite the changes lymphedema may have caused. We also provide information about support that may help you cope with challenges, including emotions.

Report Ongoing Emotional Distress

It's natural to be upset about lymphedema. You'll probably feel down about it sometimes. However, it is important to let your doctor or another health care professional know if you feel unusual anxiety or irritability, or if you are having difficulty sleeping. Emotional distress that lasts for weeks to months and interferes with your ability to concentrate, function socially or at work, or with your ability to experience pleasure may not be temporary blues about your condition; it may be clinical depression, which can be treated.

Don't Blame Yourself

You may also feel some guilt about having lymphedema and wonder if you could have stopped its development. It is critical to realize that *having lymphedema is not your fault.* Just as you did not choose to have cancer, you did not choose to have lymphedema.

Lymphedema is a result of your cancer treatment, which was essential to preserving your life. Much about lymphedema and why it is triggered in certain people remains unknown, but we continue to learn more about the triggers and successful treatment of lymphedema.

Coping with Body Changes

Changes in skin color, skin texture, or swelling can alter your appearance as well as the way you feel about yourself and your body. Body changes may affect your sexuality and relationships. A swollen arm or leg can also affect your range of motion, your clothing choices, and the activities you can pursue. Body changes may also be an unwelcome daily reminder of your cancer experience.

Some people feel self-conscious—even embarrassed—about the way their lymphedema-affected limbs look. You might worry that everyone is staring at your affected arm or leg or you might feel repulsion over touching your limb.

You may be even more concerned about physical changes than you are about the potential health complications of lymphedema.

Lymphedema does not define you. It is a physical condition, and you are working to manage its effects. Try to remember that although it takes time, lymphedema symptoms can be reduced. In the meantime you may need to make adjustments to accommodate changes in your body.

Communicate with Your Partner about Intimacy

Your desire to be intimate may be influenced by the effects of lymphedema on your body. Feeling tired, in pain, ashamed of the appearance and feel of your swollen limb, or fearful of worsening lymphedema can make you uninterested in intimacy. A drop in your libido (or sex drive) can negatively affect your self-image and make you self-conscious, which can cause you to further shy away from intimacy.

Your partner may not know how to best support you and accommodate your feelings about the changes in your body. As a result, your partner may avoid sexual contact rather than risk doing something that might harm the affected limb or cause you pain. Open communication will allow your partner to provide you with the help and understanding you need. Share with your partner your discoveries of changes in your body so you can face and address issues such as sexual intimacy as a team. Talk openly about your fears and your needs, and ask your partner to do the same. A professional counselor can also help facilitate the conversation if you feel awkward or reluctant to broach the topic.

Lymphedema may necessitate changes in your intimacy. Be open to new ways of expressing your affection. Remember that intimacy is not just sexual. Sometimes you may simply want to hug and cuddle.

Choose Appropriate Clothing

Every day when you get dressed you may face one of the difficulties of lymphedema: choosing and wearing clothing. It may be hard to find clothes that fit, and you may be uncomfortable choosing comfortable clothing if it exposes your lymphedema. To someone not facing the condition, concerns about wardrobe might seem trivial. But encountering changes in something as basic as the clothes you are able to wear can be demoralizing.

As your arm or leg swells, you may not be able to wear fitted clothing, and common-sense recommendations include avoiding constricting clothing. Women with lymphedema of the arm may not be able to comfortably wear a bra—or wear one at all. Lymphedema of the foot may require you to buy two different pairs of shoes to properly fit each foot.

If you have thickening of the skin and swelling, you may be less apt to wear clothing that bares your affected limb or the compression garment covering it. Hot, summertime weather can exacerbate the symptoms of lymphedema, yet the thought of either exposing a swollen limb with skimpy beachwear—or, conversely, the embarrassment of standing out by wearing long-sleeved shirts or long pants in the heat— may make you simply want to stay inside and away from people.

You may choose to wear looser clothing such as oversized shirts, light pants, or long skirts. Many clothing lines include less structured options that are also fashionable. A seamstress may be able to help sew or tailor clothes to accommodate a swollen limb. Others with lymphedema (see *Relying on Support* on page 132) or lymphedema therapists may be able to steer you in the right direction for clothing options.

Coping with Changes in Daily Life

In chapter 4 we explored some of the daily life and home factors that might affect treatment. Your daily activities and home life are also likely to be affected *by* treatment.

Changing your lifestyle to protect your body may sometimes pose a challenge, and you may be frustrated at times about suggested changes that are not proven to prevent lymphedema but probably provide some protection. For example, activities such as carrying a heavy bag on an at-risk shoulder or submerging the affected limb in a sauna or hot tub are thought to potentially trigger lymphedema, so you may choose to avoid them.

You may also find that it's more difficult than before for you to lift things, grip objects with an affected arm, reach or stretch your leg or arm as far as you used to, or walk and be physically active. You may have trouble sleeping because of trying to keep your affected arm or leg in a certain position or because of bandaging that can be bulky and may take some getting used to.

If lymphedema is not diagnosed and treated early, it may cause physical discomfort or disability. If this is the case, you may need to consider changes in the tasks you do at work and at home. See the sections that follow for ideas of how you might plan for and enact necessary changes in your daily life. In *Communicating with Others* and *Relying on Support* on pages 129 and 132, we explore asking others for help when you need it.

Consider Modifying Activities You Enjoy

Consider how you can preserve the things in your life that make it feel complete. Which people, activities, or places remind you of what is important, make you laugh, or make you feel refreshed and alive?

You may discover that you aren't able to do things exactly the way you always have because of lymphedema risk or effects. Explore ways of modifying your favorite activities to protect their places in your life, whether they include hiking, woodworking, playing with children or grandchildren, or spending weekends with friends.

Don't feel that you must simply abandon your regular activities. Consider fitting in fewer or shorter sessions of the things you enjoy. If you can't exercise as much or as vigorously as you did in the past, or if you feel that working in the garden puts your limb at risk, aim to spend short periods enjoying these activities, and monitor any changes in your arm or leg.

You might also think about alternative ways of remaining exposed to the kinds of things you love; if you avoid heavy gardening because you feel doing so protects you against potentially triggering lymphedema, could you give garden tours at a local arboretum instead? If you love a rough contact sport but opt out of playing it nowadays, could you coach a community team instead?

Alter Home and Work Commitments

If your daily routines have been altered by lymphedema risk, the effects of lymphedema on your limb, or the need for constant treatment, you may need to share tasks and delegate to others. You may have some difficulty carrying groceries, moving heavy items, walking the dog, carrying a pot full of water, vacuuming, or working at the computer. Consider a plan to follow through with demanding tasks in short spurts over a period of days, sharing them with someone else, or swapping tasks with a family member or coworker.

Keep in mind that your lymphedema self-care and treatment schedule may impact others and the need for them to cover your duties; talk to your lymphedema therapist about what changes in ability you might expect during and after treatment so you can think through solutions.

Communicating with Others

Share Your Limits

Understanding and setting your own limits is essential. First, think through your concerns. Are you worried about putting yourself at risk for triggering lymphedema through a certain activity, and have you triggered it in a similar way before? Are you in pain or fatigued and physically unable to complete a task?

Talk to your employer, coworkers, and family members about what you are able and willing to do and how to accommodate changes to protect your health. If you are comfortable doing so, sharing why you need to alter your schedule or duties may help others understand your condition. For example, both "My arm is fatigued and I'd like to rest it to prevent it from getting worse" and "My leg is swollen, so would you pitch in to help with the vacuuming today?" explain your limits.

Alternatively, you may want to set limits without explicitly describing your condition. Simply communicating your limits and needs is most important. Regarding a sales event and the possibility of standing up all day, for example, you might simply state, "I'm glad to work the booth in two-hour shifts or use a chair."

When deciding whether to share information with others about your lymphedema, consider whether they might be affected by your condition and your needs. For example, you might need to adjust your work schedule or take time off to accommodate a treatment regimen or because of changes in your ability to perform certain tasks, and your coworkers might need to take on additional duties while you are away from work. Being as honest as you can about your situation and educating others may prevent surprise or resentment over an increased workload.

Explain Lymphedema

Some people may feel relieved to be able to talk to friends, family members, and coworkers about their lymphedema. Others may feel uncomfortable being open about health conditions or may talk only to those closest to them.

If you want to explain your lymphedema to others but aren't sure where to begin, a few simple sentences may make people understand that you are coping with a medical condition and that it is nothing to fear. "I have a condition called lymphedema, which was caused by damage to my lymph system. It causes fluid to build up and makes my arm swell, but I bandage the arm to keep the swelling down. Certain things may make the swelling worse, so I try to be careful not to hurt my skin or strain my arm muscles." Adapting the explanation for young children may include mentioning that lymphedema is not contagious, is not painful when it is treated the right way, and that you must be careful but you are the same person as before you showed signs of lymphedema.

You may want to encourage your close friends and loved ones to read this book or to seek out other information about lymphedema so they may better understand what you are going through. Therapists and other mental health professionals may be able to help you and your family members cope with your cancer, treatment, and lymphedema together.

If Strangers Stare

Remember that even many people at risk for developing lymphedema do not know about it. The general lack of awareness about lymphedema means that strangers may be unfamiliar with your condition and therefore may be unsure how to react when they see a person whose arm or leg is bandaged, whose limb is covered with a garment, or who has one hand or foot that is larger than the other, for example.

Although people are naturally curious about things unfamiliar to them, stares and blunt questions may seem cruel or unfeeling. It's understandable that you will be irritated sometimes by stares or questions. It may help to think through probable encounters ahead of time and plan what you might say or do if questioned about your lymphedema or if someone looks curiously at your arm or leg. Try to remember that others may make abrupt comments because they are unaware of lymphedema and how to sensitively cope with it. It is not your responsibility to educate the public. But if you choose, you can help others understand the basics of the condition.

Quick Facts about Lymphedema

The depth of your experience and condition can't be summed up in a few key phrases, but the following may help others begin to understand what lymphedema is. You can tailor your explanation or comments to the person you are talking to about lymphedema. Simply keep any explanation you provide general if you do not want to share facts about your specific situation.

Who Is at Risk
- Lymphedema is a condition that allows too much fluid to collect in an area of the body.
- Hundreds of thousands of people in the U.S. have lymphedema.
- Lymphedema is not contagious.

How Lymphedema Affects the Body
- It can cause swelling and other side effects.
- It most often affects the arms or legs but can affect any part of the body where the lymph system has been damaged.

What Causes It and How It Is Treated
- It may develop after surgery or radiation treatment for cancer that damages the lymph system.
- The lymph system is a network of vessels and organs that carry fluid throughout the body.
- Lymphedema can be treated and controlled but currently cannot be cured.
- Treatment can involve special massage, bandages or sleeves/stockings that apply pressure, exercises, and skin care.
- Treatment takes time and in many cases requires a daily commitment.
- Treatment may require the help of another person.

The Need for Research and Education
- There are many unknowns about lymphedema, including how best to prevent, diagnose, and treat it. More study is needed and is ongoing.
- Many people who are at risk do not know about lymphedema, and many health professionals aren't aware of the condition.
- It's important that more people learn about lymphedema, which is why I'm sharing this information with you.

Taking Action

Follow Through with Treatment and Self Care

You are absolutely essential to the success of your treatment and self care. Being an active participant in your care is also a concrete way of coping with what is happening to you. You can be an effective participant by pursuing a treatment plan, taking responsibility for self care, understanding likely outcomes and setting goals, and taking steps to meet them.

Physical improvement due to treatment can be a powerful reminder that you can manage the effects of lymphedema. Becoming a constructive participant in your lymphedema treatment and self care may help you regain more of a sense of power over your body.

As you have read in earlier chapters, making changes in your daily life may help you guard against triggering lymphedema episodes. Being a conscientious patient and taking steps to protect your skin from infection, prevent trauma to the at-risk body area, and gently care for the limb are all positive, proactive measures that may help you feel in greater control of your condition.

Preserve Your Quality of Life

Quality of life refers to the way you perceive and value your health, including the physical, mental, and social aspects of your life; your ability to fulfill daily tasks; freedom from pain; and an overall sense of well-being. Try to make preserving your quality of life your first priority. Manage lymphedema so you are as comfortable as possible. Work with your health care team to address any discomfort or pain, and follow through with lymphedema treatment and self care to reduce your lymphedema symptoms and complications.

Ask your doctor and lymphedema therapist questions, and experiment with how you respond to certain conditions. Manage your condition step by step, without allowing your lymphedema to become more important than your quality of life.

Relying on Support

You may feel like you are the only person experiencing the physical, mental, and emotional effects of lymphedema. But you are not alone. Hundreds of thousands of people in the U.S. have lymphedema.

Coping with lymphedema can be much easier when you have a support system to lend a hand or just listen. It may help to share your feelings with others—family, friends, your health care team, or all three. Ask your loved ones to help you with bandaging, massage, household chores, or in other ways. Health care professionals can help guide you through treatment options, daily care, and ongoing management.

Those close to you may want to help but may not know how. Think about what would be most helpful to you. Do you want company, help making dinner once a week, assistance bandaging your leg each day, or distractions that take your mind off lymphedema? If someone close to you offers to help, don't be shy about providing a specific suggestion. Others cannot help you if you don't let them know what you need.

Organized Support Offers Unique Benefits

Many people join a support group to be with other people facing similar situations, such as lymphedema. Your loved ones may offer support without being able to completely relate to your experience. It may be easier for you to talk with others who have the same concerns. Not everyone is interested in a support group, but for many people, participating in a support group improves their quality of life.

Organized support groups tailored to those with lymphedema can:

- provide an opportunity for new friends
- help you understand that others are in similar situations
- help you learn more about lymphedema management
- give you a chance to talk about your feelings and work through them
- help you deal with practical or logistical problems, such as finding comfortable or flattering clothes
- help you consider how to discuss sensitive subjects with your loved ones or health care providers
- help the transfer of information about lymphedema

The National Lymphedema Network (NLN; http://www.lymphnet.org/support.html; 800-541-3259) provides a list of lymphedema support groups organized by state and nation.

Varied Options for Support

Support groups vary in format, membership, and personality. They may be led by health professionals or fellow cancer survivors. They may meet in person or online. To find groups that meet near you, look at the NLN support listings mentioned above or ask your doctor, nurse, social worker, or local cancer organization for more information.

Support for Women Treated for Breast Cancer: Reach to Recovery

Many of those affected by lymphedema are women who have been treated for breast cancer. The American Cancer Society's Reach to Recovery program, which has been helping breast cancer patients cope with their breast cancer experiences for more than 30 years, provides support for women with lymphedema.

Specially trained Reach to Recovery volunteers are breast cancer survivors who give patients and family members an opportunity to express feelings, verbalize fears and concerns, and ask questions of someone who is knowledgeable and level-headed.

For more information or to locate a Reach to Recovery program in your area, visit http://www.cancer.org or call the American Cancer Society toll-free at 800-ACS-2345.

For people with access to the Internet, Internet-based support groups (such as Netpals, accessible through the National Lymphedema Network, http://www.lymphnet.org) can be a big help, especially to people who live in rural areas, those who have trouble getting to meetings, those who want support at any time of the day or night, or those who prefer to share and read information anonymously. If you do not have Internet access at home but are interested in accessing support and information online, check with your public library. Most have computers with Internet access and staff members who can explain the process of connecting to the Internet.

Keep in mind that while support groups can provide valuable emotional encouragement, they may not always offer accurate medical information. And information provided by other patients may be factually correct but may not apply to you because of differences in your medical condition. Check with your doctor and lymphedema therapist before making changes in your self care based on what you have heard from others with lymphedema.

How to Choose a Support Group

If you are thinking about joining a support group, consider asking the group's contact person the following questions:

- How large is the group?
- Who attends (those with lymphedema, family members, lymphedema after treatment for all types of cancer, age range)?
- How often does the group meet?

Starting a Lymphedema Support Group

Lymphedema-focused support groups do not exist in every city. If you cannot find a support group either locally or online that meets your needs, consider encouraging your health care center to start one or—if you are committed to handling the logistics—creating one yourself. If you decide to start a new group or help your health center start one, consider the following issues:

Who Will Take Part

- Determine **who will lead the group**. Will it be led by a lymphedema therapist, you, or an expert and a person with lymphedema, for example?
- Consider **the group's focus**. Will it be only for people with lymphedema, or for their loved ones as well?

Planning and Logistics

- Consider **where the group will meet, how often, and for how long**. Facilities may be available through a health care center, local house of worship, or community center.
- **Determine the goals of the group and the budget**.
- **Post notices** of meeting times, location, and a contact number. Consider posting information at a local health care center or hospital or in free weekly newspapers and on local bulletin boards.

The Meetings

- **Have topics on hand** in case participants don't open up. It can take time for a group to build rapport.
- You may ask **potential experts**—doctors, therapists, and other experts at your lymphedema treatment center—to offer presentations or advice on topics of interest for the group, or you may invite participants to **share testimonials**.
- **Keep a list of members and contact information**. You may want to encourage members to talk or get together between meetings for support or companionship.

- Who leads the meetings, a professional or a survivor?
- What is the format of the meetings and how long do they last?
- Is the main purpose to share feelings, or do people also offer tips to solve common problems?

You may want to visit several support groups before deciding whether a support group is right for you, and if so, which type best suits you.

Looking Ahead

In one way, a diagnosis of lymphedema may bring relief: you finally have an explanation for what has been happening to your body. But you may also feel overwhelmed, frustrated, angry, or sad; you have coped with cancer, only to face the new challenges of lymphedema.

Consider lymphedema's impact on your life in the context of what is important and meaningful to you—for example, family, friends, or spirituality. Being actively involved in treatment, maintenance, and precautions can help you retain a sense of control over your lymphedema, your body, and your life. But don't expect to suddenly come to terms with lymphedema and shed your concerns in one dramatic moment. Seek support from those around you, maintain open communication, delegate tasks when necessary to protect your affected or at-risk limb, and let yourself take each day step by step, building your confidence that you can successfully control, manage, and live with your lymphedema.

ᔓ So many questions remain unanswered. Is anyone looking into lymphedema-related issues?

ᔓ What is a clinical trial, and what does it mean if my doctor suggests I join one?

ᔓ How do I find out if I'm eligible for a clinical trial?

ᔓ Is anyone studying how to reduce the risk of lymphedema or how to prevent it?

ᔓ Are researchers looking into potential new treatments for lymphedema?

ᔓ Are any studies focusing on proving how well lymphedema prevention and treatment really works?

ᔓ I don't have lymphedema of the arm and my lymphedema wasn't caused by breast cancer. Will lymphedema studies also help people in my situation?

ᔓ How can I get involved to advocate for lymphedema awareness, insurance coverage, legislation, and research? Are there other ways I can help?

SUE'S STORY ↝
Coping with Lymphedema

PREPARED FOR LYMPHEDEMA

I knew I might get lymphedema. My daughter, a registered nurse, told me I could have lymphedema after my breast cancer treatment (I had mastectomy, chemotherapy, and radiation). So I knew when my arm started to enlarge about 10 months after treatment that it was lymphedema.

COPING WITH LYMPHEDEMA

I cope with lymphedema as I've coped with other challenges—the best I can. My life has not been changed too drastically by lymphedema. I can't wear sleeves with elastic in them, but there are plenty of other choices out there. I lift smaller loads than before with my affected arm, but I continue to exercise it carefully. I don't have blood pressure taken in that arm, nor blood draws, shots, or IVs. I think maintaining a healthy weight is a help to those of us who have lymphedema.

TREATMENT

After I started having swelling I began to sleep with my arm elevated on a pillow each night and when I rode in the car for any significant time I kept it up on a pillow. My oncologist started measuring my arms at each visit and recommended therapy, which I did. I wear a compression sleeve when I notice swelling—I used to wear it more than I need to now.

THE RISK OF INFECTION

I've been very careful not to get cuts, pricks, or bites on my affected arm to reduce the risk of infection. I try to keep the skin very clean. I have had cellulitis twice, however. Once I stayed in the hospital two days and the cellulitis was painful, but with the proper antibiotics I was soon over it. I haven't had cellulitis in two years.

WHEN PEOPLE ASK ABOUT LYMPHEDEMA

People often ask me why my arm is larger than the other. I merely explain the situation as best I can, and it doesn't bother me at all that they ask. I think people need to understand lymphedema and know that it can develop.

I'm thankful my lymphedema isn't worse and that I can live a near-normal life with lymphedema.

—SUE
lymphedema of the arm
following breast cancer treatment

CHAPTER NINE

THE FUTURE OF LYMPHEDEMA

A person who developed lymphedema before the development of complete decongestive therapy (CDT) had few options. The development of the elements of CDT has helped many people manage their lymphedema.

Research could help us learn more about the condition, its diagnosis, and treatment. Additional study could point researchers in exciting new directions for lymphedema prevention and clarify the importance of factors that trigger the condition.

As you have read throughout this book, many essential questions remain unanswered, including:

- How many people have lymphedema? (How many have secondary lymphedema? How many have upper extremity lymphedema? Lower extremity lymphedema? Lymphedema affecting other body areas?)
- Why do some at-risk people get lymphedema while others don't?
- What characteristics affect the development of lymphedema?
- What should be the standards of diagnosis and measurement of the condition?
- How can health care providers improve patient satisfaction and quality of life?

- What is the proven value of specific lymphedema treatments? What are the outcomes of each approach, individually and combined in CDT?
- What should be the recommended and standard requirements for lymphedema therapist training?

In this chapter we explore exciting research currently underway as well as topics yet to be studied. As noted below, some of this research consists of laboratory studies (cell or animal studies), which are often the first step in research, while others are clinical trials (studies of people). In this chapter we also look at how you may be able to help raise awareness of lymphedema if you are interested in advocacy.

About Clinical Trials

Clinical trials are research studies involving human subjects that take place after studies on cells or animals suggest that a treatment or method of prevention is likely to be safe and effective. Clinical trials allow scientists to improve the way a condition is managed and thus improve the health of the population. Thousands of people take part in clinical trials each year, to the benefit of millions (often including the participants themselves).

What Makes a Study a Clinical Trial?

Clinical research studies are developed to answer a range of questions about how to reduce the impact of a condition on men and women. Clinical trials may be investigations into:

- prevention
- screening
- diagnosis
- treatment
- symptom management
- psychological impact of the condition
- rehabilitation after treatment

Despite the wide variety in topics under study, each clinical trial has a number of common factors, as described below. These factors determine if a person may be eligible for a study and if she may benefit from participating.

- **The study is designed to answer one primary question,** for example, Does treatment A help those with lymphedema more than treatment B?
- **The study examines a group of patients who meet specific criteria.** Researchers may want to evaluate a treatment's effects on people with similar health characteristics, such as gender, age, or the absence of certain physical conditions.
- **The study involves a change or an evaluation.** For most clinical trials, a specific intervention (change) or set of interventions is part of the study. For example, participants may begin receiving a lymphedema treatment. Alternatively, participants in a lymphedema prevention or screening study may go about their regular lives without intervention but be regularly evaluated in some way. For example, they may have their limbs measured regularly.
- **The study includes enough participants to answer the primary question.** Studies that do not include enough participants run two risks: (1) no effect may be noted with the intervention although an effect did exist, or (2) an effect may be noted with the intervention but it was really only due to chance.
- **The study has potential risks and benefits.** A study of a promising new treatment for lymphedema, for example, has a potential for both risks (serious side effects may occur) and benefits (lymphedema is successfully treated). Although researchers who design studies would not intentionally include an intervention with serious risks, in rare cases interventions that were expected to reduce side effects turn out to increase side effects or cause other problems.

What Are the Benefits and Risks of Participating?

The decision to participate in a clinical trial is a very personal one that depends on many things, including the benefits and risks of the study and what a person hopes to achieve by taking part. If you are interested in participating in a clinical trial, talk to your lymphedema therapist and your doctor about whether a clinical trial may be appropriate for you. Some potential benefits include:

- **gaining access to care** that may not available to the general public, including new treatments
- **receiving personalized and frequent attention** from the research team, whose purpose is to provide the very best care for the patient
- **helping others** by advancing the field of care and adding to existing knowledge

Ask questions of your therapist and the trial's researchers about how the clinical trial treatment differs from standard treatments, and make sure you understand the difference in risks, possible benefits, and procedures of the clinical trial and standard treatment.

Clinical trial participation is not for everyone. There are some potential drawbacks:

- **potential inconvenience and cost;** some clinical trials may pay for part or all of the participants' medical care during the study, but more frequent or invasive tests may be required, and a person may need to travel to a participating institution. Talk to your insurance provider about costs and coverage before you decide to participate in a clinical trial.
- **lack of control over care;** you and your health care team may not be able to select the treatment received
- **possible risks;** undergoing any medical test, procedure, or new treatment involves risk. Before participating in a medical trial, it is important to recognize that some aspects of a new treatment are unknown and may carry possible risks.

How to Find Out about Clinical Trials

The following resources will help you locate clinical trials, whether you are interested in being aware of current research or are considering participating. If you want to be part of a study, talk to your health care team about whether a clinical trial might be appropriate for you. Many hospital Web sites also include information about the clinical trials being conducted there.

American Cancer Society

The American Cancer Society provides comprehensive information about clinical trials, including questions to ask and information about state laws and clinical trials. The confidential matching service for cancer clinical trials nationwide can help you locate a research study based on your situation and personal preferences (800-ACS-2345; http://www.cancer.org/docroot/ETO/ETO_6.asp). If you search online, select your cancer type from the list (for example, breast cancer), then either search manually or use your Internet search function to find trials related to lymphedema.

National Cancer Institute (NCI)

Many clinical trials are funded by the National Cancer Institute (NCI; part of the National Institutes of Health, or NIH) through cancer centers or cooperative networks made up of research institutions, university and community hospitals, and clinics. The NCI sponsors hundreds of experimental treatment programs. Note that many of the lymphedema studies are related to breast cancer. Contact the Cancer Information Service (CIS), a program supported by the NCI, for information about ongoing clinical trials related to lymphedema (800-4-CANCER or http://www.cancer.gov/clinical_trials/ and search under breast cancer trials for the term "lymph" or "lymphedema").

National Institutes of Health (NIH)

Through the National Library of Medicine, the National Institutes of Health (NIH) runs a Web site that provides regularly updated information about federally and privately supported clinical research on human volunteers. The Web site offers information about a trial's purpose, who may participate, locations, and phone numbers for more details (http://clinicaltrials.gov/ct/gui).

Association of Community Cancer Centers (ACCC)

This is a resource that helps locate cancer centers and clinical trials, including studies of lymphedema. The up-to-date international listing of clinical trials for cancer reflects those actively recruiting patients. You can search the ACCC Web site by state to locate any trials in your area (http://www.centerwatch.com/ctrc/accc/index.shtml).

Lymphedema-Related Studies

Because a large percentage of the people affected by lymphedema have developed the condition after breast cancer treatment, much of the research currently being done concentrates on breast cancer–related lymphedema. The findings of these laboratory studies and clinical trials may ultimately benefit those with lower extremity lymphedema and lymphedema in other body areas as well. However, clinical trials focusing on lymphedema of other body areas are also needed.

Both specific studies recruiting patients and those that are closed to new participants and already underway are listed in this chapter to provide a glimpse into current trends in lymphedema research. In a few instances we also mention topics that may be studied in the future but are not currently scheduled for study. Not all current or in-progress studies are explored here. If you are interested in participating in a lymphedema-related study, speak to your doctor and lymphedema therapist, who can help you explore options that may be appropriate for you.

Prevention

Early cancer detection may allow for less invasive treatment. For example, advanced imaging tests allow doctors to diagnose cancer at earlier stages and thereby reduce the necessity of surgery or radiation. Such reduction can minimize how the lymph system is compromised and lower the risk of lymphedema.

Studying the lymph system for certain characteristics could allow for personalized cancer treatment plans. In theory, doctors could view a person's lymph system structure and functioning, using the information to tailor surgery or radiation to guard weak areas from harm and protect against lymphedema risk.

New nationwide clinical trials designed to study prevention are in development and will hopefully move forward. The cooperative groups Cancer and Leukemia Group B (CALGB) and American College of Surgeons Oncology Group (ACOSOG) will use randomized clinical trials to examine (at multiple study locations) lymphedema incidence and prevention in women treated for breast cancer. Randomized clinical trials are studies in which two therapies or approaches—a standard method and a new method—are tested and evaluated, with patients randomly assigned to one group or the other. These are the "gold standard" of clinical trials.

A current National Institutes of Health–funded study is tracking women scheduled for breast cancer treatment for 30 months following diagnosis. Additional funding has been requested to follow them for seven years after treatment, measuring arm size and evaluating how women cope with any lymphedema that develops. In this observational study, researchers will gather information about the timeline of a woman's lymphedema development and details of her cancer and lymphedema treatment. The study may provide information about early methods of preventing or treating lymphedema and help identify factors that could affect coping and care.

Can Sealing Lymph Vessels Help Prevent Lymphedema?

A multi-state National Cancer Institute study will attempt to determine whether the use of products called fibrin sealants may reduce the development of lymphedema after surgery for vulvar cancer.

Fibrin sealants use proteins from human blood—the same ones that naturally form blood clots—to stop bleeding after an injury or wound. They work by forming a flexible material over the blood vessel that can often control bleeding within five minutes. They are currently FDA-approved to help stop bleeding from small, sometimes inaccessible blood vessels during surgery.

Some study participants will have fibrin sealants applied to lymph vessels in the groin area where lymph nodes were removed; others will receive standard post-surgery care. All participants will be evaluated periodically for six months after surgery for symptoms of lymphedema. (However, lymphedema may develop years after treatment.)

Will Reducing Radiation Effects or Using MLD Prevent Lymphedema?

A U.S. Department of Defense-funded study is examining whether tailoring the delivery of radiation to protect crucial parts of the lymph system may reduce the risk of or severity of lymphedema after lymph node surgery for breast cancer. Injecting a radioactive substance and a dye (in a technique similar to that used in identifying sentinel lymph nodes; see chapter 2) could help doctors identify the critical lymph nodes that drain the arm area after axillary lymph node surgery. Researchers hope that protecting those lymph nodes from radiation will minimize the risk of radiation-induced injury to the lymph system and prevent or reduce lymphedema's effects.

An American Cancer Society–funded laboratory study at the University of Arizona in Tucson will examine risk factors that may lead to or worsen lymphedema so the condition may be better prevented. Study researchers will specifically study whether reducing exposure to radiation and/or using MLD immediately after breast cancer surgery or radiation can prevent the condition from developing.

Diagnosis

Measures that could allow doctors to diagnose lymphedema earlier could prevent its progression and allow for more effective treatment. Magnetic resonance imaging (MRI) is a method of taking pictures of the inside of the body by using powerful magnets and transmitting radio waves through the body. Currently, MRI studies are not a standard way of diagnosing lymphedema or guiding its treatment, but may identify causes of lymphedema that are not related to cancer treatment—such as tumors. However, if new versions of imaging studies were developed that were advanced enough to show the lymph system in detail, they could potentially help doctors find lymphedema at earliest stages and stop it from progressing. Current methods don't allow for this use, and no studies into developing MRI in this way are currently scheduled.

Tissues affected by lymphedema and fibrosis react uniquely to pressure. Therefore a device called a tonometer—which precisely measures how much a person's skin and underlying tissue pits (indents)—could potentially help doctors diagnose lymphedema after initial symptoms are reported. A tonometer could also be valuable in assessing a person's response to treatment or any lymphedema progression. However, further study and evaluation are needed of the reliability of tonometry and how it may be useful to doctors.

Does Bioimpedance Allow for Easier Diagnosis?

Bioimpedance, also called bioelectric impedance, involves applying a low-level electrical current to an area of the body to gauge the volume of fluid present. This could not only help doctors identify the presence of lymphedema, but also track its progression. Bioimpedance measures how much an area of the body impedes (resists) electrical flow; for example, tissue with lymphedema contains more fluid and thus shows different resistance from lower-protein tissues.

Bioimpedance is a pain-free method that has been shown to accurately gauge increased protein and limb volume as lymphedema progresses. A National Center for Complementary and Alternative Medicine–funded clinical trial will compare the effectiveness of, ease of use, and sensitivity of bioimpedance instruments to methods of water displacement.

Treatment

The topics below are scheduled for study or currently being studied. The effectiveness and safety of investigational treatments for lymphedema, such as laser therapy to reduce arm volume, have not been studied enough to warrant medical claims. No positive recommendations can be made about treatments that have not been carefully and scientifically evaluated in clinical trials.

Some studies of lymphedema treatment will also evaluate participants' responses to a questionnaire that is in development. The questionnaire lists lymphedema symptoms and may be used in the future as a tool for assessing symptom severity and tracking improvement with treatment.

Future treatment-related studies may focus on the effectiveness of compression garments and the potential for using herbal remedies as lymphedema treatment or as adjuncts to treatment.

How Effective Are CDT and MLD?

There is strong support for complete decongestive therapy (CDT) and one of its components, manual lymph drainage (MLD), but researchers are working to quantify the value of CDT through randomized clinical trials. One study, an American Cancer Society–funded three-year laboratory study at the University of Arizona, will examine the effects of both CDT and MLD. Researchers will also specifically study whether the components of MLD (stimulating lymph nodes, opening watersheds, and massage of limbs) are effective when used alone or only when combined.

How Helpful Is MLD Alone?

One widely cited study of just a few participants examined the effect of MLD combined with compression bandaging versus compression bandaging alone. Although limb volume may not have been significantly reduced with combined therapy versus bandaging alone, effects on outcomes such as quality of life and distress caused by lymphedema symptoms must also be considered.

A National Center for Complementary and Alternative Medicine–funded clinical trial is evaluating how helpful MLD is for lymphedema of the arms when used alone versus with compression bandaging. Patients will be randomly assigned to receive MLD or MLD along with self-care and compression bandaging.

Is Hyperbaric Oxygen Therapy Effective?

In hyperbaric oxygen therapy, a person lies enclosed in a high-pressure chamber and breathes 100 percent oxygen that has been pressurized 2 to 3 times normal atmospheric pressure. This is hoped to reduce arm swelling and reduce symptoms such as fibrosis through stimulating the growth of new or damaged blood vessels and improving blood flow to the affected area.

Some researchers have studied how hyperbaric oxygen therapy may benefit patients affected by lymphedema. A new study funded by the Royal Marsden NHS Trust (England) will compare the effectiveness of hyperbaric oxygen therapy to standard therapy in women with lymphedema following radiation for breast cancer. Some participants will be randomly chosen to receive hyperbaric oxygen therapy for 90 minutes 5 days a week over 6 weeks; others will receive standard lymphedema management. All study participants will be asked to complete questionnaires every 3 months for 15 months and will be evaluated about a year after treatment has begun.

Can a Botanical Extract Help Treat Lymphedema?

This National Center for Complementary and Alternative Medicine–funded clinical trial will examine the effectiveness of a botanical extract of a pine tree (Pycnogenol) as a treatment for arm lymphedema following breast cancer treatment. The extract is used investigationally in Europe and is thought to potentially constrict blood vessels and increase the ease with which fluid passes through blood vessels. Participants will randomly receive either a Pycnogenol supplement or placebo.

Could Surgery Eventually Prove Effective?

As noted in chapter 6, surgery has not been proven to provide better overall results than CDT in treating lymphedema. Surgery to treat lymphedema involves potential risk, complications, and cost, and it may further damage the lymph system or make lymphedema worse. However, some researchers wonder if surgical methods could eventually prove useful in treating lymphedema.

A few researchers have studied the effectiveness of grafting lymph vessels to bridge injured portions of the lymph system. Results have been mixed. For this reason surgery is not a widely endorsed treatment choice. No studies are currently being funded into developing operations to repair defects in lymph vessels.

As mentioned in chapter 2, there are only two pathways for the removal of fluid from tissue: veins and the lymph system. If veins are moving blood more slowly than normal or are blocked, the lymph system has to work harder to regulate fluid. There is some controversy as to whether the flow of blood through the veins directly contributes to lymphedema. However, some researchers have explored the idea that inserting a stent (a device used to keep open a structure such as a vein) in an axillary vein shown not to be moving blood normally could help reduce pressure and/or increase flow in the venous and lymph systems. More research is needed into whether this could prevent or treat lymphedema.

Economic Impact

One area that has not yet been examined is how much lymphedema costs the person with the condition, the patient's family, and the patient's employer. Current research seeks to establish a model for the cost of lymphedema treatment versus the cost of treating recurrent cellulitis infections.

What Does Lymphedema Cost?

A three-year American Cancer Society–funded study at M. D. Anderson Cancer Center in Houston, Texas, is the first attempt to establish the economic impact of lymphedema by tracking costs and treatment patterns. The economic impact of lymphedema on individuals, workplaces, and health care systems has not been determined. Lymphedema can also economically impact family members and caregivers by decreasing their productivity as they care for a person with lymphedema or take on additional tasks as a result of lymphehdema. Experts do not currently have an estimate of these lymphedema costs.

Access to Care

A City of Hope Cancer Center research study is investigating whether access to care can improve outcomes. It will examine how well a grant-funded program can meet the needs of women with lymphedema without insurance coverage through evaluating: how many women are treated, how many doctors refer patients to the program, the efficacy of lymphedema treatments, and the impact of care on women's quality of life.

The American Cancer Society's Role in Lymphedema Research

The American Cancer Society, through generous support from The Longaberger Company's Horizon of Hope Campaign (http://www.horizonofhope.com), is making available over two million dollars for grants to support lymphedema research. Through these grants, the Society aims to improve understanding of lymphedema's cause, prevention, and effective management in order to reduce discomfort and disability from lymphedema that occurs after breast cancer treatment. Potential areas of study include reducing risk through changes in breast cancer treatment; improvements in early diagnosis; ideal treatment methods, duration, and timing; the economic burden of lymphedema; and complications such as infections and skin and tissue damage due to lymphedema.

Your Potential Role in Raising Awareness

While study related to prevention, treatment, and improving understanding of lymphedema has increased in recent years, it is imperative that we support even more research into this potentially debilitating disease. Helping draw attention to the need for more attention and resources is one way people may play active roles in improving their situations. Taking part in a clinical trial or starting a support group may also contribute in important ways to others' knowledge about the condition and thus their well-being.

If you do want to push for and support advancing our base of knowledge, consider contacting your state and U.S. legislators and asking for additional funding for lymphedema research and increased awareness. You may also want to speak to your local hospital about the need for local lymphedema centers, mentioning the many cases of lymphedema that exist, outlining your personal stake, and providing literature reinforcing the value of treatment.

The American Cancer Society actively monitors cancer-related legislative and policy efforts. To find out about local and national efforts, for tips on contacting your legislators, and for information about policies and proposals that could impact you, contact the American Cancer Society (800-ACS-2345; http://www.cancer.org; search "Talk to Your Legislators").

Do not feel guilty if your main focus is to simply face your own lymphedema with grace. You are not obligated to become an activist for lymphedema-related issues. And the things you might naturally be inclined to do—including asking your insurance company about covering lymphedema treatment and explaining your condition to your loved ones—also help increase awareness. You can begin to improve widespread understanding simply by adding to the knowledge of those around you.

RESOURCES

ABOUT THE RESOURCES

Listings in this section represent organizations that operate on a national level and provide some type of service or resource to consumers related to lymphedema, cancer, or public health. This list is designed to offer a starting point for seeking information, support, and needed resources. Most of the organizations listed here can be contacted via phone, fax, or e-mail, and some through a Web site. Many of the Web sites provide much of the same information that is available by postal mail. Some organizations are solely Web-based and will require Internet access. Keep in mind that new Web sites appear daily while old ones expand, move, or disappear entirely. Some of the Web sites or content outlined below may change, and often a simple Internet search will point to the new Web site for a given organization.

There is a vast amount of information on the Internet. This information can be very valuable in making decisions about your health. However, since any group or individual can publish on the Internet, it is important to consider the credentials and reputation of the organization providing information. Internet information should not be a substitute for medical advice.

The American Cancer Society does not endorse the agencies, organizations, corporations, and publications represented in this resource guide. This guide is provided for assistance obtaining information only.

AMERICAN CANCER SOCIETY RESOURCES

AMERICAN CANCER SOCIETY
Toll-Free: 800-ACS-2345
Web site: http://www.cancer.org

The American Cancer Society is the nationwide community-based volunteer health organization dedicated to eliminating cancer as a major health problem by preventing cancer, saving lives, and diminishing suffering from cancer through research, education, advocacy, and service. Contact the American Cancer Society for more information about lymphedema, educational materials, patient programs, and services in your community, as well as information about support, advocacy, and research. The publications listed in the front of this book are available for sale though the Society's toll-free number and Web site and include information about caregiving, living well during and after cancer treatment, and many other topics.

Cancer Survivors Network
Toll-Free: 800-ACS-2345
Web site: http://www.acscsn.org

This network provides an online community that welcomes cancer survivors, friends, and families to share and communicate with others with similar interests and experiences. The program offers a community of real people supporting one another and sharing personal experiences. The Web site enables registered members to have live, private chats, to create personal Web pages to share experiences, thoughts, and wisdom, to help people create personal support communities of people who share common concerns and interests, and offers information about resources.

Reach to Recovery
Toll-Free: 800-ACS-2345
Web site: http://www.cancer.org

This program has been helping breast cancer patients (female and male) cope with their breast cancer experience for more than 30 years. It is designed to help patients with breast cancer cope with their diagnosis, treatment, and recovery and also provides support for those with lymphedema. The specially trained volunteers have had breast cancer. They offer understanding, support, and hope, as well as up-to-date information, including literature for spouses, children, friends, and other loved ones. Reach to Recovery gives patients and family members an opportunity to express feelings, talk about fears and concerns, and ask questions of someone who is knowledgeable and level-headed. Ongoing support groups are available to help deal with the challenges of breast cancer. Reach to Recovery also provides referrals to local diagnostic and treatment centers.

Lymphedema Information and Support

ASSOCIATION OF COMMUNITY CANCER CENTERS (ACCC)
11600 Nebel Street, Suite 201
Rockville, MD 20852-2557
Phone: 301-984-9496
Fax: 301-770-1949
E-mail: mmilburn@accc-cancer.org
Web site: http://www.accc-cancer.org

This national organization includes over 600 medical centers, hospitals, and cancer programs. The ACCC helps patients locate cancer centers and clinical trials, including studies of lymphedema. Use this regularly updated listing to search for clinical trials actively recruiting patients. The ACCC Web site can be searched by state so you can find trials in your community (http://www.centerwatch.com/ctrc/accc/index.shtml).

CIRCLE OF HOPE LYMPHEDEMA FOUNDATION, INC.
36 Woodcrest Drive
Prospect, CT 06712
Phone: 203-758-6138
E-mail: JT@lymphedemacircleofhope.org
Web site:
http://www.lymphedemacircleofhope.org/

This nonprofit group was started by a breast cancer survivor to promote and provide educational programs, public awareness, medical treatment, and continued research. The Circle of Hope Web site includes general information about lymphedema. You can pose questions to a lymphedema therapist through the Web site.

LYMPHEDEMA RESEARCH
FOUNDATION (LRF)
100 Forest Drive
East Hills, NY 11548
Phone: 516-625-9675
Fax: 516-625-9410
E-mail: lrf@lymphaticresearch.org
Web site: http://www.lymphaticresearch.org

The Lymphatic Research Foundation is a non-profit organization whose mission is to advance research about the lymphatic system and to find the cause of and cure for lymphatic diseases, lymphedema, and related disorders. The LRF organizes conferences, educates the medical community, advocates for research funding and support, and publishes a peer-reviewed scientific journal, *Lymphatic Research and Biology*. The LRF is planning a National Lymphatic Disease Patient Registry and Tissue/Cell Bank to provide researchers with samples and clinical data with the aim of developing improved treatments and finding a cure for lymphatic diseases, lymphedema, and related disorders.

LYMPHOLOGY ASSOCIATION OF
NORTH AMERICA (LANA)
1901 N. Roselle Road, Suite 800
Schaumburg, IL 60195
E-mail: lana@clt-lana.org
Web site: http://www.clt-lana.org

This professional organization promotes standards for lymphedema management and maintains certification requirements for medical professionals who provide lymphedema treatment. You can find out about LANA's training standards online at http://www.clt-lana.org/cert.html.

NATIONAL CANCER INSTITUTE (NCI)
NCI Public Inquiries Office
Building 31, Room 10A03
31 Center Drive, MSC 2580
Bethesda, MD 20892-2580
Toll-Free: 800-4-CANCER (800-422-6237)
Web site: http://www.cancer.gov

This government agency, part of the National Institutes of Health (NIH), provides cancer information through several services (see list below). The lymphedema-focused area of the Web site (http://www.cancer.gov/cancertopics/pdq/supportivecare/lymphedema) includes information about risk, types of lymphedema, diagnosis, and management. *Spanish-speaking staff and Spanish materials are available.*

CANCERLIT (Bibliographic Database)
Web site:
http://www.cancer.gov/cancerinfo/literature

This searchable site is maintained by the NCI and contains cancer and lymphedema articles published in medical and scientific journals, books, government reports, and articles that were presented at national meetings.

CancerTrials
Web site: http://www.cancer.gov/clinicaltrials

Maintained by the NCI, this site offers information about ongoing cancer clinical trials and explanations of what a trial is and what is involved. It allows you to search for clinical trials by state, city, and type of cancer—you may find lymphedema-related trials by searching for your type of cancer, then searching under "supportive care" for lymphedema-related trials.

Cancer Topics
Web site: http://cancer.gov/cancerinformation
Web site (Spanish version):
http://www.cancer.gov/espanol
Web site (online ordering):
https://cissecure.nci.nih.gov/ncipubs/

This comprehensive Web site contains information on diagnosis, treatment, support, resources, literature, clinical trials, prevention and risk factors, and testing. The PDQ section provides overviews for patients (look under "supportive care" for lymphedema information). Up to 20 publications can be ordered online. The publications list is searchable. *Some publications are available in Spanish.*

Cancer Information Service (CIS)
Toll-Free: 800-4-CANCER (800-422-6237)
Web site: http://cis.nci.nih.gov

The CIS provides information to consumers and health care professionals. The Web site contains a wealth of information including pamphlets and brochures about cancer, treatment, research, and prevention. *Spanish-speaking staff members are available.*

NATIONAL LYMPHEDEMA NETWORK (NLN)

1611 Telegraph Avenue, Suite 1111
Oakland, CA 94612-2138
Toll-Free (Hotline): 800-541-3259
Phone: 510-208-3200
Fax: 510-208-3110

E-mail: nln@lymphnet.org
Web site: http://www.lymphnet.org

The Web site for this nonprofit agency offers information and education about preventing and managing lymphedema, a referral service to medical and therapeutic treatment centers, and information on locating or establishing local support groups. The NLN sells videos outlining exercises as well as self-care measures, including manual lymph drainage, bandaging, and skin care for upper and lower extremities. It publishes a newsletter, *LymphLink,* which contains articles on lymphedema and related topics. The NLN includes a resource guide of treatment centers, physicians, therapists, and suppliers, and it lists over 100 support groups. *Some Spanish-language materials are available.*

PATIENT AND FAMILY SERVICES

AMERICAN DIETETIC ASSOCIATION (ADA)

120 South Riverside Plaza, Suite 2000
Chicago, IL 60606-6995
Toll-Free: 800-877-1600
Web site: http://www.eatright.org

The ADA is an organization of food and nutrition professionals. It serves the public by promoting optimal nutrition, health, and well-being. Contact the ADA for more information about dietitians or for a referral to a dietitian near you.

AMERICANS WITH DISABILITIES ACT (ADA)

United States Department of Justice
950 Pennsylvania Avenue, NW
Civil Rights Division
Disability Rights Section-NYAV
Washington, D.C. 20530
Phone: 800-514-0301
Fax: 202-307-1198
Web site: http://www.ada.gov

Specialists at the ADA information line answer questions about titles II and III of the ADA. The ADA Web site includes a text version of the ADA and available publications. Many publications can be ordered through the automated fax system; call the information line for directions. *Spanish-speaking staff and Spanish materials are available.*

DEPARTMENT OF VETERANS AFFAIRS (VA)

810 Vermont Ave NW
Washington, DC 20420
Toll-Free: 800-827-1000 (Connects to your local Veterans Affairs office)
Web site: http://www.va.gov

If you are a veteran, you may qualify for benefits from the government. Veterans' benefits are changing, and the number of veterans' medical facilities is declining. To get the most accurate information, contact the VA.

HILL-BURTON PROGRAM

Parklawn Building
5600 Fishers Lane, Room 10-105
Rockville, MD 20857
Toll-Free: 800-638-0742; 800-492-0359
  (in Maryland)
Phone: 301-443-5656
Fax: 301-443-0619
Web site: http://www.hrsa.gov/osp/dfcr
  (Click "Obtaining Free Care")

Hill-Burton centers are required to provide a specified amount of services to people who are unable to pay. If your income is less than twice the United States Department of Health and Human Services Poverty Guidelines, you may qualify for free or reduced medical care. Hill-Burton facilities include hospitals, nursing homes, and outpatient clinics. At your first visit, request the facility's individual notice, which will describe whether you qualify for this type of care and outlines the care provided.

MEDICAID

Department of Health and Human Services
Centers for Medicare & Medicaid Services
  (CMS)
Toll-Free: 800-MEDICAR (800-633-4227)
Web site: http://www.cms.hhs.gov/medicaid/

This federal and state health insurance program is designed to provide access to health services for persons below a certain income level. Medicaid provides health care to qualifying women and children and the impoverished elderly. For local numbers, call the number above or go online to http://www.cms.hhs.gov/medicaid/statemap.asp

MEDICARE HOTLINE

Department of Health and Human Services
Centers for Medicare & Medicaid Services
  (CMS)
Toll-Free: 800-MEDICAR (800-633-4227)
Web site: http://www.cms.hhs.gov/medicare/

The official U.S. Government site for Medicare provides information on eligibility, enrollment, premiums, coverage, payment and billing, insurance, prescription drugs, and frequently asked questions. Call the toll-free number to receive information about local services. For basic information about Medigap, call 800-633-4227 for "Medigap Policies, The Basics," publication 10209, or search for "Medigap policies" on the Medicare Web site.

THE NATIONAL ASSOCIATION OF AREA AGENCIES ON AGING (NAAAA)

1730 Rhode Island Avenue NW, Suite 1200
Washington, DC 20036
Toll-Free: 800-677-1116
Phone: 202-872-0888
Fax: 202-872-0057
Web site: http://www.n4a.org;
http://www.eldercare.gov (Eldercare Locator)

The National Association of Area Agencies on Aging (NAAAA) provides the Eldercare Locator, a nationwide directory assistance service designed to help older persons and caregivers find local support resources. The Eldercare Locator Web site has links to state and local agencies on aging for information on transportation, meals, advocacy, home care, housing alternatives, legal issues, and social activities.

SOCIAL SECURITY ADMINISTRATION (SSA)

Office of Public Inquiries
Windsor Park Building
6401 Security Boulevard
Baltimore, MD 21235
Toll-Free: 800-772-1213; TTY: 800-325-0778
Web site: http://www.ssa.gov

Call the toll-free number to receive information about local services or visit the Web site to learn more about benefits, disability, and other frequently asked-about topics. Call or go to their Web site (http://www.ssa.gov/disability/) to find out if you qualify for one of two assistance programs, Supplemental Security Income (SSI) or Social Security Disability Insurance (SSDI).

UNITED STATES DEPARTMENT OF LABOR (DOL)
Employee Benefits Security Administration (EBSA)
200 Constitution Avenue, NW
Room N-5625
Washington, DC 20210
Toll-Free: 866-444-3272 (To order publications or to reach a Benefits Advisor in the EBSA Regional Office nearest the caller.)
Phone: 202-219-8776
Fax: 202-219-8141
Web site: http://www.dol.gov/ebsa

The Family Medical Leave Act (FMLA) grants up to 12 weeks of medical leave to eligible employees. For more information, contact the Department of Labor (http://www.dol.gov/dol/allcfr/ESA/Title_29/Part_825/toc.htm). For information about other job accommodations, contact the DOL Office of Disability Employment Policy's Job Accommodation Network (800-526-7234; http://www.jan.wvu.edu).

GLOSSARY

A

advanced cancer: a general term describing stages of cancer in which the disease has spread from the primary site to other parts of the body.

advanced lymphedema: lymphedema that has progressed and caused severe symptoms and effects.

alternative therapy: use of an unproven therapy *instead of* standard (proven) therapy. Some alternative therapies have dangerous or even life-threatening side effects. Discuss any alternative therapies you are considering with your doctor. Compare to *complementary therapy*.

Americans with Disabilities Act (ADA): designed to protect the workplace rights of those who are disabled and receiving medical treatment for serious illnesses.

analgesic: any medicine that acts on various parts of the nervous system to temporarily relieve pain.

antibiotic: medicines such as penicillin used to kill organisms that cause disease.

artery: a type of blood vessel that carries oxygenated blood from the heart to the cells throughout the body.

axilla: the armpit.

axillary node: lymph node in the armpit.

B

benign: not cancerous; not malignant.

benzopyrones: a group of drugs including bioflavonoids and coumarin; proponents believe that benzopyrones reduce lymphedema swelling, but studies are not considered reliable.

bioflavonoids: substances that occur in fruits and vegetables. See also *benzopyrones*.

bioimpedance: also called bioelectric impedance. Applying a low-level electrical current to an area of the body to gauge the volume of protein present. It could potentially help with lymphedema diagnosis; further study is needed.

biopsy: the removal of a sample of tissue—for example, a lymph node—for examination under a microscope.

body mass index (BMI): helps doctors evaluate if a person is at a healthful weight or may weigh too much or too little. BMI = (your weight in pounds × 700) ÷ (your height in inches, squared). Talk to your doctor about evaluating your BMI.

breast cancer: cancer that starts in the breast. Surgery or radiation to the underarm lymph nodes to treat breast cancer is the biggest risk factor for lymphedema.

butchers broom: *Ruscus aculeatus*, a supplement studied in a few small clinical trials as treatment for lymphedema; it requires more study before any effectiveness in improving lymphedema treatment is established.

C

cancer: a group of diseases that cause cells to change and grow out of control.

cellulitis: inflammation or infection of the skin and the tissues beneath.

chemotherapy: treatment with drugs to destroy cancer cells.

chronic venous insufficiency: poor blood circulation.

circumference: the distance around something; for example, a limb being measured for lymphedema swelling.

clinical trials: research studies in people that take place after studies on cells or animals suggest that a treatment or method of prevention is likely to be safe and effective in people. Findings allow scientists to continually improve the way a condition is managed and thus improve the health of the population.

collagen fibers: strong fibrous proteins found in connective tissue including the skin, bone and cartilage.

comparative circumferential measurement method (CCMM): using a tape measure to measure around both arms or legs in several places and compare size to evaluate for lymphedema swelling.

complementary therapy: therapy used in addition to standard therapy to help relieve symptoms and improve the patient's sense of well-being. Therapies include relaxation techniques, yoga, guided imagery, deep breathing, biofeedback, and meditation. Discuss any complementary therapies you are considering with your doctor. Compare to *alternative therapy*.

complete decongestive therapy (CDT): lymphedema treatment that reduces the amount of fluid that builds up in the tissues through a combination of hygienic skin care, lymphatic massage, compression using special bandages or garments, and exercise. Also called complex decongestive therapy (CDT), complex physical therapy (CPT), combined decongestive therapy, and complete decongestive physiotherapy (CDP).

compression bandage: bandages wrapped around the body area affected by lymphedema to stimulate lymph flow.

compression garment: a tightly knit elasticized sleeve or stocking that applies pressure to an area to prevent backflow and accumulation of fluid in an affected limb.

compression pump: an air pressure–driven pump that exerts pressure on a limb affected by lymphedema. Many health professionals do not support their use; they may be ineffective and may even worsen swelling. Sequential pumps apply pressure in a series of chambers along the limb rather than applying pressure to the whole limb at once.

computed tomography (CT): also called a CAT scan, an imaging test in which many x-rays are taken from different angles of a part of the body. The images are combined by a computer to produce cross-sectional images of internal organs.

coumarin: one of a group of natural and synthetic compounds that inhibit blood clotting by blocking the synthesis of Vitamin K in the liver. Proponents believe it may reduce lymphedema swelling. It is not approved for medical use in the United States. See also *benzopyrones*.

CT scan: see *computed tomography*.

D

deep vein thrombosis (DVT): a blood clot that usually occurs in one of the deep veins of the lower legs.

diagnosis: identifying a condition, by physical examination and by using tests and laboratory findings.

diaphragm: the muscle between the chest and the abdomen that plays an important role in breathing and promoting lymph flow.

dietitian: an expert in food and diet who has at least a bachelor's degree and has passed a national competency exam.

Doppler ultrasound: see *ultrasound*.

E

edema: buildup of fluid in the tissues, causing swelling.

exercise therapy: an exercise plan to encourage blood and lymph flow, maintain or restore range of motion and flexibility, and encourage muscle contraction.

F

Family Medical Leave Act (FMLA): a law intended to allow employees to balance their work and family life by taking reasonable unpaid leave for medical reasons.

fatigue: an unusual and persistent sense of tiredness that can occur with cancer or cancer treatments. It can be overwhelming, last a long time, and interfere with everyday life. Rest does not always relieve it.

fibrin sealants: FDA-approved agents that help stop bleeding from small, sometimes inaccessible, blood vessels during surgery. They work by forming a flexible material over the blood vessel.

fibrosis: the formation of fibrous (scar-like) tissue. This can occur anywhere in the body.

H

Hill-Burton centers: health care centers required to provide a specified amount of services to people who are unable to pay.

hyperbaric oxygen therapy: a process in which a person lies enclosed in a pressure chamber and breathes 100 percent oxygen pressurized 2 to 3 times normal atmospheric pressure. This is not a standard treatment for lymphedema, and potential effects on lymphedema are scheduled for study.

I

imaging studies: methods used to produce a picture of internal body structures, including CT scans, magnetic resonance imaging (MRI), and ultrasound.

immune system: the complex system that provides a defense system for the body; it helps the body resist or fight infections and attacks foreign agents in the body such as cancer. See also *lymph system.*

inguinal lymph nodes: lymph nodes located in the groin.

interstitial fluid: fluid found in small spaces between cells and tissues.

intravenous (IV): a method of supplying fluids and medications using a needle inserted in a vein.

L

liposuction: surgical removal of fat from under the skin to reduce the size of an area of the body. Liposuction of or close to an area affected by lymphedema may make lymphedema worse.

lumpectomy: surgery to remove a breast tumor and a small amount of surrounding normal tissue.

lymph node dissection: surgery to remove multiple lymph nodes for examination under a microscope.

lymph system: the tissues and organs (including lymph nodes, spleen, thymus, and bone marrow) that produce and store lymphocytes (white blood cells that fight infection), and the channels that carry the lymph fluid. The lymph system drains lymph, transports lymph, filters harmful substances from lymph, and removes excess fluid.

- **lymph:** also called lymph fluid; clear fluid that flows through the lymphatic vessels and is made up of protein, salts, water, and white blood cells.

- **lymph drainage:** like watersheds, drainage regions of the body where lymph is collected and sent back into the blood.

- **lymph nodes:** also called lymph glands; small, bean-shaped collections of immune system tissue found along lymphatic vessels. They remove cell waste and fluids from lymph. They help fight infections and also have a role in fighting cancer.

- **lymph vessels:** vessels that carry lymph through the body.

lymphocyte: a type of white blood cell that helps the body fight infection.

lymphedema: a condition in which excess lymph fluid collects in an area of the body, most often the arms or legs. It occurs when the amount of fluid in the body overwhelms the lymph system's ability to transport it. This condition can be persistent and can interfere with activities of daily living.

- **acute lymphedema:** lymphedema that arises suddenly and lasts from three to six months.

- **chronic lymphedema:** lymphedema that lasts longer than six months.

- **primary lymphedema:** lymphedema that arises with no known cause (idiopathic), and is not related to any other condition.

- **secondary lymphedema:** lymphedema that occurs as a result of radiation, trauma to the lymphatic system, removal of the lymph nodes, or infection.

lymphangiography: also called lymphography, the x-ray representation of the lymph glands and vessels created using a radioactive dye.

lymphangitis: infection of the lymph system that occurs when bacteria are allowed to thrive in stagnant lymph.

lymphedematous: affected by lymphedema.

lymphoceles: firm areas of swelling due to lymph buildup.

lymphoscintigraphy: a diagnostic technique that involves injecting a radioactive solution so the flow of lymph can be seen in a two-dimensional image of the lymph system.

lymphostasis: impaired lymph drainage that precedes the development of lymphedema.

M

magnetic resonance imaging (MRI): a method of taking pictures of the inside of the body. Instead of using x-rays, MRI uses a powerful magnet and transmits radio waves through the body to produce images.

malignant lymphedema: lymphedema that is caused by slowed lymph flow due to pressure of a nearby tumor; it is not cancerous.

manual lymph drainage (MLD): a type of lymphedema therapy that uses special, light massage to transfer lymph buildup to an area with functioning drainage. A component of complete decongestive therapy.

mastectomy: surgery to remove all or part of the breast and sometimes other tissue.

Medicaid: a federal program that covers the cost of medical care for those with income and assets below a certain level, which varies from state to state. Not all health providers accept Medicaid coverage for services.

medical assistance programs: programs available for those with incomes under certain amounts. Coverage varies from state to state but they may provide money for expenses such as prescription medicines.

Medicare: federal health insurance providing basic health coverage for people who are at least 65 years old or who have been permanently disabled and/or have had a Social Security disability benefit for 24 months.

Medigap: supplemental health insurance purchased by individuals to cover services not covered by Medicare.

melanoma: a type of skin cancer.

microsurgery: a type of surgery which may be used to create new lymph channels to try to improve lymph flow.

mm Hg: an abbreviation for millimeters (mm) of mercury (Hg), a standard commonly used to measure pressure, as with compression garments.

N

node: see *lymph system*.

O

obesity: a body mass index of over 30.

P

pentoxifylline: brand name Trental, a drug that may help red blood cells more easily flow through blood vessels; studies of potential application to lymphedema treatment are needed.

perometry: a device that uses infra-red lasers (radiation that can't be seen or felt) to estimate the volume of an area of the body, such as a leg affected by lymphedema. Further study into its usefulness and how it can be used by doctors is needed.

physiatrist: a doctor who specializes in rehabilitation.

physical therapist: a health professional who recommends exercises and other methods to restore or maintain the body's strength, mobility, and function.

pitting: when skin indents under pressure and stays indented; this occurs in relatively early stages of lymphedema.

pneumatic compression pumps: see *compression pumps*.

podiatrist: a doctor who specializes in treating foot conditions.

primary source: original research or document, rather than personal comments or stories.

Pycnogenol: a botanical extract of a pine tree thought to potentially constrict blood vessels and increase how easily fluid passes through blood vessels. Under study as a treatment for lymphedema.

R

radiation therapy: treatment with high-energy rays (such as x-rays) to kill or shrink cancer cells from outside of the body (external radiation) or from radioactive materials placed directly in the tumor (internal or implant radiation).

range of motion: the extent to which a joint can go through normal movements.

recurrence: cancer that has come back after treatment.

risk factor: something that increases a person's chance of developing a condition like lymphedema.

S

selenium: an antioxidant studied in a few small clinical trials as a treatment for lymphedema; it requires more study before any effectiveness in improving lymphedema treatment is established.

self-image: the way a person feels about herself and her body.

sentinel lymph node biopsy: a procedure in which dye and/or a radioactive tracer are injected into the tumor site at the time of surgery and the first (sentinel) node that picks up the dye is removed and examined. If the node is cancer-free, fewer nodes are removed.

side effects: unwanted effects of treatment.

Social Security Administration (SSA): the federal agency that issues benefits to individuals for retirement or disability.

Social Security Disability Insurance (SSDI): a Social Security program that pays benefits to you and certain members of your family if you are "insured," meaning that you worked long enough to qualify and paid Social Security taxes.

stasis: the stoppage or slowing of fluids through the body.

subclinical lymphedema: lymphedema that has not yet caused visible symptoms but causes an arm or leg to feel full or tight.

Supplemental Security Income (SSI): a Social Security program that provides monthly checks to the elderly, the blind, and people with disabilities who are in need.

surgery: an operation; surgery may be used to treat lymphedema to improve lymph drainage or remove swollen tissue. Lymphedema surgery involves potential risk, complications, and cost and may further damage the lymph system.

symptom: a change in the body or its functions that could indicate the presence of disease; a feeling of tightness or fullness can be an early symptom of lymphedema.

symptom "cluster": a set of effects experienced at one time.

T

tonometer: a device intended to precisely measure how much a person's skin and underlying tissue indents. Further study and evaluation are needed of its reliability and how it may be useful to doctors.

transcutaneous electrical nerve stimulation (TENS): a method of applying a mild electric current to the skin to relieve pain.

trigger: a factor that stimulates lymphedema to develop in an at-risk person.

tumor: an abnormal lump or mass of tissue that can either be benign (not cancerous) or malignant (cancerous).

U

ultrasound: an imaging method in which high-frequency sound waves are used to outline a part of the body. The sound wave echoes are picked up and displayed on a television screen. A Doppler ultrasound shows the flow of blood through the body and can identify or rule out problems in the veins.

unproven therapy: any therapy that has not been scientifically tested and proven to be safe and effective.

V

vascular access device (VAD): a catheter inserted under the skin into a vein through which a person can receive injections.

vein: a type of blood vessel that carries deoxygenated blood from the cells back to the heart and lungs.

venous stasis ulcer: a sore on the leg caused by impaired blood flow.

vessel: any type of tube that carries or circulates body fluid, such as blood or lymph, through the body.

volume: the amount of space something takes up; limb volume may be measured when evaluating lymphedema-like symptoms.

W

white blood cell: also called a leukocyte, a type of blood cell that helps defend the body against infections. Lymph fluid contains white blood cells.

Women's Health and Cancer Rights Act (WHCRA): a provision requiring all group health plans that cover mastectomy to provide for coverage of physical complications such as lymphedema.

X

x-rays: a form of radiation that at low levels can produce an image of the body on film.

REFERENCES

INTRODUCTION

American Cancer Society. 2003. Lymphedema: What every woman with breast cancer should know. http://www.cancer.org/docroot/MIT/content/MIT_7_2x_Lymphedema_and_Breast_Cancer.asp (accessed April 27, 2004).

National Cancer Institute. 2004. Lymphedema (PDQ). http://www.cancer.gov/cancerinfo/pdq/supportivecare/lymphedema (accessed April 27, 2004).

National Lymphedema Network. Lymphedema: A brief overview. http://www.lymphnet.org/whatis.html (accessed April 27, 2004).

Petrek, Jeanne A., Peter I. Pressman, and Robert A. Smith. 2000. Lymphedema: Current issues in research and management. Review. CA: A Cancer Journal for Clinicians 50 (5): 292–307; quiz 308–311.

Thiadens, Saskia R., Jane M. Armer, and Davina Porock. 2002. NLN preliminary statistical analysis of survey data on lymphedema. National Lymphedema Network. LymphLink, January–March.

CHAPTER 1

American Cancer Society. 1999. Reducing lymphedema risk. ACS News Center. February 19. http://www.cancer.org/docroot/NWS/content/NWS_2_1x_Reducing_Lymphedema_Risk.asp (accessed April 27, 2004).

———. Detailed guide: Breast cancer: What happens after treatment for breast cancer? http://www.cancer.org/docroot/CRI/content/CRI_2_4_5X_What_happens_after_treatment_5.asp?sitearea=MH (accessed April 27, 2004).

———. Lymphedema: What every woman with breast cancer should know. http://www.cancer.org/docroot/MIT/content/MIT_7_2x_Lymphedema_and_Breast_Cancer.asp (accessed April 27, 2004).

———. Understanding lymphedema (for cancers other than breast cancer). http://www.cancer.org/docroot/MIT/content/MIT_7_2x_Understanding_Lymphedema.asp (accessed April 27, 2004).

Armer, Jane M. 2003. Lymphedema. In Contemporary issues in breast cancer, 2nd ed., Karen Hassey. Sudbury, MA: Jones & Bartlett.

Armer, Jane M., and Davina Porock. 2002. Self-management of fatigue among women with lymphedema. Lymphology 35 (2): 208–212.

Browse, Norman, Kevin G. Burnand, and Peter S. Mortimer. 2003. Diseases of the lymphatics. London: Arnold Publishers.

Burt, Jeannie, and Gwen White. 1999. Lymphedema: A breast cancer patient's guide to prevention and healing. Alameda, CA: Hunter House Publishers.

Kelly, Deborah G. 2002. A primer on lymphedema. Upper Saddle River, NJ: Prentice Hall.

Lasinski, Bonnie B. 2003. Question Corner. National Lymphedema Network. LymphLink, July–September. http://www.lymphnet.org/question.html (accessed November 4, 2004).

Muscari, Esther. 2004. Lymphedema: Responding to our patients' needs. Oncology Nursing Forum 31 (5): 905–912.

National Cancer Institute. 2004. Lymphedema (PDQ). http://www.cancer.gov/cancerinfo/pdq/supportivecare/lymphedema (accessed April 27, 2004).

National Lymphedema Network. 2004. Lymphedema: A brief overview. http://www.lymphnet.org/whatis.html (accessed April 27, 2004).

Petrek, Jeanne A., and Andrea L. Cheville. 2004. Lymphedema. In Diseases of the breast, 3rd ed., Jay R. Harris, Marc E. Lippman, Monica Morrow, and C. Kent Osborne. Philadelphia, PA: Lippincott Williams & Wilkins.

Petrek, Jeanne A., Peter I. Pressman, and Robert A. Smith. 2000. Lymphedema: Current issues in research and management. Review. *CA: A Cancer Journal for Clinicians* 50 (5): 292–307; quiz 308–311.

Sarvis, Connie, and Emil Vernarec, eds. 2003. When lymphedema takes hold. *RNWeb*, September 1. http://www.rnweb.com/rnweb/article/articleDetail.jsp?id=107151 (accessed April 27, 2004).

Swirsky, Joan, and Diane S. Nannery. 1998. *Coping with lymphedema: Sound, helpful information for those who must deal with the problems associated with lymphedema.* Garden City Park, NY: Avery Publishing Group.

Chapter 2

American Cancer Society. 1998. Living with lymphedema. ACS News Center. May 12. http://www.cancer.org/docroot/NWS/content/NWS_3_1x_Living_with_Lymphedema.asp (accessed April 27, 2004).

———. 2004. *A breast cancer journey: Your personal guidebook,* 2nd ed. Atlanta, GA: American Cancer Society.

———. 2004. Cancer deaths to decline in 2004. ACS News Center. January 15. http://www.cancer.org/docroot/NWS/content/NWS_1_1x_Cancer_Deaths_to_Decline_in_2004.asp (accessed March 14, 2005).

———. 2004. Detailed guide: Breast cancer: Surgery for breast cancer. http://www.cancer.org/docroot/CRI/content/CRI_2_4_4X_Surgery_5.asp?sitearea= (accessed April 27, 2004).

———. 2004. Lymphedema: What every woman with breast cancer should know: Hand and arm care following surgery or radiation therapy for breast cancer. http://www.cancer.org/docroot/CRI/content/CRI_2_6X_Lymphedema_5.asp?sitearea= (accessed April 27, 2004).

———. 2004. Understanding lymphedema (for cancers other than breast cancer). http://www.cancer.org/docroot/MIT/content/MIT_7_2x_Understanding_Lymphedema.asp (accessed April 27, 2004).

———. 2005. Breast cancer. Cancer Information Database. http://documents.cancer.org/104.00/104.00.pdf (accessed January 9, 2005).

American Society of Clinical Oncology. 2001. Optimizing cancer care—the importance of symptom management. Lymphedema. ASCO Curriculum.

Armer, Jane M. 2003. Lymphedema. In *Contemporary issues in breast cancer,* 2nd ed., Karen Hassey. Sudbury, MA: Jones & Bartlett.

Cheville, Andrea, Charles L. McGarvey, Jeanne A. Petrek, Sandra A. Russo, Saskia R. J. Thiadens, and Marie E. Taylor. 2003. The grading of lymphedema in oncology clinical trials. *Seminars in Radiation Oncology* 13 (3): 214–25.

Erickson, Virginia S., Marjorie L. Pearson, Patricia A. Ganz, John Adams, and Katherine L. Kahn. 2001. Arm edema in breast cancer patients. *Journal of the National Cancer Institute* 93: 96–111.

Hsueh, Eddy C., Nora M. Hansen, and Armando E. Giuliano. 2000. Intraoperative lymphatic mapping and sentinel lymph node dissection in breast cancer. *CA: A Cancer Journal for Clinicians* 50: 279–291.

Kelly, Deborah G. 2002. *A primer on lymphedema.* Upper Saddle River, NJ: Prentice Hall.

Muscari, Esther. 2004. Lymphedema: Responding to our patients' needs. *Oncology Nursing Forum* 31 (5): 905–912.

National Cancer Institute. 2004. Lymphedema (PDQ). http://www.cancer.gov/cancerinfo/pdq/supportivecare/lymphedema (accessed April 27, 2004).

———. 2004. Lymphedema (PDQ). Health professional version. http://www.cancer.gov/cancerinfo/pdq/supportivecare/lymphedema/HealthProfessional (accessed May 5, 2004).

National Lymphedema Network. 2004. Lymphedema: A brief overview.http://www.lymphnet.org/whatis.html (accessed April 27, 2004).

Pain, Simon J., and Arnie D. Purushotham. 2000. Lymphoedema following surgery for breast cancer. *The British Journal of Surgery* 87: 1128–1141.

Petrek, Jeanne A., and Andrea L. Cheville. 2004. Lymphedema. In *Diseases of the breast,* 3rd ed., Jay R. Harris, Marc E. Lippman, Monica Morrow, and C. Kent Osborne. Philadelphia, PA: Lippincott Williams & Wilkins.

Petrek, Jeanne A., Peter I. Pressman, and Robert A. Smith. 2000. Lymphedema: Current issues in research and management. Review. *CA: A Cancer Journal for Clinicians* 50 (5): 292–307; quiz 308–311.

Petrek, Jeanne A., Ruby T. Senie, Margaret Peters, and Paul Peter Rosen. Lymphedema in a cohort of breast carcinoma survivors 20 years after diagnosis. 2001. *Cancer* 92 (6): 1368–77.

Sarvis, Connie, and Emil Vernarec, eds. 2003. When lymphedema takes hold. *RNWeb*, September 1. http://www.rnweb.com/rnweb/article/articleDetail.jsp?id=107151 (accessed April 27, 2004).

Swirsky, Joan, and Diane S. Nannery. 1998. *Coping with lymphedema: Sound, helpful information for those who must deal with the problems associated with lymphedema.* Garden City Park, NY: Avery Publishing Group.

Weiss, Robert. 2005. Incidence of lymphedema: A literature review summary. National Lymphedema Network. *LymphLink*, January–March.

CHAPTER 3

American Cancer Society. 1999. Reducing lymphedema risk. ACS News Center. February 19. http://www.cancer.org/docroot/NWS/content/NWS_2_1x_Reducing_Lymphedema_Risk.asp (accessed April 27, 2004).

———. 2004. Lymphedema: What every woman with breast cancer should know. http://www.cancer.org/docroot/MIT/content/MIT_7_2x_Lymphedema_and_Breast_Cancer.asp (accessed April 27, 2004).

———. 2004. Understanding lymphedema (for cancers other than breast cancer). http://www.cancer.org/docroot/MIT/content/MIT_7_2x_Understanding_Lymphedema.asp (accessed April 27, 2004).

Brennan, Michael J., and Linda T. Miller. 1998. Overview of treatment options and review of the current role and use of compression garments, intermittent pumps, and exercise in the management of lymphedema. American Cancer Society Lymphedema Workshop. Review. *Cancer* 83 (12 Suppl American): 2821–7.

Harris, Susan R., and Sherri L. Niesen-Vertommen. 2000. Challenging the myth of exercise-induced lymphedema following breast cancer: A series of case reports. *Journal of Surgical Oncology* 74 (2): 95–8; discussion 98–9.

Kelly, Deborah G. 2002. *A primer on lymphedema.* Upper Saddle River, NJ: Prentice Hall.

McKenzie, Donald C., and Andrea L. Kalda. 2003. Effect of upper extremity exercise on secondary lymphedema in breast cancer patients: A pilot study. *Journal of Clinical Oncology* 21 (3): 463–6.

Muscari, Esther. 2004. Lymphedema: Responding to our patients' needs. *Oncology Nursing Forum* 31 (5): 905–912.

National Cancer Institute. 2004. Lymphedema (PDQ). http://www.cancer.gov/cancerinfo/pdq/supportivecare/lymphedema (accessed April 27, 2004).

National Cancer Institute. 2004. Lymphedema (PDQ). Health professional version. http://www.cancer.gov/cancerinfo/pdq/supportivecare/lymphedema/HealthProfessional (accessed May 5, 2004).

National Lymphedema Network Advisory Committee. 2004. Air travel. Position statement of the National Lymphedema Network. May 19. http://www.lymphnet.org/nlnairtravel.pdf (accessed December 20, 2004; expires May 19, 2006).

Petrek, Jeanne A., and Andrea L. Cheville. 2004. Lymphedema. In *Diseases of the breast*, 3rd ed., Jay R. Harris, Marc E. Lippman, Monica Morrow, and C. Kent Osborne. Philadelphia, PA: Lippincott Williams & Wilkins.

Petrek, Jeanne A., Ruby T. Senie, Margaret Peters, and Paul Peter Rosen. 2001. Lymphedema in a cohort of breast carcinoma survivors 20 years after diagnosis. *Cancer* 92 (6): 1368–77.

Swirsky, Joan, and Diane S. Nannery. 1998. *Coping with lymphedema: Sound, helpful information for those who must deal with the problems associated with lymphedema.* Garden City Park, NY: Avery Publishing Group.

World Health Organization. 2004. International travel and health: Travel by air: Health considerations. http://www.who.int/ith/chapter02_01.html#3 (accessed December 20, 2004).

Chapter 4

American Cancer Society. 1998. Living with lymphedema. ACS News Center. May 12. http://www.cancer.org/docroot/NWS/content/NWS_3_1x_Living_with_Lymphedema.asp (accessed April 27, 2004).

———. 2004. Lymphedema: What every woman with breast cancer should know. http://www.cancer.org/docroot/MIT/content/MIT_7_2x_Lymphedema_and_Breast_Cancer.asp (accessed April 27, 2004).

American Society of Clinical Oncology. 2001. Lymphedema. Optimizing cancer care—the importance of symptom management. ASCO Curriculum.

Armer, Jane M. 2003. Lymphedema. In *Contemporary issues in breast cancer*, 2nd ed., Karen Hassey. Sudbury, MA: Jones & Bartlett.

———. 2005. The problem of post-breast cancer lymphedema: Impact and measurement issues. Nursing Perspectives. *Cancer Investigation* (1): 76–83.

Brown, Jennifer L. 2004. A clinically useful method for evaluating lymphedema. *Clinical Journal of Oncology Nursing* 8 (1): 35–8.

Cheville, Andrea, Charles L. McGarvey, Jeanne A. Petrek, Sandra A. Russo, Saskia R. J. Thiadens, and Marie E. Taylor. 2003. The grading of lymphedema in oncology clinical trials. *Seminars in Radiation Oncology* 13 (3): 214–25.

International Society of Lymphology. 2003. The diagnosis and treatment of peripheral lymphedema. Consensus document. *Lymphology* 36: 84–91. http://www.u.arizona.edu/~witte/ISL.htm (accessed September 14, 2004).

Kelly, Debbie D., Jane M. Armer, Deidre D. Wipke-Tevis, and Donna A. Williams. 2002. Increasing the accuracy of arm volumeter measurements in breast cancer survivors with lymphedema. *Lymphology* 35 (2): 265–267.

Kelly, Deborah G. 2002. *A primer on lymphedema.* Upper Saddle River, NJ: Prentice Hall.

Lymphology Association of North America. 2004. North American certification for lymphedema therapists. Exam outline. http://www.clt-lana.org/outline.html (accessed October 22, 2004).

Muscari, Esther. 2004. Lymphedema: Responding to our patients' needs. *Oncology Nursing Forum* 31 (5): 905–912.

National Cancer Institute. 2003. Common Terminology Criteria for Adverse Events v3.0 (CTCAE). Cancer therapy evaluation program. DCTD, NCI, NIH, DHHS. NIH Publication #03-5410. December 12. http://ctep.cancer.gov/forms/CTCAEv3.pdf (accessed January 7, 2005).

———. 2004. After you've finished your cancer treatment. Facing forward series: Life after cancer treatment. http://www.cancer.gov/cancerinfo/life-after-treatment#2 (accessed April 27, 2004).

———. 2004. Lymphedema (PDQ). http://www.cancer.gov/cancerinfo/pdq/supportivecare/lymphedema (accessed April 27, 2004).

———. 2004. Lymphedema (PDQ). Health professional version. http://www.cancer.gov/cancerinfo/pdq/supportivecare/lymphedema/HealthProfessional (accessed May 5, 2004).

National Lymphedema Network. 2004. Lymphedema: A brief overview. http://www.lymphnet.org/whatis.html (accessed April 27, 2004).

Petrek, Jeanne A., and Andrea L. Cheville. 2004. Lymphedema. In *Diseases of the breast*, 3rd ed., Jay R. Harris, Marc E. Lippman, Monica Morrow, and C. Kent Osborne. Philadelphia, PA: Lippincott Williams & Wilkins.

Petrek, Jeanne A., Peter I. Pressman, and Robert A. Smith. 2000. Lymphedema: Current issues in research and management. Review. *CA: A Cancer Journal for Clinicians* 50 (5): 292–307; quiz 308–311.

Sarvis, Connie, and Emil Vernarec, eds. 2003. When lymphedema takes hold. *RN*, September 1.

Swirsky, Joan, and Diane S. Nannery. 1998. *Coping with lymphedema: Sound, helpful information for those who must deal with the problems associated with lymphedema.* Garden City Park, NY: Avery Publishing Group.

CHAPTER 5

American Cancer Society. 1999. Coumarin and lymphedema: Study determines coumarin does not reduce lymphedema. ACS News Center. March 4. http://www.cancer.org/docroot/NWS/content/NWS_3_1x_Coumarin_and_Lymphedema.asp (accessed April 27, 2004).

———. 1999. Reducing lymphedema risk. ACS News Center. February 19. http://www.cancer.org/docroot/NWS/content/NWS_2_1x_Reducing_Lymphedema_Risk.asp (accessed April 27, 2004).

———. 2004. *A breast cancer journey: Your personal guidebook*, 2nd ed. Atlanta, GA: American Cancer Society.

American Society of Clinical Oncology. 2001. Optimizing cancer care—the importance of symptom management. Lymphedema. ASCO Curriculum.

Armer, Jane M. 2003. Lymphedema. In *Contemporary issues in breast cancer*, 2nd ed., Karen Hassey. Sudbury, MA: Jones & Bartlett.

Gergich, Nicole L. 2002. Question Corner. National Lymphedema Network. *LymphLink*, January–March. http://www.lymphnet.org/question.html (accessed January 6, 2004).

International Society of Lymphology. 2003. The diagnosis and treatment of peripheral lymphedema. Consensus document. *Lymphology* 36: 84–91. http://www.u.arizona.edu/~witte/ISL.htm (accessed September 14, 2004).

Kelly, Deborah G. 2002. *A primer on lymphedema*. Upper Saddle River, NJ: Prentice Hall.

National Lymphedema Network. 2004. Lymphedema: A brief overview. http://www.lymphnet.org/whatis.html (accessed April 27, 2004).

CHAPTER 6

American Cancer Society. 1998. Living with lymphedema. ACS News Center. May 12. http://www.cancer.org/docroot/NWS/content/NWS_3_1x_Living_with_Lymphedema.asp (accessed April 27, 2004).

———. 1999. Coumarin and lymphedema: Study determines coumarin does not reduce lymphedema. ACS News Center. March 4. http://www.cancer.org/docroot/NWS/content/NWS_3_1x_Coumarin_and_Lymphedema.asp (accessed April 27, 2004).

———. 2004. Frequently asked questions about nutrition and physical activity. http://www.cancer.org/docroot/mbc/content/MBC_6_2x_FAQ_Nutrition_and_Physical_Activity.asp?sitearea=MH (accessed April 27, 2004).

———. 2004. Lymphedema: What every woman with breast cancer should know. http://www.cancer.org/docroot/MIT/content/MIT_7_2x_Lymphedema_and_Breast_Cancer.asp (accessed April 27, 2004).

American Society of Clinical Oncology. 2001. Optimizing cancer care—the importance of symptom management. Lymphedema. ASCO Curriculum.

Armer, Jane M. 2003. Lymphedema. In *Contemporary issues in breast cancer*, 2nd ed., Karen Hassey. Sudbury, MA: Jones & Bartlett.

Armer, Jane M., P. Paul Heppner, and Brent Mallinckrodt. 2002. Post-breast cancer treatment lymphedema: The secret epidemic. *Scope on Phlebology and Lymphology* 9: 334–341.

Badger, Caroline, Nancy Preston, Kate Seers, and Peter S. Mortimer. 2004. Benzo-pyrones for reducing and controlling lymphoedema of the limbs. *Cochrane Database of Systematic Reviews (Online)* (2): CD003140.

Brennan, Michael J., and Linda T. Miller. 1998. Overview of treatment options and review of the current role and use of compression garments, intermittent pumps, and exercise in the management of lymphedema. American Cancer Society Lymphedema Workshop. Review. *Cancer* 83 (12 Suppl American): 2821–7.

Bruns, Frank, Jens Buntzel, Ralph Mucke, Klaus Schonekaes, Klaus Kisters, and Oliver Micke. 2004. Selenium in the treatment of head and neck lymphedema. *Medical Principles and Practice: International Journal of Kuwait University, Health Sciences Centre* 13 (4): 185–90.

Burt, Jeannie, and Gwen White. 1999. *Lymphedema: A breast cancer patient's guide to prevention and healing.* Alameda, CA: Hunter House.

Erickson, Virginia S., Marjorie L. Pearson, Patricia A. Ganz, John Adams, and Katherine L. Kahn. 2001. Arm edema in breast cancer patients. Review. *Journal of the National Cancer Institute* 93 (2): 96–111.

International Society of Lymphology. 2003. The diagnosis and treatment of peripheral lymphedema. Consensus document. *Lymphology* 36: 84–91. http://www.u.arizona.edu/~witte/ISL.htm (accessed September 14, 2004).

Kelly, Deborah G. 2002. *A primer on lymphedema.* Upper Saddle River, NJ: Prentice Hall.

Lasinski, Bonnie B. 2003. Question Corner. National Lymphedema Network. *LymphLink*, July–September. http://www.lymphnet.org/question.html (accessed November 4, 2004).

Lin, Esther M. 2002. Current trends in lymph management. Matters of Life Web Cast Series. November 7. http://www.commpartners.com/mattersoflife/matter.php (accessed April 27, 2004).

Memorial Sloan Kettering Cancer Center. 2004. About Herbs: Butchers broom. http://www.mskcc.org/mskcc/html/11571.cfm?TAB=HC&RecordID=394 (accessed November 16, 2004).

———. 2004. About Herbs: Selenium. http://www.mskcc.org/mskcc/html/11571.cfm?TAB=HC&RecordID=463 (accessed November 16, 2004).

Micke, Oliver, Frank Bruns, Ralph Mucke, Ulrich Schafer, Michael Glatzel, Alexander F. DeVries, Klaus Schonekaes, Klaus Kisters, and Jens Buntzel. 2003. Selenium in the treatment of radiation-associated secondary lymphedema. *International Journal of Radiation Oncology, Biology, Physics* 56 (1): 40–9.

Muscari, Esther. 2004. Lymphedema: Responding to our patients' needs. *Oncology Nursing Forum* 31 (5): 905–912.

National Cancer Institute. 2004. Lymphedema (PDQ). http://www.cancer.gov/cancerinfo/pdq/supportivecare/lymphedema (accessed April 27, 2004).

National Lymphedema Network Advisory Committee. 2004. Air travel. Position statement of the National Lymphedema Network. May 19. http://www.lymphnet.org/nlnairtravel.pdf (accessed December 20, 2004).

National Lymphedema Network. 2004. Lymphedema: A brief overview. http://www.lymphnet.org/whatis.html (accessed April 27, 2004).

Petrek, Jeanne A., and Andrea L. Cheville. 2004. Lymphedema. In *Diseases of the breast*, 3rd ed., Jay R. Harris, Marc E. Lippman, Monica Morrow, and C. Kent Osborne. Philadelphia, PA: Lippincott Williams & Wilkins.

Stewart, Paula J. 2001. Lymphedema and wound management challenges. National Lymphedema Network. *LymphLink*, October–December. http://www.lymphnet.org/woundcare.html (accessed November 4, 2004).

Swirsky, Joan, and Diane S. Nannery. 1998. *Coping with lymphedema: Sound, helpful information for those who must deal with the problems associated with lymphedema.* Garden City Park, NY: Avery Publishing Group.

Tuppo, Catherine M. 2002. Question Corner. National Lymphedema Network. *LymphLink*, April–June. http://www.lymphnet.org/question.html (accessed November 4, 2004).

Weiss, Janet M., and B.J. Spray. 2002. The effect of complete decongestive therapy on the quality of life of patients with peripheral lymphedema. *Lymphology* 35 (2): 46–58.

CHAPTER 7

American Cancer Society. 2001. Medical insurance and financial assistance for the cancer patient. http://www.cancer.org/docroot/MLT/content/MLT_1x_Medical_Insurance_and_Financial_Assistance_for_the_Cancer_Patient.asp?sitearea=&level=1 (accessed March 9, 2005).

———. 2001. Medicare expedites access to lymphedema pumps. ACS News Center. June 14. http://www.cancer.org/docroot/NWS/content/update/NWS_1_1xU_Medicare_Expedites_Access_to_Lymphedema_Pumps.asp (accessed April 27, 2004).

———. 2004. *A breast cancer journey: Your personal guidebook*, 2nd ed. Atlanta, GA: American Cancer Society.

———. 2004. About the Commission on Cancer. http://www.cancer.org/docroot/FTC/content/ftc_1_2.asp?sitearea=ETO (accessed July 22, 2004).

———. 2004. Understanding lymphedema (for cancers other than breast cancer). http://www.cancer.org/docroot/MIT/content/MIT_7_2x_Understanding_Lymphedema.asp (accessed April 27, 2004).

———. 2004. Women's health and cancer rights act. http://www.cancer.org/docroot/CRI/content/CRI_2_6X_Womens_Health_and_Cancer_Rights_Act_5.asp?sitearea=&level= (accessed July 23, 2004).

Beck, Marcia. 2002. Question Corner. National Lymphedema Network. *LymphLink*, July–September. http://www.lymphnet.org/question.html (accessed November 4, 2004).

Centers for Medicare and Medicaid Services. 2003. *Medigap policies: The basics*. Publication No. CMS-10209 May 2003. http://www.medicare.gov/Publications/Pubs/pdf/10209.pdf (accessed January 6, 2005).

Circle of Hope Lymphedema Foundation, Inc. 2004. Finding a qualified therapist. http://www.lymphedemacircleofhope.org/therapist.htm (accessed September 10, 2004).

Muscari, Esther. 2004. Lymphedema: Responding to our patients' needs. *Oncology Nursing Forum* 31 (5): 905–912.

National Lymphedema Network. 2004. Choosing a lymphedema therapist. http://www.lymphnet.org/choosing.html (accessed September 10, 2004).

———. 2004. Resource guide. http://www.lymphnet.org/resource.html (accessed September 10, 2004).

———. 2005. Legislation. Virginia: Statewide legislation addressing lymphedema treatment passes. http://www.lymphnet.org/legislation.html (accessed January 6, 2005).

Petrek, Jeanne A., and Andrea L. Cheville. 2004. Lymphedema. In *Diseases of the breast*, 3rd ed., Jay R. Harris, Marc E. Lippman, Monica Morrow, and C. Kent Osborne. Philadelphia, PA: Lippincott Williams & Wilkins.

Swirsky, Joan, and Diane S. Nannery. 1998. *Coping with lymphedema: Sound, helpful information for those who must deal with the problems associated with lymphedema*. Garden City Park, NY: Avery Publishing Group.

Thiadens, Saskia R. J., Jane M. Armer, and Davina Porock. 2002. NLN preliminary statistical analysis of survey data on lymphedema. National Lymphedema Network. *LymphLink*, January–March.

Chapter 8

American Cancer Society. 2000. Cancer information & support available online. http://www.cancer.org/docroot/ESN/content/ESN_2_4X_Cancer_information_and_support_available_online.asp (accessed March 7, 2005).

———. 2004. Overview: Breast cancer: Moving on after treatment. http://www.cancer.org/docroot/CRI/content/CRI_2_2_6X_Moving_on_after_treatment_5.asp?sitearea= (accessed April 27, 2004).

———. 2004. Reach to recovery. http://www.cancer.org/docroot/ESN/content/ESN_3_1x_Reach_to_Recovery_5.asp?sitearea=SHR (accessed April 27, 2004).

———. 2004. *When the focus is on care: Palliative care and cancer*. Atlanta, GA: American Cancer Society.

Armer, Jane M., P. Paul Heppner, and Brent Mallinckrodt. 2002. Post-breast cancer treatment lymphedema: The secret epidemic. *Scope on Phlebology and Lymphology* 9: 334–341.

Beck, Marcia. 2002. Question Corner. National Lymphedema Network. *LymphLink*, July–September. http://www.lymphnet.org/question.html (accessed November 4, 2004).

breastcancer.org. 2004. Arm lymphedema: Emotional effects. http://www.breastcancer.org/lymphedema_emotional.html (accessed April 23, 2004).

Hull, Margaret M. 1998. Functional and psychosocial aspects of lymphedema in women treated for breast cancer. *Innovations in Breast Cancer Care* 3 (4): 97–100, 117–8.

Muscari, Esther. 2004. Lymphedema: Responding to our patients' needs. *Oncology Nursing Forum* 31 (5): 905–912.

National Cancer Institute. 2004. Joining a support group. Facing forward series: Life after cancer treatment. http://cancer.gov/cancertopics/life-after-treatment/page7 (accessed April 27, 2004).

———. 2004. Your mind and your feelings after cancer treatment. Facing forward series: Life after cancer treatment. http://www.cancer.gov/cancerinfo/life-after-treatment/page6 (accessed April 27, 2004).

Radina, M. Elise, and Jane M. Armer. 2001. Post-breast cancer lymphedema and the family: A qualitative investigation of families coping with chronic illness. *Journal of Child and Family Nursing* 7 (3): 281–99.

CHAPTER 9

American Cancer Society. 2000. *American Cancer Society's guide to complementary and alternative methods.* Atlanta, GA: American Cancer Society.

———. 2004. Targeted grants for research on the pathogenesis and treatment of lymphedema secondary to the management of breast cancer. RFA-01-2004.

———. 2005. *American Cancer Society's complete guide to prostate cancer.* Atlanta, GA: American Cancer Society.

Andersen, Lene, Inger Hojris, Mogens Erlandsen, and Jorn Andersen. 2000. Treatment of breast-cancer-related lymphedema with or without manual lymphatic drainage: A randomized study. *Acta Oncologica* 39: 339-405.

Armer, Jane M. 2003. Lymphedema. In *Contemporary issues in breast cancer*, 2nd ed., Karen Hassey. Sudbury, MA: Jones & Bartlett.

———. 2005. The problem of post-breast cancer lymphedema: Impact and measurement issues. Nursing Perspectives. *Cancer Investigation* (1): 76–83.

———. 2001. Prospective nursing study of breast cancer lymphedema. Unpublished raw data.

Bernas, Michael J., and Marlys H. Witte. In-progress clinical trial. Massage therapy for breast cancer treatment-related swelling of the arms. National Center for Complementary and Alternative Medicine Study ID 1 R21 AT01326-01. http://clinicaltrials.gov/show/NCT00058851 (accessed January 3, 2005).

Carlson, Jay. In-progress clinical trial. Fibrin sealant in decreasing lymphedema following surgery to remove lymph nodes in patients with cancer of the vulva. Gynecologic Oncology Group, National Cancer Institute (NCI) Study CDR0000069149; GOG-0195; NCI-P01-0201; NCT00028951. http://clinicaltrials.gov/show/NCT00028951 (accessed January 3, 2005).

Cheville, Andrea, Charles L. McGarvey, Jeanne A. Petrek, Sandra A. Russo, Saskia R. J. Thiadens, and Marie E. Taylor. 2003. The grading of lymphedema in oncology clinical trials. *Seminars in Radiation Oncology* 13 (3): 214–25.

Cornish, Bruce H., Marilyn Chapman, Cherrell Hirst, Bev Mirolo, Ian H. Bunce, Leigh C. Ward, Brian J. Thomas. 2001. Early diagnosis of lymphedema using multiple frequency bioimpedance. *Lymphology* 34 (1): 2–11. http://www.ncbi.nlm.nih.gov/entrez/query.fcgi?cmd=Retrieve&db=PubMed&list_uids=11307661&dopt=Abstract (accessed January 3, 2005).

Federal Drug Administration. 1998. New fibrin sealant approved to help control bleeding in surgery. FDA Talk Paper. May 1. http://www.fda.gov/bbs/topics/ANSWERS/ANS00865.html (accessed January 3, 2005).

Hutson, Paul, and Lynn VanUmmersen. In-progress clinical trial. Pycnogenol for the treatment of lymphedema of the arm in breast cancer survivors. National Center for Complementary and Alternative Medicine Study ID R21 AT001724-01. http://clinicaltrials.gov/show/NCT00064857 (accessed January 3, 2005).

Jacobs, Linda. 2004. Personal communication with Jane Armer regarding planned study by Cancer and Leukemia Group B (CALGB) and American College of Surgeons Oncology Group (ACOSOG). January 12.

National Center for Complementary and Alternative Medicine. 2004. Lymphedema clinical trials. National Institutes of Health. http://nccam.nci.nih.gov/clinicaltrials/lymphedema.htm (accessed April 27, 2004).

Shih, Ya-Chen Tina. 3-year study beginning January 1, 2005. Burden of breast cancer related lymphedema on working American families. American Cancer Society Grant RSGTL-05-093-01 CPHPS.

Siegmund, Ellen. 2005. Lymphedema treatment program for underserved women. City of Hope Study 01167. http://clinicaltrials.coh.org/_asp/study_display.asp?pid=3713539 (accessed January 3, 2005).

Weiss, Robert. 2002. Cost-efficacy of lymphedema treatment: A preliminary model. Poster paper. 5th National Lymphedema Network International Conference. Chicago, IL. August 28–September 1.

Wingert, Karen. 2003. Evidence based practice for clinical treatment of lymphedema. PhD study, Rocky Mountain University, Provo, Utah.

Witte, Marlys H. Three-year study beginning January 1, 2005. Pre-clinical model of breast cancer treatment-related lymphedema. American Cancer Society Grant RSGTL-05-090-01 CCE.

Yarnold, John R. In-progress clinical trial. Hyperbaric oxygen therapy compared with standard therapy in treating chronic arm lymphedema in women who have undergone radiation therapy for early breast cancer. Royal Marsden NHS Trust Study CDR0000349496; RMNHS-HOT; EU-20337; NCT00077090. http://clinicaltrials.gov/show/NCT00077090 (accessed October 10, 2004).

INDEX

Cancer Information Service (CIS), 154
Cancer Survivors Network, 152
Cancer Topics Web site, 153
Cancerlit database, 153
CancerTrials, 153
Care standards and language, uniformity of,
    xxi–xxii
Cause of lymphedema, 19
Cellulitis, 14, 15
Certification, lymphedema treatment, 102–104
Cervical cancer, 18, 23, 120
Challenges of lymphedema, xx–xxii
Chemotherapy, 15, 40
Circle of Hope Lymphedema Foundation, Inc.,
    152
Circulatory system, 3–5
City of Hope Cancer Center, 149
Clinical trials, 139–149
Clothing
    choosing appropriate, 127
    tight, 36–37, 52
Colon cancer, 23
Combination therapy for lymphedema, 72–94
Commission on Cancer (CoC), 104
Common sense and precautions against lym-
    phedema, 30–31
Communication
    with lymphedema therapists, 65
    with others about one's lymphedema,
        129–130
    with partner about intimacy, 126–127
Comparative circumferential measurement
    method (CCMM), 54
Complementary methods, 97, 147, 148
Complete decongestive therapy (CDT), 70, 71
    components of, 72–73
    compression bandages in, 72, 77, 78–80f, 80
    compression garments in, 32, 36–37, 81–83
    compression pumps in, 83–84
    exercise in, 84–93
    length of treatment time for, 73
    lymphedema therapists certified in, 102–105
    manual lymph drainage (MLD) in, 71, 72,
        74f, 75–76
    skin care, 93
    studies on, 147

Compression
    bandages, 77, 78–80f, 80
    complete decongestive therapy (CDT)
        and, 72, 76
    garments, 32, 36, 81–83
    pumps, 83–84
    self care and, 82–83
Computed tomography (CT), 57–58
Consolidated Omnibus Budget Reconciliation
    Act (COBRA), 113
Constriction or pressure, avoiding, 36–37, 52
Cooking, protection against burns from, 36
Coping with lymphedema, xxii, 2, 18, 62, 97,
    120, 138. See also Self care
    body changes, 126–127
    changes in daily life, 127–129
    and communicating about one's lymphedema,
        129–130
    and feelings, 124–126
    strategies for, 121–124
    support systems for, 132–135
    taking action and, 132
Costs, lymphedema treatment, 107–108, 149
Coumarin, 96

D

Daily life
    coping with changes in, 127–129
    and home factors that may affect treat-
        ment, 67
Debulking procedures, 100
Deep lymph nodes, 9
Deep venous thrombosis (DVT), 64, 102
Definition of lymphedema, 3, 9
Department of Veterans Affairs (VA), 115,
    154
Diagnosis of lymphedema
    awareness and, 21
    being aware and examining one's body in,
        44–47
    bioimpedance and, 146
    challenge of, 43–44
    general health assessment in, 49
    healthy weight and, 52

In memory of Dr. Jeanne Petrek

Jeanne Petrek, MD, directed the surgical program at the Evelyn H. Lauder Breast Center, Memorial Sloan-Kettering Cancer Center, and was attending surgeon in the Breast Service of Memorial Sloan-Kettering's Department of Surgery and a professor of surgery at Cornell University School of Medicine. She studied the prevalence and effects of lymphedema and was a pioneer in working to reduce lymphedema risk through surgical techniques such as sentinel lymph node biopsy. She was a compassionate physician concerned about patients' quality of life.

As a long-standing, dedicated American Cancer Society volunteer, Dr. Petrek served on numerous ACS volunteer committees and advisory groups focused on breast cancer, women's health, and in particular, lymphedema. In 1998 she co-chaired an international workshop sponsored by the American Cancer Society and the Longaberger Company on breast cancer treatment-related lymphedema, an event that raised awareness about lymphedema in the scientific and clinical community, and has had far-reaching effects on science and policy.

Dr. Petrek served as an indispensable advisor and contributor to this and other American Cancer Society publications, and *Lymphedema: Understanding and Managing Lymphedema After Cancer* would not have been possible without her efforts.

She will be remembered for her warmth, her good humor, her scientific and clinical contributions and leadership, and most of all, her unwavering devotion to improving the lives of women with breast cancer.

American Cancer Society
Books/Product Marketing Specialist
Fax your comments to us at 404-325-9341

No Matter Who You Are, We Can Help.

Your feedback can help the American Cancer Society help others. Please complete this very brief "reader survey" and fax it to us today. Thank you!

The American Cancer Society respects your privacy. *Your contact information will not be distributed.*
PLEASE PRINT CLEARLY.

First Name _____ Last name _____

Street _____

City _____ State _____ Zip _____

E-mail _____

Please choose one answer for each question.

❑ Yes, I would like more information about other books published by the American Cancer Society.
I prefer to be contacted via: ❑ e-mail ❑ US mail

I am ❑ a patient ❑ a caregiver ❑ a friend or family member

I am ❑ female ❑ male Age: ❑ 60+ ❑ 40–59 ❑ 20–39

I have bought or read _____ health books in the past 12 months.

Lymphedema: Understanding and Managing Lymphedema After Cancer Treatment

This book is for ❑ me ❑ someone else

How I found out about this book (please choose one): ❑ Received a complimentary copy
❑ American Cancer Society—Hope Lodge _____ (location)
❑ American Cancer Society—Local Division _____ (location)
❑ 1.800.ACS.2345 ❑ www.cancer.org/bookstore ❑ Online retailer_____ ❑ Recommendation
❑ Store display ❑ Catalog/Mailing ❑ Advertisement_____ ❑ TV/Radio

The most helpful parts of this book are:
❑ the organization of the book
❑ the stories shared by other patients and caregivers
❑ the resources provided at the back of the book
❑ the information about coping
❑ the information about lymphedema and its treatment
❑ the information about medical care and talking to my doctor
❑ the information about insurance, finances, and/or legal issues
❑ other (please specify _____)

I think that the next edition should include this topic: _____
_____

Thank you for sharing your thoughts!